W9-BJB-262

DISCARDED

LANDS AND PEOPLES

LANDS AND PEOPLES

EUROPE

Volume 4

GROLIER
INCORPORATED
DANBURY, CONN.

HATHAWAY HIGH

1138

COPYRIGHT © 1991 BY GROLIER INCORPORATED

COPYRIGHT © 1989, 1987, 1985, 1983, 1981, 1980, 1978, 1977, 1976, 1973, 1972 BY GROLIER INCORPORATED

Library of Congress Catalog Card Number: 90-22140

ISBN 0-7172-8013-6

*All rights reserved. No part of this book may be
reproduced without written permission from the publishers.*

Printed and manufactured in the United States of America.

CONTENTS
EUROPE
Volume 4

FLAGS OF EUROPE (continued)

ICELAND

DENMARK

NORWAY

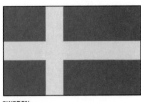
SWEDEN

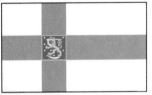
FINLAND

PORTUGAL

SPAIN

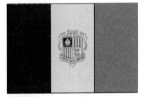

ANDORRA

ITALY

SAN MARINO

VATICAN CITY

MALTA

GREECE

POLAND

CZECHOSLOVAKIA

HUNGARY

YUGOSLAVIA

ALBANIA

BULGARIA

ROMANIA

UNION OF SOVIET SOCIALIST REPUBLICS

A church at Thingvellir, a plain south of Iceland's capital Reykjavik.

ICELAND

In A.D. 874 two Norwegian Vikings who had been exiled from their mother country set sail with their families, livestock, slaves, and other possessions to seek a new life. In their open Viking ships they sailed over 600 miles (1,000 kilometers) across the North Atlantic to the island of Iceland. They had come to a land where they would have to overcome great hardships in order to survive. Then, as now, with its vast areas of volcanoes and lava deserts, glaciers and ice fields, Iceland was a land of fire and ice. Today's Iceland is a land where elements of the Vikings' spirit and ingenuity have become part of the living present and where the past and the future exist side by side.

ECONOMY AND WAY OF LIFE

Iceland is located in the middle of one of the world's richest fishing grounds, and fish have always been the mainstay of the country's economy. Today fish and fish products account for about 70 percent of Iceland's exports. The annual catch of nearly 1,000,000 tons is made up mainly of cod, capelin, and redfish. Most of the fish is salted, canned, or quick-frozen, but some is still dried on racks in the open air—a process that dates from Viking days. The air-dried fish, or stockfish, is exported to southern Europe and in large quantities to Africa, where it supplies valuable protein for the local diet.

The Icelandic fishing fleet is one of the most modern in the world. Airplanes and radar are used to spot the best locations. Their reports, radioed back to the waiting fleet, help to insure large catches. In the summer, hundreds of students from Iceland's university and high schools spend their vacations working in the fishing industry. The boys usually sail with the fleet and the girls help in the salting, canning, and freezing plants.

Farming in Iceland can also be traced back to Viking origins. The Vikings were a seafaring people, so it was natural that they should settle on the coasts, whose deep bays and inlets offered the protection of good harbors. However, Iceland's farms also had to be near the coastal settlements, since about 75 percent of Iceland's interior is an uninhabitable region of rocks and lava formations, volcanoes, and glaciers. The main farm crop in Iceland is hay, which is used to feed cattle and the long-haired Icelandic sheep. The sheep, too, came to Iceland with the Vikings, and for hundreds of years they were the Icelanders' most dependable source of food and clothing. Farmers in Iceland also raise turnips, potatoes, carrots, and other vegetables that grow fast enough to ripen in the short summer season.

The original settlers also brought with them a special breed of small horse, somewhat larger than the Shetland pony. Because so much of the terrain is rough and difficult to cross, and because the country had no central authority to sponsor road building, the hardy, surefooted ponies were the main means of transportation on the island until the beginning of the 20th century. Icelandic horses are still used for recreation and during the great sheep roundups in the fall. In many parts of Iceland today, pony trails worn into the earth by centuries of hooves are still in use and can be seen crisscrossing moors and meadows.

THE LAND

On November 14, 1963, near the Westman Islands (Vestmannaeyjar) off Iceland's south coast, a towering plume of steam and water shot out of the sea, raining ashes and molten lava over a wide area. As the lava flow began to cool and harden, a volcanic island was formed. It was named Surtsey, for a giant of fire in Norse mythology. Then, on January 23, 1973, the earth opened near the Helgafell volcano on the island of Heimaey, the largest in the Westman group, and erupted so violently that all of the island's inhabitants had to be evacuated.

The intense volcanic activity in and around Iceland is due to its location on a great rift, or crack, in the earth. Earthquakes occur so frequently that all of Iceland's houses must be built of reinforced concrete, which has a high resistance to earth tremors. Sometimes it seems as if

Geysers occur throughout Iceland. The water that erupts from the geysers has been heated by volcanic rock.

Iceland must be very close to the hot, restless core of the earth. In fact, it has been estimated that one third of the earth's lava output in the last 500 years was produced in Iceland.

Iceland has over 100 volcanoes in all. Among the best-known is Hekla, 4,892 feet (1,491 m.) high, which was once thought to conceal one of the gates of hell. Another is Laki, near the vast Vatnajokull glacier in the southeast. In 1783 Laki killed 70 percent of Iceland's livestock and ruined most of its crops, causing a famine in which 20 percent of the population died of starvation. Dust clouds from Laki's eruption drifted across Europe, darkening the skies as far away as Finland and Russia.

But not everything in Iceland's volcanic environment is destructive. There is much that has a harsh, desolate beauty, like the surface of the moon. And, in many cases, the Icelanders have learned to tame the violence of nature and even to turn it to their use, as a servant.

Because Iceland's many rivers are too fast-flowing, too rocky, or too short, not one of them is navigable. Most of them provide excellent salmon and trout fishing, as well as hydroelectricity. Iceland has waterfalls by the score. There are delicate lacy ones and large powerful ones— which are also harnessed to produce hydroelectricity. Some have fanciful names, like Gullfoss ("golden falls"); others, like Godafoss ("gods' falls"), carry echoes of ancient legends as they crash down over their lava cliffs.

There are many beautiful lakes in Iceland; perhaps the best-known is Myvatn, in the northeast. The lake contains numerous small islands, and it is set among some of Iceland's most grotesque lava formations.

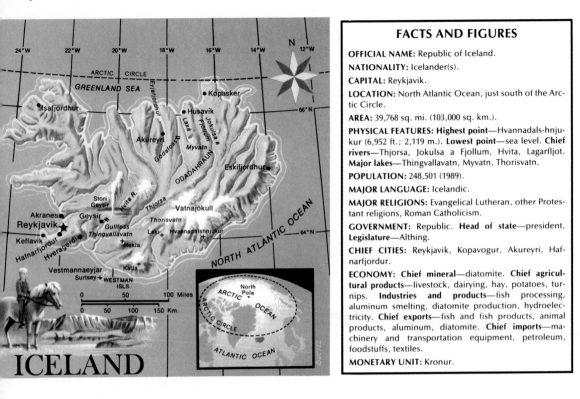

ICELAND

FACTS AND FIGURES

OFFICIAL NAME: Republic of Iceland.

NATIONALITY: Icelander(s).

CAPITAL: Reykjavik.

LOCATION: North Atlantic Ocean, just south of the Arctic Circle.

AREA: 39,768 sq. mi. (103,000 sq. km.).

PHYSICAL FEATURES: Highest point—Hvannadals-hnjukur (6,952 ft.; 2,119 m.). **Lowest point**—sea level. **Chief rivers**—Thjorsa, Jokulsa a Fjollum, Hvita, Lagarfljot. **Major lakes**—Thingvallavatn, Myvatn, Thorisvatn.

POPULATION: 248,501 (1989).

MAJOR LANGUAGE: Icelandic.

MAJOR RELIGIONS: Evangelical Lutheran, other Protestant religions, Roman Catholicism.

GOVERNMENT: Republic. **Head of state**—president. **Legislature**—Althing.

CHIEF CITIES: Reykjavik, Kopavogur, Akureyri, Hafnarfjordur.

ECONOMY: Chief mineral—diatomite. **Chief agricultural products**—livestock, dairying, hay, potatoes, turnips. **Industries and products**—fish processing, aluminum smelting, diatomite production, hydroelectricity. **Chief exports**—fish and fish products, animal products, aluminum, diatomite. **Chief imports**—machinery and transportation equipment, petroleum, foodstuffs, textiles.

MONETARY UNIT: Kronur.

Myvatn is also known for the large variety of birds that inhabit its shores, and for its excellent fishing. The lake has become a favorite vacation spot for Icelanders and tourists alike.

A major problem created by the environment is the island's lack of wood. The Vikings cut down the trees carelessly and at random for boats, houses, fences, and hundreds of other everyday uses. The trees were never replaced. Poor soil, glacial erosion, volcanic eruptions, climate, and grazing sheep (which eat tender tree seedlings) took care of the rest. Reforestation experiments, using Alaskan spruce and other conifers, are being carried out today in protected areas, such as Hallormsstadur in the east.

There are hot springs all over the island, which the Icelanders use in several ways. In Reykjavik, the capital, the natural hot water is piped to almost 90 percent of the city's homes and businesses, as well as to several year-round outdoor swimming pools. Elsewhere, especially around Hveragerdi—*hver* means "hot spring" in Icelandic—the hot springs heat greenhouses, allowing the Icelanders to raise tomatoes, cucumbers, lettuce, and flowers that would otherwise have to be imported at great cost. Some oranges, pineapples, and bananas have also been grown in the greenhouses. Plans have been made to use steam from the hot springs to generate electricity, as in Italy, New Zealand, Mexico, and Japan.

Finally, Iceland has geysers. The Icelandic word *geysir* means "gusher," and some 50 mi. (80 km.) east of Reykjavik, in a stone pool atop a deep natural shaft, there is Stóri Geysir, or "great gusher." Like America's Old Faithful and New Zealand's North Island geysers, Geysir erupts spectacularly. Unlike most of the others, however, it no longer erupts without help. It must be fed many shovel-loads of soapflakes to create the conditions that cause it to spout.

HISTORY

In many parts of the world, a country's history can be read in the remains that are left behind—a Gothic church here, a medieval fortress there, a baroque palace somewhere else. In Iceland there are very few such remains, and though the country is developing rapidly, the past lives on in the Icelanders themselves, because they are so intensely aware of their heritage.

The purity of their language, which is basically Old Norse, is one example of how the Icelanders keep tradition alive. If the word *geysir* was a gift from Iceland to the rest of the world, the Icelanders took almost nothing in return. This is because Icelandic does not easily borrow words from other languages, even for new and technical terms. So, today, the Icelandic word for "telephone" is *simi,* which means "thread" or "cord." The word for electricity comes from two old words that mean "amber power"; the lumbering tanks of World War II were "creeping dragons"; and today's swift jet planes are *thota,* or "darter." It is said that if the original settlers were to return to Iceland today, the country's appearance might surprise them, but they could speak to anyone and be understood.

The special history that produced today's proud, heritage-conscious Icelanders is long and filled with hardships. The Vikings came to Iceland to escape domination by the Norwegian king. Gradually a system of local *things,* or assemblies, developed, and finally, in A.D. 930, on a plain near Reykjavik, all the chieftains, with their families and retinues, met and established the Althing—an all-island assembly. Today that plain—the Thingvellir, or "plain of the thing"—is Iceland's national shrine. It is a major landmark in world history as well, for the Althing was the world's first democratic parliament.

But the Althing lacked the power to enforce the laws it made, and by 1262, struggles between rival chieftains had so divided the country that King Haakon IV of Norway found it ready to accept his royal authority. It was the end of the old republic and the end of independence. Iceland was under Norwegian domination until 1380, when the Norwegian royal house died out. Then both Norway and Iceland came under the Danish Crown. For Iceland, this marked the beginning of almost 300 years of decline. It proceeded slowly at first, but then at a faster and more dangerous pace. For Denmark did not consider Iceland a colony to be helped and supported. Iceland was given little or no protection against marauding pirates who raided the coasts. Supplies from abroad were erratic, and no new ships were built. Iceland soon lost contact with the tiny outpost it had established on Greenland in 985. The Greenland settlement died out completely. In 1602 Iceland was forbidden to trade with other countries. By the 18th century, Iceland's climate had entered its grimmest, coldest phase. In 1783 Laki erupted. In 1800 the Althing was suspended by the Danish. It seemed that nature and events had combined to make life in Iceland almost impossible.

The 19th century brought some improvement in Iceland's situation. The Althing was reconvened in 1843, and in 1854, after the Danish Government relaxed its trade ban, Iceland gradually began to rejoin the world of Western Europe. With the return of contact with other peoples came a reawakening of Iceland's arts—especially its literature—and of its old, proud nationalism.

Fishing boats in Husavik harbor. Fish products make up more than 90 percent of Iceland's exports.

This movement was led by Jón Sigurdsson, a statesman, historian, and authority on Icelandic literature. Sigurdsson wanted his countrymen to take pride in their past and, more important, to work realistically toward the future. He published an edition of Iceland's ancient sagas—many of them telling of the gods of Norse mythology or of the days of the Viking settlement. He also founded a political journal in which he called for a return to national consciousness and for practical measures such as co-operatives and training schools to speed up Iceland's development. In 1854 Denmark finally revoked the ban on foreign trade, and 20 years later Iceland was granted a constitution. Icelanders today still consider that Jón Sigurdsson's efforts were largely responsible for both.

Iceland gained independence in 1918, retaining only a formal bond with the Danish Crown. After the outbreak of World War II and the occupation of Denmark by the Nazis, Iceland's strategic location on the North Atlantic shipping routes became extremely important to the Allies. In 1940 the British placed Iceland under protective occupation, and in 1941 Americans took their place. The Americans built an airfield at Keflavík—an important North Atlantic Treaty Organization (NATO) base today. On June 17, 1944, after a national referendum—and after almost six centuries of Danish rule—Iceland broke its last tie with Denmark and declared itself a republic.

Reykjavik was the site of a two-day meeting in 1986 between U.S. President Ronald Reagan and Soviet leader Mikhail Gorbachev. Here they

In October 1986, Reykjavik was the site of a summit meeting between the United States and the Soviet Union.

discussed the issues that led to a 1987 agreement eliminating the medium-range missiles held by the two nations.

GOVERNMENT
Iceland is a republic. The president, who is elected for 4 years, is the head of state. Under the constitution, the president also is vested with certain executive power. In practice, however, the prime minister, who is selected by the president and leads the Cabinet, serves as the head of the government. The legislative body, the Althing, also is elected for 4 years. Icelanders elected Vigdis Finnbogadottir as their first woman president in 1980, re-electing her in 1984 and 1988. A coalition of Iceland's three main parties was also formed in 1988.

ICELAND TODAY
Iceland is an example of what a small nation with few natural resources can accomplish. In Reykjavik, the capital, modern concrete-and-steel office buildings and apartments overlook statues of heroes of Viking days. Five daily newspapers are published here, and so are the thousands of books read in Iceland each year. One of the most popular Icelandic authors, Halldór Laxness, won the Nobel prize for literature in 1955. Iceland has no army or navy and has never fought a war.

Reviewed by KARL F. ROLVAAG, Former United States Ambassador to Iceland
JOHN FISKE, Cultural Affairs Officer, United States Embassy, Reykjavik

Fredriksborg Castle, completed in 1620, now serves as Denmark's National History Museum.

DENMARK

Writers have called Denmark a kingdom of reason, a close-up of democracy, a social laboratory, a land of balance, and a toyland run by adults. Although their nation is small and lacks natural resources, the Danes are praised for their contributions to culture and crafts, industry and commerce, education and science. Aided by their strategic location in the North Sea, near the great Western industrial nations, the Danes have met the problems of their country with skill and talent. These qualities have managed to provide all of the inhabitants of this smallest Scandinavian nation with a good life.

THE LAND

Denmark is made up of the peninsula of Jutland—which faces north to Norway and points a finger toward Sweden—and 482 islands, of which only 99 are inhabited. Denmark's islands range in size from mere dots in the sea to middle-sized islands such as Zealand (Sjaelland), on which Copenhagen, the Danish capital, is built, to the world's largest island, Greenland, off northeast North America. (An article on GREENLAND appears in Volume 5.) Other important islands in Denmark are Fyn (Fünen), Lolland, Falster, and Bornholm. In addition, the Kingdom of Denmark includes the Faeroes, a group of 21 islands north of Scotland.

Almost everywhere in Denmark one breathes the sea air. Except for the 42-mile (68-kilometer) boundary with West Germany at the south of Jutland, all of Denmark is surrounded by water. This fragmented little kingdom thus has a remarkably long seacoast—over 4,600 miles (7,400 km.). To the west is the North Sea; to the north, the Skagerrak; to the east, the Kattegat and Øresund (The Sound); and on the south, the Baltic Sea. All along the shores of Jutland and the larger islands there are fiords and bays. In addition, there are numerous small rivers and lakes.

There are no mountains in Denmark. The landscape is gently rolling. In some areas low hills rise between the plains. The highest point—in southeast Jutland—is only 568 feet (173 meters). Even the 531-foot (162 m.) hill in the heart of Jutland has earned the name of "heaven mountain" (Himmelbjaerget). The west coast of Jutland along the North Sea is lined with ridges of sparkling white sand dunes. There are heaths and moors in the western part of Jutland that have been turned into needed

Ribe, on the Jutland peninsula, is said to be the oldest city in Denmark.

forests and farmland. Eastern Jutland and the islands have the best soil. About 10 percent of the total land area of Denmark is forested. Since the country is mostly plains and water, the Danes take great pride in two unusual sights. On the island of Møn are spectacular milky-white chalk cliffs, which rise more than 400 feet (120 m.) over the blue Baltic Sea. And on the island of Bornholm, which lies in the Baltic Sea and is more like nearby Sweden than the rest of Denmark, are jagged granite cliffs, the only hard rock in the whole country.

The Danes have tied together the bits and pieces of their country and connected it to the outside world with a system of bridges, highways, ferries, buses, railroads, and planes. Where there are no lacy steel bridges to connect two islands, there are spotless ferries that run like clockwork. Train and car ferries connect Zealand with Fyn, Zealand with Jutland, innumerable towns with one another, and Denmark with Sweden, Norway, Germany, and Great Britain.

Agriculture

Although Denmark's soil is not naturally fertile, it is the nation's most important natural resource. Climate also adds to the difficulty of farming. During most of the year westerly winds blowing over waters warmed by the Gulf Stream make the weather relatively mild for so northern a country. Rainfall ranges from 16 to 32 inches (40–80 centimeters) a year, but the wettest months are in late summer and early autumn, when the farmer needs fair weather for his harvest. The driest months come in the spring, when rain is needed to water newly planted crops.

In spite of these natural obstacles, the Danes today are one of the world's largest exporters of meat and meat products, of butter and eggs, and of cheeses. It was not always so.

Most farms in Denmark are small, efficiently run family operations.

FACTS AND FIGURES

KINGDOM OF DENMARK—Kongeriget Danmark—is the official name of the country.

THE PEOPLE—are called Danes.

CAPITAL: Copenhagen (Kobenhavn).

LOCATION: Northern Europe. **Boundaries**—North Sea, Baltic Sea, West Germany.

AREA: 16,629 sq. mi. (43,069 sq. km.), excluding the Faeroe Islands, 540 sq. mi. (1,399 sq. km.), and Greenland, 840,000 sq. mi. (2,175,600 sq. km.).

PHYSICAL FEATURES: Highest point—Ejer Bavnehoj (568 ft.; 173 m.). **Lowest point**—13 ft. (4 m.) below sea level at Lamme Fjord (Zealand).

POPULATION: 5,119,155 (1982 census). 5,130,000 (latest estimate).

MAJOR LANGUAGE: Danish.

MAJOR RELIGION: Evangelical Lutheran.

GOVERNMENT: Constitutional monarchy. **Head of state**—queen. **Head of government**—prime minister. **Legislature**—Folketing.

CHIEF CITIES: Copenhagen (1,377,000), Arhus (247,000), Odense (170,000), Alborg (154,000).

ECONOMY: Chief minerals—chalk, limestone, sandstone, granite, clay. **Chief agricultural products**—milk, pork, bacon, beef, butter, cheese, eggs, cereals, root crops. **Industries and products**—food processing, machinery and equipment, textiles and clothing, chemical products, electronics, transportation equipment, metal products, bricks and mortar, furniture. **Chief exports**—meat, dairy products, industrial machinery and equipment, textiles and clothing, chemical products, transportation equipment, fish, furs, and furniture. **Chief imports**—industrial machinery, transportation equipment, fuels, textile fibers and yarns, iron and steel products, chemicals, grain and feedstuffs, wood and paper.

MONETARY UNIT: 1 Krone = 100 øre.

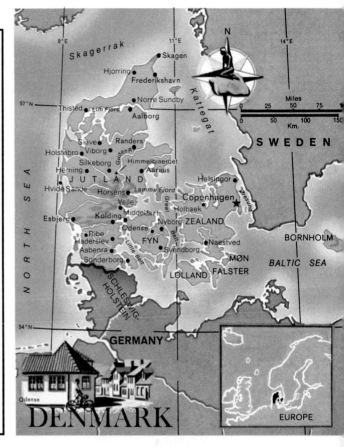

DENMARK

Until 1880 the Danes were mostly producers of grains. With the growth of railroads and improved shipping, Denmark could not compete with the giant grain-growing countries. There was also a worldwide drop in grain prices. Danish agriculture was threatened with ruin. The Danish farmers reasoned that if they could buy grain cheaper than they could grow it, it would be sensible to turn to other products. They began to specialize in butter, bacon, eggs, cheese, and ham—foods that were needed by the United Kingdom and by the other Western European nations. Denmark became known as the country that was sending breakfast to millions of people in Europe.

Co-operatives. This successful and rapid transformation of Danish agriculture was made possible by the establishment of a system of co-operatives. The original Danish agricultural co-operative grew out of the simple idea of collecting the milk from a number of small farms, processing it into butter in one central place, selling the large batches of butter, and distributing the profits according to each farmer's individual contribution. From 1882 to 1890 nearly 700 dairies became co-operatives. The movement grew rapidly to include co-operative buying of machinery, fertilizers, and feed; co-operative egg collecting, pig slaughtering, and bacon and ham processing; and co-operative exporting. From buying and selling together, it was natural to go on to establish uniform standards of quality and to benefit from centralized agricultural research. The co-operative system has been more widely applied in Denmark than anywhere else in the world. Eggs are graded, sized, and packed under rigid rules for quality and uniformity. The buyer can be certain of the same uniformity and quality in the bacon, the chickens, the butter, the many types of potatoes, the more than a dozen varieties of cheeses, and all other exported food.

Folk Schools. Where did the Danish farmers learn how to organize for such economic and social change? For the answer one must go back to a remarkable man, Nikolai Frederik Severin Grundtvig (1783–1872). A theologian, historian, educator, poet, philosopher, hymn-writer, and politician, Grundtvig was interested in educating adults to take an intelligent interest in representative government, which was then beginning in Denmark. He thought this could be done at folk high schools (folkehøjskoler). His disciple Kristen Kold (1816–70), a teacher, set the pattern for these adult schools, which were soon established all over the country. Students and teachers lived together in simple surroundings. There were no entrance requirements, no formal studies, no examinations, no diplomas, and few fees. Teaching was largely oral, relying mainly on lectures and discussions. The idea was not only to teach facts, but to arouse intellectual curiosity and an interest in social problems. No special courses in democracy or co-operatives were given, but the folk high schools are credited with transforming peasants into enlightened farmers.

Industry

The talented and energetic Danes have turned a small country with no coal, no iron, and no hydroelectric power into a modern industrial nation. Long ago the Danes learned to use fully almost every inch of their country. The bedrock of chalk and limestone is used to make cement. The island of Bornholm, which lies in the Baltic Sea, yields the hard rock used for cobblestones that pave some of the streets of the leading cities of Denmark. Bornholm also provides kaolin, the clay used in making the porcelain figurines and fine chinaware sold all over the world.

Denmark does not have enough natural forests to produce the wood needed for building and making newsprint. But since 1805, when Denmark passed the first forest protection law in the world, the Danes have managed to convert some lowland into forests of spruce and pine to fill some of their paper and building needs.

More Danes work in factories than on the land, but much of their industry is based on processing farm products. The factories are busy turning milk into butter and cheese; packaging bacon, sausage, and hams; and converting malt, hops, and grain into world-famous beer. Denmark also has a large fishing industry, with a fleet of more than 8,000 fishing vessels. About 90 percent of the catch comes from the seas around Denmark, where herring, plaice, mackerel, eel, and cod are found. Tiny, delicious shrimp, an important Danish product, come from the world's largest shrimp grounds in the waters off southern Greenland. Fishing is a year-round industry, and the Danes—in addition to selling fresh fish—freeze, can, and smoke fish and make fish meal and oil.

In recent years the Danes have made great strides in many new industrial fields and expanded ones for which they have been renowned. Their modern furniture, often made from teak imported from Southeast Asia, has won acclaim for its elegantly simple design and fine quality. The same craftsmanship and advanced design have made Danish silver, porcelain, textiles, and rugs greatly prized in homes all over the Western world. Denmark also produces ships, engines, chemicals, medicines, machinery (including electrical machinery and parts), toys, clothing, shoes, and prefabricated housing elements.

Denmark's industrial development could not have taken place without the surrounding sea. To carry on its foreign trade, Denmark has a large, modern merchant marine. The Danes perfected the diesel engine and launched the first oceangoing motor ship in the world in 1912. Copenhagen, the capital and largest city of Denmark, is also the leading industrial center and has the largest port. Ships come in carrying raw materials and fuel and leave carrying export products. Most of these go to the United Kingdom, Sweden, Germany, Norway and the United States. Denmark's entry into the Common Market (it formally joined in 1973) provided a vast market, with millions of customers.

THE PEOPLE

Almost the entire Danish labor force, skilled as well as unskilled, is organized in unions. In addition, Denmark has one of the most comprehensive social-welfare systems in the world. The Danes have simply decided that no one is to suffer any avoidable hardship. No one is to be cold, or sick and unattended; no one is to be ill-housed, ill-clothed, or ill-fed.

The beaches of Holbæk on Zealand are popular in the summertime.

Children in a state-run day care center enjoy an outing.

Denmark has achieved so many firsts in social welfare that one cannot list them all. In 1792 Denmark became the first European state to abolish slave trading. In 1814 it was the first to make elementary education compulsory. The Danes were the first people in the world to organize a complete old-age pension system and one of the first to have a superb system of municipal hospitals. In medical standards, preventive medicine, and patient care, they rank among the world leaders. As far back as 1870 Denmark converted former monasteries into comfortable, attractive homes for the elderly, and today people come from all over the world to study the charming living arrangements Denmark has provided for its older citizens.

Taxes are very high, but a large amount of the revenue is used for the support of hospitals, day care centers for children, disability payments, pensions, unemployment insurance, and education. The Danish program of social legislation has been so successful that, as an old Danish song says, Denmark is truly a land where "few have too much, and fewer too little." It has been said that if there are social ills that intelligence can cure, the Danes will take care of them.

The Danes, whether they live in modern apartment houses in the cities, in timbered farmhouses, or in whitewashed country cottages with tiled roofs, are proud of their homes. As one leaves the cities one can see neat rows of gardens, for many city-dwellers have plots where they cultivate vegetables and flowers. The Danes love flowers, and in the summertime Denmark is like one big garden. Flowerbeds and green lawns are everywhere.

The typical Danish home is *hyggeligt,* a word the Danes use to express the ideas of coziness, warmth, attractiveness, and friendliness. The home may include a shining old porcelain stove, a modern abstract art poster, inherited antique tables or chairs, and books. The Danes love to eat, and whether at home or in restaurants, their food is served attractively, and there are usually fresh flowers on the table. Many Danish housewives are good cooks, often making their own bread and baking any of the dozens of different cream cakes, tarts, and Danish pastries that delight the eye and the taste.

Nothing in Denmark is more celebrated than the famous *smørrebrød* (literally, "bread and butter"). *Smørrebrød* is a Danish invention that has become a folk art. It is an open-faced sandwich—thick, pure butter spread on a slice of delicious Danish bread and covered with tiny shrimp, liver paste, cold meats, or any of more than 100 variations of local delicacies. Other favorite foods are roast pork stuffed with prunes and apples, and *frikadeller* (meat patties). They may be followed by a dessert of any of many delicious cheeses, fresh fruits, or a marvelous pudding of raspberry and currant juices called *rødgrød med fløde*.

Whatever the Danes choose to eat, the drink is nearly always beer. Two giant breweries, Carlsberg and Tuborg, supply the delicious brew, which is known world-wide. Denmark is among the largest beer exporters on the European continent, and the profits from the sales have aided Danish art, culture, and education. The Carlsberg Foundation is Denmark's greatest cultural benefactor, using its money for museums,

Beer being made in one of Denmark's giant breweries.

statues, gardens, and a wide variety of educational and cultural events and institutions. Tuborg, a smaller company, has provided funds for foreign study grants for young Danes and for various commercial activities to benefit the community.

The Arts and Education in Denmark

Denmark's most famous export is, strangely enough, a collection of fairy tales. To readers all over the world, Denmark is known as the home of Hans Christian Andersen (1805–75). His stories are a part of the heritage of children everywhere. Another Danish writer well-known outside his country is the 19th-century philosopher Søren Kierkegaard. He is now recognized as the founder of the philosophy of existentialism. Baroness Karen Blixen, who wrote under the name of Isak Dinesen, achieved an international reputation for her work, especially for her brilliant storytelling in *Seven Gothic Tales* and for the autobiographical *Out of Africa*. Many Danish authors, including some Nobel prize winners, are not read outside Denmark because they have not been widely translated. The Danes, who are great readers of books, read even more newspapers. Cities of 20,000 people usually have more than one daily newspaper, and Copenhagen has about 10.

Children in Denmark attend school from the age of 7 to 16. After the age of 16 school is voluntary, and students who desire to continue their education by attending college may apply for admission to one of Denmark's five universities with their many associated specialized institutes. All who qualify attend free.

Continuation schools (*efterskoler*) have been set up to meet the demand for additional education for those boys and girls who have left school. These schools are residential, and they provide general education in an informal atmosphere, with no entrance tests and no examinations unless the students wish to go into specialized fields. The adult folk high schools still flourish. They are also informal and residential. Men and women may attend a 5- or 6-month winter course or shorter ones, including even 2-week summer family courses.

The Danes have made many significant contributions to research and learning as well as to education. They have produced great astronomers, such as Tycho Brahe, who discovered a new star in 1572 and whose precise observations in fixing the positions of the planets and stars were of enormous importance. There have been many world-famous Danish mathematicians, medical scientists, chemists, and physicists. Perhaps the best-known in modern times was Niels Bohr, who made historic discoveries in atomic physics. Bohr attracted scholars from all over the world to the University Institute of Theoretical Physics, which he founded in Copenhagen in 1920.

One needs neither an understanding of the language nor a knowledge of science to appreciate one of Denmark's greatest treasures, the Royal Danish Ballet. The Danes take pride in this notable company and support it generously, as they do their symphony orchestras and opera companies. The Danes also love to dance and sing. As far back as A.D. 1100, many noblemen had their own dance festivals, and to this day folk dancing as well as social dancing is widely enjoyed. Whether dancing outdoors or sailing, the Danish people love the outdoors and are dedicated sun-worshipers, as are many other northern people who have a

Young ballet students practice for the internationally known Royal Danish Ballet.

short summer. As soon as weather permits, they take to the beach—to swim, to sail, to row, to canoe, or just to sunbathe. They also enjoy bicycle races, badminton, and tennis; but their favorite non-water sport is soccer. For skiing the Danes travel to Norway and Sweden.

COPENHAGEN, THE CAPITAL

To many people Copenhagen's Tivoli Gardens, the world's most famous amusement park, is the key to Denmark. There, on 20 acres (8 hectares) in the heart of the capital, is something for everyone, old, young, rich, poor, serious, frivolous. There are restaurants and snack bars, concerts by symphony orchestras and performances by jazz groups and brass bands, ballet and pantomime, flea circuses and fun rides, playgrounds, paths on which to stroll under shady trees, and places to sit amid beautiful flowerbeds. From May to mid-September thousands of Danes and visitors "tivolate"—as one happy visitor explained—in an atmosphere that is a mixture of lightness, color, and gaiety combined with orderliness, good taste, and superb organization. At night Tivoli becomes a fairyland of twinkling lights and floodlit waters. Twice a week before closing time there is a display of fireworks that ends when the huge bell in the nearby City Hall tower strikes midnight.

About one fourth of the Danes live in Copenhagen and its suburbs. The city was founded in 1167 by Bishop Absalon on the east shore of Zealand across Øresund from Sweden. Its name means "merchant's harbor," and since its founding, Copenhagen has been the center of Danish life, although it did not become the capital until 1445. It is a windswept city of slender, pointed spires, copper-green roofs, and domes topped with gold balls, coronets, and clocks; of old and new buildings on narrow streets; and of a sparkling harbor alive with ships being built, being loaded and unloaded, and under sail.

Copenhagen's world-famous Tivoli Gardens feature everything from concerts and ballets to circuses and rides.

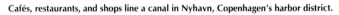

Cafés, restaurants, and shops line a canal in Nyhavn, Copenhagen's harbor district.

Amalienborg, the royal palaces in Copenhagen, dates to the 18th century.

Much of the character of Copenhagen was set by King Christian IV (1577–1648), who planned and built much of the city. Not only did he plan the unique Stock Exchange (*Børsen*) building, but while it was being erected, it is said, he himself worked on its strange spire, which is formed by the entwined tails of four copper dragons that appear to be standing on their heads. It is the world's oldest market exchange building in continuous use. Christian also built churches, the Rosenborg Castle, which is now a great museum, and the Nyboder, a group of houses for men of the Royal Navy and their families, often called the first public housing project. Four succeeding kings continued building the city. About 1750 King Frederik V permitted four noblemen to build four palaces enclosing an octagonal plaza. These buildings, Amalienborg, are now the home of the Danish royal family.

Visitors to Copenhagen flock to the National Museum; to the Glyptotek to see the collection of French art; and to the Thorvaldsen Museum to see the works of Denmark's great sculptor, Bertel Thorvaldsen (1768–1844). They also stroll through many parks, including the Langelinie, where, from a large boulder at the water's edge, a bronze statue of Andersen's fairy-tale Little Mermaid watches the ships come and go.

HISTORY

Hunters and fishermen were living in Denmark as far back as the Old Stone Age (about 10000 B.C.). Many relics of the peoples of the Stone, Bronze, and Iron ages have been found in Denmark. The oldest surviving costumes in Europe have been recovered from oak-coffin graves dating from the Bronze Age. Among the interesting relics of this period are lurs. These musical instruments—long, elegantly carved horns —are in pairs that are identical except for being curved in reverse. The lur has survived as a symbol on Danish butter.

The Danes took part in the Viking raids, which started out as pirate raids and ended as large-scale military expeditions and invasions. The Viking period—between the 9th and 11th centuries—was a time of trade and emigration and led to the settlement of thousands of Danish peasants in England, Normandy, and northern Germany. The royal line of Denmark began in the Viking period.

History tells us that the Danish monarchy, rulers of the oldest kingdom in Europe, goes back to Gorm the Old, who died in A.D. 940. Gorm and his wife, Queen Thyra Danebod, had a son Harold Bluetooth, who was the first Christian ruler of Denmark. The Danish warrior kings continued their raids until 1016, when the Danish king Canute (Knud) the Great completed the conquest of England. At his death, he was the ruler of Denmark, England, and Norway. After his death there was a period of turmoil and civil war, and the empire fell apart.

In 1397 Denmark, Norway, and Sweden were united by Queen Margrethe I, following a meeting in the Swedish town of Kalmar. This union became known as the Kalmar Union and continued officially until 1523, when it was finally dissolved. The truth is that after the death of Queen Margrethe, who had been a remarkable diplomat, the union began to disintegrate, and very little significance was attached to it. Sweden left the union in 1523, but Norway remained a part of Denmark until 1814. Norway had brought to the union the Faeroe Islands, Iceland, and Greenland. Iceland became independent in 1918. (An article on ICELAND appears in this volume.)

The Faeroe Islands remain a part of Denmark to this day. These 21 volcanic islands, whose name means "sheep islands," are in fact used for raising sheep. The Faeroe Islanders are fishermen as well as shepherds, and they make their own local laws, use their own language, and have their own flag. Greenland, which has also remained a part of Denmark, held its first elections under home rule in 1979. The Faeroe Islands and Greenland each send two representatives to the Danish parliament.

Costly Wars

From earliest times, Denmark was almost continuously engaged in some war. Many of the battles were with Sweden, and finally, in the mid-17th century, Denmark was defeated and lost the rich provinces of Skane, Halland, and Blekinge to Sweden. Norway was lost to Sweden in 1814 as a result of Denmark's involvement in the Napoleonic Wars. When war broke out in 1803 between England and France, Denmark first chose to remain neutral. The Danes rejected a demand that they turn over their fleet to the British. As a result, the British fleet bombarded Copenhagen and destroyed much of the city. The Danes were ultimately forced to surrender their fleet and angrily concluded an unhappy alliance with Napoleon. At a peace conference in Kiel, Germany, in 1814, Denmark gave up Norway.

For many years, tensions had been growing in the area known as Schleswig-Holstein, in the south of Jutland. Schleswig, an ancient Danish duchy, and Holstein, which had traditionally been German but had come

Hvide Sande on Jutland is a fishing center.

under Danish rule in the 15th century, were to create trouble with Germany that lasted through World War II. In the first war (1848–49) fought over Holstein, the Danes were victorious. But this led to a second war (1864) against Austria and the German state of Prussia. In this war many Danes were killed. The day the peace treaty of Vienna was signed—October 30, 1864—was perhaps one of the darkest days in Danish history. The Danes had to surrender not only German Holstein and southern Schleswig, but also northern Schleswig, which had always been Danish. Denmark thus lost one third of its already diminished territory and two fifths of its population.

A Danish patriot said, "What has been lost outside must be gained inside." Each time Denmark has suffered severely, the Danes have managed to turn adversity into advantage. After the Napoleonic Wars, the country was bankrupt and the people impoverished and in despair. Yet this was a time of great achievement in art, literature, and government. The beginning of compulsory education for all, important economic reforms, a movement to limit the absolute monarchy, and demands for a new constitution all followed the losses in 1814. The losses of 1864 were followed by a drive for land reclamation that created tens of thousands of new acres of farmland out of the heathlands of Jutland. It was also the time of the great agricultural revolution.

Denmark, neutral during World War I, got back part of Schleswig in 1920. The Danes insisted on a plebiscite since they wanted only the part of the country where the people voted overwhelmingly to return to Danish rule. At the outbreak of World War II, Denmark again hoped to remain neutral, but on April 9, 1940, German troops occupied the country. For 3 years the Germans tried to make Denmark a model Nazi protectorate, but as they failed to win over the Danes, more and more restraints were imposed and a strong resistance movement developed. The Germans were beset with constant sabotage and with subtle defiance and outright ridicule. The press went underground so effectively that in the last year of the war almost 180 illegal papers were published, with a total daily edition of 1,000,000 copies. People began public songfests, singing the national anthem, which begins, "There is a lovely land," until the Nazis forbade public singing. Suddenly it seemed the whole country took to wearing little woolen beanie hats, knitted in the design of the British Royal Air Force insignia, and the Nazis passed a law forbidding Danes to wear red, white, and blue beanies. When a bookstore displayed English books, the Nazis complained, and the Danish owner substituted German books with a sign saying, "Learn German while there is still time."

But no other Danish war story shows the cohesion of the people and their bravery as does the story of Denmark's rescue of almost its entire Jewish population. When word was received in September, 1943, that the Nazis planned to round up all the Jews, the Danes acted within 24 hours. Almost every citizen, young and old, participated in the rescue, in which Jews were found, warned, hidden in homes, woods, hospitals, inns, and churches, and taken by fishing boats across the narrow sound to neutral Sweden. Of almost 8,000 Danish Jews, all but a few hundred— too ill to be moved or unwilling to co-operate—were saved. This almost unbelievable feat of courage and organization was arranged in one day and night in a wholly occupied country.

The war left Denmark with a severely crippled economy, although it had suffered little physical damage. With the aid of the American Marshall Plan, it became possible to put the country back on a sound and prosperous basis in a relatively short time. Denmark became a member of the United Nations and also of the North Atlantic Treaty Organization (NATO), giving up its former neutral position.

GOVERNMENT

Denmark is a constitutional monarchy with a single-chamber parliament (the Folketing). If the royal family should fail to provide an heir to the throne, the Danes have arranged for the parliament to elect a new king. The orderly Danes have, since the Middle Ages, called their kings Christian and Frederik alternately. However, once there was a King Hans who upset the order, causing the country to be one Frederik short. Because of this, Queen Margrethe, who came to the throne in 1972 on the death of her father, Frederik IX, named her son Frederik. When he assumes the throne, the balance will be restored.

From the smallest to the largest problems, the Danes approach difficulties with logic and imagination. In a time when many countries in the world seem to be in turmoil, Denmark is often cited as a unique example of a land where the people have learned to cope successfully with their time and with their environment. The Danes are a homogeneous people. Almost 98 percent of the people living in Denmark were born there. But even in this small country, with no religious or racial divisions, it has not been simple to establish a truly democratic society where a policeman is rarely glimpsed. There is some grumbling about high prices and high taxes. But the Danes, a people with a great respect for law and a highly developed sense of justice, have shown a willingness to work hard and the courage to experiment in seeking solutions as problems arise.

CASPAR H. W. HASSELRIIS, Former Director, Danish Information Service, New York

NORWAY

A thousand years ago Vikings from Norway roamed the coasts of Europe in their dragon-headed longboats, plundering and raiding wherever they touched land. They penetrated inland by river, even sacking cities like London and Paris. The Vikings were fierce, merciless warriors. People all over Europe feared their cruelty and prayed for protection from "the wrath of the Norsemen." Today the Norwegians live in what has been called the peaceful corner of Europe, at peace not only with their fellow Europeans but with themselves. The descendant of the Vikings is a soft-spoken individual with a highly developed sense of responsibility for his neighbor.

About 100 years ago many Norwegians left their country to build a new life on the continent across the Atlantic. Altogether about 800,000 Norwegians left for the United States between 1855 and 1920 because they could not make a living in their homeland. Today, however, Norway is a prosperous member of the Western European family of nations, with one of the highest standards of living in the world.

Geiranger Fjord, one of the many fiords that indent Norway's west coast.

Norway above the Arctic Circle, part of the "land of the midnight sun."

What changed Norway over these 1,000 years, and especially during the last century? The most important answers lie in the country itself and in the people who live there.

THE LAND

Roughly speaking, Norway is one long and massive chain of mountains facing the North Atlantic. It forms the western part of the Scandinavian peninsula, which it shares with Sweden. Norway also includes Spitsbergen (Svalbard), some 400 miles (640 kilometers) to the north; Jan Mayen Island, about 640 miles (1,030 km.) to the west; and Bouvet and Peter I islands, near Antarctica.

The mainland area of about 125,000 square miles (324,000 square kilometers) is the fifth largest in Europe outside the Soviet Union. Its long coastline is cut by deep fiords, narrow arms of seawater sometimes reaching 100 miles (160 km.) inland, with towering mountains rising on each side. Fertile green valleys stretch inland along the rivers that flow from the high mountains towards the coast. The actual distance from the southernmost tip of Norway to its North Cape is over 1,000 miles (1,600 km.), but if the fiords could be straightened out, the Norwegian coastline would reach halfway around the equator. Along this coast are scattered more than 150,000 islands and skerries—reefs of tiny uninhabited rock islands.

About one third of Norway lies north of the Arctic Circle. At the North Cape, some 71 degrees north of the equator, the sun shines day and night from mid-May through the end of July and is completely absent for about 2½ months in winter. But in spite of its high latitude,

Norway does not have an Arctic climate. The warm waters of the Norway Current of the Gulf Stream system give the coastal areas of the country a temperate climate, with ice-free harbors even in the extreme north. Deep inland and in the mountains winter temperatures are more severe, but that is not where most Norwegians live. Actually only about 3 percent of the country can be farmed, while 25 percent is covered by forests. Mountains, lakes, rivers, forests, and bare wasteland—including the 340-square-mile (880 sq. km.) Jostedalsbre—take up nearly all of the land. It is not surprising that Norway is the second most sparsely populated country in Europe (after Iceland), or that most of its population lives along the coasts, close to the sea.

HISTORY

The sea was always a challenge to the Norwegians. In the early days of settlement, land communications were virtually impossible and farmland was even scarcer than it is today. The sea naturally became both the principal artery of transport and, because of its abundance of fish, a major source of food. The Norwegians soon learned to dominate the sea —the most important factor in their environment. It was the superior skill of the Norwegian Viking shipbuilders and sailors that made possible their impact on the rest of Europe, starting about A.D. 800. However, in spite of the fear the Vikings caused wherever they went, they were more than raiders. They were also discoverers and colonizers, and Viking kingdoms existed outside Scandinavia for hundreds of years. During the 9th and 10th centuries, Norwegians discovered and settled far-off Iceland, and from Iceland, Greenland was later settled. Around the year 1000 Leif Ericson and his men set sail from Greenland for the shores of North America. There they established a colony they called Vinland. Remnants of a Viking-Age settlement dating from that time were discovered in Newfoundland in the 1960's. Norwegian Vikings also invaded and settled much of Ireland, northern England, and Scotland and its surrounding islands.

About 885–890 the scattered chiefdoms and provinces that had made up the country were gathered into one kingdom by Harold the Fair-haired, who became the first king of Norway. Harold tried to replace the system of local *things,* or assemblies, with one central assembly, and he collected taxes from the lesser chiefs. (Some who were unwilling to live under his rule emigrated to Iceland.) Viking raids and conquests in the rest of Europe continued, but the conversion to Christianity in the early 11th century was an important factor in calming the wrath of the Norsemen. Gradually, instead of plundering, Norwegians went abroad to trade. Cultural influences from Europe swept through Norway and blended with the Viking heritage. During the late Middle Ages, Norway entered a period of great expansion and prosperity. Some of Norway's cities, including Oslo and Bergen, were founded or grew into important trade centers during this time.

But prosperity was not to last. Conflicts between local rulers broke out, leading to civil war. The population was growing too fast to be supported by the land, and Norway had to import all of its grain. In the 14th century the great plague known as the Black Death swept across Europe. Almost half the Norwegian population died. Agriculture, crafts, and trade came to a standstill. The powerful Hanseatic League, a group

HATHAWAY HIGH

1138

of North German cities that controlled much European shipping, took over Norway's foreign trade—its main source of income. Norway's mastery of the sea was lost, and the country sank into poverty. Iceland and Greenland, acquired a century before, could no longer be supplied. The population in Iceland survived, but the Greenland colony perished.

In 1397 Queen Margrethe of Denmark set up the Union of Kalmar, uniting Sweden, Denmark, and Norway under her rule. The union lasted until 1523, but Norway's dependence on Denmark continued for almost 300 years more.

The loss of national independence, however, did not mean loss of personal freedoms. While practically all the rest of Europe was dominated by the feudal system, which severely restricted people's liberties, most Norwegians remained free men. The free Norwegian farmer in particular became a symbol of Norway's past and of national independence. The country's forests became a new source of income when the British and Dutch sailed across the oceans in ships built of Norwegian timber. An independent middle class arose in the cities, the economy prospered, and shipping revived.

The drive for independence gained momentum in the 18th century. The turning point came with the Napoleonic Wars in the early 19th century. Denmark sided with France, while most of Norway's trade and other interests lay with England, which was suddenly called the enemy. The Norwegians resented the Danish policy that so neglected the interests of Norway. On May 17, 1814, at Eidsvoll, near Oslo, an elected assembly declared Norway's independence and signed a constitution. Inspired by the American Declaration of Independence and the ideals of the French Revolution, it was the most liberal constitution in Europe at the time. With some amendments, it is still in force today, and May 17 is still celebrated as Norway's national holiday.

Later that year, however, Norway was forced to accept a union with Sweden. But the Norwegian Constitution was retained, and the average Norwegian continued to have political liberties unknown in the rest of Scandinavia. As the 19th century went on, Norway's independent position within the union was gradually strengthened. The Industrial Revolution began to make its mark in Norway. By about 1900 Norway had regained its position as one of the world's leading shipping nations.

In 1905 the union with Sweden was peacefully dissolved by mutual consent, and a Danish prince, Carl, was elected king (as Haakon VII) of independent Norway.

During the long reign of King Haakon VII (1905–57), modern Norway took shape. Social legislation was passed, with old-age pensions and other benefits for workers. The educational system was expanded to include more vocational and technical schools. Life in Norway grew prosperous and stable.

In April, 1940, however, in spite of Norway's declared neutrality, Germany invaded in a surprise attack. King Haakon refused to surrender, and several provisional capitals were set up as the government kept moving north one step ahead of the invaders. Finally King Haakon escaped to London to set up a government-in-exile. Vidkun Quisling, a Norwegian whose name has come to mean "traitor," led the government of Nazi-occupied Norway. Throughout the 5 years of occupation practically all Norwegians participated in the resistance movement. At the

FACTS AND FIGURES

KINGDOM OF NORWAY—Kongeriket Norge—is the official name of the country.

THE PEOPLE—are called Norwegians.

CAPITAL: Oslo.

LOCATION: Western part of the Scandinavian peninsula. **Boundaries**—Barents Sea, Soviet Union, Finland, Sweden, North Sea, Norwegian Sea.

AREA: 125,181 sq. mi (324,219 sq. km.), mainland; 149,426 sq. mi (387,014 sq. km.), including possessions.

PHYSICAL FEATURES: Highest point—Galdhøpiggen (8,097 ft.; 2,468 m.). **Lowest point**—sea level. **Chief rivers**—Glomma, Tana. **Major lakes**—Mjøsa, Femund.

POPULATION: 4,122,000 (1981 census); 4,100,000 (latest estimate).

MAJOR LANGUAGE: Norwegian.

MAJOR RELIGION: Evangelical Lutheran.

GOVERNMENT: Constitutional monarchy. **Head of state**—king. **Head of government**—prime minister. **Legislature**—Storting.

CHIEF CITIES: Oslo (450,000), Bergen (210,000), Trondheim (135,000), Stavanger, (92,000).

ECONOMY: Chief minerals—petroleum, natural gas, iron and iron pyrites, copper, zinc, lead. **Chief agricultural products**—hay, potatoes, barley, oats, wheat, vegetables, dairy products. **Industries and products**—oil and gas extraction, food processing, shipbuilding, wood pulp, paper products, refined metals, chemicals. **Chief exports**—crude oil and natural gas, refined metals, pulp and paper, fish and fish products, ships, chemicals. **Chief imports**—grains and other foodstuffs, ships, fuels, motor vehicles, iron and steel, chemical compounds, textiles.

MONETARY UNIT: Krone (pl. kroner) of 100 øre.

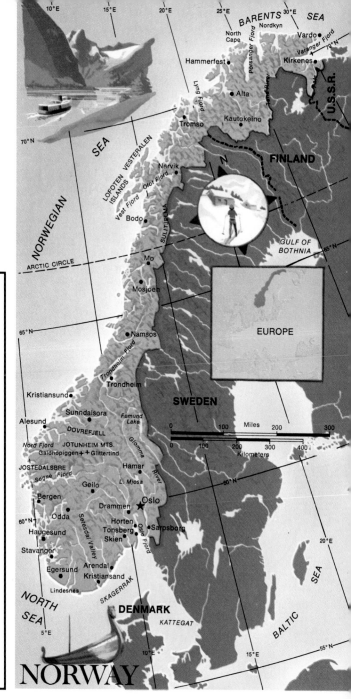

NORWAY

end of the war in 1945, King Haakon was joyfully welcomed back to a liberated Norway.

GOVERNMENT

Norway is a constitutional monarchy whose government is based on the Constitution of 1814, with subsequent amendments. The executive power held by the king is actually exercised by a cabinet headed by a prime minister. Cabinet members, although appointed by the king, govern with the approval of the Storting, Norway's legislative body, which is elected every 4 years. After each election, the Storting divides into two sections—the Lagting and the Odelsting.

ECONOMY

Beginning in the early 20th century, the thousands of rivers, waterfalls, and streams that rush down from Norway's towering mountain ranges were harnessed to produce electric power for homes and industry. Norway today has more kilowatt hours of electricity per inhabitant than any other country in the world. Because of this, whole new industrial centers have grown up across the country. Chemicals, refined metals, and high-quality finished goods such as tape recorders, office machinery, and electronics equipment are exported.

The sea is still important, however; Norway's merchant fleet is among the largest in the world. And, as in Viking days, fishing is still a major economic factor, although the number of fishermen is relatively small. Since the 1970's, moreover, the sea has yielded an enormous wealth in oil and natural gas—so great that these commodities now account for more than half of all Norwegian exports.

Because so little of Norway's land can be farmed, agriculture has been declining in importance. Most Norwegian farms are small, averaging about 12 acres (5 hectares), but they use mechanized methods and production is increasing steadily. Norway must still import most of its grain, but extensive dairy farming gives it a surplus of dairy products.

Another traditional Norwegian industry is forestry. At one time timber was the country's principal export. Forests still cover much of the country, and they are maintained by the addition of over 100,000,000 saplings every year—most of them planted by Norwegian schoolchildren and university students. Timber is processed for export and turned into paper, pulp, and a variety of other products. Wood products are Norway's third largest export industry, after crude oil and metals.

THE PEOPLE

Finally, as in Viking days, Norway's most valuable raw material is its people. The country has a population of more than 4,000,000, and statistics show that some 80 percent are blond and blue-eyed; that most are tall and athletic; and that of all the peoples in the world only the Icelanders have a longer life expectancy. But it is not possible to describe the Norwegian without giving a picture of his cultural background and the society in which he lives.

Norwegian culture today is a blend of the traditional and the modern. The Vikings had a highly developed artistic feeling, and their sense of craftsmanship has been preserved through the centuries in Norway's folk art. Though disappearing from the countryside today, folk art can be seen in Norway's many open-air museums, found all over the country.

As far back as the 9th century A.D., a form of oral literature flourished in Norway. This was later developed and written down in Iceland, including the sagas of Norway's kings, which contain most of what is known of Viking history. However, what is known abroad today of Norwegian literature dates mostly from the 19th century, when the plays of Henrik Ibsen and Bjørnstjerne Bjørnson were introduced into world literature. In this century the writers Sigrid Undset and Knut Hamsun have won the Nobel prize for literature. The 19th-century composer Edvard Grieg, the 20th-century expressionist painter Edvard Munch, and the sculptor Gustav Vigeland also won international renown.

Gabled construction was typical of Norway's medieval stave churches.

Education

Norway was one of the first countries to eradicate illiteracy, and since then Norwegians have been well aware that education holds the key to the future. The educational system is highly developed, but great efforts are being made to meet the fast rising demand for education. The young Norwegian enters school at the age of 7 and remains in school for a minimum of 9 years. Most students continue after that, going into technical, vocational, industrial, or commercial schools, or to colleges and universities. Education in Norway is free at all levels.

Tax money is used to finance the educational institutions—and taxes are higher in Norway than in most other countries. But the Norwegian feels that he is getting something back. Tax money is also used so that every citizen can live in comfort and security, without fear of misfortune. This is not a political issue in Norway. It is more a reflection of a general belief that everybody has a duty towards his neighbor if he is in trouble. This has not been left to chance and improvisation, but is part of a system that all Norwegians consider rational and fair, giving everybody an equal opportunity to live decently.

The Oslo Town Hall (right) opened in 1950 to commemorate the 900th anniversary of the city's founding.

One example is Norway's health program. Norway has a system of compulsory health insurance that covers the entire population and even foreigners who live there. It provides unlimited free medical care, unlimited free hospitalization in modern and comfortable hospitals, liberal cash allowances, and many other benefits. Doctors have their private practices and welcome the health insurance plan, which means that everybody can afford to see a doctor, whether it is the family physician or a specialist. The cost is split four ways—among the employee, the employer, the state, and the local community.

Similar plans exist in many other areas, providing insurance, for instance, against unemployment and disability. And today the retired Norwegian is entitled to a minimum pension that corresponds to about two thirds of his average annual income during his 20 best earning years.

This is the background against which the Norwegians live. Though they do not believe they have solved all their problems, they do believe that if the Norwegian can live under the best material conditions, he will also be able to give his best contribution to Norway's growth.

CITIES

Oslo. Norway's capital and its industrial, commercial, and cultural center is Oslo. It has all the characteristics of a bustling modern city as well as some of the aspects of a peaceful country town. This is largely because of its location at the end of the Oslo fiord and because of the nearby woodlands and hills.

Most public buildings are clustered around Oslo's main street, Karl Johans Gate, which leads from the main railway station up to the Royal Palace. In this town center are found the Lutheran Cathedral, the Storting (parliament), the National Theater, the National Gallery of Arts, the Museum of History, and the old university buildings. The main government buildings and the Supreme Court are only a few steps away, as is the harbor, which is guarded by Oslo's medieval Akershus Castle and the modern City Hall.

The park along the main street is called the Studenter-Lunden, the "student's grove," though most students have moved away to a new university campus built on the outskirts of the town. But the Student's Grove, dotted with open-air cafés during summer, remains the center both of cultural life and Oslo's amusement life. The Opera House is a short walk away, and the city's three repertory theaters and many movie houses are found nearby. Across the street from the grove, the Oslo Philharmonic performs in the old University Hall. Karl Johans Gate itself is lined with bookstores and fine shops. Since most Norwegians speak English, bookstores and newsstands carry a large selection of literature in English. The stores offer selections of contemporary furniture, crystal, silver, ceramics, furs, handmade fabrics, and sweaters—all the products that have contributed to Norway's reputation as a home of good design and craftsmanship. Some of Norway's best restaurants are found there, and though most offer an international menu, it is still easy to sample Norwegian food, like seafood specialties, reindeer steak, or the traditional cold table with its scores of tempting dishes.

Bergen, Norway's chief port on the North Sea, was the country's cultural center for centuries.

Vessels like the 1,000-year-old Oseberg ship were used by Norway's Viking ancestors to raid northern lands.

Among Oslo's attractions are the Vigeland sculptures in Frogner Park, a collection of more than 150 groups of bronze and granite sculptures depicting the cycle of human life. This monumental work was commissioned by the city of Oslo from Norway's best-known sculptor, Gustav Vigeland. Across the city's harbor is the Bygdøy peninsula, with a number of museums. Perhaps the most famous is the Viking Ship Museum, where three 1,000-year-old Viking ships are preserved, together with many Viking artifacts. The ships look as if they could sail today. A large open-air folk museum is also found on Bygdøy, with groups of authentic old farm buildings, as well as a stave church from the 12th century. In the Polar Exploration Museum is the *Fram*, the ship used on expeditions by Norway's explorer-statesman Fridtjof Nansen, and by Roald Amundsen in 1911, when he became the first man to reach the South Pole. Next door is the Kon-Tiki Museum, which shows the famous balsa raft on which Thor Heyerdahl crossed the Pacific in 1947.

These skiers are practicing a sport Norway is said to have invented.

Other Norwegian Cities. During Norway's early history, Bergen and Trondheim vied with each other for the designation as the nation's capital. Today they rank as Norway's second and third largest cities. The picturesque **Bergen** is located on the southwest coast, about 190 miles (300 km.) from Olso, on a small fiord surrounded by seven mountains. It has been a trade center for almost 1,000 years and is proud of its history, which can be felt everywhere—from Haakonshallen, the medieval banquet hall of the kings of Norway, to the Bryggen (Quay) from the Hanseatic period. Bergen is the home of Norway's second university and its College of Business Administration and is one of the world's leading centers of oceanographic research. Each spring thousands of visitors flock to its international festival of music, drama, and arts, when some of the concerts are held in Edvard Grieg's home, Troldhaugen ("troll's hill"), near the city. Bergen is also the starting point for tours of the great fiords, where the intense blues and greens of the crystal-clear waters reflect fruit orchards near sea-level and snow-clad mountain peaks high above.

In the Middle Ages **Trondheim**, farther to the north, was Norway's religious center. The city's skyline is still dominated by the Nidaros Cathedral, which is considered the finest Gothic church in Scandinavia. Trondheim is the home of Norway's Institute of Technology and of the University of Trondheim. The country's fourth university is in Tromso, in the far north, long a starting point for Arctic exploration.

A string of charming cities and towns lie along the Norwegian coast. **Stavanger**, in the southwest, is an important industrial center and has perhaps the most successful blend of old and modern architecture in the whole country. **Alesund**, north of Bergen, is Norway's largest fishing port and calls itself the herring capital of the world. And **Hammerfest** has the distinction of being the northernmost city in the world. All of them have good schools, libraries, and museums, and if they do not have orchestras, art galleries, and theaters of their own, visits are organized by a number of government-sponsored institutions. Even in a small place, life can be varied and full.

Daily Life in Norway

Norwegians enjoy life. They start the day with a hearty breakfast, and since there is little need for a heavy lunch, school is usually over by 1 or 2 P.M., and offices close at 4. Shops and factories close by 5 P.M. After an early dinner there is ample leisure time left over for sports and outdoor life. Many, if not most, city families have cottages on the seaside or in the mountains, which they use for swimming, sailing, fishing, and hunting. Norway's national sport, however, is skiing. Prehistoric rock carvings over 4,000 years old show skis in use in Norway, and a 2,500-year-old ski is on display in Oslo, in the world's only ski museum. In the 19th century Norwegians introduced skiing as a sport to the rest of the world. They still win many medals in the winter Olympic Games.

Though Norwegians today take modern conveniences as a matter of course, there are still some who do not lead the typical life of an industrial society. In the far north a few nomadic Lapps still lead their traditional life, following their reindeer herds from pasture to pasture. Years ago the reindeer provided food and furs for tents and clothing. Today the sale of reindeer meat is the Lapp's main source of income. But modern life has reached the Lapps, too. The Norwegian Government has built a special school and cultural center at Kautokeino, and radios and modern communications have brought the Lapps closer to the 20th century. (An article on LAPLAND appears in this volume.)

THE FUTURE

The Norwegians today lead a reasonably happy life in fair comfort, in a land that was never endowed with great riches. They have forced this land to yield a good living in spite of all natural handicaps, but they are determined that it shall not end there. They know that change will come, but they will try to make these changes themselves and not have them imposed by circumstances.

World politics place Norway in a vulnerable position. Norway also knows what it is to be occupied by a foreign power. The 5-year occupation by Nazi Germany during World War II taught Norway that security can only be found in co-operation with other democratic nations. The Norwegians therefore think that their best safeguard is to fulfill their commitments in the North Atlantic Treaty Organization and to work for peaceful solutions to international conflicts through the United Nations. They know that world peace is essential if they are to continue their own life of peace and progress, and they are willing to take the responsibilities that even a small country must shoulder.

On the world globe Norway is a small country in the far northwestern corner of Europe, but the Norwegians do not think of themselves as isolated. Through the centuries they have looked outward across the sea. From the days of the Vikings they have regarded the ocean as a "blue meadow" that is theirs to harvest, and as their lifeline to the world. Today more than ever, the Norwegians think that the sea does not divide, but unites.

LARS LANGAKER, Cultural Attaché, Royal Norwegian Embassy Information Service

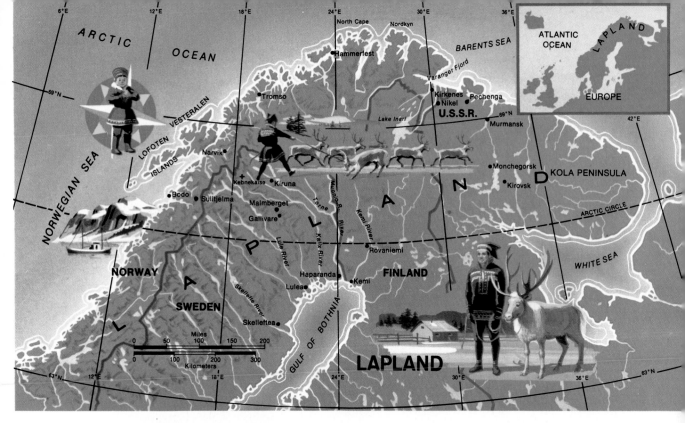

LAPLAND

Lapland is a region of some 150,000 square miles (390,000 square kilometers) that cuts across northern Norway, Sweden, Finland, and the Kola Peninsula of the Soviet Union. There, at the very top of Europe, live about 35,000 Lapps. The Lapps have made the Arctic Circle their home for thousands of years. It is a harsh environment but, over the centuries, the Lapps have adapted themselves to it. Today there are also Swedes, Norwegians, Finns, and Russians living in Lapland.

The Lapps probably arrived in northern Europe at the end of the last Ice Age. They were gradually pushed into the Arctic Circle by the Finns, Norwegians, and Swedes. The Lapps were isolated by the severe conditions in which they lived. But slowly they developed resources for making life easier in their unique northern homeland. They learned to tame and breed wild dogs and reindeer. They invented skis.

THE LAND

In the vast area above the tree line, there are seemingly endless snowfields and alpine mountains. Along the Arctic coastland there are gaunt, rocky cliffs. Inland are deep rivers with dangerous rapids and spectacular waterfalls, and sparkling finger-shaped lakes with thousands of islands. There are boundless marshlands and dense forests of pine, spruce, and birch.

The sun does not set over Lapland for 2 to 5 months in the summer. The regions closest to the North Pole have sunshine for the longest periods. The sun dips close to the horizon, filling the sky with glorious color. In midwinter, when conditions are reversed, there are a few hours

A Lapp boy in traditional costume beside the family tent.

A Lapp family admires one of its prize reindeer.

of twilight at midday, but the sun does not rise at all for 6 weeks or more.

Economy. The development of mineral resources in Lapland has brought thousands of new people to the area. One of the largest deposits of high-grade iron ore in the world is located at Kiruna in Swedish Lapland. Norway has iron mines near Kirkenes, and other metals are mined in Swedish, Russian, and Finnish Lapland. In northern Norway fish is a very valuable export. The rushing rivers are the site of many hydroelectric plants that supply power to Sweden and Finland.

THE PEOPLE

Lapps are known by the area in which they settled. The coastal or sea Lapps of Norway and the river Lapps of Sweden and Finland live in permanent homes and are mostly fishermen. The forest Lapps may have small reindeer herds, but today they combine reindeer breeding with fishing, simple farming, or working in the mining or timber industries. They do not wander far from their settlements.

Some Lapps live in cities and make their living from a thriving tourist industry. Because of the moderating effect of the Norwegian Current, Lapland has a much milder climate than parallel regions in northernmost Canada, Alaska, and Siberia. This encourages thousands of visitors to flock to Lapland to see the midnight sun, to ski, camp, and hike in the magnificent wilderness, and to observe the Lapp way of life.

Once all reindeer-breeding Lapps were nomads, with no permanent homes. Families moved south to the forests in winter. In summer they went north to escape the ferocious swarming mosquitoes and to reach the tundra, the plains on which moss and lichen—the reindeer's food—grow over permanently frozen subsoil. Today, family migrations are shorter or have almost ceased.

Not long ago skis and boat sleds pulled by reindeer provided the nomads with their only transportation over the frozen wastelands in winter. In summer the Lapps walked, but the reindeer carried their packs. The reindeer gave them milk. Some were also slaughtered for food and for their hides. The pelts, sewn with thread made from reindeer sinews, became clothing, shoes, and blankets and were used for the tepeelike tents. Reindeer bones and horns were shaped into implements and utensils. In Lapp a large reindeer herd is *aello,* "what one lives on." Today reindeer are bred for their pelts, and for their meat.

Tourists and workmen have brought the trappings of the modern world to Lapland, but the Lapps still follow many of their old ways of life. Families are close-knit, and devotion is lavished on the children. The Lapp language (which is related to Finnish) has a wealth of special ways to express affection between children and parents, between husband and wife, and between friends. The language also reflects the Lapps' deep feeling about nature. Special words describe states of weather and types of valleys, rivers, and lakes. There are countless words for the beloved reindeer, including a different name for the male reindeer for each of the first 6 years of life. Though there is little written Lapp literature, there is a rich store of legends and fairy tales that tell of the beauty and the hardship of life at the edge of the habitable world.

Reviewed by MIKKO IMMONEN
Former Consul, Consulate General of Finland, New York

Stockholm, Sweden's capital, is a city built on islands.

SWEDEN

Sweden shares the Scandinavian peninsula with its neighbor Norway. There at the top of Europe the Swedish people have created for themselves a prosperous, peaceful, democratic kingdom where they enjoy the highest standard of living in Europe.

Unlike many other European nations, Sweden has never known a large-scale foreign occupation and has not been at war since 1814. In the hope of insuring their prosperity and independence, the Swedes cling to their policy of neutrality and depend on their self-reliance and strength.

THE LAND

Sweden, the fourth largest nation in Europe (only France, the Soviet Union, and Spain are larger) is a long, narrow country. Geographers often divide it into three main parts: Gotaland in the south, Svealand in the center, and Norrland in the north. Gotaland, traditional home of the Goths, includes the most southern of Sweden's provinces, Skane. There, on 2.5 percent of the land, live 12 percent of the Swedish people. Skane, which enjoys Sweden's most pleasant climate, is a natural garden. There, amid gently rolling fields and peaceful villages, is Sweden's best agricultural land. Skane also has miles of white sandy beaches along its coast. Many resorts and the important port of Malmo are located on the coast.

North of Skane rise the Swedish highlands—a rugged, more wooded landscape. This area is damper and cooler, and the forests begin here. The land is stony and the soil thin. This is the area where most Swedish glass, furniture, and handicraft industries are located.

Svealand is considered the middle section of the country although it is still in the bottom half of Sweden. Here are the great forests that are supposed to have separated the two ancient rival tribes, the Svear and their southern neighbors, the Goths. There are also iron deposits here, and this is where most of Sweden's metal plants and steel foundries are.

Most of the more than 100,000 lakes of Sweden are in this central region. Some, such as Lake Malar, Lake Vatter, and Lake Vaner, are extremely large.

Sweden's two largest cities, Stockholm, the capital, and Goteborg, the port city, are in Svealand. They are connected by the picturesque Gota Canal, a remarkable inland waterway, only about one third of which is actually composed of canals. The remainder is a chain of rivers and lakes that form one of the loveliest areas in Scandinavia. Svealand also includes Dalarna, a historic province of Sweden, with lovely mountains and the beautiful Lake Silja.

Norrland, the third area of Sweden, covers about two thirds of the country. This sparsely populated northern land contains Sweden's highest mountains, including Kebnekaise, its highest peak. Norrland is considered the last open frontier in Europe. It is Sweden's big reservoir of natural resources. The great forests feed the string of sawmills, pulp mills, and cellulose factories on the coast. The enormous waterfalls provide the electric power for most of Sweden. The giant iron mountains give Sweden one of the world's most important sources of iron ore.

The northern highlands extend from central Sweden up beyond the Arctic Circle. This is the heart of Lapland, although Lapland is a vast area that also includes part of Norway, Finland, and the Soviet Union. Some 10,000 Lapps live in Swedish Lapland, and many still follow their herds of reindeer on annual migrations to the mountains in the spring and to the lowlands in the fall. (An article on LAPLAND appears in this volume.)

Off the east coast in the Baltic are two large limestone islands, Gotland and Oland. Oland is rich in archeological remains, Viking ship burial sites, and prehistoric forts. Both islands have a great variety of lovely and unusual flowers. Gotland is a trip back 6 centuries in history to the times of knights and monks. On the island is Visby, the only walled city in northern Europe and one of the best preserved anywhere.

Climate. Although it lies far north, Sweden has a more moderate climate than one would expect. It is warmed by the prevailing southwesterly winds and by the extension of the Gulf Stream current that brings the warm water from the West Indies to the North Atlantic.

But in such a long, stretched-out country, there is naturally a fairly wide variety of climate. "Last year summer happened on a Thursday" is the standard joke in Sweden. In the far north summer lasts only about 6 weeks, but during that time the midnight sun never sets. In midwinter, for the same period of time, there is almost total darkness. In Lapland snow lies on the ground from August to June. In the south, summer weather is mild and pleasant and lasts from about May to September. By September it is chilly, and in the winter it snows frequently.

Resources. Ore, forests, and water are Sweden's great natural riches. More than one half of the country is wooded. The favorable climate makes it possible for trees to grow everywhere except on the high mountains in the north. The major rivers of Sweden flow generally southeast from the mountains to the Gulf of Bothnia. Rivers flow through the forests, making it comparatively easy to float the logs down to factories and mills on the coast. A great deal of money, however, has been spent on building good roads, and today logs are often transported by truck.

It seems that where there are not trees in Sweden, there is water. Lakes cover nearly nine percent of the country's area, and the rapids on the rivers supply Sweden with large amounts of hydroelectricity.

Some mines are found in central Sweden, but in the northland there are whole mountains of iron ore. Northern Sweden also has deposits of copper, lead, and zinc.

Sweden does lack some important resources. It needs to import oil, coal, and coke, but the ingenious Swedes have used what they have the most of—iron ore, water, and forests—to build a great industrial nation. Since most available waterpower has been harnessed, however, Sweden has begun to utilize atomic energy. Several nuclear power plants are in operation, but further development of this power source is uncertain because questions about the safety of nuclear power production have led to political controversy.

THE PEOPLE

The Swedes are an extraordinarily homogeneous people. With the exception of the small group of Lapps in the north, the people of Sweden have the same ethnic origin. They are descended from Germanic tribes who settled the region. There are exceptions, but generally Swedes have fair skin, blue eyes, light hair, and are tall and trim.

Religion. The people of Sweden also share the same religion. Over 90 percent belong to the state church, which is the Evangelical Lutheran Church. There is complete religious freedom, but by law the king must be a member of the state church.

Language. The Swedish language is related to the languages spoken by the Norwegians and the Danes. All are related to German. The Swedish alphabet is like the English but also includes three additional vowels, å, ä, and ö, which come at the end of the alphabet.

Education. In 1842, earlier than in most countries, education was made compulsory. Students now must attend school from the age of 7 to 16. Most continue for 2 more years of academic or vocational training. At least 30 percent go on to 3-year gymnasiums, which correspond to senior high schools and junior colleges in other countries. There are now institutions of higher education at 21 locations in Sweden, including the universities of Uppsala and Lund, the former established in 1477, the latter in 1668.

Way of Life. The Swedes are extremely hardworking. But they also know how to play. In the summer they leave their offices early and often take 3-day weekends. All workers are legally entitled to 4 weeks of paid vacation.

Swedish people love sports. Soccer is the national game. Camping, bicycling, motoring, skiing, sailing, tennis, and golf are all very popular. All Swedes are required to take gymnastics in school, and many Swedes continue the exercises afterward since they take great pride in being physically fit.

About 80 percent of the Swedish people live in apartment houses. Because of the high cost of heating during the long winter months, it is more economical to build apartment houses than it is to build individual

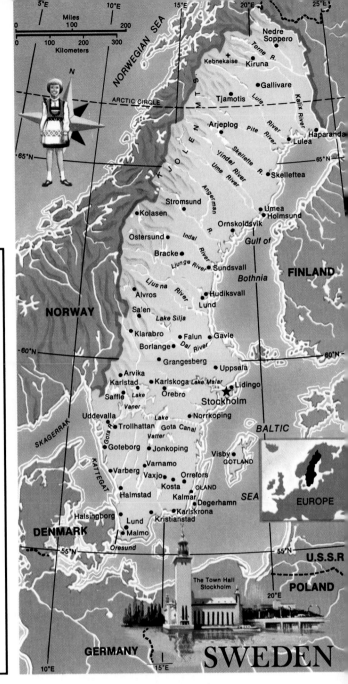

SWEDEN

FACTS AND FIGURES

KINGDOM OF SWEDEN—Konungariket Sverige—is the official name of the country.

THE PEOPLE—are called Swedes.

CAPITAL: Stockholm.

LOCATION: Eastern Scandinavian peninsula. **Boundaries**—Finland, Baltic Sea, Norway, Gulf of Bothnia.

AREA: 173,649 sq. mi. (449,750 sq. km.).

PHYSICAL FEATURES: Highest point—Kebnekaise (6,965 ft.; 2,123 m.). **Lowest point**—sea level. **Chief rivers**—Gota, Torne, Dal, Lule, Pite, Skellefte, Angerman, Indal, Ljusna. **Major lakes**—Malar, Vatter, Vaner.

POPULATION: 8,208,442 (1975 census); 8,345,000 (latest estimate).

MAJOR LANGUAGE: Swedish.

MAJOR RELIGION: Evangelical Lutheran.

GOVERNMENT: Constitutional monarchy. **Head of state**—king. **Head of government**—prime minister. **Legislature**—Riksdag.

CHIEF CITIES: Stockholm (650,000), Goteborg (430,000), Malmo (235,000), Uppsala (150,000).

ECONOMY: Chief minerals—iron, copper, lead, zinc. **Chief agricultural products**—hay, barley, oats, wheat, potatoes, sugar beets, dairy products. **Industries and products**—iron and steel, precision equipment (bearings, radio and telephone parts, armaments), wood pulp and paper products, processed foods, motor vehicles. **Chief exports**—motor vehicles, machinery, paper and board, iron and steel, chemicals, wood products, telecommunications equipment, metal manufactures. **Chief imports**—fuels, chemicals, foodstuffs, transportation equipment, machinery, clothing.

MONETARY UNIT: 1 Krona = 100 ore.

homes. However, many Swedish families have cabins in the woods to which they escape whenever possible.

Sweden is not a classless society, but because of high taxes and wide social benefits, it is a society in which differences hardly seem evident. Ways of living do not vary much from one part of the country to another. The fair-minded Swedes see to it that telephone subscribers in Stockholm pay the same rate for installing a telephone as do the Lapps, for whom it may be necessary to run 50 miles (80 km.) of wires. Most people have cars. Most people live in attractive flats. All see the same television. All go to the same state-run schools, take the same exams, draw similar social benefit grants, and earn salaries not too different from those of their neighbors.

Sweden has highly productive farms and abundant forestland, despite being as far north as Alaska.

Generally speaking, people are determined to find a way for everyone to realize his greatest potential. Many sum up the Swedish way of life by saying Sweden is a country of balance, a country of *lagom*, which means roughly: not too little, not too much, but just about right.

The Swedes have taken strides toward a real partnership between men and women. Women in Sweden probably have greater freedom than those of any other country. A large proportion of Swedish married women work full- or part-time outside the home. Since domestic help is almost unknown, the majority of married women find it necessary to stay home until their children can start school. There are free day-care nurseries, but they are used mainly by working mothers who are the sole support of their families.

Whether at home or in a restaurant, Swedish food is delicious and well-prepared. Perhaps the best-known contribution to international cuisine is the smorgasbord. This legendary feast—which has been known to defeat even the healthiest appetites—consists of a seemingly endless array of fish, meats, salads, and cheeses, from which diners select courses until they have eaten their fill. Smorgasbord is usually accompanied by beer. Should any room be left over for dessert, there are the tiny, delicate Swedish pancakes, sugared and served with whipped cream and a sauce made of lingonberries, or mountain cranberries. Swedish cooks also take pride in their preparation of the fresh fish that abound in northern waters and in such dishes as *köttbullar,* or Swedish meatballs.

Writers. Because few foreigners speak Swedish, many of the great past and contemporary writers are unknown to the rest of the world. Only through translation have their works become familiar beyond Swedish shores. Selma Lagerlöf, the first woman to receive the Nobel prize for literature, is probably Sweden's best-known writer. At her death at the age of 82, in 1940, she left a great body of work which ranges from *The Story of Gösta Berling,* a novel based on legends of her native Varmland, to the children's books about Nils, a youngster who traveled on the back of a wild goose and thus learned about the geography, culture, and history of Sweden and of foreign lands. August Strindberg's plays, such as *The Father,* and *Miss Julia,* have had a lasting effect on the development of drama in the Western world. Another great Swedish dramatist, Pär Lagerkvist, wrote stark plays about the plight of man, violence, and wars. He also wrote novels and poems.

Art. In Sweden there are some 2,000 runic inscriptions engraved by Viking artists on boulders, on the face of the bedrock, or on flat, upright stones. In these intricate patterns, done in the country's earliest days, we can see the beginning of Swedish interest in art and design.

The Swedes have always been noted for their wood carvings and sculptures. Sweden's best-known modern sculptor was Carl Milles, who died in 1955. Many of his exuberant works can be seen in a beautiful setting overlooking the waters of the Baltic in Millesgarden, in Lidingo, a suburb of Stockholm.

Sweden's architects have long designed buildings that demonstrated their feeling for the natural beauty of wood, stone, and other materials. The early medieval log buildings, the simple churches of the Middle Ages, the austere castles of the 16th century, and the mansions of later days all had the strong, clean lines and elegant simplicity that are evident in modern Swedish concrete, glass, and wood structures.

Swedish crystal is world renowned for its delicate designs and unusually vivid colors.

Films.   Swedish culture today is probably best-known to the rest of the world through the films produced in Sweden. Since the 1940's the work of Swedish directors has been acclaimed by critics everywhere. Arne Sucksdorff's *The Great Adventure* and *A Jungle Tale* and Ingmar Bergman's *The Seventh Seal, Wild Strawberries*, and *Through a Glass Darkly* are considered classics of the screen.

SWEDISH CITIES

More than 80 percent of the Swedish people live in cities and towns, and the process of urbanization is still continuing. There are three metropolitan areas: greater Stockholm, Göteborg and surrounding areas in the west, and Malmo and its neighboring cities in the south.

Stockholm.   Stockholm today is truly the center of Sweden and Swedish life. It is the seat of the government and the center of business and culture. It is an important manufacturing city as well. Seen from a plane the lovely city seems to be made of many separate pieces all floating on blue water and interlaced by an intricate network of bridges. Actually, the Queen of the Waters, as Stockholm is known, is built on a whole group of islands where the fresh water of Lake Malar meets the Baltic Sea. Founded in the 13th century, Stockholm became the capital of Sweden in 1634. The Old Town (Gamla Stan) is on an island in the center of the city, and it is from this island that the modern city grew. The Old Town, which still retains its medieval street plan, includes the Royal Palace, a masterpiece of classical design.

The rest of Stockholm is modern, busy, and crowded. All of it seems to be clean, sparkling, and carefully planned. It is hard to mention all

Pedestrian shopping mall in Stockholm combines efficiency and the best of modern design.

These are just a few of the sculptures in the Millesgarden, outside Stockholm.

the treasures of Stockholm and its environs. The museums are a delight to visit, since their collections are displayed with great technical skill.

The Royal Academy of Music, founded in 1771, is one of the oldest on the continent outside of Italy, and the Royal Opera dates from 1773. It plays one of the longest seasons in the world. Close to the city is the famous Drottningholm Court Theater. Built in 1766, Drottningholm is the world's only complete 18th-century theater that has survived and is used just as it was in earlier times for operas and ballets.

Skansen, a beautiful 60-acre (24 hectares) park a few minutes from the center of town, is really a great open-air museum. More than 100 old buildings brought from all over Sweden have been reconstructed there.

Göteborg. A seaport on the Kattegat at the mouth of the Gota River, Göteborg is Sweden's second largest city and greatest port. It is also a historic city. Dutch town planners were brought in to build it in the 17th century, and their influence is apparent in the old circular canals. The charming Gotaplatsen (Gota Square) is dominated by Carl Milles' fountain sculpture of Poseidon, the Greek sea god. Göteborg is a busy center of auto manufacturing and ball-bearing production. It has an ultramodern shipyard that produces supertankers.

Malmo. Sweden's third city is on the Oresund opposite Copenhagen. From the end of the Middle Ages until 1658, when it became Swedish, Malmo was one of the leading cities of Denmark. The central city retains its medieval street plan, but the city has spread out and also has some of Sweden's most interesting modern housing projects. An important port, Malmo is also a shipbuilding and manufacturing city. It has many notable buildings, including the finest Gothic church in Sweden, the 14th-century Church of Saint Peter.

Industry

Early in the 20th century Sweden was one of the most backward countries in Europe. Conditions were so bad that more than one fifth of the population emigrated to America. In a truly remarkable leap forward, the Swedish people in a relatively short period of time created an industrial nation with almost full employment, where labor receives the highest wages in Europe and the most lavish welfare benefits in the world, and where a large share of the national production is exported.

The Swedes managed to avoid many errors made by other countries that industrialized earlier and very quickly recognized the need for industrial planning. There has been much written about Swedish socialism. In reality the government has left the operation of industry almost entirely in private hands. Some 85 percent of Swedish industry is privately controlled, more than in West Germany, France, and Great Britain. The government does play an important role in all industrial planning.

The early industries were based on the Swedish forests and minerals. Swedish inventors aided in developing industries by devising products and perfecting techniques to aid in their manufacture. In the 19th century J. E. Lundström invented the safety match. And in 1866 Alfred B. Nobel invented dynamite and began to accumulate the fortune that enabled him to establish the famous Nobel prizes. Other Swedish inventions include ball bearings, automatic light beacons, new types of steam turbines, methods of electrical transmission, refrigerating systems, machines and methods for making cellulose, high-grade steel, and other products.

Göteborg is Sweden's leading port and home to its largest shipyards. Only Japan leads in shipbuilding.

Iron ore from the north is used to make high-quality steel—an important Swedish export.

But in recent years Swedish industries have turned more and more to highly sophisticated metalworking and engineering industries. Shipbuilding, a traditional industry, is still important, but more important today is the manufacture of cars, buses, and trucks. Some of the finest steel in the world is made in Sweden and many products made from high grade steel, such as ball bearings, cutlery, precision instruments, tools, medical instruments, and razor blades, are increasingly exported. A wide variety of complex products ranging from sewing machines to computers and airplanes are now made in quantity for export.

Agricultural Products. Only 7 percent of the land in Sweden is arable, and only about 6 percent of the people are now employed in agriculture. It is possible to grow grain and potatoes even in northern Sweden, but most of the farming is done in the southern part of the country. By the use of soil studies, improved seed, artificial fertilizers, and mechanization, Sweden has managed to produce record harvests. Most of the farms are very small, but almost all are participants in cooperatives that market products and provide farmers with equipment. It is remarkable that with so little farmland, Sweden feeds itself so well.

GOVERNMENT

Although Sweden has a king, he exerts no political power and is no longer even crowned. He is the titular head of the state, while real responsibility rests with the prime minister, who is the leader of the majority party in the Parliament. The present king is Carl XVI Gustaf, who succeeded his grandfather, Gustav VI Adolf, in 1973.

The Riksdag, or parliament, became a permanent institution in 1435. One of the oldest legislative bodies in the world, it now has one chamber elected by all citizens 18 years or older on election day. The Social Democratic Party was the ruling party almost continuously from 1932 until 1976, and it returned to power in 1983 after seven years in the opposition.

Welfare State. Since the early 20th century the Swedish people have been developing a wide range of social-welfare benefits for all citizens. A large part of the total national income is devoted to paying for these benefits. Extensive education, health, welfare, and retirement services are provided. This is expensive, and the taxes are high, ranging from 20 to 80 percent depending on the size of the income.

A person does not have to prove need in order to receive benefits, because the Swedes believe it is as important to prevent social distress as to relieve it. All citizens are protected against financial hardships resulting from illness, disability, childbirth, old age, or death of the family provider.

There are free health services both for preventive care and for hospital care if needed. Necessary medicines are free. There are allowances paid for anyone who is sick and unable to work. The Swedes rank among the top nations in terms of life expectancy.

All parents receive a monthly allowance for all children under 16 years and those up to 21 who are attending school. Education benefits are many and varied. They include free college tuition.

Provision for old age extends over a wide range of benefits. In addition to old-age pensions that go to all who reach the age of 67, there are supplemental pensions for those who need them. Special dwellings are available for elderly people. For those who wish to live alone, assistance is provided.

In 1809 the Swedes created the office of ombudsman to provide a way to protect citizens from abuses by government. The ombudsman is a government official empowered to investigate complaints by citizens against government employees. The idea has been widely copied by many countries.

HISTORY

The land that is now Sweden emerged late from the retreating ice cap. Tribes of hunters moved north and for many years two tribes, the Goths in the south and the Svear in the eastern part of central Sweden, waged war. Ultimately, in the 9th century A.D. the two tribes were united. The Swedish name for Sweden, or Sverige, means "kingdom of the Svear."

During the time of the Vikings (A.D. 800–1050), these fierce sea warriors went on long expeditions to trade and to wage war. The Swedish Vikings, unlike the Norwegian, sailed eastward across the Baltic Sea. Some of them even traveled down the Russian rivers as far as the Black and Caspian seas. By the 10th century the Swedish Vikings had established trading posts in that distant land. The name "Russia" may come from the word "Ros," which is the name of the Swedish Vikings who lived along the Baltic, north of Stockholm.

Christian missionaries visited Sweden during this time, but it was not until the 12th century that Christianity was firmly established. During the 11th and 12th centuries Sweden gradually became a united king-

Gripsholm Castle, in southern Sweden, was a favorite residence of King Gustavus I.

dom. Working to convert the Finns, the Swedes developed Finland as a part of Sweden. In 1397 the Kalmar Union united all the Nordic lands—Denmark, Norway, and Sweden—under a Danish queen, Queen Margrethe. The union was not a happy one. The Swedes feared Danish domination, and warfare broke out in the 15th century. In 1523 after a long struggle Sweden became independent. Until 1814 a long series of terrible wars between Denmark-Norway on one side and Sweden-Finland on the other marked Scandinavian history.

Gustavus Vasa, a young nobleman who had led the Swedes in their struggle against the Kalmar Union, was elected king in 1523. He took the title Gustavus I, and until his death in 1560 he did much to lay the foundation of modern Sweden. It was during his reign that Sweden broke with the Catholic Church and Lutheranism became the state religion. His grandson, known as Gustavus Adolphus, who ruled from 1611 until 1632, led an enormous political and military expansion. Under his leadership, Swedish armies played an important role in the Thirty Years War. By the end of his reign Sweden could regard the Baltic Sea as a Swedish lake.

Swedish power was constantly challenged by Russia, Saxony-Poland, and Denmark-Norway. In 1700 they joined to attack the Swedish kingdom. The young Swedish king Charles XII won spectacular victories, but his plan to attack Moscow led to a catastrophic defeat at Poltava in 1709. This marked the beginning of the end of Sweden as a great power.

Gradually Sweden was forced to give up its Baltic territories. In 1809 the Swedes lost Finland, a country they had held since the 12th century. At this time Sweden was in a desperate economic condition and feared invasion by the Danes from the south and west and by the Russians from the east. A revolution deposed the monarch, and the Swedes drafted a constitution and elected Jean Baptiste Bernadotte (1763–1844), a general in the French Revolution and later one of Napoleon's marshals, to be their crown prince. He succeeded in 1818 as King Charles XIV.

Under Crown Prince Bernadotte the Swedish armies fought against Napoleon. By the Treaty of Kiel in 1814, Sweden received Norway from Denmark. The union of Sweden and Norway lasted until 1905, when the Norwegians demanded and received their independence.

In the early 1900's Sweden embarked on a great drive for liberalized government and economic development of the country. At the same time, the Swedes became determined to make neutrality the keystone of their foreign policy. During World War I, Denmark, Norway, and Sweden declared their neutrality. When World War II broke out, they did so again. Denmark and Norway were invaded. Sweden escaped. All during the struggle, Sweden did much to aid its Scandinavian neighbors and served as a haven for refugees.

Neutrality. For more than 150 years the Swedes have been living in peace, and they wish to go on doing so. Sweden's neutral state is supported by substantial military power. The Swedes have used their natural resources to aid their defense planning. Vast underground shelters, said to be safe in nuclear attack, have been carved out of Sweden's rocky terrain. They are used in many practical ways—for parking lots, warehouses, and even gymnasiums. Defense expenditures are large for a small nation, and there is universal military service. The Swedes have decided to make it expensive and difficult for any nation to invade them.

Yet Sweden has always been in the forefront of all peace efforts. A strong supporter of the League of Nations in the past, Sweden is today a strong supporter of the United Nations. Swedish troops have served with U.N. peace-keeping missions in Israel, the Congo, and Cyprus. Count Folke Bernadotte lost his life in 1948 in Israel, where he had gone as a U.N. mediator. Dag Hammarskjöld, the second secretary-general of the U.N., died in an accident in 1961 on his way to the Congo to try to stop the civil war there.

Collectively Sweden, Norway, Denmark, Finland, and Iceland are known as the Nordic countries. Since the 1950's the Nordic Council has met to discuss and recommend parallel legislation and administrative actions. Relations between the countries are so close that any Nordic citizen may freely cross the border into any other Nordic country to take up work or residence and is entitled to social security benefits while there.

The Swedes have often been criticized for remaining aloof in their neutrality and for being smug in their accomplishments. But along the path that took Sweden from a great power to a welfare state there were great hardships. The Swedish people have attained what they have because of a willingness to work hard and to pay the price in high taxes for their improvements and benefits. They yearn to see their country as a world laboratory for technical and sociological change. Knowing they will never again be a world power, the Swedes·hope to be an example to the emerging countries of the world of what intelligent planning and peace can accomplish. They continue to experiment in better ways to live and to govern. They believe, as one of their prime ministers observed, "stability can come only from social change."

ULRICH HERZ, Editor and author

In winter in Finland, reindeer are often used to pull sleds.

FINLAND

Sisu is a Finnish word that means "spirit," "courage," "patriotism," "tenacity," and "determination," and it is the word that best describes the people of Finland.

THE LAND

Since about one third of Finland lies north of the Arctic Circle, the Finns live in one of the most northerly nations in Europe (and the world). Yet Finland today enjoys a high standard of living from every point of view—economical, social, and cultural.

Although Finland lies farther north than the distant wastes of northern Labrador, it has developed modern industry, agriculture, and cities. The Fennoscandian Peninsula, which Finland shares with Norway and Sweden, juts out of continental Europe into the Atlantic Ocean. Southwesterly winds from the Gulf Stream bring warmth and moisture to the land. The waters of the Baltic Sea and the Gulf of Bothnia also contribute to the maritime quality of Finland's climate. As a result, no part of Finland is covered by permanent snow, ice, or ground frost. Temperatures are generally mild, and even during February, the coldest month of the year, temperatures in the north average about 5 degrees Fahrenheit (−15 degrees Celsius).

Finland has an area slightly less than that of the state of Montana. Many rivers thread the land. Its coasts are heavily indented and fringed by some 30,000 islands. Along the western coast especially, another unique aspect of Finnish geography can be observed—land emergence. Since the last Ice Age, about 8,000 years ago, the land has

One of Finland's 60,000 lakes.

been rising from the sea at a rate of about 3–4 feet (1 meter) every century, adding miles of land to Finland's area every 100 years.

Lakes and Forests

Finland has over 60,000 lakes, which comprise about 9 percent of the country's area. Many of them are in central and southeast Finland, where the land was shaped and folded into ridges and depressions by the glaciers of the last Ice Age. The lakes form a vast network of clear, sun-sparkled waters set among cool, green forests, like a blanket of jewels thrown carelessly across the face of the land. The largest of Finland's lakes, and the center of its lake system, is Saimaa, near the Russian border. The Saimaa Canal, extensively rebuilt after World War II, links the industrial city of Lappeenranta on the south shore of the lake with Vyborg, a Russian port on the Baltic.

North of Lake Saimaa, near the town of Savonlinna, stands Olavinlinna ("Saint Olaf's castle"). Built in 1475 as a watchtower facing east, Olavinlinna is the best-preserved medieval fortress in northern Europe. Now, however, the castle walls echo not with the sounds of battle but with the music of the opera festival that is held there every July. Not far from Olavinlinna is Punkaharju, where a road winds for about 5 miles (8 kilometers) along a narrow rise of land topped by some of the tallest pine trees in the world. Punkaharju—the word means "primrose ridge" in Finnish—has inspired many poets, artists, and musicians. Overlooking a dazzling view of lakes and islands, it has been described as the soul of Finland. Punkaharju, one of the country's main tourist attractions, is under the protection of the Finnish Government so that it will always remain beautiful and unspoiled.

The lakes and islands are as useful as they are beautiful. Since Finland has no coal or oil, waterpower, or "white coal," is the source of

Olavinlinna, in southeastern Finland, dates from the 15th century.

much of the country's electricity. Finland lost about one third of its hydroelectric plants to the Soviet Union in 1944–45, but the production of hydroelectricity has increased greatly since World War II. The lake system's major task, however, is carrying wood, Finland's most valuable natural resource. After the timber is cut, huge rafts of logs are floated to the mills where they are turned into pulp and paper, to the factories where they are made into fine furniture, or down to Baltic ports for export. Forests cover about three quarters of Finland's total land area. Timber, wood products, and paper products account for nearly 40 percent of the nation's exports.

Agriculture—Much From Little

Almost nowhere in Finland is there deep, fertile, and naturally treeless soil ready for the plow. Less than ten percent of the land is arable, and even this small amount had to be won over the years from forests and swamps by backbreaking labor. Hundreds of years ago, farmers had to cut down and burn off the pine trees in order to gain land to raise crops. Today, though the majority of Finnish farms are small—only a few hundred are larger than 250 acres (100 hectares)—every bit of usable land has responded so well to careful tillage that the country is almost self-sufficient in food production. Most of the farms are owned and run by single families.

Finland's soil resources are modest, but because of its latitude it has the advantage of long days during the growing season. In the south in late June, the sun shines for some 18 to 19 hours daily, and the nights do not get really dark. Farther north, but still below the Arctic Circle, daylight is nearly constant during the height of summer. In the extreme north the sun remains above the horizon for over 70 consecutive days.

Hardy types of grain that ripen during the short growing season are

Forests are Finland's most valuable natural resource. Cut timber, bundled into rafts, is floated downstream to paper mills, furniture factories, or to Baltic ports for export.

raised extensively, and Finland is able to supply almost 90 percent of its own grain needs. Since the early 1900's, however, dairy farming has become more important than grain farming. Finnish farmers also raise such vegetables as beets, carrots, cabbage, turnips, spinach, and lettuce. Apples, especially cold-resistant varieties, are grown over a wide area, but pears, cherries, and plums succeed only in the south, where the climate is mildest. Potatoes are the only crop that grows in the far north.

THE PEOPLE AND THEIR HISTORY

The origin of the Finns is unknown, though linguistic studies have shown that the Finnish language is related to Estonian and, more distantly, to Hungarian. Finland's recorded history actually began during the Middle Ages, at a time when most Finns lived by hunting and farming and the country consisted of a group of settlements located mainly along the rivers, within 200 miles (320 km.) of the south coast.

Finland and Sweden

In 1155 King Eric IX of Sweden decided to convert the land of the Finns to Christianity. He sent the Bishop of Uppsala, at the head of an army, across the Gulf of Bothnia. This was the first of three Swedish crusades to Finland. Within about 100 years, most of the Finns had accepted Christianity. Since they had had no national government, there was little resistance and Finland was easily absorbed by Sweden. In this period cathedrals and fortresses were built and towns grew up around them, including Turku, on the Aura River in southwest Finland. Finland's first university was founded there in 1640. The city was also the center of Roman Catholicism in Finland and, after the Protestant Reformation in the 16th century, of the Lutheran Church. Turku was the capital of Finland until 1812, when Helsinki became the capital.

The inclusion of Finland in its kingdom was an important factor in Sweden's rise to power in the Baltic, a power it was able to maintain against all challenges through the 17th century. In 1703, however, seeking increased trade with European nations and what he called a "window looking on Europe," Czar Peter the Great of Russia founded the city of St. Petersburg (now Leningrad). He built his city on land he had taken by force from Sweden. Throughout the 18th century, Sweden fought against the new threat from the east. Finland became a focal point in the struggle between Sweden and Russia, and it was invaded and re-invaded by Russian armies. Towns and villages were burned; crops were ruined. In the 8 years between 1713 and 1721, many of Finland's people were killed, died of starvation, or emigrated from their homes.

In the 18th and 19th centuries, the first awakenings of nationalism took place in Finland. The two leaders responsible were Henrik Gabriel Porthan and Elias Lönnrot. Porthan was a historian who tried through his writings to create an awareness of Finland's own special heritage as a nation. Lönnrot spent many years traveling all over Finland, collecting the legends and tales that had been handed down by generations of Finnish folk poets. In 1835 he published the first edition of the *Kalevala,* the long poem that became Finland's national epic. Before the *Kalevala,* Finnish had been considered a language unfit for literature, suitable only for farmers and the uneducated. Now it became a source of pride and inspiration for the Finns.

Finland and Russia

By the time of the Napoleonic Wars, Swedish power in the Baltic had disappeared almost entirely. In 1808 the King of Sweden refused to join Napoleon I's blockage of England. In retaliation, Napoleon persuaded Czar Alexander I to invade Finland. In 1809, after more than 600 years, Sweden had to give up Finland to Russia.

Again the Finns were not actually conquered. Finland became part of Russia as an autonomous state. Finland was allowed to keep the constitution that had applied to all of Sweden before 1808. The legal rights of Finland's citizens remained unchanged. The Lutheran Church remained the state church. A Finnish government council was set up in Helsinki, the new capital, and a delegation of Finns was sent to the Russian capital to advise the Czar on Finnish matters. The Czar of Russia, under the title Grand Duke of Finland, ruled Finland as a constitutional monarch. So at first Finland seemed to have gained by its inclusion in the Russian Empire. At the same time, other changes were taking place. Farming was being modernized; a nationwide school system was introduced (1866); and railroads and industry came to Finland as they did to the rest of Western Europe.

Yet in the second half of the 19th century, other trends appeared. The spirit of nationalism began to spread. During the Crimean War (1854–56), some young Finns, dreaming of independence, joined the British Navy to fight the Russian fleet in the Baltic. After the war, though Czar Alexander II had granted Finland liberal reforms, Finland's self-

Highly productive family farms have made Finland nearly self-sufficient in agriculture.

FACTS AND FIGURES

NAME: Finland.

NATIONALITY: Finn(s).

CAPITAL: Helsinki.

LOCATION: Fennoscandian Peninsula. **Boundaries—**Norway, Soviet Union, Gulf of Finland, Baltic Sea, Gulf of Bothnia, Sweden.

AREA: 139,127 sq. mi. (337,030 sq. km.).

PHYSICAL FEATURES: Highest point—Mt. Haltia (4,343 ft.; 1,324 m.). **Lowest point—**sea level. **Chief rivers—**Kemi, Oulu, Tornio, Muonio, Pats, Ounas, Kokemäki, Kymi, Vuoksi. **Major lakes—**Saimaa, Oulu.

POPULATION: 4,963,592 (latest estimate).

MAJOR LANGUAGES: Finnish and Swedish (official), Lapp, Russian.

MAJOR RELIGIONS: Evangelical Lutheranism, Greek Orthodoxy.

GOVERNMENT: Republic. **Head of state—**president. **Legislature—**one-house Eduskunta.

CHIEF CITIES: Helsinki, Tampere, Turku, Espoo.

ECONOMY: Chief minerals—copper, zinc, iron. **Chief agricultural products—**animal husbandry, dairy, forestry, cereals, sugar beets, potatoes. **Industries and products—**metal manufacturing, shipbuilding, wood processing, copper refining, foodstuffs, textiles, clothing. **Chief exports—**timber, paper and pulp, ships, machinery, clothing and footwear. **Chief imports—**foodstuffs, petroleum and petroleum products, chemicals, transportation equipment, iron and steel, machinery, textile yarn and fabric.

MONETARY UNIT: Markka.

A NOTE ON PLACE-NAMES

A number of cities in Finland are often still called by their former Swedish names. This list gives some Finnish place-names and their Swedish equivalents.

FINNISH	SWEDISH
Helsinki	Helsingfors
Turku	Åbo
Tampere	Tammerfors
Lappeenranta	Villmanstrand

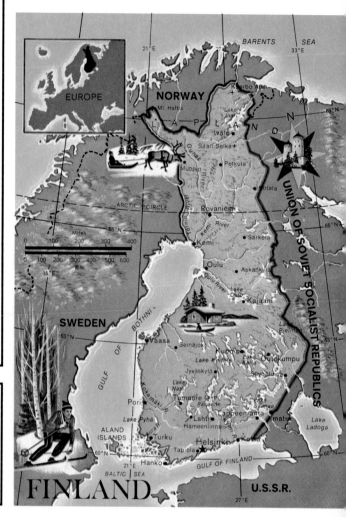

government and the freedom of its citizens were in danger. After 1890, a policy of Russification went into effect. Russian was made the official language; Finland's army was absorbed into the Russian army; the power of Finland's Diet (parliament) was restricted until it was no more than a rubber stamp of Russian policies; and strict censorship was imposed on the press. By the beginning of World War I, in 1914, the Finns had lost much of their freedom. When the Russian Revolution brought the end of czarist rule in Russia in 1917, Finland declared itself independent.

Independent Finland

The period between the two world wars was a time of progress for Finland. Land reforms were put through, and most of Finland's independent family farms date from this time. Industrial production more than tripled in volume and quadrupled in value. Finland's trade also expanded greatly. Some of Finland's other natural resources, such as copper and nickel, were first developed at this time. Finnair, the national airline, was founded. The shipbuilding industry grew, and Finland soon led the world in the construction of icebreakers and similar ships.

Though there had been an attempted revolution by Finnish Communists in 1918, in general, Finland enjoyed marked political stability after independence. Numerous welfare measures were put into effect, including accident, sickness, and disability insurance; old-age pensions; and maternity benefits and child allowances.

The national school system that had been in place since the 19th century was expanded at this time. In 1921, compulsory education was introduced; school attendance is now obligatory between the ages of 7 and 16. Finland's universities and professional schools also expanded, and the number of vocational schools and adult-education centers increased. During this period, too, the first attempts were made to bring education to the Finnish Lapps and to make them part of Finnish life without losing any of their own special cultural traditions. (An article on LAPLAND appears in this volume.)

The Winter War and World War II. Finland's foreign policy after independence had been simple—peaceful relations with all nations, faithful observance of international commitments, and absolute neutrality in case of war. In 1939, however, the Soviet Union demanded that Finland cede parts of its territory for the defense of Leningrad. Finland refused and was invaded. Although they were faced with overwhelming odds, the Finns defended their liberty so resolutely that English Prime Minister Winston Churchill said of them, "Finland alone—in danger of death, superb, sublime Finland—shows what free men can do."

The heroic resistance was led by Field Marshal Carl Gustav Emil von Mannerheim. United by love of their country, the Finns also knew the land they were fighting on and were able to withstand the unusually severe winter better than the poorly trained Russian soldiers. Using specially trained ski troops camouflaged in white, the Finns were able to hold back the Russians for about four months. Finally, though, they were forced to sue for peace, to accept the harsh treaty imposed by the Soviet Union, and to give up vital areas of southeast Finland.

In June 1941, Germany attacked the Soviet Union. Finland entered World War II fighting alongside Germany, but only to regain its lost territories. (Finland refused to take part in operations that served German, rather than Finnish, aims.) Although they were successful at first, eventually the Finns had to accept another treaty dictated by the U.S.S.R. Under the terms of the treaty, Finland paid the Soviet Union some $300 million—in ships, industrial machinery, locomotives, and, most important, fully equipped paper and woodworking factories. Within eight years, Finland had met these terms. Finland was never behind the Iron Curtain, but its independence was precarious at best during the Cold War years. In matters of foreign policy, especially during the volatile Stalin era, Finland was careful not to provoke its powerful neighbor.

Since the end of the war, Finland has been governed by a changing coalition of political parties. After 1987 elections, the conservative National Coalition Party joined the government for the first time since 1966, and its leader became prime minister. Social Democratic Party leader Mauno Koivisto was elected president in 1982 and 1988.

Government. Finland's head of government is the president, who is elected every six years by 301 electors. The electors are chosen by universal suffrage. All Finns over the age of 18 can vote. The country's single-chamber legislature is called the Eduskunta.

Helsinki, Finland's capital and largest city, is the site of the imposing Lutheran cathedral (background).

CITIES

Helsinki.   Much of Finland's history can be read in the buildings and streets of Helsinki, often called the "white city of the north." It became the capital in 1812, when Czar Alexander I decided that Turku was too far from Russia and chose instead a small city on the Baltic. He supervised much of the planning and architecture of the new capital. A German architect, C. L. Engel, was chosen to design many of the buildings, including those surrounding Great Square—the Government Palace, the University, and the Great Church, whose tower is visible from ships approaching the harbor. In 1894 a statue honoring Czar Alexander II—"Friend of Finland"—was erected in the square.

But even today Helsinki remembers its beginnings as a small port and fishing center. Every morning the traditional harbor market is still held, and among the crowded stalls sea gulls can be seen picking up scraps while ducks paddle and dive below the docks nearby.

Elsewhere in the capital there are the clean, sweeping lines that have made Finnish architecture famous around the world. The Helsinki Olympic Stadium, designed by Alvar Aalto, is used for the track-and-field events in which the Finns have excelled since the days of Paavo Nurmi, the great runner who was called the "flying Finn." The National Museum, on Mannerheimintie ("Mannerheim street"), and the Helsinki Railroad Station were both designed by Eliel Saarinen, who later emigrated to the United States. Both Eliel and his son Eero made important contributions to 20th-century architecture in the United States.

Helsinki's new, white-tile National Theater is the center of the performing arts in Finland. The works of Finnish playwrights of the 19th century, such as Aleksis Kivi, are popular, but the majority of plays put

On Aland Island in the Gulf of Bothnia, a craftsman makes pottery for the tourist trade.

A statue of Paavo Nurmi, a Finnish runner who won seven gold medals, stands by Helsinki's Olympic Stadium.

Boldly colorful Marimekko cottons are only one example of fine Finnish design.

Helsinki's Sibelius Memorial captures the spirit of his music and of Finland.

Helsinki's harbor, choked with midwinter ice.

on are by non-Finnish authors. The Finnish book industry is based in Helsinki, publishing almost 7,000 books per year, including the novels of the 1939 Nobel prize winner, Frans Eemil Sillanpää, and the contemporary Mika Waltari.

In Helsinki's restaurants, some of the country's characteristic foods can be sampled—Karelian pie, made of ground meat, rice, and melted butter; small, succulent crayfish taken from Finland's sparkling waters; desserts made from the yellow cloudberry, which grows only in Scandinavian countries; and the special golden liqueur called Mesimarja, made from the fruit of the Arctic bramblebush. The city's shops sell the pottery and glassware of Arabia and Iittala, the brightly printed fabrics and fashions of Marimekko, Artek, Vuokko, and Finn-Flare, and all the other products that have earned Finland its reputation as a home of good design.

Visitors to Helsinki can enjoy trips out to the fortress of Suomenlinna (Sveaborg), which has been guarding the harbor since the 18th century. They can take walks along the esplanade near the harbor, and relax at one of its outdoor restaurants. On May 1, they can watch the traditional May Day fun, when university students drape the statue of Havis Amanda (a symbol of Helsinki) with flower garlands and place a white graduation cap on her head. The students also take part in Finland's Independence Day celebrations every December 6. There is a torchlight procession during which one Finnish flag is carried for every year since 1917.

Visitors can also try a sauna, one of the oldest and best-known Finnish traditions. No one knows quite how the sauna got its start, but it seems to have been a part of Finnish life for centuries. It is estimated that there are close to 1,000,000 saunas in Finland today, and they are often used more as a social occasion or a form of relaxation than as a bath. Families often invite friends to enjoy their saunas together.

The word "sauna" means "dry heat bath," and in its most traditional form the sauna is a specially constructed wooden cabin, where stones are heated almost red-hot and water is thrown on them to control the humidity. There are several benches, or shelves, in the sauna, and the higher the bench, the hotter the air. The sauna is usually followed by a cooling dip in a lake or pool—or in winter, by a frosty roll in the snow.

In summer, Helsinki offers fine beaches near the city for swimming

Tapiola, near Helsinki, typifies the best of Finnish architecture.

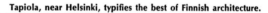

and sunbathing, and visitors and residents alike flock to sports stadiums to watch *pesäpallo* ("nest ball"). This game, which has been called Finland's national sport, is a form of baseball.

Tapiola.   Some 4 miles (6 km.) from Helsinki is Tapiola, a garden city dating only from 1960. Named for one of the legends of the *Kalevala,* Tapiola was designed by a team of architects and planners to provide the best that modern city life could offer—efficiency, comfort, and beauty in its homes and offices, streets and parks. It is another example of how the Finns not only try to make the best of what they have, but add something special to it.

Tampere.   Between lakes Näsi and Pyhä, northeast of Turku, is Tampere, Finland's second largest city and the home of many of its industries. Because all its factories are run by hydroelectricity, however, Tampere is not a typical industrial town. It, too, has wide, clean streets, many lovely parks and gardens, and modern apartment houses. Even the factories seem close to nature, built among trees, gently rolling hills, or on the lake shores. Tampere is also the starting point of many lake-steamer routes to the north and south.

Turku.   Turku, Finland's third largest city, stands near the mouth of the Aura River on the Gulf of Bothnia. Because of its location, it was natural that Turku developed into a thriving seaport. As early as the 13th century, Turku carried on trade with the cities of the Hanseatic League and other Baltic ports. Often called Finland's gateway to the West, Turku is still a busy port today, with a harbor that is kept ice-free all year round. Turku also has large shipyards, and its other industries include steel-, lumber-, and textile-milling.

Turku is Finland's oldest city and was the country's first capital. Its cathedral dates from the 13th century and contains the tombs of many great Finns. Nearby there is a statue of Michael Agricola, the city's 16th-century bishop who translated the New Testament into Finnish.

In 1827 a great fire almost leveled Turku. Today, in the Luostarinmäki section of the city, which escaped the fire, the old houses have been turned into a crafts museum and workshop. Here weaving, pottery, and other arts are still carried on in their traditional settings.

Finland's national university, founded in Turku in 1640, was moved to Helsinki in 1828. Today, however, Turku is the site of two universities, one teaching in Finnish and the other in Swedish. Turku's position as a cultural center is also maintained by its Concert Hall, one of the most modern in Finland.

Hämeenlinna.   Hämeenlinna, about 50 miles (80 km.) from Tampere, is one of the lake ports on the southern route. It is also the birthplace of Finland's great composer Jean Sibelius (1865–1957), whose music carried Finland to the world and who came to be a living symbol of his country. His tone poems *En Saga, Finlandia,* and *Tapiola* and his symphonies and other compositions all seem to contain more than Sibelius' deep love for Finland. They contain the wind howling through the pine trees and the sun glancing off the waters of 60,000 lakes; they contain the ancient legends of the *Kalevala;* they contain all of Finland's history of hardships and all the promise of its future. They contain *sisu,* which has made Finland what it is today.

JOHN H. WUORINEN, Author, *A History of Finland*
Reviewed by HALLBERG HALLMUNDSSON, Translator and Editor

Vineyards cling to the hillsides of Portugal's upper Douro Valley, the home of port wine.

PORTUGAL

Flying over the coast of Portugal, the westernmost country in Europe, one can see at the end of the long shoreline that projects into the Atlantic a point of land called Cape Saint Vincent. The cape, the southwesternmost point in Europe, was for centuries the extreme limit to which Europeans dared to venture. Beyond this point, the legends said, the sea was filled with monsters and dangers beyond description, and one was in danger of sailing off the edge of the flat earth into nothingness.

It remained for the Portuguese to show that great lands and unbelievable wealth lay across the mysterious sea. In the late 15th and 16th centuries, the Portuguese mariners—the astronauts of their day—explored two thirds of the then unknown world. Their discoveries made Portugal a leading imperial power. For a time this small country was the heart of one of the world's largest and richest empires.

Portugal held on to its overseas empire longer than any other European colonial power. It was not until 1974, when political change swept the country and a new government came to power, that Portugal decided to give up its vast territories. Today, all that remains of the once-great

Oxen help launch a traditional fishing boat. Portugal is one of the world's leading fishing nations.

empire is the tiny overseas province of Macao in southeast China. Aside from Macao, Portugal today comprises that part of Portugal lying on the continent of Europe plus the Azores and Madeira islands in the Atlantic Ocean. The African territories that Portugal governed for centuries are now independent nations, and the country's current leaders are emphasizing a future linked to Western Europe rather than faraway lands.

THE LAND

In a few hours in Portugal one may drive from the high, cold, almost barren mountainous areas to the southern coast of the country, where summer never ends. Portugal occupies about one sixth of the Iberian Peninsula, which it shares with Spain, its only neighbor. The boundaries between Spain and Portugal are formed partly by rivers, including the Minho in the north and the Guadiana in the southeast. Two other important rivers, the Tagus and the Douro, rise in Spain and flow through Portugal to the Atlantic Ocean.

The Tagus River, in the center of Portugal, divides the country into two distinct parts. The northern half of the nation is mostly mountainous and includes the highest range in Portugal—the Serra da Estrêla—whose loftiest peak, Pico da Serrá, stretches 6,532 feet (1,991 meters) above sea level. The Serra da Estrêla region is noted for its resorts and for its mineral resources. Moving west from the mountainous interior, one comes to the foothills dotted with small farms, olive groves, and vineyards.

The warm, dry, sunny upper valley of the Douro River in northern Portugal is the home of the country's most famous wine—port. There, on steep, terraced vineyards that look like giant staircases, the grapes are

FACTS AND FIGURES

OFFICIAL NAME: Portuguese Republic.

NATIONALITY: Portuguese.

CAPITAL: Lisbon.

LOCATION: Southwestern Europe. **Boundaries**—Spain, Atlantic Ocean.

AREA: 35,552 sq. mi. (92,080 sq. km.).

PHYSICAL FEATURES: Highest point—Pico da Serrá (6,532 ft.; 1,991 m.). **Lowest point**—sea level. **Chief rivers**—Tagus, Douro, Guadiana, Minho, Mondego, Zêzere.

POPULATION: 10,459,701 (1989).

MAJOR LANGUAGE: Portuguese.

MAJOR RELIGION: Roman Catholicism.

GOVERNMENT: Republic. **Head of state**—president. **Legislature**—one-house Assembly of the Republic.

CHIEF CITIES: Lisbon, Oporto, Amadora, Coimbra, Setubal, Braga.

ECONOMY: Chief minerals—tungsten, iron, uranium ores. **Chief agricultural products**—grains, potatoes, olives, grapes. **Industries and products**—textiles, footwear, wood pulp, paper, cork, metalworking, oil refining, chemicals, fish canning, wine. **Chief exports**—cotton textiles, cork and cork products, canned fish, wine, wood and wood products, resin, machinery, appliances. **Chief imports**—petroleum, cotton, grains, machinery, iron and steel, chemicals.

MONETARY UNIT: Escudo.

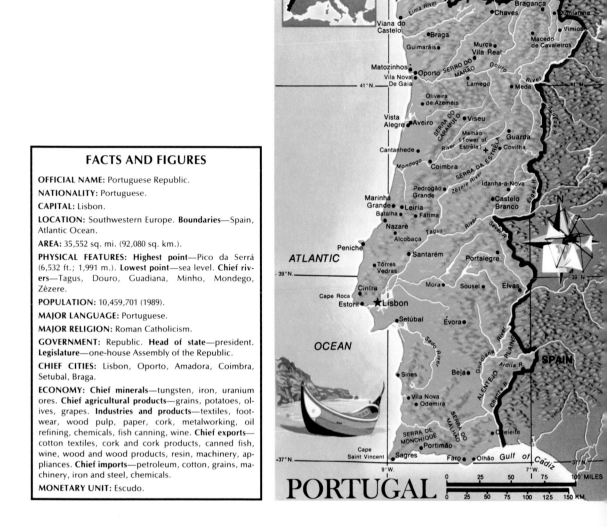

PORTUGAL

grown and harvested. After the grape juice has been allowed to ferment for a time, brandy is added, and the port is put into oak casks. The casks of new wine are brought by oxcarts to the Douro River and then floated on flat-bottomed boats downstream to Oporto, Portugal's second largest city. The wine is graded and stored in caves until it achieves the proper color and flavor for export.

South of the Tagus River, Portugal becomes a land of rolling plains and plateaus. This is the area of the latifundia, huge estates where the owners employ as many as 100 workers, who live on the estate or in nearby villages. Although the soil is poor, this is the grain-growing center of the nation. Here, too, sheep, goats, and cattle graze, and horses and bulls are bred for bullfighting. There are also olive groves, rice plantations, and forests of cork oak. Portugal is the world's largest producer of cork. There are also forests of chestnut, eucalyptus, and pine. Portugal exports much resin, turpentine, and other wood products. In the mild, subtropical climate of the Algarve in the far south, almonds, dates, figs, carobs, oranges, and pomegranates are grown.

Madeira and the Azores: the Island Provinces

The Madeira islands and the Azores are included in mainland Portugal for administrative purposes; however, both groups of islands received limited autonomy in the wake of the 1974 revolution. The Madeira islands, which lie about 600 miles (960 kilometers) southwest of Portugal in the North Atlantic Ocean, are famous for their scenery and as a year-round resort. The capital and chief city, Funchal, is on the largest island, also called Madeira. Madeira wines and delicately embroidered linens are the islands' best-known products.

The Azores, about 1,000 miles (1,600 kilometers) west of Lisbon, have also been important as a stopover place for travelers between Europe, Africa, and the Western Hemisphere. Today, their location and magnificent scenery make them a popular tourist attraction. Grains and fruit are raised on the islands, and fish are taken from the sea. A controversy erupted in 1986 when Portugal's armed forces objected to a provision in the new autonomy statute that permitted the Azores the right to have its own anthem and flag. The president vetoed the new law the day before it was to take effect. This action sparked the reemergence of a right-wing, separatist Front for the Liberation of the Azores.

The Former Overseas Territories

At one time Portugal governed overseas territories that were 23 times the size of Portugal itself. Officially these territories were considered to be overseas provinces or states. Portugal ruled a vast area in Africa: Portuguese Guinea (now Guinea-Bissau) on the west coast of Africa; the Cape Verde Islands off the west coast; São Tomé and Príncipe, a group of islands lying in the Gulf of Guinea off west central Africa; and Angola in the southwest, and Mozambique in southeast Africa.

Angola and Mozambique were by far the largest and most valuable of the overseas provinces, with fertile farmland, good fishing grounds, and considerable mineral resources, including oil, copper, and diamonds. Guinea-Bissau was the first of the African territories to win independence, in 1974. The others gained their independence in 1975. (Separate articles on ANGOLA, CAPE VERDE, GUINEA-BISSAU, MOZAMBIQUE, and SÃO TOMÉ AND PRÍNCIPE appear in Volume 1.)

Portuguese Timor, the eastern part of the island of Timor in the Malay Archipelago, was one of the Asian territories of Portugal. East Timor, as it is sometimes called, became part of Indonesia in 1976. Portugal lost its territories in India, including Goa, in 1961. The last remaining territory, Macao, is located at the mouth of the Canton River off China's southeast coast. Under a 1987 accord between Lisbon and Peking, Portugal will turn over the territory to the People's Republic of China in December 1999. It will become a special administrative zone with considerable autonomy. (An article on MACAO appears in Volume 2).

THE PEOPLE

The Portuguese people are a mixture of several different groups. The earliest people known to have inhabited the peninsula were the Iberians. They were later joined by the Celts. In time the Phoenicians, Greeks, and Carthaginians arrived and set up coastal settlements. The most aggressive of these invaders were the Carthaginians, and it was to

Women flock to dockside markets to buy freshly caught fish, a staple of the Portuguese diet.

fight them that the Celtiberian people called on the Romans for help. The Romans came, but they, in turn, tried to conquer the region. They were strongly opposed by a warlike tribe called the Lusitanians, who managed to resist the Roman conquest for nearly two centuries but were finally overcome about the 1st century B.C. The Romans were defeated by the Germanic tribes, and they, in turn, were pushed out by the Moors from North Africa in the 8th century A.D. Out of these conquests and reconquests ultimately came the nation of Portugal and a people united by their language and by their religion—Roman Catholicism.

In describing the people of Portugal writers often dwell on the profound Portuguese melancholy, which is said to stem from ages of struggles and sorrows and is eloquently expressed in Portugal's famous songs, the fados. Sung with guitar accompaniment, the fados tell of too-early death, of cruel lovers, of past heroes, of a great bullfighter killed in the arena. They are summed up in the untranslatable Portuguese word *saudade*, which describes a state of mind in which one is yearning, longing, or recalling the past with resignation.

Despite this aura of melancholy the Portuguese find joy in many things. Their heritage of riches can be seen in the tapestries, gold works, and decorative tiles—*azulejos*—in the churches and palaces. Beauty and decoration play a role in their daily life, too. The wife of a poor farmer may embroider her tablecloths exquisitely. The driver carves the yoke of his oxen and paints it in brilliant colors.

It is a treat to be invited into a country home in Portugal for a lunch that comes out of a gleaming copper kettle and is accompanied by a local wine. The items in the diet are limited, but their variations may be great. Corn is a staple, and fish is more important than meat. Codfish is the most common dish, and a good cook will claim she can prepare *o fiel amigo* (the faithful friend), as the codfish is called, in at least 365 ways—one for each day of the year.

Tourists are drawn to the many sandy beaches that line Portugal's long Atlantic coastline.

Sports

Portugal is internationally famous for the excellence of its soccer teams, some of which have achieved top listings in European and world contests. Each team has fiercely loyal and noisy fans numbering in the thousands. The soccer games and the *totobola* (football pools) based on them are among the most popular amusements of the Portuguese today.

But the major attraction for the person in the street is still the Portuguese bullfight. The traditional *corrida* (bullfight) is a contest between a charging bull and a horseback rider—swerving, turning, and always returning to a frontal attack to prove mastery over the bull. The bull is not killed in the Portuguese bullfight. *Pega*—tackling of the bull by hand —is unique to Portugal. In the bullring a team of agile and courageous young men led by a captain tackles the bull face-to-face. On foot, they defy the bull, seizing its horns in their bare hands, subduing it, and bringing it to its knees. The men are amateurs who play this dangerous game for the sport, not for money.

Education

There have been compulsory education laws in Portugal since 1911, but they were not strictly enforced until the early 1930's. Today, there is little or no illiteracy in the population under 50 years of age and approximately 20 percent in those over 50. This is because an intensive effort has been made in the field of adult education, and a certificate of primary education is required for even the lowest category of jobs.

There are six universities in mainland Portugal. The oldest, the University of Coimbra, was founded in Lisbon in 1290 and moved to Coimbra in the 16th century. Two other universities, at Lisbon and Oporto, were founded in 1911. The remaining universities are at Aviero (founded 1973), Minho (founded 1974), and another at Lisbon (founded 1974). The Technical University of Lisbon was founded in 1930, and the Catholic University was opened in Lisbon in 1967.

Cities

Ever since 1147, **Lisbon** (Lisbōa) has been the political center of Portugal. One of Europe's oldest cities, Lisbon is built on seven hills overlooking the wide mouth of the Tagus River, a great natural harbor. About one tenth of the population of Portugal lives in Lisbon, which is the commercial and industrial hub of the country.

Much of the beauty of the city is a credit to the master plan drawn up by the Marquês de Pombal, who was prime minister in 1755 when an earthquake, fires, and huge waves destroyed two thirds of Lisbon. One of Pombal's plans resulted in one of the most beautiful squares in Europe, Praça do Comercio ("commerce square"). A series of arcaded buildings, built in the late 18th century, face the square on three sides. The fourth side is open to the river.

Lisbon, like many old European cities, is a city of contrasts. There are broad avenues, handsome modern buildings, and lovely pastel stucco apartment houses. There are also old sections of narrow, twisting streets, ancient areas (some of which escaped the earthquake) with old churches, and little old shops that sell antiques. Some of Lisbon's streets are so steep that elevators take you from one level to another; others have cable cars or cogwheel-driven streetcars. The major distraction to Lisbon's charm is the widespread presence of political slogans and graffiti that began appearing on walls and buildings following the April 1974 revolution that ended a half-century of authoritarian rule.

There are many famous sights for the visitor in Lisbon. Some of the pavements of the important avenues are tiled in black and white mosaics, arranged in attractive designs. The most famous historic monuments are in the area called Belém, where King Manuel I had the great monastery church Os Jeronimos built in the 16th century. It rises on the site of a small chapel to which the early navigators came to pray before sailing into the unknown. It is a national shrine. Vasco da Gama, who is supposed to have prayed at this spot on the eve of his historic voyage to India in 1497, is buried there, as is Luis Vaz de Camões, the Portuguese poet of the 16th century who wrote the epic Os Lusíadas. The heart of this poem concerns the voyage of discovery around the Cape of Good Hope to India and the deeds of Da Gama and his band of mariners.

The church of Os Jeronimos is a masterpiece of Manueline architecture, a style developed in Portugal during the late 15th and early 16th centuries and named after King Manuel I. It is an exuberant elaboration of Gothic style that was made possible by the wealth coming from the trade with the Orient. Manueline buildings can be recognized by the masses of intricate stone carvings of ropes, seashells, anchors, compasses, globes, and other symbols of Portugal's mastery of the seas.

The suburb of Belém also has the Tower, an exotic Manueline monument built on the exact spot from which the ships sailed forth on their voyages of discovery. In 1960, to commemorate the 500th anniversary of the death of Prince Henry the Navigator, the Monument of Discoveries was unveiled. Portugal's leading maritime explorers, with the Prince at their head, are depicted on the monument.

A short distance inland from Lisbon is **Cintra,** a town of lovely old stucco houses set in magnificent gardens. At Cintra there are old palaces, for this was once a favorite place for the kings and nobility to pass the summer. Also close to Lisbon, but on the coast, is **Estoril,** the center of Portugal's fashionable resorts on the Costa do Sol (coast of the sun). There the rich, and some exiled royalty from other European lands, have built lovely homes of red, blue, pink, orange, and yellow stucco and tiles that shimmer in the brilliant sun.

Portugal has many old cities, all worth a visit. **Oporto,** the second largest city and the center of the wine industry, has several notable Romanesque churches, and it is also the home of the Museum Soares dos Reis, which displays almost all the works of the great 19th-century sculptor and painter Soares dos Reis, as well as paintings, goldsmiths' work, and porcelains.

North of Oporto is **Braga,** which is famous for its churches. The city of **Évora** traces its history to the Romans and the Moors. There are the remains of a Temple of Diana from the 1st or 2nd century B.C., the great cathedral in Gothic style from the 12th century, and many other monuments.

In central Portugal is the village of **Fátima,** with its national shrine in honor of Our Lady of the Rosary of Fátima. Roman Catholics have made pilgrimages to Fátima since 1917, when three shepherd children reported seeing the Virgin Mary there six times. Portugal's devotion to Roman Catholicism is also reflected in the fact that it is one of only a handful of nations in the world that bars divorce.

ECONOMY

The days of the great voyages of discovery and colonization have passed into history, but many Portuguese still earn their living from the sea. They are the fishermen who provide the Portuguese with the chief source of protein in their diet and the raw material for their important canning industry. The sea abounds in fish, but the open ocean is often brutal and fishing can be a dangerous occupation.

At Nazaré the fishermen take their frail boats directly through the ocean surf in search of sardines and other fish. On the southern coast, in the Algarve province, and around the Azores, they go out mainly for tuna. For centuries, Portuguese fishing fleets have set out each spring for the distant seas off Newfoundland known as the Grand Banks. They return late in summer, heavily laden with codfish. The cod is salted and stored in the ships' holds. Upon arrival in Portugal the salted fish is stripped, cured, and dried, to become the national dish, *bacalhau.*

Portugal is expanding its fishing industry by granting loans for modernizing equipment, but occasionally one can still see the women at the fishing ports mending nets, which they hold taut with their bare toes; and the *varinas* (fishwives) still take their wares from door to door, carrying the fish in baskets on their heads.

The Rossio, a square in central Lisbon, honors the heroes who helped secure Portugal's independence.

Although agriculture, forestry, and fishing are the basic economic activities of almost half the workers of Portugal, there is a considerable drive to exploit the minerals of the country and to develop its industrial potential, especially since Portugal entered the European Community (EC), also known as the Common Market, on January 1, 1986. Portugal is moderately rich in minerals, but some of them are difficult to mine. In the mountains there are wolframite (the source of tungsten), tin, copper, lead, pyrites, antimony, sulfur, arsenic, lithium, and titanium. There are mines that produce limited quantities of soft coal, but substantial quantities of hard coal, coke, iron, and steel have to be imported.

Successive development plans have provided northern Portugal with a network of dams that generate much-needed power and provide irrigation. The best-known of these dams are Castelo do Bode, Belver, and Idanha on the Tagus and its tributaries. In the basin of the Douro River a joint Portuguese-Spanish effort has built a vast hydroelectric complex serving both Spain and Portugal. Two oil refineries have been built, one at Matozinhos, near Oporto, in an area that also produces steel and petrochemicals, and another near Lisbon. A modern steel mill is located across the Tagus River from Lisbon. In 1979, a petrochemical complex began operations at Sines, south of Lisbon. These improvements, and the April 25th Bridge (formerly the Salazar Bridge) spanning the Tagus and linking Lisbon with the southern half of the country, symbolize a Portugal that is entering the modern industrial era.

In addition to the fish-canning, cork, and wine industries, Portugal now produces cotton and woolen textiles, metal products, cement, chemicals, paper, soap, glass and glassware, and drugs. However, much

Oporto, Portugal's second-largest city, lies on the terraced banks of the Douro River.

of Portugal's industry is still in small factories and workshops, such as those where textiles are made, linens woven and embroidered, and rugs custom-made. Tourism provides Portugal's economy with its largest single source of foreign exchange. In addition, substantial amounts of money are received from Portuguese who work in other parts of Western Europe, Brazil, and North America and send back earnings to their families at home.

HISTORY

Modern Portuguese history began with the wars fought against the Moors, who occupied the country in the 8th century A.D. In spite of the occupation of the country by the Muslim Arabs, the Christian faith remained firmly established. The Christian nobles had retreated to the mountainous regions of the northwest, and it was not until the 11th century that they began to push the Moors back toward the south. Many young knights, motivated by faith, warrior zeal, and ambition, came from other lands to join in the wars. So it was that Henry, a young Burgundian, came from France in the 11th century, distinguished himself in battle, and gained a bride, the Princess of the Kingdom of León, who had the territory between the Douro and the Minho Rivers. This territory was called the country of Portugal, because one of the centers of this region was located near the mouth of the Douro River at a place called Portucale. The name is probably derived from the Latin for port—*portus*—and Calle, the name of a castle that overlooked it. Portucale gave its name to the nation of Portugal.

In 1139 the able son of Henry of Burgundy, Afonso, declared himself Afonso I, the first monarch of Portugal. Afonso I rallied a group of northern European Crusaders to his cause. They had been on their way to the Holy Land when a storm swept them to the mouth of the Douro. With their help, Afonso recaptured seven Moorish citadels, including the city of Lisbon. In a daring raid, like a modern commando attack, he swept across the Moors' territory and recaptured Cape Saint Vincent.

Afonso's successors completed the work of pushing the Moors out of the peninsula, and by the middle of the 13th century the boundaries of Portugal were firmly established.

One of the most remarkable of the early Portuguese kings was King Diniz (reigned 1261–1325), who was called O Rei Lavrador—"the farmer king"—because of his interest in agriculture. Among his many achievements was the planting of pine forests to prevent erosion. These forests later provided masts and timber for the explorers' ships. Diniz also wrote poetry in Portuguese and published royal edicts and documents in Portuguese at a time when only Latin was used for such writing. He also founded Portugal's first university.

The Explorers

The actual beginning of the great Portuguese voyages of discovery is hard to pinpoint. There is no mystery, however, about the leader who inspired the great voyages. He was Prince Henry the Navigator, who founded a naval arsenal at Sagres, near Europe's southwesternmost corner, to serve as a base of exploration. He then added an observatory and a school for geography and navigation. From 1418 until his death in 1460, he surrounded himself with cartographers, astronomers, instrument makers, mathematicians, and pilots. He sent crews to chart seas, study winds and currents, draw up harbor maps, and build caravels—ships designed for long voyages. With the maps, instruments, ships, knowledge, and inspiration bequeathed to them by Prince Henry, the Portuguese gradually sailed farther and farther down the coast of Africa. In 1488, Bartholomeu Dias reached the Cape of Good Hope, at the tip of Africa, and found that the coast turned northeast there. In 1498, almost 40 years after Henry's death, Vasco da Gama found the route to the riches of India that Columbus and so many others had searched for in vain.

The Portuguese had found the way to bring to Europe the silks, spices, gold, and other treasures of Asia without risking the dangerous overland caravan route or raids by those who controlled the Mediterranean waters. The Portuguese mariners took over the spice trade of the Orient from the Arabs and amassed great wealth. They started settlements on the Indian coast. The Portuguese introduced their language, their customs, and their faith to people in distant lands. Their missionaries preached Christianity in India and as far east as Japan. They also introduced firearms to those lands. From China they brought home the use of tea and fireworks, and left behind Portuguese words that became part of Chinese and other Oriental languages.

Competition between Spanish and Portuguese explorers became intense, and in 1494 the two countries signed the Treaty of Tordesillas. They divided the non-Christian world by drawing an imaginary line from pole to pole. What lay east of the line was given to Portugal; the land west of the line was Spain's. Fortunately for Portugal, when Pedro Alvares

The Monument of Discoveries in Lisbon commemorates Portugal's leading role during the Age of Exploration.

Cabral, accompanied by Bartholomeu Dias, reached Brazil in 1500, that area fell within the Portuguese claim. Missionaries and pioneers followed Cabral, pushing deep into the Amazon jungle of Brazil to found settlements, raise sugarcane, and mine the gold, silver, and diamonds that provided Portugal's fantastic wealth for decades.

In the 16th century the Portuguese empire stretched from the coast of China to Brazil, from North Africa to the Pacific Ocean. Portugal monopolized the spice trade and sent sailors, settlers, merchants, administrators, and priests to its far-flung holdings. But Portugal was a country of only 2,000,000 people, and many of its most gifted men died in these far-off lands. Furthermore, much of the profit from the imported wealth went to guard the distant settlements and to keep open Portugal's widespread sea-lanes.

Portugal's Decline

Portugal's good fortune ended suddenly. In 1578, King Sebastian led the Portuguese armies in an expedition to Morocco. Dreaming of a new crusade, he led his men to battle the Moors in the Moroccan desert. He was killed, and only a few of his men survived the slaughter. In 1580 the weakened country, torn by internal struggles, was annexed by the Spanish, who ruled until 1640. In that year John of Braganza, taking advantage of Spain's involvement in other wars, succeeded in ousting the Spanish and became King John IV of Portugal.

During the 1700's there was again a brief time of great prosperity in Portugal, with the resources of Brazil supplying the wealth. But in 1755,

Lisbon was almost destroyed by an earthquake, and it took the country a long time to recover. During the Napoleonic Wars it was invaded by the French Army. The King and royal family fled to Brazil, and for a short time the capital of Portugal was in Rio de Janeiro. After Napoleon was defeated the royal family returned to Portugal. During this period the vast empire had begun to fall apart. In 1822, Brazil declared its independence, and thus Portugal's single greatest source of wealth was lost.

The entire 19th century and the early part of the 20th century was a time of economic and political disaster in Portugal. The sudden stoppage of wealth from Brazil caused financial difficulties that led to heavy borrowing from England. The liberal ideas of the French Revolution, brought to Portugal by the invading armies of Napoleon, inspired the people to fight against absolute rule. Violent partisan struggles, civil wars, and continuous agitation led to chaotic conditions and a growing movement towards republicanism. The King and his heir were assassinated in 1908, and two years later Portugal became a republic.

During World War I Portugal was one of the Western allies against Germany. But Portugal had such severe economic problems that freely elected governments faced great difficulties. In the 16 years after the republic was proclaimed in 1910, Portugal witnessed repeated coups d'etat, and 46 governments followed one another in quick succession. Political turmoil continued to disrupt the nation's life until 1926, when Marshal António Oscar de Fragoso Carmona took over the government.

In 1928, Carmona appointed António de Oliveira Salazar, a professor at Coimbra University, as minister of finance to help stabilize Portugal's economy. In 1932, Salazar became premier and, with his powers extended by the new Constitution of 1933, headed the government for 35 years. Forced to retire due to illness, he was succeeded by Marcello Caetano in 1968. Salazar died in 1970.

Years of Change

During Salazar's years as premier, Portugal had a generally stable but authoritarian government. Under the constitution then in effect, Portugal was described as a unitary and corporative republic. There was a president as head of state; a legislature, the National Assembly; and an advisory body called the Corporative Chamber. It was Salazar, however, who ruled Portugal during this long period. Only one political party was officially permitted.

Soon after Marcello Caetano became premier he extended the vote for women. Previously only women who were heads of families or independent professional workers were permitted to vote. In 1969 the election law was amended to place women on an equal footing with men. Caetano also curbed the political police, permitted greater freedom of discussion, and relaxed the laws of censorship.

But many Portuguese desired more widespread political and social reforms. The question of the overseas provinces in Africa also aroused great controversy. For many years the Army had been fighting a bitter and costly war against African nationalist groups in Portuguese Guinea (Guinea-Bissau), Angola, and Mozambique who were seeking independence. The war was unpopular with many people who believed that the provinces should be allowed their independence. They felt that the enormous sums of money spent in keeping them under Portuguese rule would be better spent in such areas as education, housing, and industrial development at home.

In 1974 a group of army officers opposed to the continuation of the war in Africa overthrew the government of Premier Caetano. A provisional government made up of members of the armed forces was established. One of its first acts was to recognize the right of the African provinces to independence. The new leaders of the country also promised to restore democracy to Portugal. However, conflict soon arose as to what kind of government Portugal was to have. A struggle for power developed between the Communists, allied with extreme radical groups, and the Socialists. A wave of unrest swept the country, threatening civil war, and the already weakened Portuguese economy was further disrupted by the political instability.

The Democratic Era

Even though 17 governments have held power since 1974, Portugal gradually moved into the sunshine of democracy from the shadows of turmoil that engulfed the country after Caetano's removal from office. Several factors caused this transition. Of crucial importance was the continual support for democratic forces provided by members of the European Community and by the United States. In addition, Socialist leader Mário Soares, who twice served as premier before winning the presidency in 1986, championed democratization and opposed extremists within both the armed forces and in the Communist Party. Reforms introduced by Soares in the early 1980s opened up an economy afflicted by years of high tariffs, red tape, subsidies, outdated management practices, and state intervention in economic affairs.

Entry into the European Community (EC) vastly broadened export opportunities for Portugal, where wages remain the lowest in Western Europe. The EC furnished its new member with at least $2 billion in aid for industrial modernization beginning in 1988. The combination of political stability, economic potential, and more flexible laws sparked a sharp increase in foreign investment from other EC states, particularly the United Kingdom, Spain, and Germany.

Contributing to the country's political stability were the July 1987 elections, in which Aníbal Cavaço Silva, head of the Social Democratic Party, obtained 50.2 percent of the popular vote and an absolute majority in the 250-seat parliament. A university professor and economist, Cavaço Silva pledged to end "the era of state paternalism" by encouraging free enterprise, allowing employers to fire surplus workers, and closing down or selling off unproductive enterprises. In 1989 the parliament approved constitutional reforms that removed Marxist language from the 1976 constitution. Opponents had used these provisions to impede Cavaço Silva's program of denationalization. In 1982 Cavaço Silva won revisions of the constitution that banned the military from politics and limited presidential powers.

In recent years, Portugal has strengthened its ties with the United States, and it is a member of the North Atlantic Treaty Organization (NATO). Still, the country's oldest alliance is with the United Kingdom; it dates to the signing of the Treaty of Windsor in 1386 by King Richard II and King João I.

GEORGE W. GRAYSON, College of William and Mary

The Alhambra, a Moorish palace in the city of Granada, was built in the 14th century.

SPAIN

Spain is a peninsula. This geographic fact alone suggests two basic truths about the country: its isolation and its deep historic involvement in the affairs of the world. Spain's greatness and its tragedies have been shaped by this contradiction between its geography and its history.

Spain's geographical isolation comes from the seas and the mountains. Spain is attached to the continent of Europe only by a narrow neck held in the high collar of the Pyrenees. The rest of Spain is surrounded by seas, except for the rectangle of Portugal, with which it shares the Iberian Peninsula. In the south the Strait of Gibraltar barely separates Spain from Africa. In the east its shores are bathed by the Mediterranean.

Spain's physical isolation from the world is mirrored in the isolation of one region from another within Spain—a separateness caused by the mountain chains. From the northern ranges of the Pyrenees to the southernmost peaks of the Sierra Nevada, the country is crisscrossed by mountains and creased by valleys. From the air it looks like a huge sheet of paper crumpled by the hand of God.

Spain's involvement in all the great currents of world history comes, on the other hand, from its central position at the crossroads of conquest and trade routes. From prehistoric to modern times, the Iberian Peninsula has been the prize of invading armies from Africa, in the south, and Europe, in the north. Spain has been not only the target of invasions but a pathway for invasions directed at other lands. It was occupied by the Romans, the Carthaginians, the Visigoths, the Arabs, and the French. Phoenicians and Greeks established trading posts on Spain's coasts and helped to settle some of its great towns and cities.

An historic link between Europe and North Africa, Spain is both European and North African in culture, temperament, and appearance. France's Emperor Napoleon and some geographers have said that Africa begins at the Pyrenees.

But Spain has been more than a continental stepping-stone or a victim of centuries of conquest. In its long history, Spain conquered and held together a majestic empire. Spain created new civilizations across the world. And Spain has enriched the world with its culture.

Spain has seen its own civilization and personality nearly erased by many wars during its long history and by a bloody and devastating civil war in the 1930's. But it has kept a powerful identity of its own. There are few countries in the world that offer the variety and beauty that exist in Spain.

THE LAND

Spain, the third largest nation in Europe, with which it is becoming increasingly integrated, occupies five sixths of the Iberian Peninsula. Almost square in shape, Spain measures about 500 miles (800 kilometers) from north to south and about 600 miles (960 kilometers) from east to west. At its narrow southern tip, Spain is separated from Africa by the 8-mile (13-kilometer)-wide Strait of Gibraltar. Tiny Gibraltar, at the eastern end of the strait, is a British possession. In the northeast is the tiny republic of Andorra, which is jointly ruled by the Spanish bishop of Urgel and the president of France. (Both ANDORRA and GIBRALTAR are described in separate articles in this volume.)

Metropolitan Spain includes the provinces on the peninsula, the Balearic Islands in the Mediterranean, and the Canary Islands in the Atlantic off the northwest coast of Africa.

The two most important geographical facts about Spain are its mountainous terrain and the limited rainfall that affects all except the northern provinces. The heart of Spain is the huge central plateau called the Meseta (tableland), which is divided between Old and New Castile. The Meseta is surrounded and dissected by mountain ranges. The highest mountains in Spain are the Pyrenees in the northeast and the Sierra

SPAIN

ATLANTIC OCEAN

BAY OF BISCAY

FRANCE

La Coruña • Gijón Altamira San Sebastián
Santiago de Oviedo Cave Bilbao
Compostela Covadonga Santander
CANTABRIAN Pamplona
Vigo • León MOUNTAINS ANDORRA
Pico de Aneto
GALICIAN MTS. Burgos Huesca Olot
Miño River Valladolid Douro River Zaragoza Tarrasa
Zamora Ebro River Barcelona
M E S Tarragona
Salamanca Tortosa
Segovia SIERRA DE GUADARRAMA m. Vinaroz BALEARIC SEA
Ávila San Lorenzo del Escorial
SIERRA DE GATA Escalona ★ Madrid Cuenca MINORCA
SIERRA DE GREDOS Talavera Torrijos Aranjuez Valencia Palma MAJORCA
Lagartera de la Reina Toledo Gulf of
Tagus River MONTES DE TOLEDO Valencia BALEARIC ISLANDS
IVIZA
Mérida FORMENTERA
Guadiana River Ciudad Real Alicante
Ríotinto SIERRA MORENA Murcia
Córdoba Guadalquivir River
Huelva • Seville Guadix Cartagena
Granada
Gulf of Cádiz Jerez Mulhacén
Marbella Málaga SIERRA NEVADA Almería
Cádiz Torremolinos Adra Cape Gata
Cape Trafalgar Algeciras
Tarifa GIBRALTAR (U.K.)
Strait of Gibraltar

PORTUGAL

MEDITERRANEAN SEA

MOROCCO **ALGERIA**

Gulf of Lion

Belmonte Castle, Cuenca

EUROPE

CEUTA MELILLA
CANARY ISLANDS **AFRICA**

Seville

FACTS AND FIGURES

OFFICIAL NAME: Spanish State.

NATIONALITY: Spanish.

CAPITAL: Madrid.

LOCATION: Southwestern Europe. **Boundaries**—Bay of Biscay, France, Balearic Sea, Mediterranean Sea, Gibraltar, Gulf of Cádiz, Atlantic Ocean.

AREA: 194,884 sq. mi. (504,750 sq. km.).

PHYSICAL FEATURES: Highest point—Mulhacén (11,411 ft.; 3,478 m.). **Lowest point**—sea level. **Chief rivers**—Ebro, Douro, Tagus, Guadiana, Guadalquivir.

POPULATION: 39,417,220 (1989).

MAJOR LANGUAGE: Spanish.

MAJOR RELIGION: Roman Catholicism.

GOVERNMENT: Parliamentary monarchy. **Head of state**—monarch. **Legislature**—Cortes (Chamber of Deputies and Senate).

CHIEF CITIES: Madrid, Barcelona, Valencia, Seville.

ECONOMY: Chief minerals—coal, lignite, iron ore, uranium, mercury, pyrites, fluorspar, gypsum, zinc, lead, tungsten, copper, kaolin. **Chief agricultural products**—grains, citrus fruits, vegetables. **Industries and products**—textiles and clothing, food and beverages, metals and metal products, chemicals, shipbuilding, automobiles. **Chief exports**—iron and steel products, machinery, automobiles, citrus fruits, vegetables, wine, soybean oil, barley, textiles, shoes. **Chief imports**—fuels, machinery, chemicals, iron and steel, automobiles, corn, soybeans, coffee, tobacco, wood products, hides and skins, cotton, livestock.

MONETARY UNIT: Peseta.

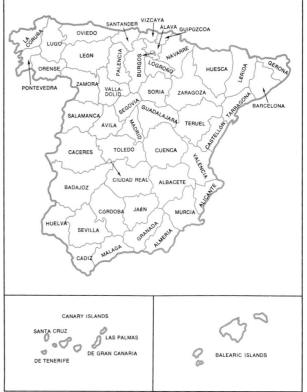

Small villages lie nestled in the Pyrenees, the mountains that separate Spain from the rest of Europe.

Nevada (snowy range) in the southeast. Mulhacén, the highest peak in Spain, is in the Sierra Nevada. The Cantabrian Mountains rise on the northern and northwestern edge of the Meseta. The Sierra Morena (dark range) is at its southern edge. The Meseta itself is divided by the Sierra de Gredos, the Sierra de Guadarrama, and the Montes de Toledo.

There are only a few lowland areas in Spain besides the narrow coastal plain. The largest lowland area is the valley of the Guadalquivir River in the south. Other rivers such as the Douro, Tagus, and Guadiana have carved their way through rocks and canyons as they flow across Spain and Portugal to empty into the Atlantic Ocean. The Ebro, in the northeast, empties into the Mediterranean Sea. The Ebro is sometimes called the Nile of Spain because, like the Egyptian river, it brings life-giving water to its parched valley. The northern coastal lowland is the site of a number of ports and industrial cities. The larger lowlands on the Mediterranean coast are the site of such important cities as Barcelona, Valencia, and Cartagena.

Climate. Northern and northwestern Spain are the only parts of the country with adequate precipitation. In this region moisture-bearing winds from the Atlantic bring rain to the land. The year-round temperatures are mild without extremes of hot or cold.

Parts of the Sierra Nevada mountains in southern Spain are snow-covered throughout the year.

As one moves south from the moist, fertile northern regions, Spain's climate becomes typically Mediterranean. Winters are usually mild and somewhat rainy. Summers are very hot and dry. The average annual rainfall for Spain is 20 inches (50 centimeters)—the lowest in Western Europe. With the exception of northern Spain, the lack of fertile soil and water continues to make life a struggle for survival.

Mineral Resources. The shortage of rain and good soil are partially made up for by Spain's impressive variety of mineral resources. They include iron, coal, and zinc in the Cantabrian Mountains in the north; copper from Ríotinto in the southwest; mercury, which is found near the Sierra Morena; as well as lead, manganese, gold, silver, and tin. Spain lacks sufficient oil, but a vast potential power source to take its place has been found in the mountain streams that are being harnessed for hydro-electricity.

The Islands of Spain

The Balearic Islands lie 50 to 190 miles (80–300 kilometers) off the east coast of Spain. The Balearics are made up of three large, densely populated islands—Majorca, Minorca, and Iviza—and several smaller islands. The capital, Palma, is on the island of Majorca. The magnificent scenery and mild climate of the islands have made them into popular year-round resorts.

The Balearics, like so many other Mediterranean islands, have a history of conquest and reconquest. Prehistoric ruins linger side by side with traces of later settlers—Iberians, Phoenicians, Greeks, Carthaginians, Romans, Byzantines, Moors, and Spaniards. Today, the income from tourism is supplemented by that from farm products such as olives, grapes, cereals, almonds, and citrus fruits. Pigs and sheep are grazed. Among the province's other products are lignite, marble, lead, salt, gravel, and timber from the extensive pine forests. Shoes, ceramics, and metal products are manufactured on the islands.

The Canary Islands lie 680 miles (1,100 kilometers) southwest of Spain and about 70 miles (110 kilometers) west of Morocco. The islands are divided into two provinces, Santa Cruz de Tenerife (which is made up of the islands of Tenerife, Gomera, La Palma, and Hierro) and Las

The Spanish island of Majorca in the western Mediterranean receives over 3 million tourists annually.

The sandy Mediterranean beaches of the Costa del Sol near Gibraltar have become a major resort area.

Palmas (which includes Grand Canary, Fuerteventura, and Lanzarote islands and six islets). For the most part the climate is warm and pleasant and a variety of crops, including bananas, sugarcane, citrus fruits, and vegetables, are raised. Shipping and tourism are increasingly important to the islands' economy. (For more information about the CANARY ISLANDS see Volume 1.)

Overseas Territories

The Spanish empire disappeared long ago, and the age of European colonialism is over. Of its once-great empire, Spain today retains only two tiny enclaves in North Africa. The geographic nearness of these small territories makes it relatively easy for Spain to govern them. There is also a touch of sentimentality about Africa, with which the destiny of Spain was interwoven for so many centuries.

At the end of World War II, Spain renounced its sovereignty over what had been Spanish Morocco, now part of the Kingdom of Morocco. Along with other European powers and the United States, Spain also withdrew from the multinational administration of Tangier on Africa's northernmost tip.

After fighting a brief war with Morocco in 1957 to retain the enclave of Ifni on Morocco's Atlantic coast, Spain ceded it voluntarily in 1969. In the previous year it granted independence to Spanish Equatorial Guinea and the island of Fernando Po (now Bioko). Together, they became the Republic of Equatorial Guinea, a tiny country in which Spain continues to have powerful interests. (There are articles about MOROCCO and EQUATORIAL GUINEA in Volume 1.)

Spain's last large territory in Africa was Spanish Sahara. It is a huge tract of desert land rich in phosphates (which are used in making artificial fertilizers) and possibly oil. The native population consists largely of nomadic Berbers, who live around a number of oases. The Berbers are a people of northern Africa who inhabited that region before the arrival of the Arabs. Spain officially withdrew from Spanish Sahara in 1976. The region, which is now called Western Sahara, was divided between the neighboring countries of Morocco and Mauritania. Mauritania later gave up its claim. (A separate article on WESTERN SAHARA appears in Volume 1.)

Ceuta and Melilla. Spain has no intention of giving up the remaining small territories that it still governs on the North African mainland. These are the small ports of Ceuta and Melilla on Morocco's Mediterranean coast. It was from Ceuta that the Nationalist troops of Generalissimo Francisco Franco crossed the Strait of Gibraltar to Spain to launch the Civil War in July 1936. They are thoroughly Spanish towns held by what remains of the Spanish Legion and are run as fortresses. Morocco has made no serious effort to claim them. The growing number of Muslims, especially illegal Moroccan aliens in Melilla, increases the possibility of turmoil in these two North African enclaves.

Gibraltar. Gibraltar, the British crown colony that controls the passage between the Atlantic and the Mediterranean, has been the subject of continuing controversy. Britain has held Gibraltar—the fortress, the port, and what has grown into a pleasant and prosperous town of about 25,000 inhabitants—since 1704, when Spain lost the War of the Spanish Succession. The Spanish government calls Gibraltar "The Last Colony in Europe" and demands its immediate return to Spanish sovereignty. The United Nations has instructed Britain to "decolonize" Gibraltar. Instead, the British held a referendum in 1967 that showed that the overwhelming majority of its inhabitants insisted, in Spanish-accented English, "British We Are and British We Shall Remain." The Spanish Government, however, declared the referendum illegal. It gradually imposed tight restrictions on the colony, cutting off all trade with the mainland. The flow of Spanish workers to Gibraltar also was cut off. In 1982 the border between Spain and Gibraltar was partly opened. It was completely opened again in 1985. Talks on the future of the colony were begun by Spain and Britain the same year; however, the lack of progress in negotiations led Madrid to block a European Community (EC) accord on air travel in order to convert Gibraltar into a European issue rather than a problem confined to Anglo-Spanish relations.

THE PEOPLE

There is, of course, no such thing as a "typical" Spaniard. In fact, there is perhaps no other country in Europe where the differences among people are as deep as among the Spaniards. The division of Spain imposed by its geography, which until recently blocked the movement of populations, has preserved the regional types. It has kept alive the different languages and dialects. And it has preserved old political and cultural differences within the nation.

In a general and oversimplified way, the Spaniards can be divided into three main categories. The northerners are descended from the Celts who came to the peninsula 12 or 13 centuries before the Christian

Narrow streets lined with sun-baked houses are typical of villages in Spain's Andalusian region.

Era and, perhaps, from the Vikings who came to the peninsula about 1,000 years ago. The southerners are strongly influenced by the effects of the Moorish rule that lasted more than seven centuries. The easterners trace their origins back to the ancient Iberian tribes and then to the Visigoths.

Despite all the physical and cultural barriers, modern labor migrations are beginning to blur the differences, particularly in the industrial areas. The southerners have spilled over into the center and the north, and the northerners into the center and the south. Dark Andalusians and short, rosy-cheeked Galicians now often work side by side with fair Basques and Catalonians. If there is such a thing as a Castilian type it defies precise description. The Madrileño, as the inhabitant of Madrid is called, is the product of what might be described as the first Spanish melting pot, since the capital has traditionally attracted people from all over Spain.

Every spring, Seville is the scene of a colorful Holy Week procession. Most Spaniards are Roman Catholics.

Language. Most nations are united by their language, and at first glance this appears to be true of Spain, whose official language is Spanish. However, three languages are widely used. Catalán, which is related to the Provençal language of France, is spoken in Catalonia in northeastern Spain, along the east coast around Valencia, and in the Balearic Islands. Basque, a language that has no known relatives, is spoken in the Basque Provinces of Álava, Guipúzcoa, and Vizcaya. Castilian, which most people know as the language of Spain, is the dialect of the Meseta, as well as the official language of Spain. Spanish is one of the world's most widely spoken languages because it is also used by almost all South Americans except Brazilians.

Religion. Religion appears to be more of a unifying factor in Spanish life than does language, but this has not always been true. The overwhelming majority of Spaniards are Roman Catholics, and Roman

Catholicism was the state religion of Spain until the adoption of a new constitution in 1978. There are several hundred thousand Muslims (concentrated in the South), a Protestant minority of about 25,000, and a small Jewish community of about 7,500. In 1965, Spanish Jews were allowed to conduct public services for the first time since 1492, the year the Jews were ordered to become Catholics or leave the country. A special law adopted in 1966 officially lifted the government ban on public worship for non-Catholics. Moreover, the Cortes (parliament) has liberalized divorce laws, and abortions are permitted under exceptional circumstances.

The Problems of Regionalism

Despite the growing mobility of the population, regionalism and nationalism have grown, rather than diminished, in recent decades. This is the case in Basque country and Catalonia, and, to a lesser extent, in Galicia and Navarre. There are, of course, deep contradictions in this regional nationalism. A Basque considers himself both a Basque and a Spaniard, and a Catalonian considers himself both a Catalonian and a Spaniard. Since 1977, many of Spain's regions have been granted autonomy, with the broadest powers conferred on Catalonia and the Basque area. This satisfies those who only desire to preserve regional traits and characteristics. But extremists still demand outright separation.

Catalonia. Catalonia's inhabitants speak both Spanish and Catalán. But in the remote villages of Catalonia, one rarely hears Spanish, even though Catalonia has been under the rule of Spain for nearly 500 years. In addition to its own language, Catalonia has developed over the centuries a distinctive culture and a rich literature dating back to the 13th century. The sense of Catalonian cultural identity was later submerged under Spanish influences and surfaced again in a powerful renaissance in the latter part of the 19th century. It has been gaining vitality ever since. This separate identity in culture extends to other aspects of Catalonian life. The Catalonians, and especially the prosperous people of Barcelona, regard themselves as more European than the Castilians of Madrid. This feeling stems from Catalonia's nearness to France and the age-old contacts of the Catalonian traders with the entire Mediterranean world. The selection of Barcelona as the site for the 1992 summer Olympic Games brought Catalonia worldwide recognition.

The industrious Catalonians, along with the Basques, believe that their contribution to the Spanish economy helps support the rest of the country. This is largely true, but not necessarily because of the merit of the Catalonians or the failing of their fellow Spaniards. Such factors as Catalonia's geographical location, which favors trade and industry, and the climate, which has blessed Catalonia with a rich agriculture, are largely responsible for its wealth.

Another factor in this relationship is that Catalonia fought on the losing side in the Civil War. Before the Civil War, under the Spanish Republic, Catalonia was virtually an independent state. Under Franco, who was bent on restoring the unity of the shattered nation at the end of the war, Catalonia lost its separate status. Therefore, Catalonian regionalism was equated with being against the government.

Catalonians have their own divisions among themselves. The Catalonians who inhabit the southern coast, where the Kingdom of Valencia once thrived, are convinced that the Valenciano language is purer than the language spoken up north around Barcelona. The people of the Balearic Islands, however, believe that only they and their cousins in the Ampurdán area on the mainland north of Barcelona have properly preserved the Catalonian language and culture. The Catalán spoken in Majorca is, in fact, rather different from the Catalán of Barcelona. But this language dispute is cultural and has no political importance.

The Basques.   The other major nationality problem in Spain is in the Basque country. The three Basque Provinces are going through a revival of Basque cultural and national identity. Because the Basques have economic power and are known for their toughness, the government is not treating Basque nationalism lightly. The Basques have developed a militant political opposition, which is led by an underground nationalist movement and a terrorist organization known as the ETA. A Basque government-in-exile operates across the border in France. There have been bombings, armed attacks on police stations, and gun battles with the authorities. All told, some 750 people have been killed during the separatist movement's 20-year campaign. It must be remembered, however, that less than 5 percent of Basques favor violence, and only 20 percent are wedded to independence. Many leading figures in the government are Basques loyal to the central regime. Greater cooperation by the French, whose territory often served as a sanctuary for terrorists, aided the Spanish authorities who cracked down on the separatists before opening talks with the ETA in 1987 aimed at ending the violence.

A parador, or national hotel, overlooks the ocean in Galicia, the most northwesterly region of Spain.

Traditionally dressed horseback riders add color to a festival in the Andalusian town of Jerez.

Navarre. The people of neighboring Navarre practice their own brand of nationalism. During the Civil War much of Franco's support came from Navarre, which remained a significant stronghold of conservative support in his favor. They favor the Carlist branch of Spanish royalty—a branch of the Borbón dynasty—that goes back to the War of the Spanish Succession in the early 18th century. The unrest in Navarre grew so great that in 1968 most of the Carlist princes were exiled from Spain. But the fiercely independent mountain folk of Navarre have not surrendered politically, and their young people are allying themselves with other Spanish rebels.

Galicia. A quieter sort of nationalism survives in Galicia, but it is mainly based on past cultural triumphs. Small groups try to keep alive their impoverished region's special identity. The government has initiated economic projects to end the age-old isolation of the region.

Contrasts and Similarities

The Spanish regionalisms, nationalisms, and separatisms in their varying degrees of intensity are a mirror of the extraordinary diversity of the Spaniards. Perhaps the most striking of all Spanish contradictions is that, despite their profound differences, there is a set of characteristics that unites the Spaniards. They come from different origins and backgrounds, many speak individual languages and dialects, and they look different from each other. Spaniards fight for separate rights and identities, and, just a generation ago, somewhere between 500,000 and 1,000,000 Spaniards were killed in a civil war. Yet, almost incredibly, together they add up to a nation of people who share eternal virtues and eternal sins.

Pride is one characteristic trait that is shared by all Spaniards. One becomes aware of it as soon as one meets the Spaniards. This does not mean that every Spaniard has delusions of grandeur. It means, instead, that each person has a quiet sense of personal dignity. Since the loss of the empire in the early 19th century, or even before that, Spain developed something of a national inferiority complex in relation to the rest of Western Europe and, later, the United States. But few Spaniards have a personal inferiority complex.

Pride and personal dignity have always been vital for Spaniards, whose lives were always fitted into highly organized and authoritarian societies. The Spaniard accepts a king, a duke, a great landlord, and even a dictator, but never grovels before him. It is a peculiar kind of social democracy that has its roots in Spain's earliest origins. It has survived triumphs and defeats, and may find its death only at the hands of a super-technological society.

The king was simply addressed as Señor (mister). The highest title of nobility in Spain was grandee. The title was always desirable, not for the riches or land that might come with it, but because two special privileges went with the title. A grandee could remain with his head covered in the royal presence, and he was free to call on the king, unannounced, in the middle of the night. A rural landlord still shakes hands with his farmhands when he surveys his domain. It is said that the Spaniard would be less resentful of a man who tried to kill him than of the man who would be rude to him, that is, failed to show respect for his human dignity.

This Spanish pride has its side effects. One of them is anger. The Spaniard is probably the world's most courteous person—his courtesy may be light and casual to his peers but grave to a stranger. But there is an even ratio between a sense of pride and a capacity for anger. Defied, challenged, or insulted, the Spaniard is quick to react. "Honor" is one of the most commonly used words in the Spanish language, and reaction is quick if a Spaniard's honor is questioned or blemished. All of this tends to explain the stubbornness of the Spaniard at war with a foreign invader or in disagreement with a fellow Spaniard.

Courage, too, is related to pride in the Spanish character. It was a blend of these two traits that kept alive the seamen of Christopher Columbus in their voyages of discovery to the West Indies and permitted the conquistadores to overrun the Inca and Aztec empires with just a small band of men. It made it possible for Vasco Núñez de Balboa to cross the isthmus of Central America and for other discoverers to sail the wild Orinoco River in South America. This courage and pride was present when Spanish soldiers fought across Europe; when King Philip II launched his ill-fated Armada against England; and when Spaniards killed each other in the Civil War.

Pride and courage inevitably breed a sense of romance and adventure as well as the belief that the Spaniard can succeed in any enterprise. The conquest of America seems an impossible venture today. One looks back in amazement at how it was accomplished. But the Spaniards succeeded. It was no accident that in creating Don Quixote as his idealistic but impractical hero that the 16th-century novelist Miguel de Cervantes Saavedra revealed himself as one of Spain's deepest and most perceptive philosophers. He had a profound understanding of the heights and depths of the Spanish soul.

On a different level, all these Spanish traits of character go far to explain why bullfighting is the nation's most beloved public spectacle. Standing alone in the middle of the arena facing the wounded and enraged bull, the matador, glorious in his *traje de luces* (suit of lights), personifies the pride, the courage, and the romanticism of the Spaniard. And the ''moment of truth,'' the instant when death may befall either matador or beast, is the essence of the Spaniard's attitude toward life. It is no wonder that Spain's great heroes, even in this technological age, are matadors—Manolete, who was gored to death in the bullring, and Antonio Ordoñez and Manuel Benítez, ''El Cordobes,'' who continued their colorful careers into middle age.

Way of Life

The Spaniards may be mystical and fatalistic, but they are also the world's most sociable people. A day in any Spanish town, village, or city makes this clear. Every street in every town has its share of bars and cafés and *tascas* (places where one stands at the counter drinking a brandy, a glass of wine, or a beer while eating shrimp, cheese, ham, or sausage and throwing the debris on the floor). No self-respecting village, no matter how poor, would lack a café, and Spaniards will always find a minute during the day to drop in for a drink, a bite, and a chat. It is still common for a worker or a clerk to spend the evening in their favorite café playing cards or chess and discussing the bullfights and soccer. The purpose is simply to be sociable.

Spaniards and tourists alike flock to see the vivid spectacle of the bullfight.

Spaniards like to eat and to eat well. Late and leisurely lunches and dinners are not at all the monopoly of the rich. They are part of the Spanish culture. Each region has its own cuisine. Madrid is famous for tripe and its *cocido,* a rich plate of boiled beef. Valencia and Murcia are the land of the paella, the dish of saffron rice, shellfish, and chicken. The south and Estremadura offer gazpacho, the cold soup of bread, tomatoes, and cucumbers. Catalonia is known for its casseroles, and the Basque country, the delight of the epicure, specializes in fish and seafood. The Basques also patronize eating societies.

One of the outlets for the Spaniard's energy is travel. Since the automobile, the rapid train, and the jet airliner have long since replaced the mule and the donkey as the means of national transportation, the entire country seems to be moving constantly from place to place and from country to country. There seems to be no end to family visits, to calls on faraway friends, and to vacation travel.

The new ideas introduced by the growth of travel, communications, and the immense numbers of foreign tourists have deeply affected Spanish society. The economic growth and the change in the economic patterns have also made themselves felt in ways that were foreshadowed in other industrial nations. For example, thousands upon thousands of young women from the countryside and the lower urban classes have left traditional servant occupations to take better-paying and more respected factory jobs. The rising cost of living, the desire for a car and appliances, the need for money for vacations, recreational activities, and so on are leading young wives to seek office jobs. Unmarried women from the so-called good families have also entered the labor market, something that was almost unthinkable less than a generation ago.

Running the bulls through the streets of Pamplona is the highlight of the city's Fiesta de San Fermin.

Flamenco is an expressive, mostly improvised Spanish dance accompanied by guitar and sometimes by drums.

The growing economic independence of the young Spanish women has, in turn, led to a change in age-old customs and social habits. More and more women drive cars. The institution of very long engagements is giving way to quicker marriages, more on the Western European model, although this is not yet true in the smaller towns and villages. These and other changes are the despair of tradition-minded families and the government. The Franco regime always concerned itself with the protection of Spanish morals. The Ministry of Information and Tourism could issue a ban for moral as well as political reasons.

But the overwhelming reality of present-day Spain is the pace of deep change. It is felt in the universities and the churches. It is affecting the new middle classes. It is reflected in the rebel workers' organizations. It is obvious in the daily lives of millions of Spaniards.

CITIES

The contradictions that make the Spanish character and the Spanish landscape so attractive are faithfully reflected in the nation's cities, which harmoniously blend ancient and modern, Moorish and Spanish elements.

Puerta del Sol is the historic center of Madrid, Spain's capital city.

Madrid

Since the mid-1950's, Madrid has grown from a quiet and traditional European capital into a thriving, modern metropolis with almost ten percent of the national population. Three quarters of a million automobiles create serious traffic jams where once pedestrians walked serenely. Office and government buildings soar along the Paseo de la Castellana, Madrid's most elegant avenue, which was once lined by the handsome mansions of the nobility. La Castellana has been made longer, and the city itself has expanded outward into rings of suburbs.

A settlement of little importance in Roman times, Madrid was called Madjirith by the Moors who came to Spain in the eighth century. The name and a handful of inhabitants were all the city had until the 16th century, when the site of the future capital was still a forest where wild boar and bears were hunted. The transformation of the forest on the Meseta began in 1561, when King Philip II declared that Madrid was to be the capital of the Spanish kingdom. Although many of his successors considered moving the capital elsewhere, Madrid, with its approximately central location, remained the seat of government, and the city began to grow.

The oldest surviving parts of the city are on and near the Plaza Mayor. Here is the Casa de Panadería—Baking House—built in 1672 as a royal box from which the king and his nobles could comfortably watch fiestas, bullfights, tournaments, and even public executions. The law required the inhabitants of the other houses on the plaza to allow members of the court to sit by their front windows to watch these spectacles if they wanted to. The Plaza Mayor was filled on the great day in the 17th century when five saints—Saint Theresa of Ávila, Saint Ignatius of Loyola, Saint Francis Xavier, Saint Isidore (San Isidro), and Saint Philip Neri—were canonized simultaneously.

A short distance from the Plaza Mayor is Madrid's cathedral, the Church of San Isidro, Madrid's patron saint. Madrileños have a special affection for their saint because, according to legend, one day as he lay sleeping on the farm where he worked, a group of angels came from heaven to finish his chores—a bit of relief city-dwellers hope for also.

The center of Madrid is the Puerta del Sol (gate of the sun). Once a city gate, it is now in the heart of Madrid and is a central point from which all Spanish distances are measured, and from which ten of Madrid's avenues radiate. Following one of them, the Calle de Alcalá, one comes to Madrid's most famous fountain, the Cibele, the Mother Goddess. Farther along, on the Paseo del Prado, is one of the world's greatest museums. Its proper name is the Museo de Pinturas (museum of paintings), but it is almost always called the Prado. It contains an incredible wealth of art, including the work of such great Spanish painters as Velázquez, El Greco, and Goya, as well as a vast collection of Italian, Flemish, French, and German masterpieces.

The abundance of the Prado is complemented by the beauty of the nearby Botanical Gardens with its 30,000 different species of trees, and the Parque del Retiro—a green island in the city that is filled with fountains and has shaded walks, a rose garden, and even a small zoo. The

The Prado, Spain's national museum, houses one of the most important art collections in the world.

Retiro, which was begun by Philip II, is only one of hundreds of sites in the city that were embellished by the Spanish kings. The newest is the Ciudad Universitaria (City University), the vast University of Madrid complex, which was begun by the Spanish king Alfonso XIII in 1928. The university buildings were heavily damaged during the Civil War in the 1930's but have since been rebuilt and are still being expanded, like Madrid itself.

Cities and Monuments Near Madrid

About an hour northwest of Madrid is the Valle de los Caídos—"valley of the fallen"—a stark memorial to the victims on both sides in the Civil War. Not very far from this impressive monument is the Royal Monastery of San Lorenzo del Escorial, which Philip II built as a memorial to his father and to honor a Spanish victory. It is in this vast building—a mixture of royal splendors and monastic simplicity—that Philip spent his last days.

Ávila, west of the Escorial, is one of the great religious centers of Spain and because of its remarkable old walls is one of the most photographed places in the nation. Ávila, which was the birthplace of the great 16th-century mystics Saint Theresa and Saint John of the Cross, won the name of "the fortress that threw back the Reformation" largely because of the tireless efforts of its two saints. Ávila's 11th-century walls, with their 88 towers and 9 gateways, still give the city a fortresslike appearance.

Toledo, southwest of Madrid, is the most splendid of the cities near the capital and is so packed with historic treasures that it has been designated a national monument. As Toletum, the city was important in Roman times and later became a capital of the Visigoth invaders from the north. In A.D. 712 the city passed to the Moors and then in 1085 to Alfonso VI of Castile, who made it the capital of his kingdom. Until Philip moved the court to Madrid, Toledo was the Ciudad Imperial y Coronado —"imperial and crowned city"—a title it is still permitted to use.

The most famous painting of the city, El Greco's *View of Toledo,* is in the Metropolitan Museum in New York City, but the painter's greatest work, *The Burial of Count Orgaz,* and his home, which is now a museum, are in Toledo.

Other evidences of Toledo's colorful past are visible everywhere. Outside the city walls, for example, are the remains of the Roman colony, a medieval castle, and the Fábrica de Armas (arms factory), where the steel weapons for which Toledo has been known since the Middle Ages are still made. Within the walls there is a vivid lesson in Spanish architectural history—the great cathedral, which is called Gothic because it was begun in the 13th century, but which incorporates other Spanish architectural styles as well. Among them are Mudejar, plateresque, Churrigueresque, and neoclassic. Mudejar is the name given to the style influenced by the Moors; plateresque is an early 16th-century form that resembles the delicate work of silversmiths. Churrigueresque is named for José Churriguera, whose extravagant designs marked the high point of Spanish architecture in the late 17th and early 18th centuries. Other notable religious buildings in Toledo are the former mosque, dating from the 11th century and now called Santo Cristo de la Cruz, and the synagogue of El Tránsito.

Spain has had a strong artistic tradition for centuries. One of its most noted painters was Francisco Goya, who painted "Majas on a Balcony" in about 1810.

Daydreamers who have been accused of "building castles in Spain" will discover why when they see the magnificent castles in **Segovia,** which are fully fantastic and beautiful enough to inspire even the most down-to-earth. The most famous is the fortress-castle, the Alcázar, which was

The historic city of Toledo is dominated by its cathedral (center) and the restored Alcázar (right).

El Greco ("the Greek") was one of the world's greatest expressionist painters. His famous "View of Toledo," painted in about 1610, is still renowned for its dramatic imagery.

The Alcázar in Segovia is an outstanding example of Spanish castle architecture.

once the home of Queen Isabella I, and is still a fitting home for royalty —real or imaginary. Segovia is also known for its remarkably preserved Roman aqueduct, which has brought water to the city since the 1st century A.D.

Barcelona

There is less of a fairy-tale atmosphere but equally as much history in Spain's second largest city and leading seaport, Barcelona. The city's location on the Mediterranean and its people's *seny*—common sense— are usually given as the chief reasons for Barcelona's long and successful history as a center of commerce.

Barcelona has the reputation of being Spain's most European city, but actually its history has been typically Spanish and reflects the usual procession of conquerors, who seem more often to have been won over by their supposed victims. Barcelona is different in that it became so powerful at one point in its history that even the fish in the Mediterranean were said to be wearing the red and yellow colors of the Catalán capital. Barcelona, like the rest of Spain, started declining in importance in the 16th century, but with the dawn of the Industrial Revolution it began to grow—a process that is still going on.

Financial success has not dulled the charm of the city, with its splendid location on a slope leading down to the sea. In the oldest part of the city, the Gothic Quarter, there are abundant relics of the Roman occupation, including parts of the old city wall. Nearby is the beautiful 14th-century cathedral with its cloisters and gardens, where geese consecrated to the city's patron saint, Eulalia, wander happily. The center of the Gothic Quarter is the Plaza del Rey (king's square) with the Palacio Real Mayor (great royal palace), in whose halls Columbus was presented to Ferdinand and Isabella on his return from his first voyage to America.

Today, as in the 15th century, the seaport is the most important part of the city. Along the Calle de Moncada near the harbor are fine mansions that were formerly the homes of aristocrats. The Pablo Picasso Museum, the future home of the private collection of Spain's most famous modern painter, will be housed in two of these mansions. In the harbor itself there is a replica of Christopher Columbus' flagship, the *Santa Maria*, along with modern ships, large and small, including the coastal craft called *golondrinas* (swallows) and *gaviotas* (sea gulls).

Real birds, as well as flowers, books, magazines, and merchandise of every kind, are for sale along Las Ramblas, an avenue extending from the center of the city to the harbor. Scattered throughout Barcelona are the 15 extraordinary buildings designed by the architect Antonio Gaudí y Cornet (1852–1926), whose works have been hailed as the products of a genius or of a madman because of their remarkable appearance. His most famous work is the Templo Expiatorio de la Sagrada Familia—Temple of the Holy Family—a church, which will, when it is completed in about a century, have 12 towers—one for each of the Apostles—plus a

Las Ramblas, one of the most famous avenues in Europe, is the center of Barcelona's shopping district.

Barcelona's unfinished Church of the Holy Family was designed by architect Antonio Gaudí y Cornet.

higher tower for the Holy Family. Even now the church seems an appropriate symbol of the vital city in which it stands.

Seville

Seville, in southern Spain, is the city that probably best captures the foreigner's imaginary idea of what Spain is like. Here a perfect fusion has taken place between the setting, the climate, and the events of the past, resulting in a city that is as beautiful as it is rich in life, color, and history.

Seville is known to readers as the birthplace of Cervantes' knight, Don Quixote, and to opera-goers as the setting of Mozart's *Don Giovanni*, Bizet's *Carmen,* and Rossini's *Barber of Seville*. But the city is, and has been always, far more than a backdrop for imaginary events. Seville is Spain's leading seaport on the Atlantic, to which it is connected by the Guadalquivir River and by a canal for oceangoing ships. Seville is also an important manufacturing center that produces a variety of goods ranging from armaments to tobacco.

Seville was a thriving commercial center even in Moorish times. In fact, a Muslim historian reported: "If one asked for the milk of birds in Seville it would be found." After the city's reconquest by Ferdinand III of Castile in 1248, it continued to grow, although the mosque and minaret of the Muslims became the cathedral and bell tower of the Christians. The discovery of the New World in 1492 ushered in Seville's greatest period of prosperity because the city held a monopoly on trade with the colonies until the 18th century, when the monopoly passed to Cádiz.

The older part of the city with its narrow, winding streets and handsome plazas retains the face of the proud past. The Cathedral—the third largest Christian church in the world after St. Peter's in Rome and St. Paul's in London—is known for its art treasures. It is also claimed as the burial place of Columbus. The nearby bell tower, which is called the Giralda, is as familiar a symbol of the city as the Eiffel Tower is of Paris or the Empire State Building of New York City. Other buildings such as Torre del Oro (tower of gold) guarding the river, the Columbus Library with its collection of manuscripts, and the 14th-century Alcazár have given Seville its well-earned reputation for beauty.

The architecture in Seville uniquely blends Spanish and Moorish influences.

Seville's annual Ibero-American fairs celebrate Spain's enduring links with the New World.

Each evening during the Holy Week before Easter, the great cathedral becomes the focus of the processions of hundreds of *pasos*—floats—carrying magnificently carved religious figures. The *pasos* are followed by bands of trumpeters and drummers playing music that has been specially composed for the solemn and magnificent ceremonies. Other festivals throughout the year are highlighted by music, dancing, and bullfighting, which for many people are the essence of all that is most beautiful and dramatic in Spanish life.

Spain's automotive industry is one of the fastest growing manufacturing sectors in the country.

THE ECONOMY

Although the economy of Spain has improved remarkably in recent years, hundreds of thousands of men and women continue to emigrate from the countryside to the big cities and to foreign countries in search of jobs. Like many other nations, Spain is increasingly caught in the squeeze between the rise of modern technology and the lag in over-all development.

Economists and sociologists divide Spain into three basic regions—the seven industrial provinces, the central provinces, and the south. The seven main industrial provinces have the highest degree of prosperity. The central provinces are an area of generally average incomes. The south is a depressed area.

The Industrial Provinces

The principal industrial provinces are Madrid, Barcelona, the Basque Provinces—Álava, Guipúzcoa, and Vizcaya—Santander, and Oviedo. Madrid, Barcelona, and Vizcaya together produce more than all the other provinces of Spain.

Madrid, the province in which the country's capital has been situated for four centuries, derives its power and wealth from its political status. As the seat of the government and a trading and financial center, Madrid requires a high level of services. As a result it provides considerable employment, including work in the construction industry. Since the middle 1950's, Madrid has grown from a quiet and traditional European capital into a thriving modern metropolis. Madrid has an increasingly important industrial complex, emphasizing electronics, food processing, and the manufacturing of consumer products. The rest of the province, however, remains backward. The mountainous topography of the Castilian plateau, the dryness of the rocky soil, and the inadequacy of the water supply in the dry climate is responsible for the generally poor agricultural production.

Barcelona has always been prosperous. This is due to the mild Mediterranean climate and the fact that there is enough rain for rich farm production. In addition, there is the trading skill of its people, plus the industrial growth that began in the 19th century. Today Barcelona is, among other things, Spain's automotive production center. The city has spilled out into a chain of industrial suburbs and satellite towns. South of Barcelona and down the Valencian coast, the wealth is in the great orange groves, and the export of the fruit provides much of Spain's foreign exchange earnings. North of Barcelona is the Costa Brava—"wild coast"—a popular vacation region and an important source of tourist revenues.

Vizcaya, Guipúzcoa, and Álava—the Basque Provinces—benefit from a fairly benign climate and considerable rainfall brought by the winds and the mists of the Atlantic, though the winters tend to be severe. The Basque country is the greenest in Spain. For the Basques the mountains that separate them from the rest of Spain have also served to isolate them in their prosperity. But new highways and air travel are doing away with the isolation. The Basque coast of the Bay of Biscay, which joins the

Valencia oranges originated in Spain. Seedlings are cultivated indoors and later transplanted in orchards.

Cork harvesting in Andalusia. Spain is one of the world's leading suppliers of cork.

Atlantic, and the ports of Bilbao and San Sebastián have oriented this region toward France, Britain, and northern Europe.

The three Basque Provinces hold more industry than the rest of Spain put together. Taken as a whole, the Basque area, with its banks, steel industry, and shipyards, enjoys the highest revenues and personal incomes in Spain. The Basque Provinces, along with Madrid and Barcelona, absorb the bulk of the migrations from the poorer regions. Santander, which adjoins the Basque country, is a rapidly developing industrial province. Oviedo, which is also in the north, has coal mines and industry.

The Central Provinces

The central provinces around Madrid include the agricultural areas of La Mancha, the Estremadura region adjoining Portugal, and Galicia. The small shipbuilding industry and fishing in Galicia do not make up for the poor soil. The mountain-dwellers of Navarre also belong economically to this region.

Aside from the south, these two areas have the highest rates of unemployment, and many people migrate from there to industrial centers in Spain and abroad in search of work. The difference in incomes and living standards between the seven industrial provinces and the central provinces is sharp. But even the central provinces seem to enjoy a degree of relative prosperity compared to the depressed south.

The South

At first sight, the south is the most striking, beautiful, and romantic part of Spain. It has the extraordinary cities of Seville, Granada, Córdoba, Cádiz, and Málaga, where some of Spain's greatest art and architecture are on display. History still seems to live in the shade of the monumental cathedrals, churches, and mosques and in the narrow, winding streets where the shuttered old houses open up on patios full of flowers. The south is the home of the flamenco and the beautiful women who sing and dance it. The region is part of Moorish Africa in Europe. It also is one of the playgrounds of Europe, with the famous resorts of the Costa del Sol—"coast of the sun"—Torremolinos, and Marbella, and has a surface appearance of affluence.

But it is in the south—from Cádiz to Almería and Alicante—that topography and nature and climate have been the most cruel to the Spaniards. The mountain ranges and the lack of roads isolate the poor

Sherry, a white wine fortified with brandy, originated in the Spanish city of Jerez de la Frontera.

villages. The stone-strewn fields produce little, if anything. Riverbeds are often dry the year round; some of them have not seen water in years. Rain—the plague of tourists and the joy of peasants—just does not come. What there is of good land in Andalusia is held by the owners of the vast latifundia—estates—where bulls are raised for the bullfights, horses are bred for the select few, olives are raised, and grapes are grown for the sherry industry. The Andalusian peasants are farmhands or tenant farmers. In provinces like Almería—where, near the village of Palomares, the United States Air Force lost four hydrogen bombs in 1966—there is no good land to speak of. Individual irrigation schemes help to make life possible, as does the land reclamation project along the Guadalquivir Delta, where villages have been built for resettled farmers and their families.

Inevitably, then, the southerners leave the south. During the Spanish age of conquest, they went to the New World as seamen and settlers. Today, they migrate to Madrid, Barcelona, the Basque country, or abroad. But neither the Spanish of the south nor their neighbors in Galicia, Estremadura, or Castile have been broken by hardship. On the contrary, they have emerged as tough, imaginative, and often talented individualists.

HISTORY

An ancient legend says that the first settlers in Spain were Tubal and Tarsis, nephews of Noah. Little, in fact, is known about the beginnings of Spanish history. Evidence of the Paleolithic settlers in the north is contained in the caves of Altamira, near Santander. Here about 15,000 years ago artists decorated the cave walls with remarkable drawings that still retain their beauty. Slightly younger relics of these ancient times are burial mounds of the New Stone Age that were probably made by the people who gave their name to the peninsula—the Iberians.

Beginning in about 900 B.C., Celts crossed the Pyrenees into the peninsula, where they mixed with the Iberians to form the Celtiberian people, whom one Latin historian called *robur Hispaniae*—"the oak of Spain." The strategic location of the peninsula and its resources, such as tin, attracted other peoples as well. The bold, seafaring Phoenicians are known to have established trading posts in the Guadalquivir Valley and along the southern coast. The most important of these was Gades, now called Cádiz. Still another seafaring people, the Greeks, established their own outposts on the peninsula. The Greeks are credited with introducing to the Celtiberians olive and wine-grape culture, coinage, and improved ways of making ceramics.

The Carthaginians, a North African people, also set up trading posts along the Spanish coast, including Cartagena (New Carthage) and Barcelona, which is said to have been named for Hamilcar Barca, the 3rd century B.C. Carthaginian general. As a leading Mediterranean power, Carthage presented a serious threat to its chief rival, Rome. The result was the long and bitter conflict known as the Punic Wars (about 264–146 B.C.). Much of the war was fought on the Iberian Peninsula. Other important actions such as Hannibal's advance over the Alps against Rome were launched from the peninsula. Ultimately, however, the Romans drove the Carthaginians out of the peninsula and made it a Roman province called Hispania, from which the name Spain comes.

The ancient aqueduct at Segovia bears witness to Spain's past as a province of the Roman Empire.

Roman Spain

The mountainous terrain and the independent spirit of the Celtiberians made the complete conquest of the new province a difficult task that took the Romans nearly 200 years. With the rather enlightened rule of the Romans the people of Hispania were given civil and political rights under Roman law. Schools were established, and Latin became the language of the people. The products of the peninsula's mines and farms played an important role in Rome's economy. Cities such as Hispalis (Seville), Caesarea Augusta (Zaragoza), Emerita Augusta (Mérida), Brigantium (La Coruña), and Tarragona were established. About 18,000 miles (29,000 kilometers) of roads, as well as immense aqueducts (such as the one at Segovia) and amphitheaters were built, and many are still in use, a testament to the Roman genius for building. Four Roman emperors—Trajan, Hadrian, Marcus Aurelius, and Theodosius—were born in Hispania. During the so-called Silver Age of Latin literature, from about A.D. 14 to 130, such Spanish-born writers as Seneca, Martial, and Quintilian gained fame throughout the Roman world.

The period of Roman rule from about 200 B.C. to A.D. 400 was the longest era of peace and prosperity Spain has known to this day. A high degree of unity was achieved under Roman leadership that may be thought of as forming the basis of the Spanish nation. As Roman power declined, it was replaced by another unifying force—Christianity. The

Spanish Catholic Church claims to have been founded through the mission of the Apostle Saint James the Greater, whose shrine at Santiago de Compostela still attracts pilgrims from all over the world. Many scholars believe, however, that it was probably Saint Paul who founded the church in Spain on a mission there between A.D. 63 and 67. Whatever the truth may be, from that day to this the Church has been a powerful force in Spanish life.

The Visigoths

In the early 5th century A.D., the Visigoths—West Goths—a Germanic tribe, crossed the Pyrenees and made an easy conquest of the people, whose fighting skills had been submerged during their long, peaceful years as Roman subjects. But even as the Visigoths were extending their conquest of the peninsula, they were being absorbed into the Ibero-Roman culture. Latin remained the language of the people, and Christianity finally became the faith of the invaders as well. After the Visigoth king Reccaredo was converted to Christianity in A.D. 589, members of the higher clergy and the nobility were given a voice in the councils of state. Education, instead of being state-run as in Roman times, was carried on by the Church. On the peninsula, as elsewhere in Europe during the early Middle Ages, the Church helped to preserve classical learning.

The Moors

One more important strain was added to the Spanish melting pot when the Moors invaded Spain in A.D. 711. These Muslims from Morocco had been asked to help settle a conflict concerning which of the

Alhambra Palace in Granada reflects the city's heritage as the last Moorish stronghold in Spain.

Visigoth rivals should reign as king. Within 7 years the Moors and their Arab allies had conquered the peninsula except for isolated pockets of resistance, mainly in the northern mountains. It was there in the north that the Christians began to mobilize for the reconquest—a goal that was not achieved for 8 centuries.

The Muslims gained their greatest power in southern Spain. There, the greatest of the Muslim rulers, Abd-er-Rahman III (891–961), who called himself Caliph of Córdoba and Commander of the Faithful, helped to make the city of Córdoba one of the great European centers of culture and commerce. In addition, agriculture and industry advanced under the Muslims. The cultivation of such products as figs, oranges, lemons, sugarcane, melons, and rice was introduced and remains important today. The old Roman irrigation systems were expanded and improved. Mines were worked. Armor and swords from Toledo and Córdoba, Spanish silks and woolens, leather, and ceramics were traded all over Europe.

The Muslims left only a handful of architectural monuments—the great mosque at Córdoba, the Alhambra at Granada, and the Giralda Tower at Seville. Their most enduring legacy was intellectual. The Muslims brought to Spain and to Europe the culture of ancient Greece, whose last intellectual center, Alexandria, had been conquered by the Arabs in 642. As historians, philosophers, grammarians, and astronomers the Muslims made important contributions to the development of European thinking. Pharmacology and botany became formal sciences as a result of the Muslims' work in these fields, and two forms of trigonometry—plane and spherical—were developed by them in Spain.

The Reconquest

Great as their achievements were, the Muslims were often divided among themselves. As they fought among themselves, they were increasingly susceptible to attack by the Christian forces seeking to reunite the peninsula under the Cross. As the Christians fought their way south, various kingdoms were established—Galicia, Asturias, León, Castile, Aragón, Navarre, and Catalonia. Through marriages and wars, the kingdoms were gradually united.

The steps leading up to the unification of Spain are immensely complicated and are perhaps best summarized in dates—from the first skirmish at Covadonga in 718 through the recapture of the important cities of Toledo (1085), Córdoba (1236), Seville (1248), and finally Granada in 1492. The turbulence and even the romance of the period is perhaps best portrayed in the epic *Poema del Cid,* which describes the heroic deeds of the 11th-century knight-adventurer Roderigo Díaz de Vivar, known as the Cid, who fought both Christians and Muslims but never his overlord, King Alfonso VI of Castile.

Even as the Cid's deeds were becoming legendary, disunity among the Christian kingdoms seemed to make the formation of one nation impossible. The strongest of the Spanish kingdoms were expanding their power in other parts of Europe. Catalonia conquered the Balearic Islands in the early 13th century, and at the end of the same century the King of Aragón took over Sicily, thus beginning Spain's long and complicated adventures in Italy. In the course of the 14th century, Catalán seapower came to the rescue of Constantinople against the Turks and helped make Catalonia a major power in the Mediterranean. In 1443, Aragón added

Exquisite mosaic designs embellish castles and palaces in areas once under Moorish rule.

the Kingdom of Naples to its territories. The stage was set for a powerful, united Spain to become a major power in Europe and in the world for several centuries to come.

Imperial Spain

The marriage of Isabella I, Queen of Castile, to Ferdinand II of Aragón in 1469 symbolized the union of Spain, although that union was not an accomplished fact until 1492 when Granada was recaptured from the Moors. In the same year, Christopher Columbus discovered the New World for Spain. The nation was at the beginning of its greatest era of prosperity and grandeur.

In 1496, Pope Alexander VI rewarded Isabella and Ferdinand with the title of Los Reyes Católicos—The Catholic Monarchs—for their past services to the Church and as an incentive to side with him in Italy. As early as 1478, Isabella had established the Holy Office, or Inquisition, whose chief duty was to make Spain a Christian nation. Non-Christians were told to become Catholics or to leave Spain. Most of the Jews left Spain, but those that remained, and many of the Muslims as well, pretended to be converted while secretly following their old beliefs. The expulsion of the Jews from Spain had serious repercussions on the nation's life. Spain's religious unity was saved, but since the Jews had given the country some of its most distinguished writers, physicians, and almost all of its merchants, both scholarship and the economy suffered when they were driven out of the country.

At the same time, Spain was becoming a world power. Regarding France as their chief rival, Ferdinand and Isabella managed to encircle France through alliances and marriage. Isabella and Ferdinand's children were united in marriage with the royal houses of Portugal, England, and

Austria. The marriage of Ferdinand and Isabella's daughter Juana to Philip of Burgundy, a son of the Habsburg Emperor Maximilian of Austria, resulted in the union of the two crowns; their son began his reign as Charles I of Spain in 1516 and became the Holy Roman Emperor Charles V in 1519.

The Spanish Habsburgs.   The results of this royal and imperial splendor in the person of the Spanish king marked at once Spain's most glorious era and the beginning of its decline. Charles V's deep involvement in European affairs cost Spain dearly in manpower and in wealth. Recruitment and taxes increased as Charles battled Francis I of France in a succession of wars, fought to protect Vienna from the Turks, and tried vainly to turn the tide of the Protestant Reformation. Simultaneously, Spanish explorers, seamen, soldiers, and priests were extending the overseas empire. Mexico was conquered by 1522, Peru became a Spanish territory in 1535. By the middle of the 16th century, Spain's flag flew over colonies in California, Florida, Central and South America, and the Philippines, as well as on the coast of Africa.

In 1556, Charles V gave up the throne of Spain in favor of his son Philip II, who also became King of the Indies, the Kingdom of Naples, and the Low Countries. Philip's 42-year reign is noteworthy for great achievements, which seem matched by equally dismal failures. Philip made Madrid the nation's capital. He made the entire peninsula Spanish when he took over the throne of Portugal in 1580, and helped defeat the Turks in the sea battle of Lepanto in 1571. In his other endeavors, Philip was less fortunate. He was engaged in a long and finally unsuccessful struggle to keep the Low Countries Catholic and Spanish. This led him into conflict with England. It was Philip who dispatched the Invincible Armada against Queen Elizabeth I's fleet in 1588—an adventure that ended disastrously for the Spanish Armada and seriously diminished Spain's position as an international power.

The decline of Spanish power continued slowly throughout the reigns of Philip III and Philip IV. Like other monarchs of the time they entrusted much of their power to their advisers who governed for them. In fact when the kings acted on their own the results were often disastrous, as was the case when Philip III expelled almost 500,000 Moriscos —converted Muslims—from his kingdom in 1609. The loss of these able, hardworking citizens had serious economic consequences for Spain. At the beginning of Philip IV's reign, however, Spain was still a great power in Europe. By the time of his death, in 1655, France had become the leading power on the continent and Spain had lost its European territories.

Curiously, it was against this background that the arts in Spain flourished so magnificently that the period from about 1550 to 1680 has come to be known as the Golden Age. Writers, artists, architects, and sculptors, supported and encouraged by the nobles, provided the world with works of authentic genius. The theater gained enormous popularity through the work of such playwrights as Lope de Vega and Pedro Calderón de la Barca. It was in this period, too, that Cervantes published *Don Quixote,* which is considered one of the masterpieces of world literature. In painting there was an equally impressive array of creative talents, including José Ribera, Bartolomé Esteban Murillo, and Francisco de Zurbarán. The giants of art were, however, Kyriakos Theotokopoulos, who is known as El Greco (the Greek) because he was born in Crete, and Diego de Silva y Velázquez.

The Spanish Borbóns. The last Spanish Habsburg king was Charles II, a sad, imbecilic man who could scarcely think, let alone manage a kingdom. When he was near death, he was persuaded to bequeath his realm to Philip, Duke of Anjou, a member of the French house of Bourbon. The immediate result was the War of the Spanish Succession, but the Duke ultimately came to the throne as Philip V. His unsuccessful military activities did little to help Spain back to its former glory. His successors were slightly more successful in their efforts to administer the empire and Spain. Attempts were made to strengthen the economy, improve education, commerce, and industry. But the dominance of France in Europe and the recurrent wars into which Spain was drawn drained away the modest progress provided by these steps. The last of the Spanish Borbóns to reign in the 18th century was Charles IV, an incompetent king, whose wife, together with his chief minister, Manuel de Godoy, ran the kingdom.

The Long Crisis

Goya's graphic portrayals of the brutality of war reflect events in Spain during the period of Napoleon's domination of Europe. Inevitably Spain was drawn into the conflict, first as an ally of France. The results of the alliance included the destruction of the French and Spanish fleets at Trafalgar in 1805 by England's Lord Nelson and then in 1808 the invasion of Spain by French forces. Napoleon's brother Joseph was made King Joseph I of Spain, but this honor was short-lived, as the Spanish people began to wage a heroic guerrilla war against the French. With the help of British forces under the Duke of Wellington, the Spanish were able to drive the French troops out of Spain by 1814.

At the end of the war the Borbóns returned to the Spanish throne, but there was no end to the nation's problems. Strong forces gathered to overthrow the monarchy—a threat met by King Ferdinand VII with reactionary and repressive measures. The struggle between these same forces in Spanish America led to the loss of all the colonies in South America by 1825. Only Cuba, Puerto Rico, and the Philippines remained, and they were lost as a result of the settlement following the Spanish-American War in 1898.

In Spain itself the 19th century continued to be a time of strife and upheaval. A republic was briefly established in 1873, but the next year King Alfonso XII was asked to return to the throne. His son, Alfonso XIII, had the dubious distinctions of having a long reign—1886–1931—and of being the first Spanish king to abdicate without bloodshed. As the century closed, the workingmen of Spain turned hopefully to socialist and other labor parties as a way of solving their problems. Strikes and uprisings were ruthlessly put down by the government.

Revolutionary ideas were widespread and grew in intensity in the early 1920's. A strike in Catalonia prompted the King to permit General Primo de Rivera to become the military dictator of Spain. The Cortes (parliament) was dissolved, although the King remained on the throne. Rivera, who was never popular with the liberals in Spain, was finally overthrown in 1929. In 1931, as the result of a general election, the King was deposed and a republic was established.

The leaders of the republic began the enormous job of providing Spain with political and economic reforms, but it was an almost impossible task in the face of conservative traditions, attacks from the landowners, the Church, and the Army, and the steady radicalization of the left. In 1936, an election was held in which the Popular Front—an alliance of republicans, Socialists, labor, and Communists—won an impressive victory. The victory of the Popular Front was followed by general disorder and triggered a revolt by the Army against the government.

The Civil War of 1936–39 pitted Spaniard against Spaniard, as the Republican followers of the Popular Front battled the troops under the leadership of Francisco Franco. The Nationalists, led by Franco, were supported by the German and Italian dictatorships, while the Soviet Union provided aid to the Republicans. City after city fell to the Nationalists until in 1939, at the cost of between 500,000 and 1,000,000 lives and terrible devastation, Franco became the head of the Spanish state.

Transition From Franco. Franco, who took the title of Caudillo (leader), became the chief of state, the chief of the armed forces, and the leader of the only legal political party, the Falange. In 1947, Franco announced that the monarchy would be restored after his death. Prince Juan Carlos of Borbón y Borbón—the grandson of Alfonso XIII—assumed the throne as King Juan Carlos I after Franco's death, in 1975.

Modern Spain

Political change has come to Spain, but the scars of the Civil War are barely healed. In 1981, firm action by the King put down an attempted rightist coup. Victories in the 1982 and 1986 parliamentary elections ensured the dominance of the Socialist Party, which under Franco had spent more than 40 years of underground existence and opposition.

Madrid's National Palace was built in the 18th century on the site of an ancient Moorish fortress.

Felipe González, the Socialist leader who became premier in 1982, epitomized the new generation of successful Spanish politicians. He was youthful, attractive, cosmopolitan, and pragmatic. González, fully backed by King Juan Carlos, who formed an important bridge between the old order and modern Spain, proved himself to be an activist. He launched initiatives to reduce the size and influence of the armed forces, to preserve his nation's membership in the North Atlantic Treaty Organization (NATO), and to obtain Spain's entry into the European Community (Common Market) along with Portugal on January 1, 1986.

González viewed membership in the European Community as essential both to diminishing his nation's political isolation and to continuing the economic boom that characterized the Spanish economy in the 1960s and 1970s. Large foreign investments coupled with the Spaniards' hard work have helped to industrialize what had been an agricultural country. There has also been the growth of a better-educated managerial class. As a result, hundreds of thousands of new jobs have been created. While living standards for most Spaniards have risen, economic problems still exist. A general strike in 1988 was honored by two-thirds of Spain's workers as a way to protest economic policies. Unemployment remains high in spite of an economic growth rate that is one of the highest in Europe.

The achievements of recent decades are only a first step in the solution of Spain's basic economic problems. Along with a burgeoning middle class, Franco left his political heirs aging government-controlled steel and shipbuilding industries that registered heavy losses. To prepare these sectors for Spain's entry into the EC, González closed outmoded plants and laid off some 60,000 workers in a move that excited vigorous protests from trade unions. He also believed that membership in the European Community would force private corporations—many of which had become complacent and uncompetitive during the dictatorship—to modernize their facilities and improve their production techniques in order to face the challenge of increased imports.

A 7-year transitional period was established to ease Spain's full participation in the European Community. During this period, Madrid could continue—although at decreasing levels—protecting its industry, agriculture, and fishing sectors. Meanwhile the EC would provide special economic assistance to nine poorer autonomous regions beset by especially serious and prolonged unemployment. These areas are Andalusia, the Canary Islands, Castilla-León, Castilla-La Mancha, Estremadura, Galicia, Murcia, and the enclaves of Ceuta and Melilla. Soon after joining the Common Market, Spain elected 60 members to the 518-seat European Parliament. After centuries of isolation and ambivalence toward its neighbors, Spain had finally cast its lot—politically, economically, militarily, and socially—with Western Europe.

Government

In 1977, Spain held its first free elections in 41 years. A new constitution ratified in 1978 made Spain a parliamentary monarchy. The king is head of state and appoints a premier as head of government. The Cortes (parliament) consists of a Senate and a Chamber of Deputies.

GEORGE W. GRAYSON
College of William and Mary

Sparkling streams rush through Andorra's valleys.

ANDORRA

At Christmastime in the Spanish town of Seo de Urgel, the bishop sits down to a princely feast of crisply roasted capon, delicious smoked ham, and fresh mountain cheese. It is an excellent meal, and if the bishop wants to enjoy it again in the new year, he can, for there are still 11 hams and 23 cheeses in his larder. The food comes to the bishop's table from a place high in the Pyrenees to the northeast—the tiny, mountain-bound country called Andorra.

HISTORY AND GOVERNMENT

Andorra has always charmed those who happened to hear of it or visit it. As long ago as 1806, when Napoleon I passed through Andorra on his way to conquer Spain, someone suggested that he incorporate the little country into France. He refused, declaring that Andorra was a "political curiosity" that "must be preserved."

Andorra's capital, Andorra la Vella, seems dwarfed by the mountains around it.

Small Andorran farm villages cling to the land's rocky slopes.

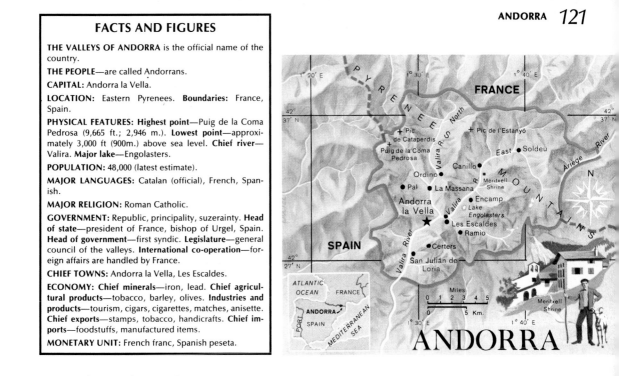

FACTS AND FIGURES

THE VALLEYS OF ANDORRA is the official name of the country.

THE PEOPLE—are called Andorrans.

CAPITAL: Andorra la Vella.

LOCATION: Eastern Pyrenees. **Boundaries:** France, Spain.

PHYSICAL FEATURES: Highest point—Puig de la Coma Pedrosa (9,665 ft.; 2,946 m.). **Lowest point**—approximately 3,000 ft (900m.) above sea level. **Chief river**—Valira. **Major lake**—Engolasters.

POPULATION: 48,000 (latest estimate).

MAJOR LANGUAGES: Catalan (official), French, Spanish.

MAJOR RELIGION: Roman Catholic.

GOVERNMENT: Republic, principality, suzerainty. **Head of state**—president of France, bishop of Urgel, Spain. **Head of government**—first syndic. **Legislature**—general council of the valleys. **International co-operation**—foreign affairs are handled by France.

CHIEF TOWNS: Andorra la Vella, Les Escaldes.

ECONOMY: Chief minerals—iron, lead. **Chief agricultural products**—tobacco, barley, olives. **Industries and products**—tourism, cigars, cigarettes, matches, anisette. **Chief exports**—stamps, tobacco, handicrafts. **Chief imports**—foodstuffs, manufactured items.

MONETARY UNIT: French franc, Spanish peseta.

What makes Andorra a curiosity is the fact that there are at least three correct answers to the question "What kind of country is it?" It is a republic, because it has its own elected parliament. It is a principality, because it has two princes. And it is a suzerainty—a form of government much more familiar 700 years ago than it is today—for its two princes are also feudal overlords, or suzerains.

One of the two princes is the bishop of Urgel; the other is the president of France. As feudal overlords, both men still receive an annual tribute from their domain. Because the president of France lives so far from Andorra, he receives 960 francs (about $210) a year. The bishop receives 460 pesetas (about $6.50) and the food. The bishop receives his annual tribute of food each Christmas. It consists of two capons, two hams, and four cheeses from each of the six districts of Andorra—a total of 12 capons, 12 hams, and 24 cheeses. And it is up to each district to make sure that the food is of high quality. This payment is called *la quistia* in Catalan, the language of Andorra, and it dates back to 1278.

In that year a treaty was signed at Les Escaldes, Andorra, ending a long struggle over the territory by the Bishop of Urgel and the Count of Foix. By the terms of this treaty the Bishop and the Count became co-princes of Andorra. In succeeding centuries, the property of the counts of Foix went to the kings of France and, finally, to its presidents. Otherwise, the treaty has been observed almost without change since the day it was written. It is one of the oldest treaties presently in force.

Andorra's history before the 13th century is not so much fact as it is long-accepted tradition. Andorrans believe that Charlemagne granted them their independence in the 8th century, in return for their help in fighting the Moors in Spain. They also believe that Charlemagne or his son King Louis I named the country—possibly for the Biblical land of Endor. However, the name Andorra may come from the Moorish word *al-dorra*, which means "a thickly wooded place."

WAY OF LIFE

The Andorrans are a proud, independent people. Though Spaniards call them *cerrada* ("closed"), and the French say that someone who is tight-lipped "acts the Andorran," it may be that Andorrans have developed a certain quiet strength through centuries of living in a difficult land.

Farming is Andorra's traditional way of life, but so much of the land is mountainous that only about 4 percent can actually be farmed. This tiny percentage explains the country's official name—Valleys of Andorra—for the valleys are where the good land is and where Andorrans grow tobacco, grain, fruits, and vegetables. Whole families work side by side on their farms, and schools often do not open in the fall until harvesttime is over. Children also help to tend the many sheep and cows that grow fat grazing the high Andorran pastures in summer.

ECONOMY

Since the 1950's, hydroelectric plants have been harnessing the tumbling mountain streams for power, and Andorra has several small factories that manufacture cigars, cigarettes, matches, sandals, and anisette liqueur. All these are used in Andorra and exported to France and Spain. Andorra's two most famous "exports," however, are not products at all, and both are easier to send over long distances. One is Radio Andorra, which broadcasts in French and Spanish. This station, whose programs consist largely of recorded music, is very popular in both France and Spain. Andorra's other well-known export is its stamps. These are issued by France and Spain and are prized by stamp collectors all over the world. Money from the stamp sales helps to support Andorran schools.

For years, stamps and radio have been carrying Andorra to the world beyond the mountains, but recently much of that world has been coming to Andorra. Approximately 7,000,000 tourists visit Andorra annually to delight in its landscape of twisted pines, ancient oaks, glistening lakes, and lush meadows. The roads from France and Spain are kept open in winter, so more skiers can reach Andorra's slopes. Visitors also enjoy annual fiestas like the Bal de Morratxa (held in San Julián de Loria), which features a dance representing the signing of the treaty so long ago.

ANDORRA'S CAPITAL, MINIATURE OF A MINIATURE

The country's tiny capital, Andorra la Vella, has some 8,000 residents. It is the site of the 16th-century Casa de la Vall ("house of the valley"), where Andorra's 24-member parliament meets. A 4-pound (2 kilograms) key unlocks the door of the old building, which also serves as Andorra's courthouse and prison. The town's shop windows are crowded with attractive merchandise, much of it imported from all over the world. And Andorra la Vella's streets swarm with cars—enough to require a traffic policeman at the busiest intersection.

Like its capital, Andorra is a place where reminders of the past still wait around every corner. It is a country that has enjoyed peace among its mountains for more than 700 years—a country that has been described as "the most peaceful . . . in the world."

Reviewed by PRESS AND INFORMATION SERVICE OF THE FRENCH EMBASSY, New York

GIBRALTAR

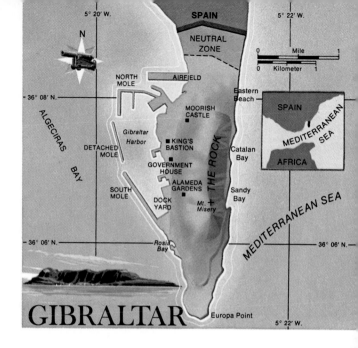

GIBRALTAR

Gibraltar, which covers only 2.3 square miles (6 square kilometers) of land, juts out from southern Spain at the entrance to the Strait of Gibraltar, the narrow waterway that separates Europe from Africa. It is one of the Pillars of Hercules, the ancient name given to the great cliffs flanking the strait. In A.D. 711 Tarik, an Arab Muslim warrior, captured the rock and built a fortress there. The Moors named it Djebel al-Tarik ("rock of Tarik"), which evolved into "Gibraltar." After 7 centuries of Moorish rule, the Spanish seized the rock in 1462. In 1704, during the War of the Spanish Succession, the British overran Gibraltar, and in 1713 Spain ceded the fortress to Great Britain "to be held and enjoyed absolutely with all manner of right forever."

Gibraltar is a British crown colony. The commander of the fortress serves as governor-general. There is an elected legislative council and an elected city council to deal with municipal affairs. The language of the more than 26,000 Gibraltarians is English, but most of them also speak Spanish. The inhabitants are descendants of British soldiers who married Spanish women, Maltese who came there to work, Jews who were driven out of Spain and Portugal at the end of the 15th century, and Italians who came to escape conscription into Napoleon's armies. In the 1967 referendum held to allow the people to choose between Spain and Great Britain, they voted 12,138 to 44 to remain British.

Since the 1960's Spain has been claiming that the British occupation of Gibraltar is illegal. For centuries Spanish laborers from nearby towns came daily to work in Gibraltar, but the border was closed by Spain in 1969, and in 1985 the remaining border restrictions were lifted. Despite continuing negotiations between the governments of Spain and Great Britain, however, no agreement on the future of Gibraltar has yet been reached.

Gibraltar has no agriculture and very little industry. Its income derives mainly from servicing the ships that use the port and from tourism, which has been greatly developed in recent years. The town on the lower slope of the rock has a museum, a Roman Catholic cathedral, and the ruins of a Moorish castle.

Reviewed by SIR JOSHUA HASSAN, C.B.E., M.V.O., Q.C., Chief Minister of Gibraltar

The scenic Amalfi coast south of Naples is one of Italy's most popular summer resort areas.

ITALY

Italy, an ancient land in south central Europe, is one of the great wellsprings of Western culture. Here the Romans built the capital of their vast empire and where later the Roman Catholic Church chose to make its spiritual headquarters. The Renaissance, or rebirth of classical art, architecture, and philosophy, began in Italy in the 14th century.

All these and other landmark achievements in European history were made against a background of warfare and bloodshed that pitted Italians from one part of the peninsula against those from another and against a seemingly endless succession of invaders. Somehow, in spite of these repeated upheavals, the Italian people survived, united by language and culture. In the mid-19th century, the unity became political as well, and the nation we know as Italy was born.

For the visitor from abroad, Italy provides one surprise after another. The tourist prepared to visit a nation that could well have become a vast museum of Western history finds instead a modern industrial nation. The surprises multiply as one finds Italy more warmhearted, more fascinating, indeed, more of everything than one had expected. At the same time it is one of those unique countries where nearly everybody feels at home immediately. The fine blend of ancient and modern in a setting of beautiful landscapes and exciting cities is an invitation in itself. It is perfectly matched by the Italian people themselves, a nation of born hosts.

THE LAND

The name "Italy" is extremely old. It seems to have been used first in documents of the 5th century B.C. to describe a small territory at the tip of the boot-shaped peninsula that extends into the Mediterranean Sea. Historians used to think that the name came from that of a legendary king, Italo. Many other ingenious and improbable theories have been suggested to explain the origin of the name. No matter what its origins, the name of that small territory at the tip of the boot spread, little by little, to indicate the whole peninsula. By about A.D. 1000 the name designated a region, a dialect, and a culture. But it was not until the mid-19th century that the many separate nations on the peninsula were united into one nation to which the ancient name "Italy" was given.

In the north, where the Italian peninsula joins the European continent, the Alps form an almost continuous natural boundary. The Alps divide Italy from France in the northwest and from Switzerland and Austria in the north. Italy's northeastern neighbor is Yugoslavia.

The Italian peninsula stretches southeast into the Mediterranean Sea from Europe to Africa, with its heel to the east and its toe pointing west. The boot seems poised to kick its largest island, Sicily, from which it is separated by the narrow Strait of Messina. In addition to Sicily, Italy includes the islands of Sardinia and Elba in the Tyrrhenian Sea off its west coast. The island of Corsica in the Tyrrhenian is a department of metropolitan France. There are about 70 smaller islands scattered along the coast in both the Adriatic and Tyrrhenian seas.

Italy's long seacoast is better-known for its beaches and resorts than for its ports, of which only Genoa and Naples are important to international shipping. However, Italy's location with easy access to North Africa, the Balkans, and the Middle East and to the Atlantic, has been vitally important in shaping the country's history and culture.

Two small independent states are within Italy's borders. One is the Republic of San Marino in the northeast, which claims to be the oldest and smallest republic in the world. The other state within Italy is Vatican City, which covers 108.7 acres (44 hectares) in the capital city of Rome. This, the smallest independent nation in the world, is the spiritual center of the Roman Catholic world. (Both SAN MARINO and VATICAN CITY are described in separate articles in this volume.)

Hills, Mountains, and Volcanoes

The most important geographical fact about Italy is that two-thirds is covered with mountains and hills. Considering that the peninsula extends for about 600 miles (970 kilometers) and has an average width of about 90 miles (140 kilometers) from coast to coast, it is easy to visualize how rugged the landscape is. In fact, the mountains and hills have served until recently to keep one region of Italy quite isolated from another. Without traveling too many miles one can still find differences of outlook, custom, dialect, and cuisine. The development of modern transportation and communication facilities is slowly erasing these differences, but it is still quite easy to tell the regional origin of an Italian.

The Alps contain the highest peak entirely within Italy, the 13,323-foot (4,060-meter) Gran Paradiso. But the Wall of Alps has never acted as an effective barrier to aggressive or peaceful invaders. Since earliest times the passes through the Alps into Italy have been used by warriors

FACTS AND FIGURES

NAME: Italian Republic.

NATIONALITY: Italian(s).

CAPITAL: Rome.

LOCATION: Southern Europe. **Boundaries**—Austria, Yugoslavia, Adriatic Sea, Ionian Sea, Mediterranean Sea, Tyrrhenian Sea, Ligurian Sea, France, Switzerland.

AREA: 116,305 sq. mi. (301,230 sq. km.).

PHYSICAL FEATURES: Highest point—Gran Paradiso (13,323 ft.; 4,060 m.). **Lowest point**—sea level. **Chief rivers**—Po, Adige, Tiber, Arno. **Major lakes**—Garda, Maggiore, Como.

POPULATION: 57,557,767 (latest estimate).

MAJOR LANGUAGES: Italian (official), German, French, Slovene.

MAJOR RELIGION: Roman Catholicism.

GOVERNMENT: Republic. **Head of state**—president. **Legislature**—Parliament.

CHIEF CITIES: Rome, Milan, Naples, Turin.

ECONOMY: Chief minerals—mercury, potash, marble, sulfur. **Chief agricultural products**—fruits, vegetables, cereals, potatoes, olives. **Industries and products**—machinery and transportation equipment, iron and steel, chemicals, food processing, textiles. **Chief exports**—textiles, chemicals, footwear. **Chief imports**—petroleum, machinery and transportation equipment, foodstuffs, metals, wool, cotton.

MONETARY UNIT: Lira.

and visitors alike. In the 3rd century B.C. the Carthaginian general Hannibal was able to lead a fully equipped army with elephants across the Alps into northern Italy. This famous invasion was followed by others, each of which has left its mark on the land and people of Italy.

Today, only the most rugged tourists would consider crossing the Alps on foot because excellent highways, tunnels, and railroads link the Italian peninsula with its transalpine neighbors. Among the best-known passes are the Brenner from Austria; the Saint Gotthard, Bernina, Great Saint Bernard, and Maloja from Switzerland; and the Mont Cenis, Mont Blanc, and Little Saint Bernard from France.

Italy's "spine" is formed by the Apennine Range, which stretches from the Ligurian Alps in the northwest down to the Strait of Messina in the south. The mountains of Sicily are considered an extension of the Apennines. Corno Grande, a peak that is in the Gran Sasso d'Italia group east of Rome in the Abruzzi region, rises to 9,560 ft. (2,910 m.) and is the highest point in the Apennines. However, the average height of the range is considerably lower. Although the Apennines were once thickly forested, centuries of indiscriminate tree cutting for building and for fire-

Dramatic mountain formations dominate the Dolomite region of the Alps. Many local residents speak German.

ITALY

SWITZERLAND — AUSTRIA — HUNGARY

EUROPE

Lake Geneva — Bolzano — San Daniele del Friuli
Mont Blanc — Trent — Monfalcone — Trieste
Val d'Aosta — Lake of Lugano — Morostica — Murano Burano
Gran Paradiso — Lake of Orta — Lago Maggiore — Lago d'Iseo — Lago di Garda
Magenta — Cantu — Brescia — Venice
Turin — Milan — Adige River
Pavia — Solferino — River
Po River — Cremona — Mantua — Po River
COTTIAN ALPS — Ferrara
LIGURIAN ALPS — Bologna — Ravenna
Genoa — Chiavari — Castel San Pietro — Faenza — Bertinoro
Carrara — APUANE ALPS — SAN MARINO
Viareggio — Pisa — Florence
San Remo — Arno River — Urbino
MONACO — Leghorn — Gubbio
Larderello — Siena — Perugia
LIGURIAN SEA — Lake Trasimeno
ELBA — Bolsena Lake — Terni
CORSICA (FRANCE) — Lago di Vico — GRAN SASSO D'ITALIA
Lake Bracciano — ABRUZZI APENNINES
VATICAN CITY — Rome — San Marco in Lamis
Albano Lake — Bari
La Maddalena — Anzio
Olbia — Portici — Vesuvius
Sassari — Naples — Salerno — Brindisi
ISCHIA — Torre Annunziata — Amalfi — Taranto
SARDINIA — CAPRI — GULF OF TARANTO
TYRRHENIAN SEA
Iglesias — Cagliari
MEDITERRANEAN SEA
USTICA ISLAND — LIPARI ISLS. — STROMBOLI
VULCANO — STRAIT OF MESSINA
EGADI ISLANDS — Palermo — Messina — Reggio di Calabria
Segesta — CONCA D'ORO — Mt. Etna
SICILY — Catania
Agrigento — Augusta — Syracuse
PANTELLERIA
IONIAN SEA
FRANCE — LIGURIAN SEA — ADRIATIC SEA — YUGOSLAVIA — ALBANIA
ALGERIA — TUNISIA

Miles 0 50 100 150 200
Kilometers 0 100 200 300

TRENTINO-ALTO ADIGE
VAL D'AOSTA — LOMBARDY — VENETO — FRIULI-VENEZIA GIULIA
PIEDMONT — EMILIA-ROMAGNA
LIGURIA
TUSCANY — UMBRIA — THE MARCHES
LATIUM — ABRUZZI E MOLISE
SARDINIA — CAMPANIA — APULIA
BASILICATA
CALABRIA
SICILY

Since Roman times, the sheltered shores of Lake Como have provided popular resort sites.

wood have left the mountains nearly bare and very badly eroded. To combat this erosion and to provide Italy with a much needed timber source, the government has launched a long-range reforestation program.

The Apennines are known for their volcanic characteristics—lava fields, earthquakes, and active volcanoes, such as Vesuvius near Naples and Mount Etna near Messina, Sicily. The earliest recorded eruption of Vesuvius occurred in A.D. 79 and destroyed Pompeii. Earthquakes often rock the Italian peninsula and Sicily, wiping out towns and lives in minutes. The most recent, in 1980, left 5,000 dead and 250,000 homeless.

Lakes and Rivers

In addition to the volcanic crater lakes in the Apennines—Bolsena, Bracciano, Albano, and Vico—Italy is noted for its magnificent lake district south of the Alps. The beautiful lakes Garda, Maggiore, Como, Iseo, and part of Lugano are world-famous tourist attractions. Garda is the largest lake in Italy; Maggiore and Como rank as the second and third largest, respectively. Maggiore is known also for its Borromean Islands, one of which, Isola Bella, was transformed by a nobleman from a barren islet into a terraced wonderland rising to surround a palace filled with fine painting and sculpture. Still another lake, Trasimeno, in central Italy, is known for its beauty and because it was there that Hannibal won an important victory against the Romans in 217 B.C.

Italy has many rivers, but only two—the Po and the Adige—are navigable. The 405-mile (650-kilometer)-long Po is Italy's longest river and has the largest drainage basin. The Po rises in the Alps, flows in an easterly direction across the plain between the Alps and the Apennines, and empties into the Adriatic south of Venice. The Po, its tributaries, and an intricate system of irrigation help to make the large north Italian plain the most fertile farmland in the nation.

The Adige rises in the Alps and empties into the Adriatic. Although it is navigable for only about 70 miles (110 kilometers), it has been harnessed to provide hydroelectricity. Other Italian rivers such as the Arno, Tiber, Piave, and Isonzo are well-known because of the cities along their banks and the events that have taken place nearby. The Arno, which is the river of Florence, the leading city of Tuscany, rises in the Apennines and empties into the Tyrrhenian Sea, as does the Tiber, the river that flows through Italy's capital city, Rome. The Piave in the north and the Isonzo in the northeast, both of which empty into the Adriatic, were the sites of fierce battles during World War I.

Islands

Sicily. The largest of Italy's islands, Sicily ranks as the largest and most populous of all the Mediterranean islands. Since 1947 Sicily and such nearby islands as the Lipari and Egadi groups have been governed as an autonomous region of Italy. Mountainous Sicily is known for its magnificent scenery, fine climate, and mineral wealth. Scenically, the most outstanding landmark is Mount Etna, the highest active volcano in Europe. The trip to the edge of the volcano's main crater can be made by cable car, then jeep, and, finally, for the last few yards, on foot. Once atop Etna there is a stunning view of the island, the surrounding sea, and, of course, the awesome crater itself. Etna's first recorded eruption took place in 475 B.C., when the island was colonized by Greeks.

The island has been occupied successively by the Romans, Byzantines, Arabs, Normans, and Spaniards. In the 18th century Sicily, with Naples, became part of the kingdom of Two Sicilies, and it was made part of the newly formed Italian kingdom in 1861. One of Sicily's attractions is the wealth of relics and monuments left behind by some of the earliest settlers. One of the best-preserved Greek temples is at Agrigento; other notable Greek legacies are at Syracuse and Segesta.

Today, however, Sicily is fast recovering from the centuries of foreign occupation, bad government, and the neglect of absentee landlords who once owned much of the land. The fertile island now leads Italy in the production of citrus fruits. Corn, barley, olives, almonds, grapes,

Crowded housing adjacent to sandy beaches is characteristic scenery along the Sicilian coastline.

The small, picturesque island of Ischia guards the approaches to the Bay of Naples.

and cotton are also grown. Tuna and sardine fishing are important to the island's economy. Since World War II, the government and private companies have greatly helped the industrial development of the island. Sicily now produces about two thirds of Italy's sulfur, as well as important quantities of asphalt, rock salt, sea salt, and pumice. Sicily's economic future has been made even brighter by the discovery of one of Europe's largest oil fields.

Sicily's Islands.   The Lipari (Aeolian) Islands, Egadi Islands, Ustica, and Pantelleria are part of the autonomous region of Sicily. The Lipari Islands, a volcanic group, take Aeolian, their other name, from Aeolus, the Greek god of the winds, who was believed to store the winds in a cave on one of the islands. Another Lipari island is called Vulcano in honor of the Roman fire god, Vulcan, whose workshop was believed to be there. Stromboli, also in the group, has an active volcano. In the past the islands were used as detention centers for political prisoners, but they are better-known today for their scenery and as a unique place to go skin diving because of the unusually clear water and underwater caves.

Capri and Ischia.   These two islands in the Bay of Naples are among Italy's most famous resorts. Capri's scenery, vegetation, and climate have attracted generations of tourists. Even in Roman times, the emperors Augustus and Tiberius found Capri lovely enough to build vacation villas there. Modern visitors seek out the Blue Grotto, which is famous for the strange luminescence of the seawater and can be visited by boat.

Ischia is a volcanic island whose warm mineral springs and superb landscapes have made it a popular health resort. A castle built on 5th-century Greek foundations and the always inviting sea also attract visitors.

Sardinia.   About 115 miles (185 kilometers) off the west coast of Italy is Sardinia, the second largest Italian island. Mountainous Sardinia is one of the most dramatically beautiful and least populated parts of Italy. Its dry climate, dense growth of shrubs, cork oak, and heather, and the clear surrounding sea are making it a popular resort. The capital city, Cagliari, is older than Rome. Prehistoric stone fortress-houses called nuraghi are scattered all over the island, but archeologists have been unable to determine exactly who inhabited them.

Sardinia, like Sicily, is an autonomous region. And also like Sicily it is one of Italy's richest mineral resource areas. Zinc, lead, lignite, copper, iron, and salt are mined. Corn, barley, grapes, olives, and tobacco are grown, and cork is exported.

Elba.   This small island only 6 miles (10 kilometers) off the coast of Tuscany, is not known either for its iron mines, which have been worked since Roman times, or for its pleasant scenery. Its fame comes from the fact that for one year in its long history of occupation by foreign powers it was a sovereign principality. The brief moment of sovereignty came in 1814–15 when the European leaders banished the French emperor Napoleon there and gave him the tiny island as his own. When he escaped from Elba and failed to reconquer his kingdom, Napoleon was sent to St. Helena, a much more remote island in the South Atlantic, and Elba eventually became a part of Italy.

Natural Resources

Italy lacks most of the resources needed for a modern industrial economy. The fact that Italy's economy is modern and industrial is the result of importing many basic resources, as well as continuous exploration to find existing resources. The ingenious use of outside resources helps to explain how Italy has transformed itself from a predominantly agricultural nation into an industrial one in recent years.

The energy from natural steam jets is harnessed at a giant complex near Pisa and used to create electricity.

One of Italy's important power resources is hydroelectricity produced by harnessing swift-flowing alpine streams. Much electricity is also generated by nuclear reactors. Oil and natural gas are found on the Adriatic coast near Ravenna, on the southern edge of the Po plain, and in Sicily.

Another source of power comes from a unique complex in the Larderello area near Pisa in Tuscany. There the natural high-temperature steam produced by the *soffioni*—steam jets erupting through the earth's crust—has been tapped through deep wells. The steam is then piped to power installations through thermally insulated pipelines and used to operate steam turbines that produce electricity.

Visitors speeding by train from Milan and Genoa to Rome, or vice versa, rarely know that their electric locomotive is powered by steam gushing in geyserlike jets from deep in the earth. And even fewer realize that Larderello—because of its huge, noisy steam jets and boiling mud wells—was for a long time considered a corner of hell on earth. Today, Larderello is a model modern industrial center employing about 2,000 people in a variety of industries—such as power stations (which have been nationalized), chemical plants, and salt refineries. This intelligent exploitation of natural resources is studied by specialists and scientists from all over the world. New Zealand, Iceland, Japan, and Mexico, in fact, have similar installations based on geothermal power.

Only three minerals—mercury, sulfur, and marble—are mined in large enough quantities for export. Italy is, in fact, the world's leading producer of marble. The most famous Italian marble comes from the quarries of the Apuane Alps, a branch of the Apennines that runs along

The Apuane quarries in Tuscany have been a rich source of choice marble since Roman times.

Goats graze near a Sicilian sulfur plant. Sicily was formerly the world's leading supplier of sulfur.

part of the Tuscan coast. The Apuane are a startling sight, rising to about 6,000 feet (1,800 meters) and seeming, even in summer, to be covered with snow. The "snow," of course, is made up of millions and millions of marble chips. Today, the Apuane quarries produce over one third of the world's marble and employ over 100,000 people. The best marble in this region comes from around Carrara. Its beautiful white statuary marble was used by the 16th-century artist Michelangelo.

Climate

Artists, songwriters, and picture-postcard photographers have all contributed to the worldwide fame of the blue Italian sky and the mild climate. Actually it is a little dangerous to make generalizations about the Italian climate because of the length of the peninsula from north to south and the presence or absence of such important geographical features as mountains and lakes. In the north, for example, the Alps act as a shield that keeps the most intensely cold winds out of Italy. At the foot of the Alps, around Lake Como and Lake Garda, the climate is so mild that there are gardens with lemon and orange blossoms.

South of the lakes, in the Po River plain, the climate is more continental. Winters are cold, and summers are hot. In fact, the average winter temperature of Milan, on the northern edge of the Po plain, is colder than that of Paris. Except for the Apennines, central Italy has a typical Mediterranean climate with the heaviest rains falling in spring and autumn. Winters are mild, and summers are hot and dry. It is this part of Italy where the blue skies, indeed the quality of the light, make the land attractive to visitors. In the mountains winter snowstorms are often heavy, but summers tend to be dry, sunny, and pleasant.

As one goes farther down the peninsula to southern Italy and Sicily the climate becomes more and more African, with intense heat in summer and mild, often rainy winters. Occasionally the hot, dust-laden wind called the *sciròcco* blows up from the deserts of North Africa across Sicily and southern Italy.

THE PEOPLE

The Italians of today are descended primarily from the ancient Etruscans and Romans. Throughout the centuries various other peoples have been added to the Italian population, so that mixed with the familiar dark-haired, olive-skinned Mediterranean faces one sees blonde, blue-eyed Italians whose forebears probably came from the north during the barbarian invasions, or later during the various periods of occupation by foreign armies.

Modern Italy is a crowded country. The population is quite homogeneous. A substantial group of German-speaking people, however, live in the province of Bolzano in the north, and a smaller number of Slovenes make their home near Trieste at the northern tip of the Adriatic Sea. These groups and the French ethnic minority in the Val d'Aosta are protected by special statutes. There are also small old communities of people of Greek and Albanian origin. The overwhelming majority of Italians are, however, united by their language, religion, and education.

Language

The Italian language comes from the Latin of the ancient Romans. In fact, a knowledge of Latin helps one to learn Italian because the modern language bears a close resemblance to classical Latin.

Even in Roman times, however, two kinds of Latin were spoken—the language of the educated class and the language of the people who had no schooling. This division grew after the Roman Empire fell in the 5th century A.D., and the Italian peninsula was divided up into many separate states, each of which developed its own dialect. It was not until Dante Alighieri's epic masterpiece, *The Divine Comedy,* appeared in the early 14th century that the Italians began to have a national language. Dante, a native of Florence in the region of Tuscany, wrote his poem in the language spoken by the common people of his city so that more people would be able to understand it than if it were written in Latin. Because of *The Comedy*'s immense popularity its language became the language of all Italy.

Literature, schools, radio, and television have done much to standardize the Italian language, but a visitor who knows Italian from formal lessons may be a bit surprised by what he hears in Italy. A southern Italian may casually drop the final vowels from words or double the initial consonants, especially "b" and "p." A Tuscan farmer may cheerfully change "c" to "h" so that he goes to his hasa—home—perhaps to have an internationally known beverage he calls "hoha hola." There are also regional vocabularies, so that it is interesting to know, for example, that to get watermelon in Florence you ask for *cocomero,* but in Trieste you must request *anguria.* Yet, whatever the words or dialect, Italian is a very musical language because of its beautiful vowel sounds and clearly pronounced consonants. It is appropriate that Italian was the language of the first operas.

The Leaning Tower of Pisa is actually a bell tower in a complex that also includes a cathedral (foreground) and a baptistery (not shown). The tower deviates about 17 feet from the vertical.

Religion

The majority—99 percent—of the Italian people are Roman Catholics, but the Constitution guarantees religious freedom. There are also about 100,000 Protestants, 50,000 Jews, and a small number of Greek Orthodox in Italy.

Since Vatican City, the spiritual headquarters of the Roman Catholic Church, is a separate state within the city of Rome, the Italian government has worked out its relationship with the Church in a series of treaties. Once a vast influential state stretching across central Italy, the Vatican is now a minute, independent state with no temporal power in Italian affairs. The influence of the Church, although declining in recent years as Italy has rapidly become more secularized in its cultural attitudes, remains important. Religious instruction is an optional part of the program in elementary and intermediate schools.

The life of the Italian people is infused with its centuries-old association with Roman Catholicism. This is most obvious in the magnificently designed and decorated cathedrals and churches that are among the nation's most beautiful and inspiring monuments. From the elaborate spires of Milan's Duomo to the smallest country chapel, Italy's churches offer a constant invitation to worship.

The Church calendar is filled with holidays honoring the saints and the great festivals of the religious year. Although each village and city has its patron saint, none has gained such popularity as Naples' San Gennaro, whose day is celebrated also by Neapolitans who have emigrated to other countries. The Feast of the Assumption of the Virgin on August 15th is both a great religious holiday and a signal for the beginning of the two-week period called Ferragosto when many Italians go on summer holiday, and a large number of shops and businesses close.

Each year more Italians are celebrating Christmas in the northern European way, with ornamented trees and the exchange of gifts on December 25th. Many people, however, still keep the older tradition, saving the exchange of gifts for January 6, the Feast of the Epiphany, recalling the gifts of the Three Magi. The Easter holiday is celebrated with church services and at home by feasts of roast lamb or roast kid followed by chocolate eggs and special cakes.

Education

All Italian children must attend school until they are 14 years old. After the five elementary school years, students go on to a *scuola media* —intermediate or junior high school—for three years. This may be followed by five years of secondary school. At this level students have a choice between schools offering courses that emphasize the classics, science, teacher training, or art, and those that emphasize technical studies such as agriculture.

To be admitted to one of Italy's universities to study for the *laurea,* or doctor's degree, a student must pass a difficult examination given by a group of professors appointed by the Ministry of Education, since the government directs all education in Italy. The successful student may choose among some of the oldest and most distinguished universities in the world. They include Salerno, whose medical school dates back to the 9th century; Pavia, whose law school dates from the same century; Bologna, which is younger by about a century; and Florence, a mecca for students from all over the world because of its distinguished faculty.

Pizza, Pasta, and Other Pleasures

When one mentions Italian cooking to most foreigners they almost automatically think of pizza and spaghetti. This is a sad oversimplification, because Italian cooking is as diversified as it is delicious. The centuries during which Italy was a collection of separate kingdoms, duchies, and republics has given the modern Italians a cuisine with many subtle variations. Pizza, for example, is a regional dish that was once served because it was inexpensive, simple to make, nourishing, and tasty.

The ancient Romans both borrowed recipes they discovered all over their large empire and distributed their ideas about cooking wherever their armies went. The best of the Roman recipes survived and were modified during the centuries that followed. In addition, Italy's position at the crossroads of the Mediterranean made it a natural entry point for the foods of the Near East and Africa. Cane sugar, ice cream, sherbet, and such candy bases as almond paste and marzipan were introduced to Italy by the Arabs. The Crusaders returned from the Holy Land with a variety of additions, including the use of lemon juice as a flavoring. By the late Middle Ages the Italians were making leavened bread and some

The Italian culinary tradition is world-renowned. Every region of Italy has its own special dishes.

types of pasta (dough). In fact, dough for making pasta was probably developed in Italy before the 13th century. This is important only because of the widespread belief that the Venetian traveler Marco Polo brought spaghetti to Italy from China.

By the 16th century cooking had acquired the status of an art in Italy. Refinements such as the table fork were introduced. Meals composed of many courses were popular with those who could afford them. And, perhaps most significant of all, two daughters of Florence's leading family, the Medici, married kings of France. Both these noblewomen took their finest chefs to the French court, which thus was introduced to the highly developed Italian cooking.

The introduction of such foods as corn, tomatoes, red peppers, potatoes, and turkey from the New World rounded out the resources of the Italian cook. A typical Italian meal now represents the best of a long tradition of cooking with deep roots extending into the past.

One can begin a meal with one of the delicious antipasti (hors d'oeuvres) such as the rosy, thin slices of prosciutto (ham), mortadella (a kind of bologna), or salami that are particularly popular in the north, or *caponata,* the eggplant appetizer from Sicily. Soups range from thick vegetable soup called minestrone to the peppery *caciucco* of Livorno (Leghorn), which is like a fish stew. The plainest broth is usually made tastier by the addition of cheese and small pasta.

Pasta opens the next course of the meal and sums up the basic Italian food. In fact, there are estimated to be more than 100 different pasta shapes. They can be divided into four categories, depending on whether they are destined for soup, for boiling, for stuffing, or for baking. An ABC of pasta goes from *agnolotti, bucatini,* and *cannelloni* to *ziti.* Most pasta names are colorful descriptions of shapes: *agnolotti* ("little fat lambs"), *bucatini* ("little holes"), and *cannelloni* ("big pipes"). Others, like *vermicelli* ("little worms") and *farfalle* ("butterflies"), taste far better than they sound. There are many delicious ways pasta can be prepared, which range from the elaborate lasagne stuffed with meat and cheese and baked in a sauce to the simplest *fettucine al cacio e burro* with its butter, cream, and grated cheese sauce. Internationally, no pasta compares in renown with spaghetti, even though it requires intricate maneuvers to get the long threads from the plate to the mouth. In northern Italy corn flour and rice share the spotlight with pasta as starches.

Beef has always been in short supply in Italy, so the famous *bistecca alla Fiorentina* ("Florentine beefsteak") is the exception to the more general rule that Italians eat little beef. However, fish, pork, chicken, and veal are cooked in a wide variety of ways, including delicate lemon-flavored veal dishes and the more pungent *pollo alla cacciatora* ("chicken, hunter's style"). As accompaniments there is an abundance of vegetables and greens that Italy has made famous.

No meal is complete without bread, which varies in shape and flavor from region to region. There are the golden sticks of *grissini* from the Piedmont, the huge round loaves of Apulia, and the small delicate rolls of Ferrara, to name only a few. Cheese also varies from place to place, as do the wines. And each meal is crowned with fruits: apples from the Trentino-Alto Adige, peaches, pears, and cherries from Romagna, figs and golden plums from Calabria, oranges and tangerines from Sicily, apricots from near Naples. For special occasions there are rich desserts like *zuppa inglese* ("English trifle")—a layer cake drenched in rum with custard and whipped cream—or some excellent ice creams.

Fairs, Feasts, and Festivals

It should be perfectly clear by now that Italians like to eat well. But their joy is complete only if they are in good company. For this reason, Italian folklore—even in the poorer regions—often concerns food and feasts. The smallest town and the largest city, have a fair, or *sagra*, whose main feature is eating. For example, at the *Sagra della Braciòla* ("fair of mutton chops") in Castel San Pietro, a village near Bologna, everybody who comes is given a free, delicious mutton chop that has been roasted over an open fire. At the Ham Fair of San Daniele del Friuli in northeastern Italy, thick slices of the almost-sweet local ham are distributed to whoever happens to be there. At Torre Annunziata, near Naples, there is a Festival of Spaghetti where huge portions of steaming spaghetti in tomato sauce are given away.

Hospitality, as well as sheer joyful eating, is at the core of almost all popular festivals in Italy. There is, for example, a Hospitality Fair celebrated each year at Bertinoro near Forlì in Central Italy. It commemorates the medieval tradition according to which a knight who chanced to pass through the town could tie his mount to a ring on the Column of Hospitality (which still stands in the middle of the piazza). On each ring there was a different coat of arms, so that one could choose his host and be assured of free and lavish hospitality in the palace or castle of the owner of the ring. The tradition has been renewed so that summer visitors can place their cards on the rings and be invited to a home for a dish of pasta and a glass of the good local wine.

Italy's wealth of traditions includes games and pageants that have been handed down unchanged from father to son over the centuries. One of the oldest of these is Florence's *Calcio in Costume* ("costumed soccer"), which has been played in the city since it was a Roman colony and is said to be the ancestor of football. The game was originally Greek and was adopted by the Romans, who, in turn, introduced it in Florence. Today, this spectacular football game is played annually with much of its antique glory revived.

One might say that the Italians—a people whose theatrical tradition goes back at least to the times of the Romans—use games as an excuse to put on a show. *Partita a Scacchi*—"chess game"—is played on the pink and white marble squares of the piazza in Marostica in the Veneto, which is a model of a chessboard. The game is played to commemorate a famous *partita* in which the stake was the daughter of the governor, Parisio. Parisio had forbidden his daughter's two suitors to joust in a tournament for her hand, as was customary then. Instead, he suggested the contest be resolved on a chessboard.

Probably the best-known of all these traditional festivals is the *palio* —a rather wild horse race—run on July 2 and August 16 each year on Siena's oval-shaped Piazza del Campo in the historical center of the town. In this show, music and color play an important role. The *palio* opens with a parade of standard-bearers from each *contrada*—"quarter" —of Siena juggling their banners, whirling and throwing them in the air, and catching them before they touch the ground.

Yet the tourist who comes only to see the horse race may miss the most curious and genuine part of this tradition, which is the ancient ritual that takes place before the race. On the morning of the *palio*, the church

Horse races are the highlight of the Corsa del Palio, a medieval festival held twice each summer in Siena.

Italians are avid sports enthusiasts. Organized bicycle races are common throughout the country.

in each *contrada* is decked with flags, banners, and insignia won from rival *contrade* over the years. At 11 o'clock a special Mass is celebrated in the church, which is attended by all the citizens of the *contrada*, and most important, by the horse that represents the *contrada*. During the rite, the silence and concentration are great, but have nothing to do with devotion. Instead, everyone is anxiously watching the behavior of the horse to see whether or not the omens will be favorable and foretell the horse's victory. In fact, the race is as good as won if the horse's droppings fall in the church. No one would dream of calling this act a sacrilege, let alone of suspecting the priest, himself an ardent supporter of the colors of his *contrada*, of slowing down the service in order to help the horse give a favorable omen.

Sports, Music, and Movies

Clearly, even traditions have their backstage secrets, which perhaps helps one to understand the spirit of a people a little bit better. This is, of course, a difficult job, especially for foreigners, who tend to be impressed by the obvious aspects of Italian life and have little time to investigate what lies behind such a striking mixture of religion and semipagan superstition, ancient wisdom and youthful gaiety.

The Italians' gaiety shows itself in many ways. Their joy in living well is clear from the enthusiasm that marks ordinary events like meals and extraordinary ones like festivals. But it is even more obvious in their passion for sports. Soccer is the national sport, and rival teams have their vocal supporters packing the stadiums. The most popular players are virtually national heroes. Italian athletes also regularly win medals in the Olympics and other international competitions in such events as skiing, bobsledding, and tennis. Long-distance bicycle racing is another sport that has a devoted following in Italy. And in almost every town and resort you can see people of all ages playing bocce, a form of lawn bowling.

The words "Italy" and "music" are almost synonymous, and it is true that nearly all Italians enjoy music. Since Italy is the birthplace of opera, it is probably not too surprising that seemingly every Italian is able to sing at least one aria from the works of 19th- and 20th-century composers Gioacchino Rossini, Giuseppe Verdi, or Giacomo Puccini. Classical music now shares the spotlight with jazz and rock music. The transistor radio, portable phonograph, jukebox, and television have a firm place in the Italian cultural scene. Popular singers have their legions of followers, and huge music competitions, such as the one at San Remo, are held annually.

Since the end of World War II, Rome has become a center of movie production. The first postwar films, with their realistic portrayals of people and their problems, were imitated all over the world. Nowadays Italian movie producers make films of every kind, including some of the best and most realistic Westerns. The works of such serious directors as Vittorio de Sica, Luchino Visconti, Federico Fellini, Michelangelo Antonioni, and Bernardo Bertolucci have won an international audience and international acclaim.

CITIES

Italians joke that they have three capital cities—Rome, the political capital; Milan, the financial capital; and Turin, the industrial capital. One could add Naples and Venice as the tourist capitals. And the list really

Milan, the commercial center of northern Italy, also played a leading role in ancient and medieval times.

Milan's top tourist attraction is the Galleria Vittorio Emanuele II, a covered arcade of shops and cafés.

should be extended to include Genoa, the seafaring capital; Florence, the nation's undisputed cultural capital; and Palermo, which really is a capital—of Sicily; as well as many other cities.

These eight cities are Italy's largest—an important distinction in a country that has been called "a nation of cities" because it has a total of more than 150 towns and cities with a population of over 30,000 each. No matter how great their local pride, the citizens of all the Italian cities now look to Rome as their capital and as the true center of national and political life. (There is an article about ROME in this volume.)

Milan

Milan, the second largest city in Italy and the capital of the province of Lombardy, is not too well loved by the majority of Italians. The Milanese are considered by other Italians to suffer from a self-destructive mania for overwork and success. And the Milanese are often compared to New Yorkers because they seem to run instead of walk. Milan is the one Italian city where one really feels the steady pulse of a productive economy at work. With its skyscrapers, subways, wide avenues, fine shops, and elegant restaurants, Milan is a city solidly planted in the 20th century. It is the most important commercial and banking center in Italy and leads the nation in the production of textiles, chemicals, and metal products, and in printing and publishing. But there is more to Milan than banks and industries. Like all Italian cities, Milan has its great cultural and historical landmarks.

The heart of Milan is the huge Piazza del Duomo ("cathedral"), which was laid out in 1861 at the feet of the magnificent Gothic cathedral. On one side of the piazza is the arcaded Galleria Vittorio Emanuele II with its fine shops, cafés, and restaurants. There the immaculately and dashingly uniformed *carabinieri* (a special army corps that has police duties) watch over an ever-changing parade of Milanese. If one crosses through the Galleria, one comes out on the Piazza della Scala and its most famous building—the Teatro alla Scala. La Scala, as it is called, is probably the most famous opera house in the world.

The city's other important landmarks include the Basilica of Sant' Ambrogio—the 11th-century church built in honor of Milan's first bishop, Saint Ambrose. The Church of Santa Maria delle Grazie is known to art lovers because it is here that Leonardo da Vinci painted his most famous fresco, *The Last Supper*. There are several fine art collections in Milan, including one of Italy's largest, in the Pinacoteca di Brera. The Ambrosian Library and three universities are among the city's best-known contributions to Italy's intellectual life.

Naples

According to an ancient legend, Naples was founded by the siren Parthenope. It was, in fact, founded by the Greeks in the 4th century

In Naples, the narrow streets of the Old Quarter are lined with small, family-owned businesses.

The Bay of Naples is dominated by Mount Vesuvius (right), an active volcano that last erupted in 1944.

B.C. Neapolis, the Greek name for it, means "new city." Naples has always been a vital center of art, learning, and commerce. It ranks as Italy's third largest city. Its magnificent setting on the northern part of the Bay of Naples has inspired great poets like Vergil and street-corner philosophers who have said again and again, *Vedi Napoli e poi muori*— "See Naples and die." The implication is that there is nothing more wonderful to be seen on this earth after one has seen Naples.

Many people have agreed with this idea. The French writer Stendhal said more than a century ago that Naples was "a capital as great as Paris. . . . There is more life here; more noise; the talk is often so shrill, it deafens me. Naples is the real capital of Italy." And to this day, Naples, with its magnificent architectural monuments, crowded markets, and sadly overcrowded slums, is a city of immense vitality. There is a constant noise of traffic, of songs, of voices in energetic conversation.

Today, as Italy's third largest city and second largest seaport, Naples is a market center for the surrounding countryside, as well as the home of such industries as metal production and food canneries and crafts such as glove and jewelry making. The National Museum has a remarkable collection of artistic and historic treasures. The Archeological Museum houses the relics of Pompeii and Herculaneum—the cities destroyed by the eruption of Vesuvius in A.D. 79. The more recent past is recalled in the Church of San Domenico Maggiore, next door to which Saint Thomas Aquinas, the medieval Catholic scholar, once taught. The San Carlo Opera House has been host to some of the greatest musical talents of all time since it was first opened in the 18th century. The city's institute of marine zoology and its aquarium are considered among the best in the world.

Turin

It takes less than two hours to go from Milan, Italy's second largest city, to Turin, the fourth largest, but arriving in Turin, one feels that one is in a new land. This is more surprising because of the fact that Turin is truly Italy's industrial capital and has over 20,000 factories. The largest is FIAT (Fabbrica Italiana Automobili Torino), the biggest privately owned industrial organization in Italy. The FIAT group, which was founded in 1899, ranks among the world's top 10 automobile manufacturers.

Neither the auto industry nor the manufacture of clothing, leather goods, chocolate candy, and vermouth has yet succeeded in over-shadowing Turin's old-fashioned stylish charm. Even its shops and restaurants have an air of elegance. In Turin it is easy to feel that France and Switzerland are very near—in fact, they are just across the Alps. Turin's mood is thus a little different from that of any other Italian city. It seems somehow more subdued, more sophisticated and elegant.

All this is in keeping with Turin's important place in Italian history, for it was here—at the Palazzo Carignano—that the idea of a united kingdom was born and proclaimed. The city's most important landmarks are associated with unification. The Palazzo Reale was the residence of the kings of Sardinia, of the House of Savoy, and later, of the kings of Italy. The Basilica of Superga was the royal burial chapel. All these historical landmarks have not overshadowed the present, however, and the Torinese is probably equally proud to tell you that his city has one of the largest sports stadiums in Europe.

The 506-foot-tall Antonelliana Tower soars above the skyline of Turin, a northern industrial city.

Genoa, Italy's leading port, also serves as an important Mediterranean outlet for much of northern Europe.

Genoa

Genoa is Italy's leading seaport and fifth largest city. Its one rival for the claim of being the chief Mediterranean port is Marseilles, France. Millions of tons of cargo annually pass through the port's modern harbor facilities, which can handle 100 ships at a time. In addition, Genoa is Italy's leading shipbuilding center and has iron and steel works. It also produces one-quarter of the nation's soap.

Genoa, like Naples, has a magnificent setting on a large harbor, and, also like Naples, its history goes back to ancient times. Genoa reached the height of its power as a maritime republic during the Middle Ages. During the Crusades, Genovese merchants had warehouses in such remote outposts as the Crimea, Constantinople, Syria, and North Africa. Genoa was defeated by its rival, the republic of Venice, in the 14th century, but beautiful palaces, churches, and stately gardens still recall Genoa's past glory. Mementos of Genoa's most famous son, Christopher Columbus, include the house in which he is supposed to have been born.

Palermo

Palermo, the sixth largest Italian city, is the capital of Sicily and the seat of the regional government. This lovely city with its gentle climate and marvelous location on the Conca d'Oro—a fertile plain at the edge of the sea—has had a tormented history. The city's founders, the Phoenicians, were followed by a long procession of invaders. After the Phoenicians came Carthaginians, Romans, Vandals, Visigoths, Ostrogoths, Byzantines, Arabs, Angevin French, Swabian Germans, Norman French, and Spaniards. The Byzantine, Arab, and Norman styles of art and architecture are still evident in buildings, among which the most famous are the Palatine Chapel of the Royal Palace, with its exquisite Byzantine Mosaics, and the Chiaramonte and Sclafani palaces.

The once drowsy provincial capital, dozing amid the ruins of the past, has become a bustling center of trade and industry. In addition to its important seaport, Palermo has a number of industries that range from the production of steel and macaroni to that of furniture, textile, glass, cement, chemical, and perfume. It is the city's beauty and wealth of historic sites, however, that attract an increasingly large number of tourists each year. Regional and national government officials are still struggling to eradicate the city's poverty-ridden slums and its organized crime operations.

Venice

Venice, considered one of the world's most beautiful cities, was founded by refugees fleeing from barbarian invaders in the 5th century A.D. The refugees chose well. Their hiding place grew into a city built on over 100 islands in the Lagoon of Venice at the northern end of the Adriatic Sea. Venetians called their city the Bride of the Adriatic and proudly spoke of being wedded to the sea, for it was the sea that brought them wealth. With its strategic location at the crossroads of east-west trade, Venice grew into a great maritime power. Its fleets reached the distant ports of the Near and Far East and returned laden with silk and

In Venice, gondolas ply the canal beneath the Bridge of Sighs, across which prisoners were led to interrogation.

brocades, gold and spices. The wealthy traders built superb palaces along the canals that run through Venice in place of avenues and streets. During the 15th and 16th centuries such famous artists as the Bellini family, Giorgione, Paolo Veronese, Titian, and Tintoretto lived and worked in Venice.

The discovery of a sea route around Africa in the 15th century marked the beginning of Venice's decline because the city no longer had a monopoly on the spice trade. Yet the city's splendor has lasted. Its inhabitants practically live on the water and are connected to the mainland only by a railroad bridge and an automobile causeway.

Today the sea, once the source of Venetian wealth and greatness, threatens the city's existence. The magnificent buildings facing the water are all endangered by the current of the canals, which is increased by the motorboat traffic, and by the seawater that slowly erodes the foundations of buildings. The city as a whole is believed to be sinking at the rate of a foot a century, a much faster rate than when only gondolas and rowboats carried people along the canals. Now also the vibrations caused by the *vaporetti* (water buses) and other motorboats strike at the city's foundations. Industries in the area around Venice are slowly draining the underground water, thus helping the formation of depressions. Gas fumes, added to dampness, and the salt air itself are slowly eating into the marble and stone facings of the buildings and the bronze of the monuments. An army of experts is racing against the tides to find a remedy that will save the city from the sea that made it great.

Florence

Florence, the birthplace of the Renaissance in Italy, also unwillingly had its destiny changed by water—not by sea, however, but by the Arno River, which cuts the city into two unequal portions.

Piazza San Marco, the largest square in Venice, is noted for its Byzantine basilica and lofty clock tower.

Birthplace of the Renaissance, Florence has countless art treasures, including its bell tower and cathedral.

On the night of November 4, 1966, while everybody was alseep, the river broke its banks, completely flooding the part of the city that is richest in history and art and covering everything with a thick layer of water, mud, and oil. In several places downtown, the level of the water was over 30 feet (9 meters). Monuments, works of art, unique and irreplaceable masterpieces, churches, elegant shops, museums, and libraries full of invaluable manuscripts and texts, were flooded and defiled.

After a few days, when the waters finally receded, it was possible to evaluate the damage suffered by the city. Called the Athens or the Citadel of Italian culture, Florence has throughout history been the home of many of the greatest artists, poets, scientists, and architects of all times. The list extends from Dante Alighieri to Michelangelo to Galileo, and many of their works were damaged—some almost beyond repair.

In the days of the flood, Florence received touching proof that its place in the history of art and ideas was recognized all over the world. Students and workers, specialists and laymen, poor people and rich people worked shoulder to shoulder. They succeeded in rescuing from the dirty mud many precious documents, many great works of art. The National Library of Florence is indebted to them for saving many of its 4,000,000 volumes.

Today, Florence has regained its former appearance. Many of the most visible ravages of the flood have been repaired. There remains only a dark line on the walls of many buildings. And in many downtown streets there is a small plaque with a blue wavy line and the simple inscription, "Here the Arno, November 4, 1966," to mark the level reached by the waters on that terrible night.

Florence seems to be growing outward in rings of highways and upward in blocks of apartment houses. The heart of the old city, however, has remained unchanged for centuries. Narrow streets are now thronged with cars, creating a new problem for all who want to save the city's treasures from gas and noise pollution. Yet the city remains unrivaled in art and architecture. Within the span of a very few blocks there are some of the world's greatest masterpieces. The skyline is dominated by the tower of the Palazzo della Signoria (city hall), Brunelleschi's graceful dome for the Cathedral of Santa Maria del Fiore, and Giotto's campanile. Ghiberti's doors for the nearby baptistery are works of art. The Church of Santa Croce is known for its works by Giotto, Andrea del Castagna, Luca della Robbia, and Donatello, as well as works by many other painters and sculptors. The Church of San Lorenzo, the burial place of the Medicis, who ruled the city-state of Florence from the 14th to the 16th century, is famous for its sculptures by Michelangelo. Florentines and the city's many visitors are constantly discovering new treasures in their city and its distinguished museums—the Bargello, the Pitti, the Uffizi, and many others.

Italy's vineyards and groves produce a billion gallons of wine yearly and a quarter of the world's olives.

The sizable Italian automotive industry, concentrated in Turin, produces many world-famous sports cars.

ECONOMY
Agriculture and Industry

Until quite recently Italy was a predominantly agricultural country. Thanks to *Il Boom*—the post-World War II growth of industry—only about one tenth of the working population is now employed in agriculture. The south is the only part of Italy that is still mainly devoted to farming. But farming on the worn-out, rocky soil is difficult and not very productive. Legislation in the post-World War II years has largely eliminated the old system of vast, landed estates (*latifundia*) owned by absentee landlords. The government, through its *Cassa per il Mezzogiorno* ("Southern Italy Development Fund"), a long-range plan for the development of the Italian South, has encouraged industries to move there by offering them lower taxes and loans. The South is steadily modernizing its economy, although many of its people still move out to seek employment in the industrial northern cities or in other countries within the European Community, to which Italy belongs.

The most prosperous farms are in the Po Valley and in the valleys of central Italy. In central Italy the old system of sharecropping (*mezzadria*) has almost completely given way to privately owned or leased farms. Grains, sugar beets, vegetables, fruits, olives, and wine grapes are among the most important products. Although Italy exports fruits and vegetables, it must import the hard wheat used for making spaghetti and other pasta products.

Stylish Italian clothing is made from the high-quality wool and cotton woven at mills in the Po Valley.

Italy's largest, oldest, and most important industry is the manufacture of textiles. Silk is cultivated in the regions of Lombardy, Piedmont, and Friuli-Venezia Giulia. Wool and cotton mills are found in the Po Valley. An offshoot of Italy's textile production is its emergence as a leading clothing exporter. Italian-made suits, dresses, bags, hats, and shoes are sold all over the world.

In addition to textiles, Italy manufactures a wide variety of products including chemicals, petrochemicals, foods and beverages, furniture, and transportation equipment. Lambretta motorcycles, Vespa motor scooters, and FIAT and Alfa-Romeo automobiles have worldwide markets. Ships from the yards at Genoa and Monfalcone, railroad equipment from Milan, and arms from Brescia are other important Italian products. Steel, TV sets, washing machines, refrigerators, computer equipment, typewriters, and tires also are produced in great volume and exported.

Since 1933 about one sixth of the Italian economy has been financed by a system of state holding companies (the IRI: Institute for Industrial Reconstruction). Many economists complain, however, that this "para-state" sector of the economy is the least efficient part.

Participation in the European Economic Community (Common Market) and an increasingly good balance between imports and exports have helped the Italian economy. The annual peaceful invasion of over 50,000,000 tourists a year adds over $5,000,000,000 a year to Italy's earnings. A further help to the economy comes from huge amounts of currency sent home each year by the several million Italians who are working outside the country. Italy's currency is part of the new European Monetary System.

The labor force in post-World War II Italy has been highly organized along ideological lines. Thus, the Communists have a powerful CGIL (Italian General Confederation of Labor); the Socialists have UIL (Italian Union of Labor); and the Christian Democrats have the CISL (Italian Confederation of Organized Workers). The big industrialists have their own *Confindustria* (Confederation of Industrialists). In the 1980's, organized labor lost much of its strength as the nation shifted from an industrial to a more service-centered kind of economy.

Transportation and Communication

Italy's railroads, postal, telegraph, and telephone systems, and some of its radio and television stations are state-owned. The railroad system, which began with a 5-mile (8-kilometer) track·linking Naples and Portici, is now a modern network covering nearly 12,500 miles (20,100 kilometers) and is mostly electrified.

Within Italy a network of *autostrade*—"superhighways"—has been built since World War II. Considered one of the world's best highway systems, this network has helped to break down the ancient regional differences and literally paved the way for economic growth all over the country. Planned to cover 4,350 miles (7,000 kilometers), the Italian highway network eventually will be linked to Sicily by a bridge across the Strait of Messina. Italy's national airline is Alitalia, and it has one of the largest merchant fleets in Europe.

GOVERNMENT

From the time of its unification until 1946, Italy was officially a monarchy. However, from 1922 until 1943, Benito Mussolini's Fascist dictatorship held all real power, and the king ruled in name only. In June, 1946, the Italian people voted to make their government a republic.

According to the Constitution that went into effect in January, 1948, Italy is "a democratic republic founded on work." Italy's Parliament is made up of two houses, the Chamber of Deputies (630 members) and the Senate (315 members). All members of Parliament are elected for five-year terms by universal suffrage on the basis of proportional representation (that is, each party gets seats in proportion to its popular vote). Additional special members of the Senate include ex-presidents and others who may be appointed by the president for special merit in such fields as science, the arts, and economics.

The president of the Italian Republic is chosen for a seven-year term by a two-thirds majority of Parliament. The president appoints the prime minister, who in turn selects the heads of the various ministries. This government then must win approval from both houses of Parliament. The Constitutional court has the power to pass on the constitutionality of all legislation.

Italian politics still are full of differences, and a large number of political parties are represented in Parliament. There are about ten national parties and several minor ones. They range from the neofascist Italian Social Movement (MSI) and the very conservative Monarchist Party on the far right to the small, hard-line Proletarian Democratic Party, which stands to the left of the large Italian Communist Party (PCI). The neofascist and monarchist parties never have been allowed to hold ministerial positions in any of the postwar governments, and the Communists have been kept out since 1947.

As a result, Italy's more than 50 governments since the war have had to be formed from a coalition of parties in the democratic center. The largest of these is the Christian Democratic Party, which has been a major presence in every coalition government since the war.

Italy's Communist Party has traditionally been one of the largest in Europe. Originally pro-Soviet in its policies, it underwent a significant transformation in the 1970s, adopting a Eurocommunist position that is quite independent of the Soviet Union. With the decline of Communism throughout Eastern Europe, the Italian Communist Party has lost considerable strength. Some voters also felt that the party was indirectly responsible for the kidnapping and murder in 1978 of former premier Aldo Moro. Although centrist parties have had to seek support from the Communists on certain issues, the party has been excluded from the government, and it is undergoing major reform in an effort to establish broader support.

The constitution provided for the use of the initiative and referendum. Since the 1970s, these lawmaking tools have been used often. For example, they have upheld such controversial measures as the legalization of divorce and abortions under certain circumstances, and they have made it difficult for the government to build more nuclear power plants.

The Constitution of 1947 authorized the creation and election of 20 regional governments, thus reversing the highly centralized system of administration that had been borrowed from France in 1861. Initially, however, such governments were actually set up for only five "special status" regions (Sicily, Sardinia, Trentino–Alto Adige, Val d'Aosta, and Friuli–Venezia Giulia). Not until 1970 did legislation implement the remaining 15 regional governments. Some people had hoped that by decentralizing the government, reforms would be achieved more rapidly.

The constitution left intact the 94 provincial governments, each with its prefect from Rome and its own parliament and executive, even though many of their functions have been transferred to the new regional system. The most important units of local government are the communes, run by mayors and councils. Their financial resources are limited, and they depend heavily on appropriations from the central government.

HISTORY

Little is known about the early history and settlement of Italy. It is known definitely, however, that invasions were part of Italy's story from the beginning. Greek colonies probably were established in Sicily and southern Italy in the 8th century B.C.

It is also known that a remarkable people called the Etruscans were living in central Italy by about 800 B.C. These mysterious people, whose language has been only partly deciphered, had a highly developed culture. They may have introduced the wine grape, olive, and chariot to Italy. Their skill at working metals such as iron, bronze, and gold provided the basis of their trade. The Greek name for the Etruscans, *Tyrrhenoi*, lingers in the name of the Tyrrhenian Sea off Italy's west coast and in the name of their chief region, Tuscany.

Ruins at Selinunte from the 7th century B.C. bear testimony to the Greek influence on pre-Roman Italy.

The Gauls from the north and the Romans from the south conquered the Etruscans, whose last important stronghold fell in 396 B.C. It was the threat of further Gaulish invasions from the north that brought the peninsula under Roman rule. From this base Roman power grew until it included most of Europe and parts of the Near East. The approximately 1,000 years of Roman rule made Italy the center of the known world, and long after the Roman Empire fell to the barbarian invaders in A.D. 476, the Roman ideal of a Europe united by one law and one language—Latin —lived on, mainly through the Roman Catholic Church.

The Dark Ages

During the 5th and 6th centuries the Roman Catholic popes tried to provide political and spiritual leadership for the people of the peninsula. It was mainly through their efforts that the Lombards, a Germanic tribe who had taken over most of northern and central Italy, were kept out of Rome. The Lombards' final defeat came with the help of the Franks, led by Pepin and then by his son Charlemagne. As a reward for his services, and to extend the authority of the Church, Pope Leo III crowned Charlemagne as the first emperor of the Romans on Christmas Day, 800.

After Charlemagne's death, the kingdom he had built was divided and subdivided. The only continuous power remained in the hands of the popes. Italy itself was chopped into a thousand fragmented units that were poorly governed, and invaders struck from all sides.

Although the peninsula seemed ungovernable, various nobles took the title of King of Italy. The last to do so for many centuries was Berengar II, the Marquis of Ivrea in the Piedmont. When Berengar failed to unite the people behind him, he ceded "the kingdom" to Otto I of Germany. In 962, Otto, like Charlemagne before him, was crowned emperor. His vast domain, the Holy Roman Empire, was to survive in one form or

Pompeii, buried by a volcano in 79 A.D. but now excavated, provides a portrait of life in Roman times.

another, with one or another German or Habsburg king on the throne, until the early 19th century.

In actuality, the empire was impossible to rule efficiently in those days of poor roads and primitive communications. Few of the emperors had the time to rule their German domains and the land across the Alps as well. The result was that Italy was part of the empire in name only and developed quite independently.

Just how ineffective the empire was in unifying the Italians soon became clear. The fortified northern cities, the popes' domain, and the separate kingdom of the Two Sicilies in the south each represented what amounted to a distinct country. The cities were moving toward independence. The papacy struggled to retain its power. And the south, in the hands of French and Spanish overlords, slowly sank beneath the weight of a strict feudal rule that made the majority into poor peasants and only a few into rich landholders.

The Growth of the City-States

Throughout the 12th and 13th centuries, the north grew increasingly prosperous as a result of the increased trade that had begun with the Crusades. Cities like Venice, Florence, Genoa, Pisa, and Milan grew into powerful independent city-states. Trade with the cities of northern Europe and the Orient in turn stimulated the growth of such industries as textile manufacturing, metal processing, and shipbuilding and eventually the growth of banking. The new rich loaned money at enormous rates of interest and became not only richer, but more powerful, as the Medici banking family of Florence proved by becoming the rulers of the city between the 14th and 18th centuries.

By the 14th century, the wealthy people of the city-states had more money and more leisure. A rebirth of interest in classical Greek and Roman literature, art, and ideas stimulated a period of unparalleled artistic and scientific growth in Italy. This period, which in Italian was called the *rinascimento*—"rebirth" or "renaissance"—made Italy a center of European culture between the 14th and the 16th centuries. In literature the Renaissance began with Dante's *The Divine Comedy* in the early 14th century. The poet Francesco Petrarch, the storyteller Giovanni Boccaccio, and the political commentator Niccolò Machiavelli are probably the best-known of his successors. In art the period opened with the paintings of Giotto and the sculpture of Nicola Pisano and reached its greatest heights in the works of Sandro Botticelli, Paolo Uccello, Fra Angelico, Masaccio, Leonardo da Vinci, and Michelangelo.

Foreign Rulers

The magnificence of the Renaissance cities and the arts they fostered were not matched by political developments. Unity was as remote as ever. The powerful cities engaged in petty wars for supremacy. Within the cities, two political parties vied for power. They were the Guelfs— the supporters of the Pope—and the Ghibellines—the supporters of the emperor's party. This constant fighting finally weakened the cities and made them easy prey for foreign conquest.

Throughout the first half of the 16th century, Italy was a pawn in the political chess game played to determine whether Spain, France, or Austria would rule the peninsula. By the end of the Italian wars in 1559, Spain had won. But when Spanish power declined during the 18th century, Austria took over the rule of most of Italy.

Stone and brick buildings are typical of many Italian hill towns including Assisi, the home of St. Francis.

Italy was in the forefront in the development of operatic music and the ornate baroque architecture of the 16th and 17th centuries. Galileo, the great astronomer and physicist, gained international acclaim in the face of the papal Inquisition, which denounced him for arguing that the sun is the central body around which the earth and other planets revolve.

In the 18th century, intellectuals from several parts of Italy were conspicuous in the Enlightenment, a movement that sought to bring about rational legal and economic reforms by enlightened despots. Cesare Beccaria of Milan, an advocate of more humane punishment for criminals, was perhaps the most influential Italian writer of this period.

The French Revolution of 1789 had a profound effect on the Italians. The establishment of the French republic made them aware of the need for national unity among the Italian people. When Napoleon Bonaparte led his armies into Italy in 1796, he was welcomed as a liberator. Although French rule was often strict and ruthless, reforms were made that had an important effect on Italian history. Republics were founded with constitutions and representative assemblies. For the first time since the fall of Rome, Italians saw that they could live together as one nation.

Napoleon's defeat at Waterloo in 1815 seemed at first to turn back the clock. At the Congress of Vienna in the same year the European powers met to determine the details of the peace settlement. Austria's Prince Metternich scornfully dismissed Italy as "a geographical expression." In the south the Bourbon kings of French origin, who had been settled in Naples since 1735, became the rulers of Naples and Sicily. The Papal States were restored to the popes. Lombardy, Veneto, and some smaller states were returned to Austria. The House of Savoy was given the rule of Piedmont, Sardinia, and Savoy as the kingdom of Sardinia.

But the movement for national unity did not die. The *Risorgimento* ("resurgence"), as the movement for unification was called, was divided into three groups. The radicals, under Giuseppe Mazzini, hoped to establish an Italian republic. Conservative Catholics wanted to unify the country under the popes. The moderates rallied behind the House of Savoy. Although the Austrians tried to suppress these movements, it was too late. Even opera-goers expressed their sentiments by shouting "Viva Verdi," which not only stood for the patriotic composer, but also meant "Long live Vittorio Emanuele, Re d'Italia."

Vittorio Emanuele (Victor Emmanuel) II, King of Sardinia, did become the king of Italy, largely as a result of the efforts of his prime minister Conte Camillo Cavour. Cavour sought to have the constitution made more liberal, raised taxes, and strengthened the army. He won a place for his kingdom as a European power by sending troops to fight on the side of Britain and France in the Crimean War of 1854. In 1858, Cavour made an agreement with Napoleon III of France by which France would supply troops to help the Italians drive the Austrians out of Italy. In return, Sardinia would cede Nice and Savoy to France.

When Austria declared war in 1859, the Italian and French forces won victories at Magenta and Solferino. Austria's power in Italy was broken. By 1860 all of northern Italy, except Veneto, became part of the kingdom of Sardinia. In the same year, Giuseppe Garibaldi landed on Sicily and defeated the army of the kingdom of Naples, crossed to the mainland, and took Naples. With the exception of Rome and Veneto, all of Italy was united. In 1861, Vittorio Emanuele was declared King of Italy.

Bologna combines the typically Roman checkerboard pattern of streets with distinctly medieval architecture.

The Kingdom of Italy: 1861–1922

The last steps of unification were completed when Veneto was annexed in 1866 and the Papal States in 1870. In July, 1871, Rome became the kingdom's official capital. The Pope withdrew to the Vatican, the small part of Rome that includes the St. Peter's Church. It was not until 1929 that the Vatican City was recognized as independent.

The formation of the kingdom did not solve Italy's age-old problems: the lack of basic industrial resources such as iron and coal, a population too large for the country to support, and the sheer weight of years of foreign occupation, leaving little experience of self-government. However, the new government worked quickly to make Italy a 19th-century power. Railroads were built, a merchant fleet was soon sailing, and the economy was sound. Thousands of emigrants left to settle in other lands, thus reducing the problem of overpopulation. But the Italian government wanted more: It wanted the nation to be like the other great powers, which meant having colonies in Africa. Hoping at the same time to solve its remaining overpopulation problems, Italy chose to expand into Eritrea and Somaliland, a move that drained it of money and manpower. The Italian forces suffered a serious defeat at Aduwa in 1896. In Italy itself the closing years of the century were marred by workers' unrest.

The new century began ominously with the assassination of King Umberto (Humbert). He was succeeded by his son Vittorio Emanuele III, and a degree of stability was gained under the political leadership of Giovanni Giolitti, who helped develop democratic parties and processes in Italy. In 1911, however, Italy went to war with Turkey to gain Tripoli in North Africa. This is sometimes considered the first step toward the Balkan Wars that led to the still more terrible World War of 1914–18.

Italy entered World War I on the side of the French and British in 1915, when it was promised certain Austrian territories in the north and northeast. After suffering a heavy setback in 1917, the Italians won a decisive victory at Vittorio Veneto in 1918, which led to the surrender of Austria-Hungary.

The Fascist Regime: 1922 to 1943

The Paris Peace Conference of 1919 granted to Italy the Trentino and the adjacent South Tryol (Alto Adige), Trieste and its province as far as the Julian Alps, Istria, and some of the islands off the Yugoslav coast. But some Italians wanted more. Thus, the poet and war veteran Gabriele D'Annunzio led a group of volunteers in 1919–20 to seize the city of Fiume on the Adriatic. It was not until 1924 that Yugoslavia relinquished it to Italy.

In the parliamentary elections of 1919 the Socialist Party became the largest political force, while the Catholics (newly organized in the Popular Party) emerged as the second largest group. The Liberals, who had dominated politics, were now in sharp decline.

There was also economic turmoil. Militant labor unions called numerous strikes in the industrial cities. In the rural areas of the Po Valley there was also much unrest among the newly-organized farm workers, who had expected land ownership. Both the landlords and factory owners objected to any concessions to the strikers. Thus, revolution seemed almost inevitable.

At this point it was relatively easy to accept the promises of Benito Mussolini, an ex-Socialist who had organized in 1919 a Fascist party of war veterans and had promised to destroy "bolshevism" and restore "law and order." When his black-shirt militias started to march on Rome in October, 1922, the timid king appointed him premier.

Under Mussolini, all other parties and the independent labor unions were dissolved. Many of their leaders were arrested or forced into exile. Parliament was restructured into a Fascist corporate system that regulated both industry and labor. The press was censored, and schools were made instruments of Fascist teaching. In spite of this repression, the theatrical Fascist leader (*Il Duce*) and his dictatorship were supported enthusiastically for many years by most Italians.

Mussolini negotiated agreements with the Pope in 1929 that recognized the independence of Vatican City and made Roman Catholicism the "official" religion of the Italian State. In 1933, during the global economic depression, Mussolini established the Institute for Industrial Reconstruction (IRI), which provided state financial aid for banks and industries in danger of bankruptcy. This led to a system of state capitalism in Italy that embraced about one-sixth of the economy and provided well-paying jobs for members of the ruling party. Mussolini's other accomplishments included the draining of malarial marshes and the construction of highways, port facilities, stadiums, and government buildings.

But Fascism led to war. In international affairs Mussolini conquered Ethiopia (1935–36), withdrew from the League of Nations, allied with

Rome's Vittorio Emanuele II Monument, dedicated in 1911, centers around the Tomb of the Unknown Soldier.

Hitler's Germany, intervened on the side of General Franco in the Spanish Civil War (1936–39), and seized Albania (1939). In June, 1940, Mussolini belatedly joined Hitler's Germany in World War II. In October, 1940, Italy invaded Greece and in 1941 declared war on the Soviet Union and the United States.

By mid-1943, Fascist Italy had lost its African territories, its economy was in a shambles, and its armies were almost destroyed. In July, Allied troops landed in Sicily and soon conquered the island. This led to Mussolini's arrest by King Vittorio Emanuele and Army Marshal Pietro Badoglio on July 25, 1943. The Fascist era was over. In September the new government signed an armistice with the Allies.

For the next 20 months, Italy was split in two and torn by civil war. The Allies liberated southern Italy and persuaded the royal government to declare war on Germany. In the northern half of the peninsula, Hitler seized control, rescuing Mussolini and setting him up as the head of a new Italian Social Republic. This puppet regime was strongly resisted by anti-Fascist "Committees of National Liberation" and by an underground network of Italian partisans who, with arms parachuted in by the Allies, helped to pin down the enemy. In late April, 1945, as Allied forces finally liberated the north, Italian partisans caught and executed Mussolini.

The Postwar Democracy

War-torn Italy made a dramatic economic recovery with help from the United States. By the end of the 1940's the country had straightened out its finances, rebuilt its transportation system and industries, launched land reforms, and was ready to begin the modernizing "economic miracle" of the 1950's.

Although it had helped the Allied cause from 1943 to 1945, Italy was treated as a defeated country when the peace conference met in Paris in 1947. It lost all its overseas colonies, and it had to turn over to Yugoslavia the city of Fiume and some of the Slavic-populated provinces of northeastern Italy. The disputed city of Trieste at the head of the Adriatic Sea finally reverted to Italy after years of difficult negotiations between Italy and Yugoslavia.

The major political question was what to do with the monarchy. The country voted in favor of adopting a republican form of government. The voters also elected a constituent assembly to draft a new constitution, which went into effect on January 1, 1948.

Italy's more than 50 postwar centrist governments have been dominated by the Christian Democrats, who retained a monopoly on the premiership from December, 1945 until 1981. After the war, five men— Christian Democrats Alcide DeGasperi, Amintore Fanfani, Aldo Moro, Mariano Rumor, and Giulio Andreotti—served as prime minister five or more times.

Italy's centrist parties have been deeply committed to the cause of European economic, military, and political integration. Thus, Italy was a charter member of the Organization of European Economic Cooperation that administered Marshall Plan aid (1947–51), an original signatory of the North Atlantic Treaty Organization (1949), of the European Coal and Steel Community (1951), and of the European Economic Community (Common Market) (1958). Italy benefited greatly from these organizations, as its investments, workers, and products could now move freely within this immense trading bloc.

Massive population shifts were among the most important aspects of postwar Italian history. The desire of Southerners to improve their standard of living led in the 1950's to the outmigration of more than 1,000,000 young men and their families. Similar numbers moved out in the 1960's, the 1970's, and the 1980's. Moreover, people in the mountains migrated to the plains, and there was also a movement from east to west in Italy. Most of the migrants settled on the edges of large industrial cities in northern Italy, but others moved on across the Alps to seek jobs in northwestern Europe. Meanwhile, Italy itself became a place of immigration for thousands of Moslems from North Africa and the Middle East.

The Modern Era

The years 1968–69 marked the onset of a chaotic, violent period in Italian history. The postwar "baby-boom" generation was reaching maturity, only to find that the overcrowded universities were unable to accommodate them adequately. The unrest quickly spread into the labor unions, which in 1969 extracted from employers huge wage increases that were to be linked to the rising cost of living. The Italian government sought to reduce some of the unrest by restructuring and expanding the universities, lowering the voting age to 18, introducing tax reforms, and setting up the 20 regional governments provided for in the Constitution.

The worst crisis occurred in 1978 when terrorists kidnapped and murdered Aldo Moro, a Christian Democratic leader who had served

Modern hotels and service areas are found along the *autostrade*, Italy's superb highway system.

several times as prime minister and was slated to be elected president of the republic. The nation was shocked. Parliament quickly elected a respected socialist, Sandro Pertini, to be president (1978–85), and the center-left government redoubled its police measures. The police also launched massive campaigns against the Mafia-controlled drug traffickers in Sicily and against terrorist actions by Middle Eastern immigrants.

Meanwhile, in 1978, the government responded to the growing women's movement and legalized divorce and abortion under certain circumstances. The Vatican agreed in 1984 to revise the Lateran Concordat of 1929 with the Italian state. As a result, Roman Catholicism would no longer be Italy's "official" religion, and the state would no longer enforce ecclesiastical laws on social issues.

The decline of the influence of the Church in Italy was especially visible in the cities. This secularization of life also greatly affected politics. Republican Party leader Giovanni Spadolini was prime minister in 1981–82, while Bettino Craxi, the Socialist Party leader, held the office from August 1983 until July 1987. The Christian Democrats, under Ciriaco De Mita, reclaimed power as head of a five-party coalition in April 1988, remaining until 1989, when veteran politician Giulio Andreotti was brought to power to end political turmoil. In 1990, the Italian Communist Party held a special congress to approve reforms aimed at achieving broader popular support.

Whatever Italy's shortcomings in the political sector have been, there can be no doubt that the nation has achieved wonders in the economic field. From the 1970s, Italy was in the ranks of the Big Seven industrial powers of the free world. By the 1980s, Italy ranked very high in the world of fashion design, cinematography, automobile production, high technology, and international finance.

CHARLES F. DELZELL, Vanderbilt University

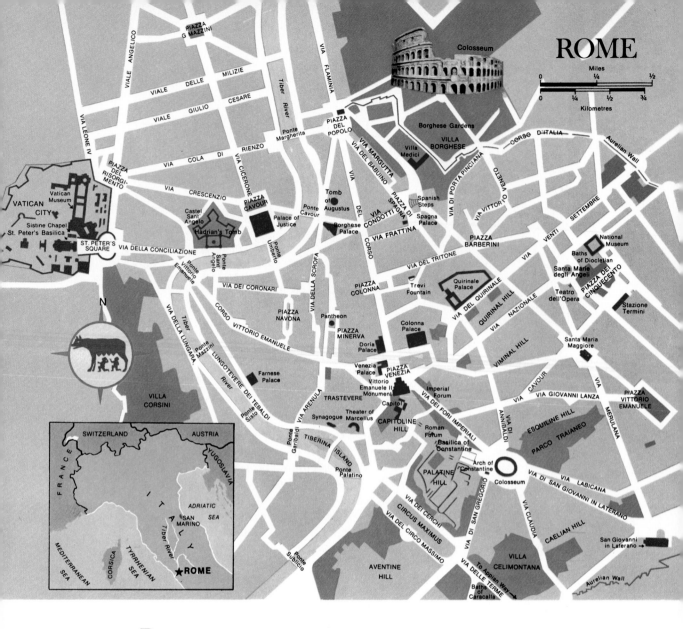

Rome

Rome, Italy's capital and largest city, is a magical mixture of ancient and modern, pagan and Christian, which annually attracts millions of visitors from every country of the world. Inevitably the founding of so great a city has been surrounded by myths and legends. According to the best-known of these, Rome was selected by the gods as the site of a new capital after the fall of Troy. Aeneas, a Trojan prince, was told by the gods to take his followers to the west. After suffering terrible hardships, the Trojans settled near the present city of Rome.

The legend goes on to tell of events in the 8th century B.C. when a priestess, who had been sworn to chastity, gave birth to twin sons whose father was the god of war, Mars. As punishment for her sin, the priestess was ordered to abandon her children on the banks of the Tiber River. A she-wolf found Romulus and Remus, the twins, and nursed them until they were taken in by a shepherd who raised them. The boys vowed that when they grew up they would build a city on the Tiber.

It was Romulus, so the legend goes, who drew the first boundaries of the city with his plow. The twins and their nurse, the she-wolf, have become the symbols of the ancient city's beginnings. A statue of the babies being suckled by the wolf—a copy of the original—stands atop the Capitoline Hill, one of the seven hills on which the city was first built.

From the original seven hills (the Aventine, Quirinal, Capitoline, Palatine, Caelian, Viminal, and Esquiline on the left bank of the Tiber) Rome grew to cover other hills on the right bank. Almost as if it had been inspired by Romulus' words—"My Rome shall be the capital of the world"—the city grew in size and splendor. From a collection of rough shacks at a bend in the river, Rome became the capital first of a republic and then of a great empire. Its motto was *Senatus Populusque Romanus*—"The Senate and People of Rome." The initials SPQR are still used in Rome today and can be seen on everything from taxicabs to manhole covers.

It was during imperial times—the early centuries of the Christian Era—that Rome reached its greatest importance and magnificence. The Romans proudly called their city Urbs—The City—implying that it was the ideal city. When the empire embraced nearly all the known world at the peak of its power, Rome was known simply as *caput mundi*—"the head of the world."

The Emperor Augustus, who ruled from 27 B.C. to A.D. 14, boasted that he had found a city of bricks and left a city of marble. The imperial city was, in fact, a mixture of handsome public buildings, elegant private homes, and slums. As the center of the vast empire the city was the home not only of the ruling classes but of merchants prospering from building and trade, emissaries from all over the empire, nobles, soldiers, slaves, and country people who hoped to find wealth in the capital. The tourist of ancient times would have been shown many of the landmarks the modern visitor seeks.

Atop the Palatine Hill were the palaces of the emperors Augustus and Tiberius. (It is from "Palatine" that the word "palace" comes.) At the base of the hill was the Forum Romanum, the first of the city's public squares. Built on the site where Romulus was said to be buried, the Forum became a city within a city, with public buildings, temples, and shops. In the Forum is the Golden Milestone from which the remarkable network of Roman roads fanned out. And it was in the Forum that the Senate met and that Julius Caesar was assassinated on the Ides of March, 44 B.C.

Later, emperors extended the Forum Romanum into the larger and more stately Imperial Forums. This was the center of the city that ruled the world. Nearby was the enormous Colosseum and across the river the tomb of the 2nd-century A.D. emperor Hadrian, which is now called Castel Sant' Angelo. Marvels of the city were the aqueducts that brought the Romans water and the great sewer called the Cloaca Maxima, part of which is still in use. The approximately 1,000,000 people who lived in the imperial capital were protected by police and fire fighters. The homes of the wealthy were heated and had a system of running water. Truly, for the wealthy, as the Roman writer Cicero observed, "There [was] no place more delightful than home."

St. Peter's Basilica, the largest church in the world, stands near the Tiber River. Although Rome enjoys a generally mild Mediterranean climate, the city is nonetheless subject to an occasional snowfall.

By day a popular diversion was going to the public baths. The largest, the Baths of Caracalla, named for the 3rd-century emperor, is now being used as an open-air opera house. Besides offering Romans cold, warm, and steam baths in the *frigidarium, tepidarium,* and *caldarium,* the building contained stores, libraries, gymnasiums, and offices —everything a Roman gentleman might need.

The wealth that poured into Rome from all over the empire was far from universally distributed. By the 2nd century A.D. one half to one third of the population was on the equivalent of what is now often called welfare. They were given bread to eat and circuses to attend to distract them from thoughts of revolution. As many as 385,000 Romans of all classes would pack into the Circus Maximus to watch chariot races, acrobats, clowns, and bands of musicians. An even more popular spectacle was the combat between gladiators and such wild animals as lions, tigers, and panthers at the vast Colosseum.

THE CENTER OF CHRISTENDOM

The wealth and power that had made Rome the capital of an empire and a rich and cosmopolitan city disappeared under the repeated attacks of barbarian invaders from the north. The imperial court was moved to Constantinople in the 4th century A.D. Christianity, which became the official religion of the empire in A.D. 380, provided the city with its new leaders. From the 6th until the late 19th century, Rome was ruled first by the bishops of Rome and then by the popes. Rome became the focus of the Christian world—a mecca for devout pilgrims who risked every kind of danger to reach the city that was for them a holy goal. No longer citadels of imperial power, the ancient monuments decayed. The great buildings of the emperors were stripped of their marble facings to make lime. Water was taken from the Tiber while the aqueducts fell into ruins. The Forum Romanum became a haven for squatters and pastureland for cattle.

The rebirth of interest in ancient times during the Renaissance in the 15th and 16th centuries led Italians to turn to their ancient capital for inspiration. Under the leadership of enlightened popes, the treasures of the ancient city were systematically uncovered, classified, and restored. The study of the arts and archeology was encouraged. Artists were employed by the popes to design and decorate churches.

The historic and strategic importance of Rome, rather than artistic considerations, made the city and the Papal States, of which it was a part, an early target for Napoleon Bonaparte's troops. The city was involved in a seesaw battle between the Pope and Napoleon for supremacy between 1798 and 1814. In the years between 1815 and 1861, during the political maneuvering and wars that led to the unification of Italy, Rome remained under papal rule except for a brief period in 1848–9. Nearly a decade passed after the Italian kingdom had been formed before the King's troops took possession of the city. Finally, in 1871, Rome was declared the capital of Italy. The Pope considered himself a prisoner of the Italian King in the city that used to be his own. This was the beginning of the so-called Roman Question that was not resolved until the Lateran Treaty was signed in 1929. The treaty created the independent state of Vatican City under the sovereignty of the pope. (See the article in this volume on VATICAN CITY.)

The Pincian Hill affords a dramatic view of the Piazza del Popolo (foreground) and the Roman skyline.

ROME AT WORK

Rome, unlike such other capitals as Paris or London, is neither an industrial nor a commercial center. It is, in fact, the heart of the vast and complicated bureaucratic activities of the Italian Government. Rome was chosen as the capital of the newly united nation a century ago because it was the city that best symbolized Italian unity, not because of its industrial leadership. Even so, many Italians, especially in the highly industrialized north, continue to criticize Rome for being essentially a nonproductive city. "Milan produces and Rome eats," they say, but they overlook the historical and political reasons for the city's condition. As a matter of fact, after Rome was annexed to the kingdom of Italy, the first governments made and maintained a policy of keeping industry out of the city because they thought it was unbecoming to the capital.

Many Romans work for the national government or are involved in the large tourist industry. A substantial number of residents of Rome are members of the Roman Catholic religious orders that have their headquarters in the city. Other important activities are printing and publishing, banking and insurance, clothing and fashion, and moviemaking.

Throughout its history Rome has been the chief tourist goal in Europe. From ancient times to the present the city has been a magnet for artists, writers, pilgrims, and people who wanted simply to see what could provoke even such a restrained and dignified man as Henry James to say on his arrival in Rome: "At last—for the first time—I live!" Satisfied by the city's abundant beauty and vitality, or exasperated by its noise and traffic, visitors continue to swarm over the city, providing employment for thousands of Romans, from hotel-keepers to guides.

The Italian movie industry centers around Cinecittá, southeast of Rome. Moviemaking was begun in 1937, but the coming of World War II and then bomb damage delayed the center's development. It was not until the 1950's that the movie industry began to grow, making the names of such directors as Federico Fellini, Michelangelo Antonioni, and Vittorio De Sica synonyms for fine movies. The addition of a special Italian product, the so-called "spaghetti Westerns"—accurate replicas of the American Westerns down to the last branding iron—helped expand and enrich the Italian movie industry to the point where it is a very important industry in Rome.

The growth of Rome, as well as internal Italian migration, stimulated the building industry, which now employs the largest number of workers. Vast new apartment complexes, office buildings, and shopping centers have been built since the end of World War II. Even so, building has not kept pace with the city's growth. A city of a little more than 690,000 inhabitants in 1921, Rome is now home to more than four times that many Italians and is continuing to grow at a rapid rate each year. Many of the newcomers are from impoverished regions in the south of Italy and are unable to find employment. As a consequence, several thousand people still live in *baracche*—shabby shacks—on the outskirts of the city. Some of the migrants find work in the city's smaller industries—food processing, glass manufacturing, pharmaceutical production, and similar activities—but many remain unemployed or find only part-time work with which to support their families.

As the nation's capital, Rome is naturally the center of the Italian communications industry. Another of Rome's well-known industries, high-fashion clothing, is also one of its youngest, since it only developed in the years after World War II. Rome now vies with Paris and New York as a producer of pace-setting styles. Related industries such as the design and manufacture of accessories and cosmetics have also developed.

Luxury apartment buildings line the streets of Parioli, a fashionable suburb of Rome.

THE ROMAN'S ROME

Administratively, Rome is divided into districts called *rioni* in the city and boroughs, *borgate,* in the suburban areas. The inhabitants of the picturesque Trastevere district, on the right bank of the Tiber, claim to be the *romani di Roma,* the only "true Romans" in the city. As a matter of fact, today the population of Rome is made up predominantly of *burzzurri* (as government officials and other newcomers are called). The "true Romans" have found some consolation in forming a club, the Association of the Romans. Yet Rome has been an effective melting pot where newcomers are able to blend into a Roman way of life.

The Romans are essentially optimistic, gay, and easygoing. They are among the least nosy and most tolerant people in the world. A major contradiction in their easygoing nature becomes apparent when they drive cars. A Roman behind the wheel or riding a motorscooter seems to have no concern whatsoever with traffic rules or the right-of-way of other drivers. The Roman seems to base his driving exclusively on speed and noise, aiming at bypassing whatever vehicle precedes him and counting essentially on his "good eye" and reflexes, which in most cases, luckily, are excellent. For the visitor, driving in Rome is usually a nightmare, unless he decides to put into practice the old saying, 'When in Rome do as the Romans do.''

The Romans speak *romanesco,* a dialect very close to the Italian language, although rich in words of its own and marked by its own peculiar accent. Even well-educated Romans tend to drawl and to speak with a basso voice that seems to come from somewhere in the belly.

Good company, conversation, open air, food, and wine are the basic ingredients of the joy of life to the Romans. Roman cuisine is delicious, but not particularly refined or elaborate. In fact, it comprises a variety of savory dishes that originated in the countryside around Rome. One eats well everywhere in Rome, in the deluxe restaurants as well as in the most humble trattorias. There seems to be a sudden mushrooming of restaurants in summer, when their tables invade the sidewalks. Musicians walk from restaurant to restaurant, playing and singing popular Roman songs. At night it is not uncommon to see entire families sitting outside an inexpensive trattoria to which they bring their food in paper bags, limiting their orders to wine and occasionally a huge portion of pasta to be shared by everyone.

The Romans like outings very much. In the city one of their favorite goals is the Borghese Gardens with its well-known museum and world-famous zoo. Among their favorite places are the beaches or the pine forests near the sea outside the city limits. Other attractive places near Rome are the towns of the Castelli Romani (Roman castles) on the Alban Hills, which contain the Pope's summer residence at Castel Gandolfo, an astronomical observatory, and a nuclear research center. The hills also are known for the delightful local wine produced there.

The entire city is served by buses and streetcars. There is also the Metropolitana, the subway system that runs from Termini railroad station in the center of Rome through E.U.R. (Esposizione Universale di Roma), a suburb to the south of the city, to the port of Ostia. The subway's growth has been delayed because subway excavations reveal ancient treasures that must be saved or because vibrations from drilling threaten the existence of monuments above ground.

Since the time of the Roman republic, roads have radiated from Rome, each named after the consul that built it. Connecting Rome with many other commercially and militarily important cities of the peninsula, most of them ended on the west or east coast. The consular roads, which were masterpieces of engineering, are still used today. For centuries they formed the major national road network. It is only in recent years that they have been surpassed by modern highways. Rome is linked to all the major roads converging on it from all parts of the country by a loop encircling the city. Rome is also the heart of the national railroad network and is thus connected with the major Italian and European cities. Leonardo da Vinci International Airport at Fiumicino, near the sea, links Rome to all the countries in the world.

THE VISITOR'S ROME

Rome is an enormously colorful and alluring mixture of the old—the Rome of ancient times, the Middle Ages, the Renaissance—and the new.

For example, arriving in Rome by train, one enters the city through the modern Stazione Termini. A few yards from the entrance are the remains of the Servian Walls, named for the legendary 6th-century B.C. king, Servius Tullius. Across the large Piazza dei Cinquecento facing the station are the Baths of Diocletian, part of which is now an archeological museum, and part the 16th-century church of Santa Maria degli Angeli.

Indeed, almost everywhere in Rome there is this rich mixture. In addition, cultural life is intense. Rome is the site of the largest university in Italy, a Catholic university, and some other religious universities, as well as many Italian and foreign cultural and scientific institutions, among which is the American Academy. There are several very important museums, art galleries, and libraries. The old artists' district near Piazza di Spagna, where many famous Italian and European writers,

Many famous artists and writers have lived in the buildings alongside the magnificent Spanish Steps.

The ancient Colosseum was the scene of the famous gladiator fights in the early days of the Roman Empire.

such as the 19th-century English poet John Keats, lived, still houses many studios where painters and sculptors are working.

Theatrical and musical activities are also popular, with a concert season at the Teatro Argentina (Argentina Theater) and an opera season at the Teatro dell'Opera. In summer open-air concerts are held at the imposing 4th-century Basilica of Maxentius and Constantine and operas at the spectacular remains of the 3rd-century Baths of Caracalla, which has one of the world's largest open-air opera stages.

Although Rome today is a vast city, its traditional center is an area of about 1 square mile that extends from Piazza Venezia and touches the Tiber, Piazza del Popolo, and Piazza Barberini. Here are the fashionable boutiques and jewelry and shoe shops of Via Condotti and Via Frattina; the antique dealers of Via dei Coronari; the art galleries and studios of Via del Babuino and Via Margutta. One can find respite a few hundred yards away from the main avenues and streets in some quiet, almost deserted street or a small square where the silence of centuries seems to hover. This can happen in the very heart of the city, or in more remote spots such as the old Appian Way, which is studded with ancient Roman relics.

Even the busiest streets seem to take a rest in the early part of the afternoon. Offices and shops close between 1 and 4 P.M., while the Romans enjoy a meal and perhaps take a little siesta at home unless they join the crowds in the busy restaurants and outdoor cafés. In summer, these are the hottest hours of the day. Rome appears almost

Legend holds that tourists who cast coins into the Trevi Fountain will return to Rome one day.

deserted, except for a few isolated people roaming the streets or the flock of tourists that bravely carry on with their guided or self-guided tours. Most visitors quickly learn the secret of mastering these hot hours. They walk on the shady side of the street, watching out for the first quiver of the tree leaves, a sure indication that the *ponentino,* a cool breeze, is blowing from the sea.

Rome at night is fascinating. Most of the city is silent, although the silence may be broken suddenly by a car horn, the buzzing of motor-scooters, or the howling of members of Rome's enormous colony of cats.

At night such familiar places as the Trevi Fountain and the Piazza Navona, the long oval baroque square with its three central fountains, seem to grow larger and more beautiful. The Via dei Fori Imperiali, flanked by the Forums and facing straight towards the massive Colosseum, seems to regain its stately grandeur under the floodlights. There are, of course, places like the Via Veneto with its outdoor cafés, where life still goes on as if it were daytime, and there is an endless procession of sports cars and people walking to and fro who want to see and to be seen.

Day and night, visitors are drawn to the Trevi Fountain, where according to tradition, they must throw a small coin to insure that they will return to Rome. The basin of the beautiful, baroque fountain is always full of the coins of travelers who are sad to leave and hopeful that they will be able to return soon to the bewitching city on the Tiber.

NELLO SPADA, Author, *Garibaldi and the Red Shirts*

SAN MARINO

The Most Serene Republic of San Marino is the oldest republic in the world. This tiny country is set on the peak and slopes of craggy Mount Titano in north central Italy. A story is told about one occasion in the republic's history when it was saved because the mountain was wrapped in such heavy fog that an invading army could not find it. When the sun burned the fog off, the invading army was so weary from hunting for its goal that it went to sleep instead of to battle.

San Marino's history has been a mixture of good luck with the important additions of hard work and modest ambitions. The nation traces its beginning to the year A.D. 301, when a Christian stonecutter named Marinus settled on the mountain with his followers to escape religious persecution. The San Marinese regard Marinus as their patron saint, and each year on September 3 they celebrate his memory with a pageant. According to legend, his bones are buried in the Basilica of San Marino.

The republic grew slowly from its mountaintop perch down the slopes to include part of the valley floor. But the people wanted no more land for themselves. When Napoleon I offered the San Marinese additional territory in 1797, they refused, because, as they explained, San Marino's small size and poverty protected it from its larger and greedier neighbors.

Just as Mount Titano provided an island of safety for Marinus and

The tiny nation of San Marino is atop Mount Titano in Italy.

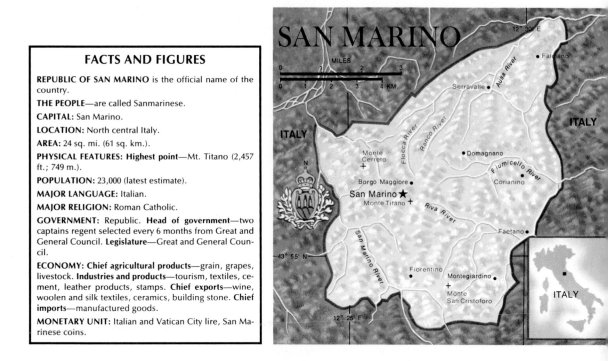

FACTS AND FIGURES

REPUBLIC OF SAN MARINO is the official name of the country.

THE PEOPLE—are called Sanmarinese.

CAPITAL: San Marino.

LOCATION: North central Italy.

AREA: 24 sq. mi. (61 sq. km.).

PHYSICAL FEATURES: Highest point—Mt. Titano (2,457 ft.; 749 m.).

POPULATION: 23,000 (latest estimate).

MAJOR LANGUAGE: Italian.

MAJOR RELIGION: Roman Catholic.

GOVERNMENT: Republic. **Head of government**—two captains regent selected every 6 months from Great and General Council. **Legislature**—Great and General Council.

ECONOMY: Chief agricultural products—grain, grapes, livestock. **Industries and products**—tourism, textiles, cement, leather products, stamps. **Chief exports**—wine, woolen and silk textiles, ceramics, building stone. **Chief imports**—manufactured goods.

MONETARY UNIT: Italian and Vatican City lire, San Marinese coins.

his followers, the citizens of the republic have repeatedly given sanctuary to exiles and refugees. During the battles leading up to the unification of Italy in 1861, Giuseppe Garibaldi and some of his followers hid briefly in San Marino. During World War II San Marino remained neutral but provided a temporary home for hundreds of thousands of refugees from all over Europe. Neutrality did not save San Marino from bombings, but the people went right on sharing their homes, their food, and their wine with the homeless.

GOVERNMENT

In 1862 San Marino and Italy signed a treaty of friendship. The two nations have a customs union. San Marino uses the Italian language and currency. However, San Marino has an entirely independent government. The heads of the government are two captains regent who preside over the 60-member Great and General Council for a term of 6 months. The same men may not be re-elected to the office until a period of 3 years has passed. The captains must accept the office to which they are elected or their citizenship and possessions will be taken away from them.

The tiny republic with its love of medieval laws and ceremonies surprised the world in 1945 when it voted in a Communist government. The only Communist government in Western Europe stayed in power for 12 years, but there were no collective farms or state controls. Since 1957 San Marino's government has moved along more familiar democratic paths.

ECONOMY

Today, as for many years past, San Marino's economy is based on its income from tourists, agriculture, and a variety of products. Tourists pour into San Marino from nearby parts of Italy by auto, bus, and heli-

The Government Palace, one of many attractive buildings in San Marino.

copter to spend a day or more looking at the mountaintop capital city, with its narrow old streets, turreted medieval buildings, the 14th-century Church of St. Francis, the Government Palace, and the museum in the Valloni Palace. Another attraction for visitors is the opportunity to write and mail postcards bearing the beautiful and highly prized stamps that annually add a considerable amount of money to the republic's income.

Agriculture and cattle raising are the main sources of income. The slopes of San Marino are covered with vineyards and meadows where cattle graze. The factories of San Marino produce a variety of products for export, such as woolen and silk textiles, tiles, varnishes, ceramics, and building stone. Only a handful of San Marinese still practice Saint Marinus' craft of stonecutting, but all of them honor his dream of freedom and independence.

Reviewed by CHARLES RÉ, Consul of San Marino (New York)

VATICAN CITY

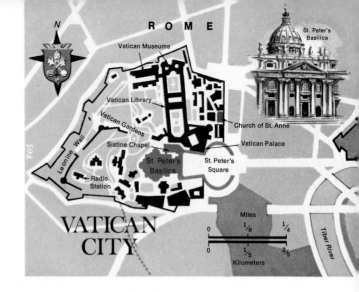

Vatican City is not a city at all, but a sovereign state. The smallest independent nation in the world, Vatican City covers only 108.7 acres (44 hectares) and is entirely surrounded by Rome, the capital of Italy. Vatican City is ruled absolutely by the Pope, who is also the Bishop of Rome and the spiritual head of the world's more than 500,000,000 Roman Catholics. The present Pope is John Paul II (Karol Wojtyla), of Poland, who was elected in 1978.

The tiny nation and its estimated 1,000 inhabitants are all that is left of the centuries-old Papal States. The Papal States once had a population of over 3,000,000 and covered some 17,000 square miles (44,000 square kilometers) that stretched across the center of Italy from the Adriatic to the Tyrrhenian Sea. In 1870 the armies of the kingdom of Italy entered Rome. The Pope, Pius IX, felt that the new Italian Government held his territory illegally. As a public protest he became a voluntary prisoner in the Vatican. His four successors continued this act of protest until 1929. In that year the Lateran Treaty was negotiated by representatives of the Vatican and the Italian Government. The treaty recognized Vatican City as a sovereign and independent state. The Pope was given a payment of money for his abandonment of all claims to the former Papal States. After the treaty was signed the Italian Government rebuilt the main road from St. Peter's Basilica to Rome. The road was given an appropriate name: La Via della Conciliazione—"the avenue of reconciliation."

A STATE WITHIN A CITY

Since 1929 Vatican City, like other nations, has had a diplomatic corps. Its envoys, appointed by the Pope, are known as nuncios or inter-nuncios. The Vatican maintains diplomatic relations with over 50 nations. In 1984, after a 116-year interruption, the United States restored full diplomatic relations with the Vatican.

The Vatican even has "colonies." They are several basilicas or churches, residences, administration buildings, seminaries, and universities in Rome and the Pope's summer villa at Castel Gandolfo in the Alban Hills outside Rome. Many of the Vatican's colonies can be recognized by plaques displaying the tiara (crown) and crossed keys that symbolize the Pope's office. These colonies enjoy extraterritoriality; that is, independence of the governments of Rome and Italy.

Pope John Paul II, protected by brightly costumed Swiss Guards, addresses a group in St. Peter's Square.

Most of the people who live in Vatican City itself are priests and members of religious orders. Several hundred lay persons—Church and civic officials, secretaries and clerks, tradesmen, domestics, and their families—also make their home in Vatican City.

The governor of Vatican City, who is appointed by the Pope, is at the head of the executive and legal offices as well as the postal, telegraph, telephone, technical, and economic services. He is assisted by the counselor general to the state, judicial tribunals (the legal system is based on canon, or Church, law and the laws of the City of Rome), and the Victualing Board. This board, as its name suggests, buys all the food necessary to feed the inhabitants (Vatican City is too small to produce foodstuffs) and provides the state's hygiene services.

Vatican City has its own guards. They are the Swiss Guards, which were organized in the 16th century as the personal guard of the Pope. Then as now the guards were Swiss Catholics. Their colorful Renaissance uniforms of blue, gold, and red are said to have been designed by the great Italian Renaissance artist, Michelangelo.

Like other, much larger states, the Vatican coins its own money and issues its own stamps (with the same values as Italian currency and postage). The Vatican also has its own car registration plates, as well as a bank, post office, electric power station, and a railway station served by the Italian railroad. In addition the small state includes large gardens, a variety of civic buildings, the offices of the Roman Catholic Church, and homes and apartments.

The Vatican's radio station, which has the call letters HVJ, is one of the most powerful in Europe. It was designed by the inventor of the radio, Guglielmo Marconi, and was supervised by him until his death in 1937. Today the station, with its staff of about 200, broadcasts to nearly every country in the world in over 30 languages. The Vatican daily newspaper, *L'Osservatore Romano,* deals with religious and political news and is widely read because it is considered to reflect the official views of the Pope on world affairs.

PLACES OF INTEREST

Vatican City takes its name from its location on Vatican Hill. The state is bounded on the southeast by St. Peter's Basilica and the great square of St. Peter's. The rest of its borders are formed by walls that were built between the 9th and the 17th centuries. Within these walls lies not only the spiritual and administrative center of the Roman Catholic Church, but also a library and museums containing extraordinary treasures.

St. Peter's Basilica, the world's largest church, is built over the tomb of Saint Peter, chief of the 12 Apostles, who were the first followers of Jesus Christ. Tradition has always held that Saint Peter, whom Roman Catholics consider the first Pope, was martyred on Vatican Hill and buried there in A.D. 67. This tradition was given substance in recent years by the discovery of what some experts believe to be the Apostle's tomb and bones. In the 4th century A.D. Constantine, the first Christian emperor of Rome, built a basilica on the spot where the Apostle's tomb was believed to be. The present basilica was begun in 1506 and was completed in the early 17th century, according to the designs of master architects, including Michelangelo, who is responsible for the magnificent dome, and Giovanni Lorenzo Bernini. The magnificent church is the burial place of numerous saints, popes, kings, queens, and princes. St.

St. Peter's Square is formed by a stately oval colonnade designed by Italian artist Giovanni Bernini.

The Vatican Library contains priceless artistic and literary treasures.

Peter's also contains priceless works of art, of which the most famous is Michelangelo's *Pietà*. Strangely enough, the parish church of Vatican City is not St. Peter's, but a much smaller church dedicated to Saint Anne.

The huge square in front of the basilica is really an ellipse formed by two great colonnades designed by Bernini. The square, which can accommodate 200,000 people, is always crowded to capacity on the Christian holy days, as it also has been on many historic occasions.

Alongside St. Peter's are the Papal Palace, where the Pope lives and receives distinguished visitors from all over the world, the Sistine Chapel, the Vatican Museums, and the Vatican Library. The chapel, which takes its name from Pope Sixtus IV (1414–84), for whom it was built, is one of the outstanding artistic attractions in Vatican City. In addition to frescoes by some of the greatest artists of the 15th century, the Sistine Chapel is the setting of Michelangelo's superb ceiling and wall paintings. The ceiling portrays Michelangelo's vision of the Creation, the story of Adam

The interior of St. Peter's Basilica is magnificently decorated.

and Eve, and the Flood. Twenty-two years after he completed these paintings, Michelangelo returned to depict the *Last Judgment* on the wall behind the altar. It is considered one of his most powerful and awe-inspiring works. The museums contain one of the world's greatest collections of ancient sculpture and vast collections of paintings by the Old Masters. The Vatican Library, which was founded in the 15th century, is the oldest public library in Europe and one of the outstanding libraries of the world. It contains an estimated 1,000,000 printed books, 7,000 incunabula (the earliest printed books), and 90,000 manuscripts.

As the heart of the Roman Catholic Church and as one of the great cultural treasure houses of the West, Vatican City is nearly always filled with lay and religious visitors from every corner of the globe. It is not only the center of one of the world's great religions, but an inexhaustible source of beauty and inspiration.

FATHER JOSEPH I. DIRVIN, C.M., Assistant to the President, St. John's University

Valletta, Malta's capital, has two natural harbors. Its fortifications were built by the Knights of St. John.

MALTA

About 60 miles (96 kilometers) south of Sicily in the Mediterranean Sea is the island of Malta, a rocky oval 17 miles (27 km.) long and 9 miles (14 km.) wide. There, at one of the narrowest points in the Mediterranean, halfway between Gibraltar and the Suez Canal, is one of the finest natural harbors in the world. Malta, this strategic dot of land, together with the nearby islands of Gozo, Comino, and the rocky, uninhabited islets of Cominotto and Filfola, became the independent nation of Malta on September 21, 1964. For 30 centuries Malta had been under foreign rule. For the last 160 years of that time it had been ruled by the United Kingdom, and Malta today remains allied to Britain as a member of the Commonwealth of Nations.

THE PEOPLE AND THEIR HISTORY

Malta may have been part of the land bridge that once linked North Africa to Italy. It is filled with the archeological, architectural, and artistic treasures of the people who once lived there. Stone Age temples have been unearthed, and remains of Neolithic and Bronze Age men

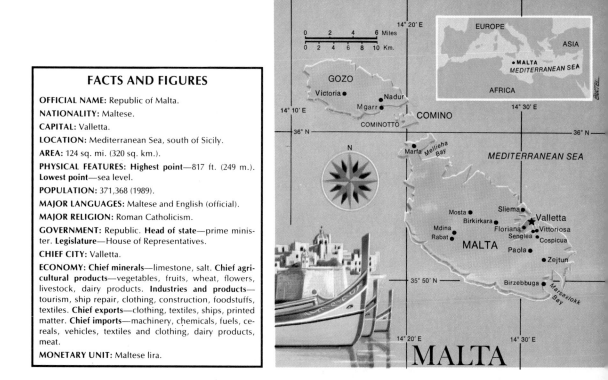

FACTS AND FIGURES

OFFICIAL NAME: Republic of Malta.

NATIONALITY: Maltese.

CAPITAL: Valletta.

LOCATION: Mediterranean Sea, south of Sicily.

AREA: 124 sq. mi. (320 sq. km.).

PHYSICAL FEATURES: Highest point—817 ft. (249 m.). **Lowest point**—sea level.

POPULATION: 371,368 (1989).

MAJOR LANGUAGES: Maltese and English (official).

MAJOR RELIGION: Roman Catholicism.

GOVERNMENT: Republic. **Head of state**—prime minister. **Legislature**—House of Representatives.

CHIEF CITY: Valletta.

ECONOMY: Chief minerals—limestone, salt. **Chief agricultural products**—vegetables, fruits, wheat, flowers, livestock, dairy products. **Industries and products**—tourism, ship repair, clothing, construction, foodstuffs, textiles. **Chief exports**—clothing, textiles, ships, printed matter. **Chief imports**—machinery, chemicals, fuels, cereals, vehicles, textiles and clothing, dairy products, meat.

MONETARY UNIT: Maltese lira.

MALTA

have also been found. The island was held in succession by Phoenicians, Carthaginians, and Romans. The Maltese still take pride in an event that occurred during Roman domination of the island. In A.D. 60 Saint Paul, on his way to Rome, was shipwrecked on Malta, at a bay that now bears his name. This is the traditional date of the conversion of the island to Christianity. Today most Maltese are members of the Roman Catholic Church.

In the 9th century the Arabs began their 220-year domination of Malta. Maltese, the language of Malta, is akin to Arabic, with traces of Italian and other languages. In 1090 a Norman count subdued the Arabs in Sicily and took the island of Malta. For 440 years Malta was an appendage of Sicily. Eventually it came under the control of the Holy Roman Emperor Charles V.

In 1530 Charles V gave Malta to the religious and military order of the Knights of St. John of Jerusalem (known also as the Knights of Malta). The Knights, originally a hospital order established to defend and care for wounded Crusaders, came to Malta after they had lost their bases in Jerusalem and Rhodes. For 268 years they policed the Mediterranean, making Malta a military base in their fight to halt the expansion of the Ottoman (Turkish) Empire. In the year 1565 the Turks laid siege to Malta with an army of about 30,000 men in nearly 200 ships. The islanders were outnumbered five to one, but they managed gallantly to hold the island as an outpost of Christian Europe. Shortly thereafter, Jean Parisot de La Valette, Grand Master of the Knights and the leader of the defense, built a great harbor-fortress on the rocky promontory and named it Valette, or, as it is now known, Valletta. It is the capital of Malta and a living memorial to the great wealth and artistic taste of the Knights.

Napoleon I seized Malta in 1798, and in 1800 the British came into control. Until 1959 Malta was a key link in the defense of the British Empire. The island prospered, with most of its inhabitants directly or indirectly involved in the life and work of the British Royal Navy. During World War II, Malta was attacked in over 2,000 bombing raids by Italian and German planes. In memory of the terrible suffering and heroic action of the people, the entire population of Malta was awarded the George Cross in 1942 by King George VI of Great Britain.

Independent Malta is unlikely to play such a role. British forces withdrew in 1979. A 1987 constitutional amendment forbade foreign military bases and declared Malta a nonaligned and neutral state. Italy and the Soviet Union have guaranteed Malta's neutrality. In 1989, Malta ended military ties with Libya after more than 20 years.

Politics have been bitter and sometimes violent. Under Dom Mintoff, prime minister between 1971 and 1984, the Labor Party moved the country to the left and curtailed the influence of the Roman Catholic Church. The opposition Nationalist Party boycotted the parliament for 15 months because in 1981 elections it outpolled Labor by 51–49 percent but won only 31 of the 65 seats. The results were exactly the same in 1987, but because of a constitutional amendment the Nationalists were awarded four extra seats and came to power.

GOVERNMENT

Malta won internal self-government in 1947 and complete independence in 1964. It became a republic in 1974. The legislature is the House of Representatives. The House elects the president, who is head of state, for 5 years. The president appoints as prime minister, or head of the government, the leader of the majority party in the House.

ECONOMY

Malta is without rivers, lakes, minerals, or raw materials, except for the yellowish limestone that is used for building. There are few trees. Winters are occasionally cold; summers are hot, dry, and cloudless. The rainfall, which varies from year to year, comes mostly in the fall and early winter. The number of sunny hours the islands enjoy is a major asset. The islands' rocky surfaces are thinly covered with 3 or 4 ft. (about 1 m.) of earth. Maltese farmers have to struggle to grow anything, but they do manage to raise potatoes, tomatoes, onions, melons, cereals, grapes, citrus fruits, and other vegetables, as well as clover and hay to feed their cattle, sheep, and goats. They also raise and export flowers, and there is a small fishing industry. In 1989, Malta was the center of international attention when it hosted an offshore summit meeting between the United States and the Soviet Union.

The Maltese have found a good natural resource in the happy combination of a reliably good climate and great historical richness. Tourists are coming in ever-increasing numbers to visit the great relics of the past —the storehouse cave of fossil remains of prehistoric animals and aquatic birds, the temples of the Stone Age peoples, the medieval palaces and cathedrals of the Knights, and the tombs of the Crusaders. And the calendar is always crowded with colorful *festas* featuring fireworks, regattas, races, music, and an abundance of delicious foods.

Reviewed by HUGH H. SMYTHE, Former United States Ambassador to Malta

The Parthenon, one of the greatest achievements of classical Greece, overlooks Athens from the Acropolis.

GREECE

Greece occupies a unique place in the minds of modern people. The ancient Greeks played a dominant role in the development of classical civilization and helped lay the basis for all European and European-inspired civilizations throughout the world. Thus modern Greece is regarded as the fountainhead of Western civilization. The Greek city-states of the classical era are remembered for their contributions to art, architecture, literature, religion, philosophy, and education. And above all, ancient Greece is looked upon as the inspiration for our modern theories of democracy.

It is not just classical Greece, however, that has influenced the modern world. Toward the end of the classical era the Greek city-states fell under the domination of Rome; but in conquering the Greek world the Roman Empire absorbed and adapted much of the Greek culture, thereby expanding and making permanent Greek ideals. Furthermore, out of the Roman Empire of the East there eventually developed a Greek medieval empire that we today call the Byzantine Empire. This empire, one of the most durable political entities ever to exist, lasted from A.D.

A canal now cuts through the Isthmus of Corinth. In ancient times, ships were dragged across the isthmus.

330 to 1453. Initially the empire's rulers used Latin in administration, but by the 7th century the empire had been reduced to essentially Greek-speaking areas of Europe, Asia, and southern Italy. The Byzantine Empire left its imprint not only on modern Greece but also on all European civilization. Its capital at Constantinople (modern Istanbul) was for many centuries the greatest city in Europe and surpassed Rome as the center of Western culture and learning.

During the 11th century the Byzantine Empire started to weaken militarily and economically. It lost many of its major core territories to outsiders (especially the Muslims) who sometimes themselves left their impact on Greek culture. As the years went by, the disintegration of the empire continued. From the late 13th century the Ottoman Turks, a people who had come out of Asia, began encroachments that became ever more successful. By 1453 the Turks had taken Constantinople, and the Byzantine Empire collapsed. Thereafter until the 19th century, Greece was under Turkish domination, but as the years went by opposition to Ottoman rule grew. Finally, independence triumphed; in 1821 the Greeks revolted, and in 1832 a tiny independent Greek kingdom was founded. From this kingdom the modern Greek state developed and expanded.

THE LAND

Geographically, Greece is located in southeastern Europe at the southernmost tip of the Balkan Peninsula and encompasses hundreds of islands scattered through the eastern end of the Mediterranean Sea. To the north, mainland Greece borders Albania, Yugoslavia, Bulgaria, and Turkey. In other directions, it is surrounded by the Mediterranean and its various subdivisions: the Ionian Sea, the Aegean Sea, and the Sea of Crete.

It took more than 100 years to bring together the lands—both continental and island—that constitute the modern Greek state. When Greece first became an independent kingdom in 1832, the state consisted of the Peloponnesus, the Cyclades, and a little territory to its north, including Euboea. The Ionian Islands were ceded by Great Britain in 1864; Thessaly and a tiny part of Epirus were handed over by the Ottoman Empire in 1881; Crete, Epirus, Macedonia, and many of the Aegean islands came from the Turks with the settlements of the Balkan Wars of 1912 and 1913; Western Thrace came from Bulgaria after World War I; and finally (1947) the Dodecanese Islands were ceded to Greece after World War II.

Throughout Greece, small squares and parks are favorite places to meet friends and pass the time.

FACTS AND FIGURES

NAME: Hellenic Republic.

NATIONALITY: Greek(s).

CAPITAL: Athens.

LOCATION: Southeastern Europe. **Boundaries**—Albania, Yugoslavia, Bulgaria, Turkey, Aegean Sea, Mediterranean Sea, Ionian Sea.

AREA: 50,942 sq. mi. (131,940 sq. km.).

PHYSICAL FEATURES: Highest point—Olympus (9,570 ft.; 2,917 m.). **Lowest point**—sea level.

POPULATION: 10,041,414 (latest estimate).

MAJOR LANGUAGES: Greek (official), English, French.

MAJOR RELIGIONS: Greek Orthodoxy, Islam.

GOVERNMENT: Republic. **Head of state**—president. **Legislature**—one-house parliament (Vouli).

CHIEF CITIES: Athens, Salonika, Piraeus, Patras.

ECONOMY: Chief minerals—bauxite, lignite, magnesite, oil, marble. **Chief agricultural products**—wheat, olives, tobacco, cotton, raisins, fruit. **Industries and products**—foodstuffs, tobacco products, textiles, chemicals, metal products. **Chief exports**—tobacco, minerals, fruits, textiles. **Chief imports**—machinery, automobile equipment, petroleum and petroleum products, consumer goods, chemicals, meat, live animals.

MONETARY UNIT: Drachma.

The Mainland

Mainland Greece is divided into two uneven parts by the Gulf of Corinth. To the north of this gulf are the historical subdivisions of Attica, Boeotia, Thessaly, Epirus, Macedonia, Western Thrace, and the Chalcidice Peninsula. To the south of the gulf is the Peloponnesus, a peninsula that until modern times was connected by land to the northern areas by the Isthmus of Corinth. In 1893, the Corinth Canal was opened, cutting through that isthmus and connecting the Gulf of Corinth with the Saronic Gulf to its east. Today, the Peloponnesus is completely surrounded by water, and ships travel directly from the west through the Corinth Canal to the Aegean Sea. The Peloponnesus itself includes areas with such ancient names as Arcadia, Laconia, Achaea, Argolis, and Messenia. In medieval times, the Peloponnesus was called the Morea, a name that is still occasionally used.

The topography of mainland Greece varies, but mountainous conditions prevail over much of the territory. The Pindus Mountains dominate in the northwest and the Taygetus Mountains in the southern Peloponnesus. Although mountains, hills, and valleys are to be found throughout the country, there are quite fertile areas suitable for farming in places like Thessaly, Arcadia, and Boeotia. Nonetheless, there has generally been insufficient fertile land to sustain the population. This is one reason why many Greeks either turned to the sea for their livelihood or emigrated to territory around the Mediterranean and later all over the world. Emigration from Greece in the late 19th and 20th centuries has been particularly high, resulting in substantial numbers of Greeks settling in the United States and elsewhere.

Mainland Greece, like Italy and Spain, reflects the climatic conditions of the Mediterranean. Many of its areas are extremely hot during the summer months. In the winter mountainous areas, especially in the north, can be very cold with considerable snowfall. Even the mountains of the southern Peloponnesus suffer severe cold and winter conditions at times. Most of the rain falls in the spring, and the summer and fall tend to be extremely dry.

The Greek Islands

Mainland Greece is bracketed by hundreds of islands that, like the continental part, vary greatly in topography and climate. The two largest islands are Crete to the south and Euboea to the east. Euboea, also

Mykonos and other Greek islands are noted for lovely harbors and dazzling white buildings.

With its mild climate and ancient and medieval ruins, the island of Rhodes is a major tourist mecca.

known as Negropont (the name given it in medieval times), lies to the east of the mainland and is separated from it by a narrow channel.

Some of the Greek islands are included in groupings that have their own distinctive names. To the west are the Ionian Islands, of which the best known are Corfu, Cephalonia, Ithaca, and Zakynthos (or Zante).

The Cyclades.   In the Aegean Sea are the Cyclades (which comes from the Greek word for circle, because the ancient Greeks considered them a circular group of islands with Delos as the great commercial and political center). The largest island in the Cyclades is Naxos. It is associated with the ancient story of Theseus, who killed the Minotaur on the island of Crete with the help of Princess Ariadne, whom he abandoned on Naxos.

Another of the Cyclades, Thera, also called Santorin, is noted for its geological formations and its many volcanic eruptions. An ancient city, believed to have been destroyed by the great volcanic eruption of 1400 B.C., is being systematically excavated.

The Sporades.   Two other groupings of islands in the Aegean Sea are the Northern Sporades and the Southern Sporades. Euboea is one of the Northern Sporades. Another is the island of Skyros, most famous perhaps because the English poet Rupert Brooke (1887–1915) is buried there. Also in the Northern Sporades is Mykonos, which is notable for its windmills and numerous whitewashed churches, chapels, and houses. Mykonos is one of the most popular of the Greek islands with summer tourists.

The most important islands of the Southern Sporades are the Dodecanese, which in Greek means "twelve." In fact, there are 12 main islands and a number of smaller ones in the group. They lie off the southern

Turkish coast, and the most important of them is Rhodes. There in ancient times was built the great bronze statue of the sun god Helios, which has come to be known as the Colossus of Rhodes, one of the Seven Wonders of the Ancient World. No trace of it survives. Rhodes has seen many conquerors over the centuries. In 1309 it was taken by an order of Crusaders, who fortified the island and established their headquarters there. In 1522 the island was surrendered to the Ottoman Turks. On Rhodes some of the medieval fortifications and other buildings have been restored.

The island of Patmos is important in Christian history. Church tradition holds that around A.D. 95, St. John the Evangelist was exiled to Patmos. There he saw his vision of the Apocalypse and dictated his account of it to his disciple St. Prochorus. The Apocalypse, also called the Book of Revelation, is part of the New Testament.

To the north are three islands famous in Greek history: Samos, Chios, and Lesbos. Samos was a great cultural center in the 6th century B.C. and claims Pythagoras as a native son. Chios, which claims to be the birthplace of Homer, was noted in ancient times for its fine sculptors and poets. In the late Byzantine period, Chios fell (1261) into the hands of the Genoese. The Ottoman Turks captured it in 1566; and in 1822, during the Greek Revolution, it was the scene of a great massacre when the Turks murdered the entire Christian population. The massacre was widely publicized and did much to bring Europeans and Americans to the side of the Greeks in their quest for independence from the Turks.

Lesbos (also known as Mytilene) is included by some geographers in the Southern Sporades. Its name is forever associated with the great woman poet Sappho and other poets of the 7th century B.C.

On the island of Astypalaia, whitewashed houses climb a hillside to the ruins of a centuries-old citadel.

Crete. In the southern Aegean is the largest Greek island, Crete. Crete has a splendid heritage from ancient times to the present. It was the site of an early Mediterranean civilization called the Minoan, after the legendary King Minos, whose palace was in the city of Knossos. The Minoan civilization influenced other parts of the Greek world. The palace at Knossos was excavated and restored in the early 20th century and is today one of the top tourist attractions of Greece.

Crete remained part of the Greek world in the classical era, and later it fell under the Roman and Byzantine empires. From 823 to 960 it was held by the Arabs. The Byzantines retook it but later lost control to Venice early in the 13th century. In 1669, it was surrendered to the Ottoman Turks after a long war. During the period of Venetian occupation, Crete produced one of the greatest artists of all time. His name was Kyriakos Theotokopoulos, but he is best known to the world by his Spanish nickname, El Greco.

Crete, the largest Greek island, is largely agricultural. Modern farming methods are not widespread.

In modern Greece, traditional costumes and folk dances are generally limited to holidays and celebrations.

THE PEOPLE

The Greeks refer to themselves as Hellenes, and Greece can be referred to as Hellas, the Greek word for the country. The inhabitants of Greece live in widely divergent locales, from the tiniest villages to great, sprawling cities like Athens. With the advent of advanced technology in transportation and communications, distinctions between city and country people have almost disappeared. Information is accessible to almost everyone throughout the country. The usual dress in urban settings is much like that known everywhere in the rest of the world. In agricultural and remote rural areas forms of dress are sometimes based on the old styles, but in general the traditional Greek costumes are worn only at festivals, parades, and other social events. The famous Evzones that guard the presidential palace and the Tomb of the Unknown Soldier in Athens wear a distinctive *fustanella* uniform; it is distinguished by a kiltlike skirt and distinctive shoes called *tsarouhia*. At one time, a century or more ago, the *fustanella* was the customary men's wear.

Modern Greek culture and civilization are an amalgam of the many influences that have been combined through the centuries. The classical tradition is visible in the remnants that abound in the country and in the reverence the Greeks show toward their heritage. The Byzantine influence is seen in the living presence of the Greek Orthodox Church as an integral part of society as well as in the architectural and artistic works that continue to be inspired by Byzantine forms. Folk traditions, music, literature, and crafts exhibit influences that stem from the classical, Byzantine, and modern periods.

It is the Greek language that binds all of this together, so that in the 20th century, Greek civilization has emerged as a multifaceted yet vibrant whole. One only needs to cite the works of three Greek writers: the poet

George Seferis, who won the Nobel Prize for Literature in 1963; Odysseus Elytis, another distinguished poet, who won the Nobel Prize in 1979; and Nikos Kazantzakis, author of *Zorba the Greek* and numerous other works and Greece's most famous modern novelist. The influence of such writers extends beyond the borders of their native Greece to the whole world.

Religion

It is estimated that about 98 percent of the Greek population belongs to the Greek Orthodox Church, a Christian denomination that is an integral part of the Eastern Orthodox Church, which was separated from the Roman Catholic Church in 1054. At that time each branch excommunicated the other.

Over the centuries the two churches for the most part merely tolerated each other. Gradually, relations between them improved. Though still separate, in 1965 both "committed to oblivion" the excommunications of 1054; and thus there is at present greater cooperation between them. In the same spirit of cooperation the Greek Orthodox Church has developed friendly relations with Protestants and non-Christian sects outside the country.

Special breads and other delicacies are prepared for Easter, the major feast of the Greek Orthodox Church.

For Greeks generally, membership in the Orthodox Church is seen not only as a matter of religious devotion but also as a part of being ethnically Greek. There is special pride and reverence in the fact that the New Testament was written originally in Greek, and it is this untranslated form of the Bible that is still used in Greek Orthodox services in Greece today.

The Greek Language

The modern Greek language is the result of developments over many centuries. At the time of Greek independence in the 19th century two forms of modern Greek were espoused by different factions. The purist form, called the *katharevousa,* was used for literary endeavors and not for everyday conversations; it tried to emulate classical Greek as much as possible. The other form was the language of ordinary speech, called the demotic, or *dimotiki,* which varies greatly from classical Greek but is still recognizably its offshoot. At times the whole question of which form—*katharevousa* or *dimotiki*—should be given precedence in literature and education became intertwined with Greek political issues. Recently, however, the demotic has gained wide acceptance in written as well as in spoken discourse.

Education

Today, universal education in Greece is strongly stressed, and the curriculum of primary and secondary schools is closely monitored by the national government. As a result of those efforts the country today has a literacy rate of 95 percent. At the top of the education system is the University of Athens, founded in 1837, only a few years after Greece gained independence. It became a catalyst for a nationwide system of higher education that today includes a number of other universities and numerous technical, trade, and specialized colleges. Under Greek law, no private universities can exist.

Cities

Athens.   As the capital city and the economic and cultural center of Greece, Athens plays a dominant role in all aspects of Greek life. Named for the goddess Athena and once the jewel of classical Greek civilization, Athens was much less important in Byzantine times and was reduced to little more than a village during the Ottoman period. It was not even the first capital of the Greek republic; Nauplia, on the Peloponnesus, was. But the seat of government was soon removed to Athens, and from that point the growth of the modern city began. Although it grew throughout the modern era, it had its greatest explosion of growth in the period after World War II. In village after village all over Greece, the young people deserted the family home in search of jobs and economic advancement in Athens. Often, they were followed by the rest of the family. As a result, today Athens is a sprawling, overcrowded city with inadequate public services and serious pollution problems. Yet the city still remains a magnet for Greeks from the rural areas and possesses a vibrancy found only in the world's great cities. It is the center of Greece's economic life, and much of the nation's shipping passes through its port of **Piraeus.**

Athens is the site of many world-famous relics from Greek history. The best known of these is the Parthenon. It is located, along with other

Despite its ancient roots, modern Athens has a contemporary look much like other European capitals.

glories of classical Greece, on the Acropolis, the ancient citadel of the city. It was originally a shrine dedicated to the goddess Athena, and it was converted to a Christian church during the Byzantine era. Incredibly, the building survived in almost perfect condition until the 17th century. Unfortunately, however, during an Ottoman-Venetian war in 1687 the Turks used the Parthenon as a storage site for munitions, and Venetian gunboats bombarded it, reducing it to the ruins we know today. Its frieze, known today as the Elgin Marbles, was removed in the early 19th century by the English Lord Elgin and is today in the British Museum. Athens boasts many other famous remnants from its classical, Roman, and Byzantine eras. Among the relics of the classical era are the Agora, the Erechtheum, and the Theater of Dionysos. From the Roman period, Hadrian's Arch dominates its location. From the Byzantine era is the 12th-century Small Cathedral, or Old Metropolitan Church. The Kapnikarea Church is another outstanding example of Byzantine architecture. The National Museum in Athens displays glorious art from all over Greece.

Among the modern structures in Athens is the Parliament Building, located on Syntagma (Constitution) Square, the city's most important public space. Originally built as a royal palace for King Otto I (reigned

1832–62), the first king of modern Greece, it was converted to a building to house the Greek parliament in the 20th century. It was in front of this building in 1844 that revolutionaries forced King Otto to grant the nation a constitution. Athens is also the site of the Olympic Stadium, which was built for the first modern Olympic Games in 1896.

The Plaka, at the base of the hill on which the Acropolis sits, is the old section of Athens. Its winding, narrow streets give an idea of what the city must have been like toward the end of the Byzantine era, the period of the Crusades, and during the Turkish occupation. The Greek government has recently paid much attention to the restoration and preservation of the Plaka, and it is one of the favorite tourist attractions of Athens, with many shops, restaurants, and night clubs.

Salonika. The second largest city in Greece is the great Macedonian city of Salonika, also known as Thessalonica. Throughout its long history it has been the cultural, religious, and commercial capital of the north. It was especially important during the Byzantine era, and its museums are filled with masterpieces of Byzantine art that rival those found in Istanbul. Modern Salonika remains an important commercial center, and its port is second only to Piraeus.

Patras. The greatest seaport in the Peloponnesus, Patras is also a major industrial center. It produces textiles, paper, tires, wines, and chemicals. Led by its bishop, Patras was the first city in the Peloponnesus to rise against the Turks in the Greek revolution of 1821.

Pandrosou Street in the Plaka, an older section of Athens, is lined with shops selling handmade goods.

The monastery atop Mount Athos has twice as many monks as all the other Greek monasteries put together.

Mount Athos. A fascinating locale in northern Greece is the Christian community of Mount Athos, located on the tip of the Chalcidice peninsula. This all-male religious community consists of 20 monasteries and is governed under a theocratic system that functions as a separate administrative entity within Greece. The first monastery on Mount Athos was founded in 963, and its religious communities have survived since that time.

Historic Cities. **Delphi**, on the mainland northwest of Athens and situated between Mount Parnassus and the Gulf of Corinth, was one of the most significant religious centers of ancient Greece. It was here that the Delphic Oracle was consulted on great matters of state. Many elaborate temples were built at Delphi and filled with treasures by various Greek city-states.

The Peloponnesus is the site of several of the most important cities of ancient Greece. **Olympia,** like Delphi, was a religious center, and it was here that the original Olympic Games were held. **Tiryns** is the location of the ruins of an important 13th century B.C. military fortress. **Mycenae** is one of the most ancient cities in Greece. It flourished from about 1600 B.C. to 1100 B.C., during the Bronze Age, and was the legendary capital city of King Agamemnon. **Corinth** was probably founded in the 9th century B.C. and became a bustling commercial center. It was destroyed in 146 B.C., and in 44 B.C. Julius Caesar built a new city on the same site. Corinth continued as an important city during the Byzantine, Venetian, and Turkish eras. Much of the city was destroyed by earthquake in the 19th century and modern Corinth was built in 1858 inland from the ancient site. Although modern **Sparta** is quite a small city, it is the site of the most important city-state on the Peloponnesus during classical times.

THE ECONOMY

The multifaceted Greek economy includes agriculture, industry, shipping, mining, and tourism. Even more than most economies, that of Greece has always been vulnerable to outside pressures. In the 20th century it has felt the effects of the Balkan War of 1912 and 1913, World War I, the Greek-Turkish War of the 1920's, the worldwide depression of the 1930's, World War II, and the Greek Civil War of the 1940's.

Agriculture remains a significant part of the Greek economy despite insufficient arable land and the fact that many young people do not seem to want to go into farming, opting instead for life in the city. Major crops include grapes for wine and raisins, olives, figs, wheat, and citrus fruits. Other fruits, rice, and vegetables are also grown. Cotton and tobacco are important crops for export. Sheep are the primary livestock.

Greece is not blessed with rich mineral resources. Bauxite is an important mineral. Marble, lignite, magnesium, and nickel are also mined. Recent discoveries of oil near the Aegean island of Thassos have led to serious disputes with Turkey over oil rights in the area.

The much-indented coastlines of Greece and its islands have made fishing an important way of life.

Shipping remains an important factor in the Greek economy, and most of the great fortunes made in Greece come from the flotillas of tankers sailed by Greek shipowners. Industrial production lags behind that of the nations of Western Europe. Greece does produce cement, steel, textiles, refined sugar, and ships. Greece entered the European Community (Common Market) in 1981 with the expectation that the nation's industrial production would increase and that other areas of the economy would be helped by a close association with other members of the Community.

Tourism. At least since the 18th century, adventurous European travelers have sought out the glories of classical and Byzantine Greece. Today, tourism is a major factor in the Greek economy. Foreigners still come to Greece to seek out its magnificent ruins and historical sites; but many more come to enjoy the swimming, fishing, boating, and cruising among the Greek islands. Fostered by governmental support, the Greek tourist industry has grown enormously since World War II. The Athens international airport is one of the busiest in the world, with regular and charter flights from all over Europe and from America. Luxurious cruise ships carry foreign tourists from one Greek island to the next.

THE GOVERNMENT

Since 1974, when the monarchy was overthrown, Greece has been a republic; its official name is the Hellenic Republic. By its constitution, ratified in 1975, the head of state is the president. Legislative authority is vested in a unicameral parliament (*Vouli*), or national assembly. Parliament, made up of 300 deputies elected by universal suffrage, chooses

The volcanic island of Thera is thought by some to be the site of the legendary continent of Atlantis.

The spectacular Palace of Minos at Knossos, Crete, discovered in this century, was built before 1400 B.C.

the president for a five-year term. Although the president has some very limited powers, the actual executive power rests with the prime minister and the cabinet of ministers, who form the government. They are chosen from among members of the parliament.

Administratively, Greece is subdivided into 52 prefectures, or departments (*nomoi*). They in turn are divided into smaller units. The minister of the interior appoints a governor, or prefect (*nomarchis*), for each department; thus there is a great deal of central control of local governments. Mayors and other officials are elected locally.

Greece has a highly structured, complicated judicial system. Included are the Special Supreme Tribunal, which specifically deals with constitutional issues; the Council of State, which serves as an appellate court for administrative acts; and the Supreme Court, which despite its name does not function like the U.S. Supreme Court. There are also various specialized judicial bodies, such as tax courts.

HISTORY

Greek-speaking peoples first migrated down the mainland of what is now Greece around 1900 B.C. Coming in contact with the already thriving Minoan civilization of Crete, they developed their own civilization, now known as the Mycenaean. This flourished from around 1600 B.C. to around 1150 B.C. This era of periodic instability was the setting for the two great masterpieces of ancient Greek literature, the *Iliad* and the *Odyssey*. Both poems were written down between 800 B.C. and 750 B.C., based on oral traditions. The blind poet Homer has always been credited with writing them. They form the first great literary works of the ancient Greeks and two of the most influential works in Western civilization. In the *Iliad*, Homer describes the siege of Troy to secure the

Ancient Greeks flocked to Delphi to ask advice of the oracle, through whom the gods spoke.

release of the exquisitely beautiful Spartan queen, Helen, who had been captured and carried away by Paris, son of Priam, king of Troy. Thus the stage was set for the Trojan War, an event that most historians accept as having taken place about 1250 B.C. The *Odyssey* traces the wandering of Odysseus, ruler of Ithaca, in his efforts to return to his home after the end of the Trojan War.

Greece's Golden Age

The ancient Greeks did not establish one unified country. Instead they established city-states, each called a *polis,* which were self-governing and independent. Often they warred with one another, the two most persistent enemies being Athens and Sparta. All the city-states, however, would from time to time go to war with another *polis.*

Although the Greeks are credited with inventing the democratic form of government, not all of the city-states were democratic in form. Sparta, for example, was during most of its predominance an aristocratic and a military regime. Even Athens, the most famous of all the democratic city-states, relied on slavery for its economic well-being. Only male Athenian citizens participated in the democracy.

All the Greek city-states had high levels of culture, and Greek civilization spread to colonies throughout the Mediterranean world: from the Black Sea to Spain and from Italy and southern France to North Africa.

Athens served as a kind of catalyst among the city-states, and what emerged was one of the greatest civilizations the world has ever seen. Architecture reached splendid levels. The Parthenon, built between 447 and 432 B.C., was the most spectacular of many beautiful temples that were erected throughout Greece. Seldom has any period in time seen such a profusion of talented people as in classical Greece. Among them were the Athenian leader Pericles; the philosophers Socrates, Plato, and Aristotle; the sculptor Phidias; the dramatists Sophocles, Aeschylus, Euripides, and Aristophanes; the poet Pindar; and Herodotus, the "Father of History."

The rivalry between Athens and Sparta erupted into the Great Peloponnesian War in 431 B.C. It finally ended in 404 B.C. with a great victory for Sparta, which emerged as the ruler of all of Greece. It was to be a short-lived rule. Wars with Persia to the east and with the Greek city Thebes left Sparta—and all of Greece—open to conquest from the north.

The Hellenistic Period

In 338 B.C., King Philip II of Macedonia was able to bring the once-proud Greek city-states under his control. The Macedonians were a kindred people to the Greeks. They spoke a form of Greek, and their rulers considered themselves to be true Greeks. Philip's son, Alexander the Great (reigned 336–323 B.C.), conquered vast areas of Europe, Egypt,

Tourists walk through the ruins of the agora in Corinth, one of ancient Greece's leading city-states.

Steps leading to a church at Mistras are typical of the architecture required by the stony Greek terrain.

and Asia, reaching as far as India. Alexander's conquests spread Greek civilization and language throughout the Middle East. The Greek-based civilization that then developed is called Hellenistic to distinguish it from the classical Greek period that ended with the Macedonian conquests.

After Alexander's death his empire was divided among his generals. The Greek city-states formed several leagues and by the 220's had become mostly independent again. Clashes with the Macedonians and the expansion of Rome hindered these attempts to maintain independence.

The Roman Period

With the decline of Macedonian power and the rise of Rome the Romans intervened repeatedly in Greek affairs particularly from the 220's B.C. By 146 B.C. the Greeks were effectively under Roman domination and would remain so for centuries. The Romans, however, were captivated by the beauties of Greek civilization, and Greek forms and ideals had such an important influence on Roman culture that even today people speak of the fusion as Greco-Roman. Christianity was fostered among the Greeks by the missionary journeys and works of St. Paul. He preached at such places as Athens, Corinth, Philippi, and Thessalonica (Salonika). It was in the first centuries of Christianity that the Roman period melded into the Byzantine era of Greek history.

The Byzantine Empire

In 330 A.D. the Roman Emperor Constantine I founded the city of Constantinople, which he erected on the site of the ancient Greek city of Byzantium. Constantinople became the capital of what was to become the Byzantine Empire. Greek had always remained the language of culture in the eastern Roman Empire. Following Constantine's reign the eastern parts of the empire increasingly separated from the western territories. Gradually they split into two parts: the Western, with its capital at Rome, and the Eastern, with its capital at Constantinople. As the Roman Empire weakened, much of its eastern territories were lost to Islamic conquerors. By the 7th century A.D. what had been the Eastern Empire was reduced to an essentially Greek-speaking core centered around Constantinople.

For many centuries this still-powerful Byzantine Empire had an enormous impact on Europe and the world around the Mediterranean basin. As Rome declined, Constantinople became the center of art, architecture, literature, education, commerce, and religion. At Constantinople resided the most important bishop of the Eastern Church, the Ecumenical Patriarch; even today members of the Greek Orthodox Church and other Orthodox churches consider the Ecumenical Patriarch the spiritual leader of the Church. Missionaries sent out from the Greek Church in Constantinople converted many people of Eastern Europe to Christianity, including the Russians, the Serbs, the Rumanians, and the Bulgarians. Thus, through the Church, Greek influence covered virtually all of Eastern Europe.

By the 11th century the Byzantine Empire had begun to weaken internally in the face of increasing outside pressures. Christian Crusaders, who came from Western Europe initially to take over "infidel lands" in Palestine, annexed lands controlled by their fellow Christians, the Byzantine Greeks. Westerners like Normans, Venetians, and Genoese took over great sections of Byzantium. Even the capital city of Constantinople was held by Western Europeans from 1204 to 1261, when the Byzantines retook it.

By that time the empire had lost its momentum, however, and the Byzantines were never able completely to dislodge Western European leaders who had set up their own little states in parts of what is today modern Greece. Athens became the Duchy of Athens and Thebes, ruled by people of Western origins. Most of the residents of the Greek islands became vassals of various ruling princes of Western Europe. And a new power had emerged in the area; from the 14th century the Ottoman Turks began encroaching on both the Byzantine Empire and its Western European conquerors.

The Ottoman Turks

Constantinople fell in 1453, thus ending the political existence of the Byzantine Empire. Subsequently, the Turks brought under their control all the Greek-speaking parts of Europe and Asia Minor except for one major area, the Ionian Islands. These remained under Venetian domination for hundreds of years (until 1797). After the Napoleonic era, they became a British protectorate.

Otherwise, the Greeks came under the domination of the Ottoman Turks. Sultan Mohammed II the Conqueror, the Turkish ruler who took Constantinople in 1453, gave to the Ecumenical Patriarch certain political and religious rights over the Greek Orthodox subjects of the empire. This helped the Greeks retain a recognizable ethnic identity in an empire that was otherwise almost wholly Muslim. Relatively few Greeks were converted to Islam, and the Greek Orthodox Church thus helped keep alive a separate national feeling among the Greeks.

The conditions of the Greeks varied from place to place in the Ottoman Empire. Some were downtrodden and exploited; others grew wealthy in commerce. Still others reached high position in the government even though they remained Christian.

The Quest for Independence

Still, many Greeks chafed under Ottoman domination, and as the ideals of nationalism that were unleashed by the French Revolution in the 18th century spread into Greek-speaking areas, the revolutionary spirit developed among the Greeks. The result was a full-fledged revolution against the Turks in 1821. With the help of Great Britain, Russia, and France, and after numerous bloody battles, Greece became an independent kingdom in 1832.

During the revolution many foreigners who were pro-Greek, including a few Americans, either helped the cause from outside or went to Greece to fight with the rebels. They were called Philhellenes, and the most famous of them was the English poet Lord Byron. His death in Greece in 1824 made him a Greek national hero, inspiring many others to join the Greek cause.

The Greek Kingdom

With independence, a Bavarian prince named Otto was chosen by the Western powers to be the first king of modern Greece. It may seem strange that the Greeks would accept a foreign-born king after they had thrown off the Turkish yoke. There were several reasons for this, among them that no Greek rebel had emerged as the clear leader of the country. Perhaps most important, it was believed that an outsider connected by birth to the great royal houses of Western Europe would give the struggling new nation the prestige it would need among the other royal rulers of Europe. Otto was the son of King Ludwig I of Bavaria, the first European monarch openly to support the Greek cause. Lastly, Otto was young enough so that he could acclimate himself to the country and become, in effect, Greek.

Otto turned out to be a strong Greek patriot. He supported a concept called the Great Idea, which envisaged tiny Greece as the nucleus for a larger Greek state that would recreate the old Byzantine Empire at the expense of now weak Ottoman Turks. Although mild-mannered, Otto was also authoritarian. An uprising in 1843 forced him to accept a national constitution. Nevertheless, his authoritarianism increased, and in 1862 he was forced from the throne.

In medieval times, the Crusaders built castles in Greece to protect their routes to the Holy Land.

Otto was replaced in 1863 by a Danish prince—elected by the Greek National Assembly—who assumed the Greek throne as George I of the Hellenes. The new king, like King Otto, espoused the Great Idea and in fact saw his kingdom enlarged three times during his reign.

During the last years of his rule, King George entrusted the prime ministership to one of the most remarkable leaders of modern Greece. Eleutherios Venizelos, a Cretan by birth, had fought the Turks on his native island, where he won wide acclaim. As prime minister, Venizelos rejuvenated Greece; he paid attention to internal administration and built up the army and the navy. He oversaw the revision of the constitution, and he skillfully built up a network of connections with Greece's northern neighbors against the Ottoman Turks.

The Balkan Wars. It was under these circumstances that the first Balkan War broke out in 1912, and Greece was a major participant in it. With Venizelos as the political leader and King George's son, Crown Prince Constantine, at the head of the army, Greece won unparalleled victories. As soon as Constantine had taken Salonika from the Turks, King George went to reside there to show that even before the peace treaty, Greece considered the city Greek. It was in Salonika that the king was assassinated by a madman in March, 1913 as he walked through the streets.

Constantine I came to the throne as a martyr's son and as the first Greek-born king in centuries. In June 1913 a second Balkan War commenced. Again Constantine and Venizelos worked together to secure enormous victories and new territories for Greece.

World War I. Unfortunately, World War I broke up the close relationship between king and prime minister. Venizelos favored joining the Allies (Great Britain, France, and Russia) against Germany, Austria-

Just off the lush Ionian island of Corfu lie several tiny islets, one of which houses a small monastery.

Hungary, and the Ottoman Empire. Constantine, whose wife, Queen Sophie, was a sister of the German Emperor William II, wanted Greece to remain neutral. Constantine was branded pro-German; Venizelos resigned from office, led a revolution, and forced the king to abdicate in 1917. Constantine's second son then became King Alexander I of the Hellenes. Venizelos returned to office as prime minister and won a brilliant series of military and diplomatic victories. They culminated in Greek troops entering Constantinople along with the other Allied forces when the Ottoman Empire lost the war and faded from history. In addition, Venizelos won from the Allies the right to occupy the Greek-inhabited city of Smyrna, in Asia Minor, thus signaling the fact that Turkish territory in Asia Minor was not immune from the Great Idea.

The 1920's and 1930's. Then everything collapsed. King Alexander died tragically as the result of an infection from a monkey bite. Venizelos lost at the polls, and King Constantine was restored to the throne by popular vote. The Turks, despite their defeat in World War I, attacked the Greeks at Smyrna and drove them out. Constantine was forced to abdicate once again (1922), this time in favor of his oldest son, who became King George II of the Hellenes. The military disaster in Asia

Minor had left Greece a weakened, disrupted country. The Great Idea was destroyed forever, and George II was forced to leave Greece in 1923.

From 1924 to 1935, Greece was a republic. Most of those years were turbulent, except for a period from 1928 to 1932 when Venizelos once again gave the country a stable government. The monarchy was restored in 1935 in the person of George II, but the following year all governmental power fell into the hands of a military dictator named John Metaxas.

World War II. Metaxas was still at the helm in October 1940 when Fascist Italy under Benito Mussolini invaded Greece. The valiant defense by the Greeks, which continued after Metaxas' death in early 1941, led to a German invasion from the north in 1941. King George II and his government were forced into exile.

During the Nazi occupation, resistance groups developed, the most important being EAM with its army ELAS. They were communists who tried unsuccessfully to take over the government in 1944 when Greece was liberated.

The Greek Civil War and Cyprus. At the end of World War II, King George II was once again restored to the throne in a 1946 plebiscite. He died in 1947, and his brother, the youngest son of Constantine I, became king as Paul I. In the meantime the communists had begun a civil war that lasted until 1949 when, with decisive American aid, it was crushed.

During King Paul's reign there emerged a man who ranks with Venizelos as one of the two great modern Greek statesmen. Constantine Karamanlis became prime minister in 1955. He stressed economic development and a settlement of the Cyprus question. Cyprus was a British

Plays in ancient Greece were performed in semicircular theaters, the ruins of which can still be seen.

colony with a population about 80 percent Greek and 17 percent Turkish. The Greek Orthodox Archbishop of Cyprus, Makarious III, became the leader of a movement for *enosis,* or union, with Greece. *Enosis* was bitterly opposed by both the Turkish Cypriots and by Turkey. Karamanlis negotiated with the British, Turkey, and the Cypriots; the final result was that Cyprus became an independent republic in 1960. Hostility over this issue continued to impair Greek-Turkish relations and continues to do so. After a quarrel with King Paul I and his German-born wife, Queen Frederica, Karamanlis resigned in 1963.

The Rule of the Colonels.   The absence of Karamanlis marked the beginning of a long, serious political crisis in Greece. King Paul died in 1964, and his son succeeded as Constantine II. Constantine found it increasingly difficult to cope with an unstable political situation. In April, 1967, Constantine faced a rebellion by a group of military officers known as the Colonels; they took over the government and established a dictatorship. The king valiantly tried to oust them from power in December 1967, but his efforts failed and he was forced into exile. The Colonels remained in power until 1974.

Meantime, the Cypriot problem would not go away. Despite independence, the two factions (Greek and Turkish) could not live together harmoniously. The Greek Colonels foolishly tried to force union on Cyprus, and Turkey invaded Cyprus in 1974, taking over about 40 percent

From this palace in Corfu, the British administered the Ionian islands during the 19th century.

In 1932, the Old Palace in Athens, formerly the monarch's residence, became the Parliament Building.

of the island. In Greece, the Colonels' failure cost them their power. Karamanlis returned from his long exile, became prime minister again, and reestablished democracy.

The Greek Republic

In 1974, the monarchy was rejected by plebiscite, and Greece was declared a republic. A new constitution was ratified in 1975. Karamanlis remained as prime minister until 1980, placing emphasis once again on economic development. His foreign policy was focused on a close relationship with Western Europe and the United States. In 1981, Greece became a member of the European Community (Common Market).

In 1981, a Socialist government came to power. Andreas Papandreou served as prime minister until 1989. A series of inconclusive elections ended in April 1990 with the selection of Constantine Mitsotakis of the New Democracy Party as premier. Papandreou and several of his close associates were later arrested on corruption charges. Mitsotakis reached agreement in 1990 with the United States on extending the leases for U.S. military bases in Greece, an issue that had previously caused friction. The Papandreou Socialist government had also raised questions about Greece's membership in the European Economic Community (EEC) and NATO. The new government faced severe economic problems that made cooperation with European allies crucial as both the EEC and the International Monetary Fund (IMF) called for austerity measures. Regardless of difficulties, Greece continues today as a democratic state, one of the countries that gives its people freedom and civil liberty.

GEORGE J. MARCOPOULOS, Tufts University

Vast, gently rolling plains cover nearly the entire Polish countryside.

POLAND

Since the beginning of its history more than 1,000 years ago, Poland has often suffered because of its geography. Poland, which takes its name from *pole*, a West Slavic word meaning "field," is in fact one vast plain with no natural frontiers or defenses on the east or the west. Only the Sudetes and the Carpathian Mountains, in the south, and the Baltic Sea, in the north, provide natural boundaries. For centuries the somber landscape of Poland has been the setting for warring armies. Since the 17th century the nation has been conquered, partitioned, and destroyed time and time again. But throughout Poland's history its people have given vivid meaning to their national anthem, which begins, "Poland will not be forsaken while we live. . . ."

THE LAND

On the north of Poland is the 326-mile (525-kilometer)-long Baltic Sea coastline. The rest of the country is part of the great plain that extends from the North Sea across Europe to the Ural Mountains, in the Soviet Union. The gently rolling plains rise gradually to the south, where, at the border with Czechoslovakia, they meet the low Sudetes and the lofty Carpathian Mountains. This is one of the most picturesque regions of Eastern Europe. Skiing in the High Tatra range of the Carpathians is excellent. In the range, which is a national park, one may see chamois, red deer, bears, lynx, wolves, eagles, and black storks. The nearby Ojców National Park, with its great woods and high cliffs, has about 50 caves in which primitive men probably lived, and where remains of prehistoric giant deer, hyenas, lions, and mammoths have been found. Just northeast of the Tatra range is the Pieniny range, where in another national park there are plants found nowhere else in the world and more than 1,800 species of butterflies.

Deep woods still cover more than one fourth of Poland. The country is also dotted with thousands of lakes. The Masuria region, in the northeast, with dense, high trees and countless sparkling lakes, is a fine hunting, fishing, boating, and camping area. In the Białowieża Forest, in eastern Poland, are 485 square miles (1,256 square kilometers) of the last remaining lowland primeval forest in central Europe. It includes a famous national park, once the private property of Poland's kings, where bison roam in complete freedom, fantastic lime trees grow, and huge eagles swoop and soar overhead.

The winters are cold, damp, and snowy and the summers cool in this land of fields, woods, and rivers. The mighty Vistula (Wisła), the main river of Poland, rises in the Carpathians, carves a roundabout route that forms a huge letter S, and empties into the Baltic Sea after traveling 680 miles (1,094 kilometers). The Vistula with its tributaries, the Bug and the Pilica, drains about two thirds of the land. Light boats can sail up the Vistula as far as Cracow, except during the winter months when the river is frozen. Warsaw, the nation's capital, is situated on the west bank of the

A religious procession in Podhale. The Catholic Church plays a vital role in the lives of Polish citizens.

river. Coal and lumber are transported on the river. West of the Vistula are the Oder and Neisse rivers, which rise in the Sudetes, flow separately, and then combine to empty into the Baltic. Canals link the main river systems, and they serve as important industrial delivery routes.

THE PEOPLE

Poles are noted for their Old World gallantry. Men habitually bow and kiss women's hands and present roses on every possible occasion. Most of the people are also devout Catholics and great patriots. Attendance at masses is among the highest in the world; after Italy, Poland is probably the most Catholic country today. About 90 percent of children are baptized in the Church, the number of priests is increasing, and new churches are being built.

By the late 1980s, Poles had become bitter and exhausted from years of economic hardship and the inability of the Communist government to govern effectively. The discontent was reflected in growing labor unrest, and increasing support for political dissidents. There was an increase in alcoholism and a drop in life expectancy. Women were the greatest victims of the overall deterioration of the quality of life: Most of them not only went to work, but after work had to stand daily in long lines to buy the basic items. Another problem was housing. Young couples had to wait years for new apartments and meanwhile had to live with their parents.

Education. There is virtually no illiteracy. Education is compulsory for eight years, after which a student can enroll in a general secondary school or a vocational school. Poland has almost 100 institutions of higher learning, including 11 universities.

The struggle between the church and state extends to education. The last church-run elementary school was closed in 1962, but children can attend special religious classes outside the schools if their parents demand it. Poland also had the only private Catholic university in the Communist world, in Lublin.

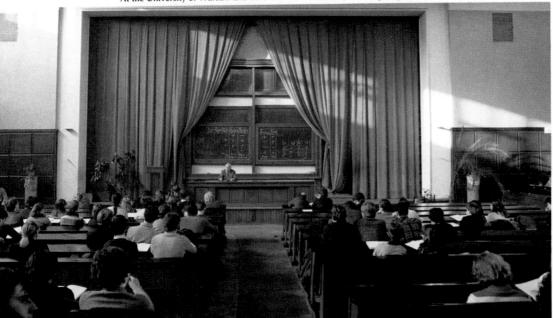

At the University of Warsaw and other Polish universities, teaching long adhered to Marxist principles.

Scores of modern buildings have been built in Warsaw since World War II, when the city was nearly leveled.

Literature and Music. Poland has a distinguished literary tradition. Adam Mickiewicz (1798–1855) is best known for the epic *Pan Tadeusz* (*Sir Thaddeus*). Poland claims three Nobel laureates in literature—Henryk Sienkiewicz, who won the 1905 prize for his novels, including *Quo Vadis?*; Władysław S. Reymont, author of *The Peasants,* who won the prize in 1924; and the poet Czesław Milosz, who lived in the United States from 1960 and who received the prize in 1980. Several authors born in Poland but writing in other languages have also won international acclaim: Joseph Conrad at the turn of the century; Isaac Bashevis Singer, who left Poland in 1935 and received a Nobel Prize in 1978 for his stories about the world of Polish Jews; and Jerzy Kosinski, who lived in the United States from 1957. The best-known contemporary Polish authors are the science-fiction writer Stanislaw Lem and the dissident novelist Tadeusz Konvicki.

Poles have always enjoyed theater. There are many large repertory theaters and countless small theaters and cabarets noted for their political satire. The Polish movie industry has won international fame, particularly with films by Andrzej Wajda, which include *Man of Marble* and *Man of Iron* (the latter about Solidarity).

Some say that to hear the truest voice of Poland's tragedies and triumphs one must listen to the music of Frédéric Chopin (1810–49), whose waltzes, études, ballades, sonatas, and nocturnes were often based on old folk themes. Polish folk songs are lighthearted and sad at the same time. There are many folk dances, such as the polonaise, mazurka, krakowiak, and others. At the same time, today there is a contemporary music club in almost every Polish village. Western rock and movie stars are well-known and popular.

Cities

Warsaw. For centuries the Poles prided themselves on their intellectual ties to the West, especially France and Italy, and for many the capital, Warsaw, was an eastern, smaller edition of Paris, the elegant French capital. Warsaw, located in the heart of Poland, is the largest city, the center of trade and industry, and one of the liveliest capitals in Eastern Europe. It is famous for its institutions of higher learning, especially the University of Warsaw, its theater and concert halls, and its great museums and libraries. Its music festivals, especially the Chopin competition, attract some of the most gifted young artists from all over the world.

Nearly all of Warsaw was left in ruins by the Germans at the end of World War II. The rebuilding of the Old Town was modeled on over 300 pictures of Warsaw that had been painted by the Italian artist Bernardo Belotto (1720–80). Warsaw's reconstructed palaces and handsome 18th-century mansions today house government agencies and academies of arts and sciences. Among the city's best-known landmarks are the Cathedral of Saint John, which dates from 1360, and Casimir Palace, the home of the University of Warsaw, founded in 1818. One of the finest modern buildings is the radium institute and hospital built in honor of Marie (Marja) Skłodowska, the Polish girl who went to France, married Pierre Curie, and with him discovered radium. They shared the Nobel prize in physics in 1903. Eight years later Marie Curie won the Nobel prize in chemistry.

Cracow. The capital of Poland until 1609, Cracow remains one of the intellectual centers of the country and is one of Europe's most beautiful and historic cities. There the charm of a medieval town blends with the bustle of the 20th century. The royal castle of Wawel, on a hill overlooking the Vistula, was begun nearly 1,000 years ago. Its majestic chambers

Cracow, the former capital of Poland, retains much of its medieval charm.

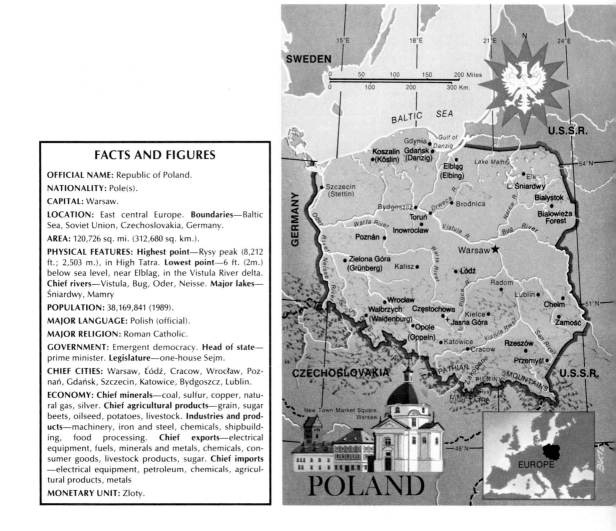

FACTS AND FIGURES

OFFICIAL NAME: Republic of Poland.

NATIONALITY: Pole(s).

CAPITAL: Warsaw.

LOCATION: East central Europe. **Boundaries**—Baltic Sea, Soviet Union, Czechoslovakia, Germany.

AREA: 120,726 sq. mi. (312,680 sq. km.).

PHYSICAL FEATURES: Highest point—Rysy peak (8,212 ft.; 2,503 m.), in High Tatra. **Lowest point**—6 ft. (2m.) below sea level, near Elblag, in the Vistula River delta. **Chief rivers**—Vistula, Bug, Oder, Neisse. **Major lakes**—Śniardwy, Mamry

POPULATION: 38,169,841 (1989).

MAJOR LANGUAGE: Polish (official).

MAJOR RELIGION: Roman Catholic.

GOVERNMENT: Emergent democracy. **Head of state**—prime minister. **Legislature**—one-house Sejm.

CHIEF CITIES: Warsaw, Łódź, Cracow, Wrocław, Poznań, Gdańsk, Szczecin, Katowice, Bydgoszcz, Lublin.

ECONOMY: Chief minerals—coal, sulfur, copper, natural gas, silver. **Chief agricultural products**—grain, sugar beets, oilseed, potatoes, livestock. **Industries and products**—machinery, iron and steel, chemicals, shipbuilding, food processing. **Chief exports**—electrical equipment, fuels, minerals and metals, chemicals, consumer goods, livestock products, sugar. **Chief imports**—electrical equipment, petroleum, chemicals, agricultural products, metals

MONETARY UNIT: Zloty.

are filled with a rich collection of tapestries and other medieval art objects. The Gothic cathedral next to the castle contains the tombs of most of the country's kings and other famous men. Many poets are buried there, since according to old Polish tradition great poets are equal to kings.

Cracow is also the home of the Jagellonian University, which was founded in 1364 and has become a leading center of culture and learning in Eastern Europe. It has produced some of the world's greatest scholars, including Nicolaus Copernicus (1473–1543), the astronomer who first declared that the earth revolves around the sun. His laboratory has been preserved in the medieval part of the campus, still used by the university.

ECONOMY

Before World War II, Poland was largely an agricultural country. Today, because of the growth of industries and the movement of young people to the cities, only 40 percent of the population remains on the farms. When the Communists came to power, they immediately began setting up collective farms, but the Polish peasants did not want to be forced into a Communist mold. In 1956 most cooperatives were dismantled, and today nearly all the cultivated land is tilled by independent farmers, mostly in small, uneconomical farms that cover less than 25 acres (10 hectares). Polish farmers, who have few modern farm machines, often sow by hand and reap the grain with long-handled scythes, and many a peasant woman can still be seen milking a cow in the middle of a meadow. Even so, Poland grows more rye and potatoes than any other country in Europe except the Soviet Union. Although wheat, barley, and sugar beets are grown, the soil is not well suited to their cultivation, and much grain and fodder must be imported.

Potatoes, cabbages, beets, mushrooms, dairy products, and some meat—mostly pork—form the bulk of the Polish diet. Favorite Polish dishes include *bigos,* a mixture of sauerkraut and sausage; *kielbasa,* smoked sausage; *barszca,* beet soup served with many meat and vegetable accompaniments; *kolduny,* pastry with meat filling; and many delicious fish dishes. Polish ham and bacon are widely exported, as is Polish vodka, made from potatoes and grain.

The task of turning an agricultural nation, almost destroyed by war, into a major industrial country has not been easy. Poland has extensive coal deposits and is the world's fifth largest producer of coal, but must import petroleum and iron ore. Other natural resources include lead, zinc, natural gas, lignite, salt, copper, manganese, uranium, phosphates, and sulfur.

When the Communists came to power, all industry, trade, and banking were nationalized. Iron, steel, chemical, and electrical output increased enormously. Nowa Huta, a city built in recent decades, is

Miners end their shift at an Upper Silesian mine. Coal is one of Poland's most important exports.

The clothing industry in Poland has grown dramatically since World War II.

completely devoted to the manufacture of steel. A large textile industry is centered around Łódź. Huge shipyards on the Baltic produce ships for sale all over the world.

For many years, Poland has traded largely with the Soviet Union and other Communist nations, and the Soviet Union still supplies most of Poland's raw materials. After workers staged a series of demonstrations and riots in the 1970s to protest the low standard and high cost of living, the government began to import machinery from the Western world. It drew up ambitious plans to modernize Polish factories and produce high-quality goods for export beyond the Soviet bloc, but industry remained highly centralized and inefficient. The Communists were unwilling to introduce economic reforms despite strong internal pressure from the Solidarity labor movement, and from the 1970s, the economy was in a state of continual crisis. With the introduction of a free-market economy by the new government in 1989–1990, inflation soared as subsidies on basic foodstuffs were gradually eliminated. Massive financial aid from the West has been promised and an international bank for the reconstruction and development of Eastern Europe has been established to help with the transition to democracy.

GOVERNMENT

The new government in Poland is controlled by the Solidarity movement. Its candidates won a majority of seats in the Sejm, or parliament. The prime minister was an early leader of Solidarity before it was outlawed by the Communists.

Although some collective farms persist, most Polish land is cultivated by independent farmers.

HISTORY

Slavic tribes probably inhabited some regions of present-day Poland as early as 2000-1000 B.C. In the 10th century, Prince Mieszko married a Christian princess from Bohemia (today part of Czechoslovakia) and accepted her faith for himself and his people. The conversion to Christianity marked Poland's entrance into the world of Western civilization.

In the next few centuries, under the rule of the Piast dynasty, Poland fought numerous wars with its neighbors and suffered from internal conflicts. In 1386, however, the Poles united with the Lithuanians and emerged, under the powerful Jagiellowian dynasty, as one of the strongest states of Eastern Europe.

The 16th century was Poland's golden age. The commonwealth stretched from the Baltic to the Black Sea and reached almost to the gates of Moscow. Universities were built. A brilliant literature was created. The Church had great influence in state affairs. Many Jews driven out by neighboring countries found a welcome in Poland, where the gentry, uninterested in handicrafts and trading, encouraged the Jews to become shopkeepers and traders.

During this period the nobility, who made up about 10 percent of the population, acquired immense independent political power. After 1572 they elected the king. Theoretically each member of the nobility was eligible to be chosen as king. In addition, any member could stop the proceedings of the parliament (Sejm) or block any law by saying *veto*, the Latin for "I forbid." The unrestrained use of this veto power gradually paralyzed the entire government. The weakness of the government and internal disorders (such as the peasant uprising against Polish domination in Ukraine in 1648–49) invited foreign intervention from neighboring Russia, Prussia, and Sweden. These wars drained the country's scattered strength and poorly used resources. Even so, there were occasional victories. The Poles believe they were saved from Swedish conquest in 1655 by the Miracle of Częstochowa. A 40-day siege of the fortified monastery

Warsaw's Old Town has been restored to the way it appeared centuries ago.

at Jasna Góra is said to have ended because the abbot held up a portrait of the Madonna that the people believed had been painted by Saint Luke. To this day, the monastery, the holiest Polish shrine, is visited each year by about 200,000 pilgrims. Poland's last important ruler, King John III Sobieski, was a brilliant military leader. He helped to save Europe from the Turkish invaders by defeating them at Vienna in 1683.

Decline and Downfall

But Sobieski could not save his own country from internal decay. From the time of his death in 1696 until early in the 20th century the Poles had no real self-government.

In 1772 part of Poland was divided among the Russians, Prussians, and Austrians. A second partition by Russia and Prussia in 1793 carved up most of the rest of the country. There were various attempts at revolt. In 1794, Thaddeus Kosciusko, (Tadeusz Kościuszko), a Polish general who had fought in the American Revolution, tried to unite his countrymen to drive the Russians and Prussians out of Poland and to free the peasants from serfdom. The Poles fought fiercely but were defeated, and in 1795 the country was partitioned for a third time by Russia, Prussia, and Austria. Poland disappeared from the map of Europe. In the part controlled by Russia, Poles repeatedly rebelled against their overlords but were always defeated. During these difficult times it was only the Roman Catholic Church that kept alive the spirit of the Polish nation.

Independence and Two World Wars.

In the late 19th century groups were formed by Polish emigrants in Paris, London, and New York to work for a free Poland. They cooperated with various political groups inside the partitioned country. At the beginning of the 20th century this drive for independence was led by Józef Piłsudski, founder of the Polish Legions during World War I; Ignace Paderewski, the famous Polish pianist; and Roman Dmowski, leader of the National Democratic Party.

The treaty of Versailles, in 1919, established Poland as a fully independent republic, and Józef Piłsudski became the first president of the new state. In the next two decades economic and political problems and boundary disputes with the neighboring countries plagued Poland. In 1926, Piłsudski seized power and then ruled as a virtual dictator until his death in 1935.

Although Poland concluded a 10-year nonaggression treaty with Germany in 1934, Nazi forces attacked the country on September 1, 1939, without formally declaring war. Two days later, Great Britain and France, which had promised to protect Poland, declared war on Germany. World War II had begun. While German forces launched their blitzkrieg ("lightning war") on Poland from the west, the Soviet Union struck at Poland from the east. Again the Poles fought stubbornly but in vain. Germany took the western part of Poland, the Soviet Union the eastern part. In 1941, when Germany attacked the Soviet Union, all of Poland came under German occupation.

Hitler had sworn he would obliterate the country, and he almost succeeded. More than one fifth of the people were killed or died as a result of the war. Of the major cities in Poland, Warsaw was 84 percent destroyed, Wrocław 80 percent, and Gdańsk and Gdynia 50 percent. Every third person lost his farm, home, or apartment. Despite the suffering, many thousands of Poles were involved in a large, well-organized resistance movement, which supplied the Western Allies with information about Nazi troop movements and sabotaged German war efforts.

No group in Poland suffered more than the Polish Jews. In 1940 the Germans herded 500,000 Jews from Warsaw and nearby areas into a part of the city around which high walls were built. In April 1943, the surviving Jews rose in revolt. The battle of the Warsaw Ghetto lasted one month, and only 200 Warsaw Jews survived. Near Cracow is Oświęcim (Auschwitz), the site of the most infamous Nazi concentration camp, where Dr. Josef Mengele performed his appalling human medical experiments and where about 2,500,000 Jews and 1,500,000 non-Jews were systematically murdered in gas chambers.

Other camps at Birkenau and Treblinka were also huge "death factories." Poland lost most of its political leaders, its educators, and its intellectuals in concentration camps. Poland also lost more than 1,000,000 of its workers, who were deported to slave labor camps in the Soviet Union.

When the Germans were finally turned back by the Russians, the Soviet Army invaded German-controlled Poland. Late in the summer of

1944, as the Soviet armies approached the Polish capital, the people of Warsaw rose up against the Germans, expecting the advancing Soviet troops to come to their help. But the Russians stayed on the east bank of the Vistula River while Warsaw was reduced to rubble.

Rule by the Communists.

As a result of the war, Poland was "moved" to the west: The Soviet Union took over former eastern Polish lands, and Poland was given former German territories east of the Oder and Neisse Rivers. The shift involved a huge population transfer, with about 6,000,000 Germans leaving the country and some 7,500,000 Poles moving from east to west.

Another result of the war was the gradual Communist takeover, which had become complete by December 1948. Mass political arrests followed, and a Soviet-style constitution was adopted in 1952—but curiously, Poland was one of the few Soviet satellites that never built a monument to Joseph Stalin. In 1956 worker riots in Poznań foreshadowed the

A monument in the former Warsaw Ghetto honors Jews killed in the 1943 uprising against the Nazis.

pattern of subsequent Polish developments. The riots led to the elevation of Władysław Gomułka, a nationalist Communist leader who had been jailed in Stalin's time, to the post of the first secretary of the party and to gradual liberalization of the regime. Most importantly, the collective farms were broken up and returned to individual farmers, and the relations with the Catholic Church were improved.

The trend toward liberalization was reversed in the late 1960's, and an increase in food prices led to another wave of worker riots, in December 1970. At least 44 people were killed during this outbreak of violence, and Gomułka was replaced by Edward Gierek as head of the party. Gierek became an energetic promoter of détente with the West: During his term, three American presidents visited Poland (Richard Nixon, Gerald Ford, and Jimmy Carter), and Gierek in turn visited the United States and several West European countries.

Meanwhile, however, Poland was becoming increasingly indebted to the West. An announcement of food price increases in 1976 had to be revoked because of widespread strikes. Two years later the rising Polish nationalism was tremendously boosted when the archbishop of Cracow became Pope John Paul II. The pope visited his homeland in 1979, and everywhere he went he was welcomed by hundreds of thousands of people.

In June 1980, the government announced meat price increases, which again provoked widespread strikes and eventually led to the fall of Gierek. This time, however, the workers were much better organized and coordinated and soon won the right to form trade unions independent of the government. This was the first time that such unions had

Portraits of Lenin along city streets reflect the close ties between the Polish government and the USSR.

The labor union Solidarity led the struggle for more freedom for the Polish people.

been permitted in a Communist country. In October, Solidarity, a national confederation of trade unions led by Lech Wałęsa, was granted legal status. In February 1981, after further labor unrest, Defense Minister Wojciech Jaruzelski was named premier, and in October of the same year he became the first secretary of the Communist Party. Following a series of confrontations between Solidarity (the membership of which had grown to about 10 million workers, including about 700,000 party members) and the government over economic reforms and calls for democratic political changes, Jaruzelski declared martial law in December 1981. Solidarity was suspended, and about 10,000 people were arrested, including Wałęsa and other Solidarity leaders, and all freedoms and rights that had been gained in the previous 15 months were abolished. The United States protested and imposed economic sanctions on Poland.

Conditions continued to deteriorate, even after the government ended martial law in 1983. By 1989, Jaruzelski, in an effort to end the growing economic crisis, was forced to seek the help of Solidarity leaders, whose stature rose after Wałęsa received the Nobel Peace Prize in 1983. In a stunning series of events, the Communists were forced to relinquish more and more power until they agreed to free multiparty elections. Solidarity-backed candidates won a solid parliamentary majority and longtime Solidarity leader Tadeusz Mazowiecki was named prime minister. Jaruzelski retained the presidency, but his power was greatly restricted; some experts predicted that Lech Wałęsa would seek the presidential post in coming elections.

Reviewed by M.K. DZIEWANOWSKI, Boston University

Cesky Krumlov is a town in Bohemia, the most highly developed and populated region of Czechoslovakia.

CZECHOSLOVAKIA

Czechoslovakia's location in the heart of Europe has had a profound effect on the nation's history and its way of life. Czechoslovakia is wedged between Poland and Hungary. It shares a frontier with Germany on the west and with the Soviet Union on the east. Along Czechoslovakia's southwestern border lies Austria.

Czechoslovakia was, for decades after World War II, firmly locked into the Communist bloc of Soviet satellite nations. When Czechoslovakia tried to liberalize its policies in 1968—a time known as the "Prague Spring"—it suffered an invasion by Soviet and other Warsaw Pact forces. Of all the East European countries that were within the Soviet orbit, Czechoslovakia has the greatest historical, educational, and traditional links to the Western world.

THE LAND

Czechoslovakia was formed in 1919 from the former Austro-Hungarian territories of Bohemia, Moravia, Silesia, Slovakia, and Ruthenia.

Bohemia, in the west, is a plateau region of rolling land encircled by the Bohemian Forest, the Erzgebirge (Ore Mountains), and the Sudetes mountains. This part of Czechoslovakia is drained by the Elbe River and its main tributary, the Vltava. Prague, the capital of Czechoslovakia, is on the Vltava. Other well-known towns in the region are Plzeň, which is famous for its beer and its industries; Jáchymov, with its uranium deposits; and the resorts Karlovy Vary and Mariánské Lázně. Fertile farms and large industries flourish in Bohemia.

Moravia lies east of Bohemia. It is bordered on the north by Silesia, on the east by Slovakia, and on the south by Austria. This rolling lowland region is an important farming and industrial region, like its western neighbor Bohemia. The Moravian lowland is drained by the Morava River, which flows into the Danube, giving Czechoslovakia an all-water route to the Black Sea. Ostrava and Brno, the largest cities in Moravia, are important centers of industry.

Silesia, north of Moravia, lies partly in Poland and partly in Czechoslovakia. The narrow, mountainous slice of Silesia in Czechoslovakia is a popular resort area and a vital source of coal and iron for Czechoslovak industries.

Slovakia, which lies east of Moravia and Silesia, is a mountainous region whose best-known peaks are in the High Tatra of the Carpathian mountains. Although Slovakia has a generally mild climate and fertile soil, it was long the poorest of the provinces that became part of Czechoslovakia. Now crops ranging from wheat, barley, and sugar beets to paprika, melons, and sunflowers are raised. Many industries in Slovakia are connected with food processing, and in recent years other industries based on the region's mineral resources have grown up. The most important cities in Slovakia are Bratislava, Košice, Trnava, and Nitra.

Ruthenia, which was once the easternmost province of Czechoslovakia, became part of the Soviet Union in 1945.

THE PEOPLE

The Czechs and Slovaks are descended largely from Slavic tribes that settled in the area during the 5th and 6th centuries. Their languages are similar; most people who speak either Czech or Slovak understand the other language, although they may not be able to write it. There are several minorities: Poles in the north, Hungarians in Slovakia, and about 300,000 Gypsies. For decades the government has been trying to suppress the nomadic ways of the Gypsies, and most of them now hold menial jobs.

Slovakia had been dominated by Hungary until 1919, but contacts between Czechs and Slovaks developed during the 19th century, and it was the Slovaks who first began to talk about uniting the two nations. After the formation of the republic, however, the differences between the Czech and the Slovak ways of life and the contrasts between the overall political and economic development of the two parts of the new state caused problems. The Czechs neglected the Slovak economy and treated the Slovaks in a rather patronizing way, which they in turn deeply resented. This animosity eventually led to the formation of an independent Slovak state during World War II (independent in name only, because it was actually a puppet government of Nazi Germany).

After the Communist takeover in 1948, the Czechs again treated the Slovaks like poor relations, and the old resentments were kept alive. The constitution of 1960, proclaiming Czechoslovakia a socialist republic, further limited Slovak political power and strengthened the centralism of

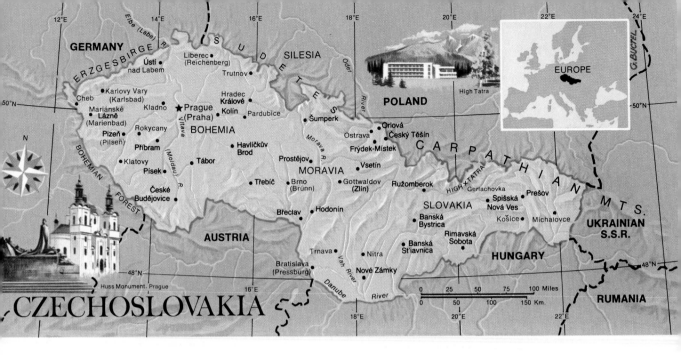

A NOTE ON PLACE-NAMES

A few cities and one river in Czechoslovakia are often still called by their former German names. This list gives Czechoslovakian place-names and their German equivalents.

Czechoslovak	German	Czechoslovak	German
Bratislava	Pressburg	Liberec	Reichenberg
Brno	Brünn	Mariánské Lázně	Marienbad
Jáchymov	Joachimsthal	Plzeň	Pilsen
Karlovy Vary	Karlsbad	Vltava River	Moldau River

FACTS AND FIGURES

OFFICIAL NAME: Czech and Slovak Federative Republic.

NATIONALITY: Czechoslovak(s).

CAPITAL: Prague (Praha).

LOCATION: East Central Europe. **Boundaries**—Poland; Ukrainia, Soviet Union; Hungary; Austria; Germany.

AREA: 49,371 sq. mi. (127,870 sq. km.).

PHYSICAL FEATURES: Highest point—Gerlachovka (8,737 ft.; 2,662 m.). **Lowest point**—535 ft. (163 m.). **Chief rivers**—Elbe, Oder, Vltava, Danube.

POPULATION: 15,658,079 (latest estimate).

MAJOR LANGUAGES: Czech and Slovak (official), Hungarian.

MAJOR RELIGION: Christianity.

GOVERNMENT: Emergent democracy. **Head of state**—president. **Head of government**—premier. **Legislature**—bicameral Federal Assembly.

CHIEF CITIES: Prague, Bratislava, Brno, Ostrava.

ECONOMY: Chief minerals—coal, coke, lignite, uranium, magnesite. **Chief agricultural products**—timber, wheat and other grains, vegetables, livestock. **Industries and products**—iron and steel, machinery and equipment, cement, sheet glass, transportation equipment, military supplies, chemicals, ceramics, wood, paper products. **Chief exports**—machinery and equipment, consumer goods, fuels, minerals, metals. **Chief imports**—fuels, minerals, metals, machinery and equipment, consumer goods.

MONETARY UNIT: Koruna.

Prague. Slovak dissatisfaction then became one of the important factors in a general political crisis that preceded the short-lived liberalization period called "Prague Spring" in 1968. The federalization law, which went into effect in January, 1969, was the only reform of the Prague Spring that survived the Soviet occupation of August 1968. This law gave the Czech and Slovak regional administrations comparable powers and responsibilities and made Czechoslovakia a federal republic. In a reversal of traditional attitudes, it is the Czechs who now tend to resent the Slovaks, because of their alleged expansiveness (particularly in Prague).

Czechoslovakia was officially atheistic during the years of Communist rule. There has been a resurgence of religious activities in recent years with more than 300,000 people signing a petition in 1988 asking for full religious freedom. The revolution of 1989 achieved new religious freedoms along with political liberalization.

Education

Since most mothers are employed, children usually start school at a very early age, often before they are 3 years old. Nurseries and pre-kindergartens are available everywhere, even in small villages. Free compulsory education begins at the age of 6 and lasts 9 years. The curriculum is uniform throughout the country, and the training is quite rigorous. Even well-educated parents often complain that they are unable to help their youngsters with their homework. Russian is taught as a second language from the fourth grade up, and other languages are taught as well, particularly English.

There are several types of secondary and vocational schools, and some 35 institutions of higher learning, including 5 universities. The competition for admission to universities is fierce. Students need to have excellent grades in their secondary schools, and a premium is put on technical skills that will help in the drive for development and increased trade with the West. Many thousands of foreign students also study in Czechoslovakia.

Music, Spas, and Sports

Czechoslovakia's spirit, a beautiful mixture of homesickness, happiness, and melancholy, is expressed perfectly in the music of its two foremost 19th-century composers, Bedřich Smetana and Antonín Dvořák. Smetana's *Má Vlast* (*My Country*) is Bohemia's musical life story, and

Karlovy Vary, noted for its many thermal springs, also hosts an international film festival each July.

his comic opera *Prodaná nevěsta* (*The Bartered Bride*) is known to every child. The foremost 20th-century composer is Leoš Janáček, whose symphonies and operas often are performed in the West. People love the moody folk songs and sing them in both city and country pubs. Music also is performed in the now public gardens of former aristocratic palaces. Young people look to the West for musical inspiration, and Western rock stars are quite well known.

All over Europe, Bohemian musicians are found both in great symphony orchestras and in obscure dance bands. In fact, Bohemian musicians are exports as well-known as Bohemian glassware and beer. Small villages have their brass bands, small towns their orchestras, and most of the larger cities have an opera house. Even the spas—mineral-springs resorts—have their orchestras.

The great Bohemian spas of Karlovy Vary, Mariánské Lázně, and Jáchymov have given real or imaginary relief to countless people from all over the world who came there suffering from a variety of afflictions. The most famous spa, Karlovy Vary, is popular with people who have lived too well and not too wisely during 11 months of the year and go there for the 12th month to atone for their gastronomic sins. At neighboring Mariánské Lázně, the overweight can lose pounds fast by drinking the waters and taking long walks. One of the loveliest and smallest of the resort towns is Jáchymov, which has been known for more than 500 years for its mineral deposits, including silver, and for its mineral waters.

Ideal conditions for winter sports are found especially in the High Tatra, a magnificent range that culminates in the 8,737-foot (2,663 meters) Gerlachovka. Among the rugged granite formations lie shimmering, deep, blue lakes, clear trout streams, and lovely valleys. Charming chalets stand in the midst of vast forests. The cost of a holiday is low, since part of it is paid by the national insurance system.

Winter sports have always been popular in Czechoslovakia, especially skiing and ice hockey. Many cities and towns have skating rinks. Large factories have their own teams, which they support on a large scale. Tournaments and international games are followed with nationwide interest. Czechoslovak amateur ice hockey teams long have been among the best in the world. Ice hockey competes in popularity with soccer, the traditional national sport of Czechoslovakia. Fans of rival clubs often get into heated discussions over the merits of their respective teams and then cool their tempers by drinking beer.

In recent years Czechoslovakia has become internationally famous for its tennis players, although the best-known among them, Martina Navratilova, is now a U.S. citizen. The government's national tennis program employs over 2,500 coaches to train some 30,000 players. The pressure to perform is great, but the program has been clearly successful.

PRAGUE, THE CAPITAL

Prague always has been a music-minded city. Wolfgang Amadeus Mozart wrote *Don Giovanni* for the Tyl Theater in Prague and conducted the first performance there. He once wrote that in Prague the people understood his music better than anywhere else. His wonderful *Le Nozze di Figaro* was a failure in Vienna but a smash hit in Prague. Today, the music of Mozart and other composers can be heard at countless concerts, particularly during the annual spring music festival.

Wenceslas Square, Prague's main thoroughfare, is named for the saint who brought Christianity to the area.

Prague is a thousand-year-old city. Around 965 a Jewish merchant from Spain described it as a busy town built of stone, where Slavs, Muslims, Jews, and Turks traded their goods. The brightest periods of Prague's history were always those times when the city opened itself to the world. During the reign of Emperor Charles IV in the 14th century, Prague attracted famous architects and sculptors from the rest of Europe. Another cosmopolitan period is connected with the reign of Emperor Rudolf II, around 1600. Rudolf invited well-known astronomers, artists, and musicians to his imperial court in Prague. In the 19th century, Prague became a cultural center for the national Czech revival, and after 1918 it was again a bustling, vigorous place, full of old charms and contemporary attractions. The shops were as beautiful as those of Paris and Vienna, and the restaurants were among the best in Europe. Prague's automat buffets with vast shelves of open-faced sandwiches were open 24 hours a day and were almost always crowded.

Prague had dozens of theaters, classical and experimental, serious and satirical. One of the greatest books of that period, *The Good Soldier Schweik,* is a devastating satire on narrowness and pettiness in both military and government life. Written by Jaroslav Hašek, the book relates the adventures of a Prague dogcatcher. He is drafted into the Austrian Army during World War I and disrupts army life by stubbornly carrying out stupid orders to the letter. Franz Kafka, a Prague German Jew, wrote his novels and stories about the absurdities of modern life at about the same time.

The atmosphere of the 1920's is gone, but Prague continues to be a lively city, with a rich cultural and social life. Many old buildings have been restored beautifully and several sections in the city's center are now pedestrian zones. The beauty of Prague is not as dazzling as that, for instance, of Paris, but it is a magical city that can possess your soul. Situated on seven hills like Rome, it has been called "Mother Prague of a Hundred Spires." Among its landmarks is one of Europe's oldest synagogues, with 13th-century Gothic architecture. Behind it is a Jewish cemetery, which may have been founded in the 11th century. Prague also has great palaces of baroque splendor, romantic squares with stone fountains, mysterious passageways, and old churches with tombs sunk deep in the ground.

But not all is old in Prague: the elegant modern subway, a few scattered glass-walled structures in the center, traffic jams, and pollution remind everyone that this is indeed the 20th century.

Other Czechoslovak Cities.   Today, two-thirds of Czechs and Slovaks live in the cities. After Prague, the largest city is Bratislava, the capital of Slovakia. Situated on the Danube, it is a leading river port. Almost as populous is Brno, the largest city in Moravia and a major industrial center. Other cities are Ostrava, in the coal-mining area of Silesia; Plzeň, with noted automobile works and famous Pilsner beer; and Kosice, an industrial city in eastern Slovakia.

ECONOMY

For centuries the Erzgebirge, running astride the border between Czechoslovakia and what was East Germany have yielded valuable minerals—not only silver but tin, lead, bismuth, zinc, and antimony. In 1727 large deposits of pitchblende, a greasy-looking ore that ranges in color from dirty-brown to asphalt-black, were discovered there. Pitchblende contains uranium and radium. It was from Jáchymov pitchblende that the Curies, after years of experimentation, extracted radium.

In the 19th century, Bohemia and Moravia became the most industrialized parts of the Austro-Hungarian Empire. After the formation of Czechoslovakia in 1918, the country began to build up worldwide markets for such products as glassware and textiles. Production of coke,

The iron and steel industry has become the most important branch of manufacturing in Czechoslovakia.

The manufacture of shoes, an early Slovak enterprise, was nationalized when the Communists came to power.

iron, steel, chemicals, and cement increased again. Czech plants manu-factured anything that could be made of steel, from railroad rolling stock to machine tools. Four automobile works—Praga, Aero, Skoda, and Tatra —began to produce and export cars. The Batǎ shoe factories in Zlin (now Gottwaldov), Moravia, became the largest enterprise of its kind in Eu-rope, selling inexpensive mass-produced shoes to many countries. Tomáš Batǎ, the founder of the company, had spent some time in the United States and became an admirer of Henry Ford, whose industrial practices he then adapted in Czechoslovakia. (After World War II, Batǎ's works were nationalized, but his descendants still manufacture shoes—in Latin America.) The trademark "Made in Czechoslovakia" became well-known throughout the world and was a guarantee of quality and precision.

The Depression of the 1930's hit the country very hard. Some recov-ery occurred after 1934, but the political upheavals of the following years made a full economic recovery impossible. In September 1938 the most industrialized border regions were taken over by Nazi Germany, which proceeded to mobilize the industrial resources of dismembered Czecho-slovakia for the German war machine.

Soon after the end of the war, more than 2,000,000 Sudeten-Ger-mans, who had lived for centuries in the Sudeten mountains near the German border, were expelled from Czechoslovakia. The expulsion was a bitter result of wartime hostilities, but it dealt a heavy blow to the Czechoslovak economy because many of the expelled Germans were highly skilled craftsmen and technicians.

Meanwhile, Russian visitors, almost unknown before, appeared in the resort spa of Jáchymov. Soon the region was sealed off and the "sightseers" began to develop uranium mines. Jáchymov ore has a very high pitchblende content—so high that for a time the estimated 50,000 miners (some of them prisoners) there were producing more uranium than the Soviet-operated mines in East Germany, where about 10 times as many people were working.

Agriculture in Czechoslovakia promises to be de-collectivized in the coming years.

After the Communist victory in 1948, virtually all economic activities were taken over by the state: railroads, banking, heavy and light industry, and services. Although the country recovered from the war years and new industries were developed, the centralized economy did not work well. In the 1960s, economists at the Czechoslovak Academy of Sciences prepared a series of reforms in order to make the economy more efficient and productive, but the implementation of these reforms was interrupted by the invasion of the Warsaw Pact armies in August, 1968.

Despite serious economic mismanagement under the Communists, Czechoslovakia is a highly industrialized country with a well-trained work force. It had one of the highest standards of living in the former Soviet bloc, and goods and services were often available through political connections and the black market. The new government has made progress toward a free-market economy a high priority. As outdated industrial equipment is replaced and foreign investment grows, the economic picture will continue to improve.

An important source of income is tourism, with well over 10 million tourists visiting the country each year. A number of super-modern hotels have been built to accommodate the flow of foreigners.

Farm Life

Cooperatives and state farms hold more than 95 percent of the arable land. Sugar beets are planted in the Elbe basin, northwest and east of Prague, and in Moravia. Wheat and barley are grown in these regions, and there is much dairy farming. In Moravia and Slovakia, wheat and barley are the chief crops below an altitude of about 1,300 ft. (400 m.); rye and oats take over on the higher slopes. Grain and potatoes are grown in southern Bohemia, and in the mountains surrounding the country there is livestock farming.

Under the Communists one-third of the agricultural area belonged to the state farms. Members of the state cooperatives grew fruits and vegetables on small private plots. Many families also raised poultry and pigs. Roast pork with dumplings and sauerkraut is the traditional national dish. For centuries Czechs have been raising carp in numerous ponds, particularly in southern Bohemia. The carp, much tastier than its wild American cousin, is a traditional food for Christmas Eve dinner virtually everywhere.

Farmers in Czechoslovakia live quite well, and there is a great surge of building activity in many villages, particularly in Slovakia. Typically, a new family home is a two-story brick house, often with a detached garage and usually with an informal garden full of flowers.

The best-known agricultural cooperative in Czechoslovakia was Slušovice, near Gottwaldav. Since the 1960s, it had grown into a kind of "state within a state." It had only a few thousand members, but in addition to its agricultural activities, it owned several restaurants, a car-rental service, a computer center, a horse racetrack, and an automobile racecourse. The cooperative also dealt directly with Western firms and had its own pension plan. Interestingly, Slušovice was located in the former "Baťa region."

HISTORY

The earliest known inhabitants of Czechoslovakia were two Celtic groups, the Boii and the Cotini. The Boii lived in the Bohemian basin and gave it the name it still bears today. In the middle of the 5th century Slavic tribes from the east settled in the valley of the Elbe. During the following 5 centuries various kingdoms were established, but the land knew little peace, since it was constantly being fought over by the Slavs, Germans, and Magyars.

In 1310 a German prince, John of Luxemburg, was elected king of Bohemia, the best-known of the provinces that were to become part of Czechoslovakia. Under the rule of his son Charles, the Czechs experienced the most brilliant chapter of their history. Charles became king of Bohemia in 1346 and Holy Roman emperor in 1355. Although brought up in France, he fell in love with Bohemia and made it the center of the empire. Prague's architecture still recalls this era.

The most famous of Prague's many spans across the Vltava River, Charles Bridge, was completed in 1357 and is a magnificent structure with its tower gateways and statues of saints. The bridge connects the Old Town, part of which dates from the 10th century, with the Lesser Town, whose beginnings date from the 13th century. The Gothic silhouette of Hradčany Castle still dominates the timeless beauty of Prague.

Charles was patron of a Prague school of painting. He ordered the making of a Latin-Czech dictionary, and in 1348 he founded Charles University of Prague, today one of the oldest in Europe.

One of the greatest Czechs of all time, John Huss, was elected rector of Charles University in 1402. A forerunner of the Protestant movement, Huss was a religious reformer, and his teachings brought on a long struggle, partly religious and partly political, called the Hussite wars. Two outstanding leaders of the Hussites were Jan Žižka of Trocnov and George of Poděbrad. George was king for a time. After his death in 1471, the fortunes of Bohemia took a turn for the worse.

Prague Castle, once home to the Bohemian kings, now houses the president of Czechoslovakia.

By that time the Habsburgs, the German-Austrian ruling family, were becoming ever stronger. They had held sway in Austria since 1278 and had taken over the reins of the Holy Roman Empire in 1438. Thus the Habsburgs were on the side of the Roman Catholic Church when, early in the 16th century, various groups began to split off to form Protestant sects. In history this period is called the Reformation.

In 1620, the Hussite armies were defeated by Habsburg forces in the battle of the White Mountain, at the gates of Prague. With that defeat, Bohemia and Moravia lost their independence. It was not to be regained for almost 300 years. The battle was one of the first engagements in the Thirty Years War, which wracked Europe from 1618 to 1648.

During the late 18th and early 19th centuries many of the subject peoples living in the Austrian Empire began to dream of and work for more freedom and autonomy within the empire. In 1848 there were revolutions in many parts of Europe, including Bohemia. The Czechs did not win all they hoped for, but by the end of the century they did obtain a number of political rights. Meanwhile, an intellectual revival and the growth of industry helped create a strong middle class, and the Czechs were reawakening as a nation.

The First Republic

When World War I broke out in 1914, various groups of Czech intellectuals and other leaders immediately closed ranks. They saw their opportunity and were determined to take it. Czech troops, who had been forced to fight in the Austrian army on the Eastern Front, escaped into Russian territory and formed the Czechoslovak Legion.

Czechoslovakia's greatest leader was Tomáš Garrigue Masaryk. During the war, Masaryk and his pupil Eduard Beneš worked actively for the establishment of an independent Czechoslovak state. Their efforts were crowned in October 1918 when the independence of Czechoslovakia was proclaimed. Masaryk became president of the new republic.

During the time of the so-called First Republic (1918–1938), Czechoslovakia was a relatively healthy, democratic state, with a full range of political and economic freedoms—while its neighbors were plagued with unrest, civil war, and dictatorship. The Czechoslovak constitution combined the best features of the constitutions of France and the United States. But the emerging threat of German Nazism in the 1930's soon undermined the republic. Czechoslovakia's large Sudeten-German minority—about 3,000,000 persons—resented the Czech political domination, and although they were prosperous, they quickly became prey to Nazi propaganda.

In September 1938, England, France, and Italy yielded to Hitler's demands and signed the infamous Munich agreement, granting him the so-called Sudetenland. The appeasement did not bring peace, however. In March 1939, Nazi troops marched into the remnants of Czechoslovakia, and Bohemia and Moravia became the Protectorate of Germany, while Slovakia was proclaimed an "independent" Slovak State. A few months later World War II started.

Eduard Beneš, president since 1935, went into exile after the Munich agreement and began once again to work for his country's independence. He set up a government-in-exile in London.

The Growth of Soviet Influence.   In 1945, during the closing months of the struggle in Europe, when the Germans were being pushed back on all sides, Soviet troops poured into Czechoslovakia. Beneš and his government had returned to Czechoslovakia after Germany's defeat, but they were soon forced to grant concessions to the Soviet Union, including the yielding of Ruthenia, the easternmost province of Czechoslovakia. Also, at least partly as a result of the wartime alliance with the Soviet Union, there was now a strong Czechoslovak Communist Party. It won 38 percent of the votes in the free general election of 1946.

The country was being drawn irresistibly into the Soviet sphere. The final blow fell in February, 1948, when the Communists, led by Klement Gottwald, took over the country in a fast, well-organized, bloodless coup d'état. Jan Masaryk, the son of the country's founding father, had been retained as foreign minister, but soon after the coup he died mysteriously after jumping, or being pushed, from a window of his office in Prague's Czernin Palace. Masaryk's death sealed the fate of the country. A Soviet-type constitution was adopted, and President Beneš was forced to resign. Gottwald became president.

What happened in Czechoslovakia thereafter follows the pattern of all the countries that fell into the Soviet orbit. Within a few years, the Communist Party became the only ruler in Czechoslovakia. All industries and businesses were nationalized, a strict censorship was introduced, and many people were imprisoned. A series of purges and show trials in the early 1950's strengthened the party's position.

As early as 1956, a few courageous and idealistic Communists began to call for policy changes, and in 1962 the Twelfth Congress of the Czechoslovak Communist Party decided to "investigate and correct" the "excesses" committed during the Stalinist era. But the investigations and corrections were undermined and delayed by Antonín Novotný, an arch-Stalinist, who had become head of the Communist Party in 1953 and president in 1957.

"The Spring Between Two Winters"

It was the writers, students, scientists, and intellectuals who led the movement for economic and political reforms in the late 1960s. In January 1968, Novotný was replaced as head of the Communist Party by Alexander Dubček, a soft-spoken Slovak, and the country plunged into a hectic 5-month period known since then as the Prague Spring. While the reformers within the Communist Party were formulating far-reaching programs in order to give socialism "a human face," numerous political and social groups began to form and voice their particular interests. General Ludvík Svoboda, an old, respected soldier, was elected president in March 1968; thousands of people persecuted during the Stalinist period were rehabilitated, and censorship was formally abolished.

As the changes in Czechoslovakia progressed, however, the Soviet Union became concerned that the reforms might prove contagious and "infect" the other socialist countries. The leaders of Poland and East Germany were also afraid that the winds of freedom from Czechoslovakia would threaten their regimes. Finally, on the night of August 20–21, about half a million Soviet and Warsaw Pact troops poured into Czechoslovakia and put a temporary end to the effort to change a repressive, centralized Communist system into a democratic socialist one.

Soon, all reforms were dismantled, reformers were expelled from the Party, and thousands of people lost their jobs. It is estimated that some 150,000 persons emigrated to the West. The new leadership of the country, under Gustáv Husák (who became both the head of the Communist Party and the president of the republic), introduced the policy of "normalization," which best can be described as a continual suppression of all change, innovation, free thought, and initiative. People reacted to this situation by retreating into their private lives. One of the most popular pastimes in the 1970s and 1980s was the construction of summer houses: most city dwellers seem to have a place in the country to which they devote all their weekends and most of their energy.

Among those who suffered most under the "normalization" were writers, scholars, and journalists, with the best among them blacklisted and repeatedly harassed. Nevertheless, dissident activity continued to grow and in 1977 the Charter 77 movement was born. Repression continued by the hard-line authorities and, until 1989, Czechoslovakia was considered one of the more staunchly Communist regimes in the Eastern bloc. In 1989, with change sweeping neighboring countries, Soviet president Mikhail Gorbachev admitted that the 1968 invasion had been a mistake. The Slovak Communist Party split with the National Party and the new Civic Forum opposition movement grew in size and influence, forcing reform and reorganization within the regime of Gustáv Husák. By December 1989, there was a noncommunist coalition government in power, and Husák had resigned under pressure. Two of Czechoslovakia's most respected dissidents rose to political prominence: Václav Havel, a playwright and signatory of the Charter 77 manifesto, and Alexander Dubček, the architect of the 1968 Prague Spring. The two men

The historic bridges and churches of Prague survived World War II virtually undamaged.

agreed to join forces in new elections. Havel was elected president of Czechoslovakia, and Dubček was selected as the president of the National Assembly. It was an astonishing turnaround of political fortunes that captured the attention of audiences around the world.

GOVERNMENT

After the collapse of the Communist regime in 1989, Czechoslovakia joined the ranks of multiparty democracies. It is a federated republic of two nations—the Czechs and the Slovaks. The Federal Assembly is composed of the Chamber of the People and the Chamber of Nations. Each of the two nations has a national council, which elects members of the Chamber of Nations, while the deputies in the Chamber of the People are popularly elected.

JOSEPH WECHSBERG, Foreign correspondent, *The New Yorker*

Budapest, Hungary's capital, was originally two cities, Buda and Pest, separated by the Danube River.

HUNGARY

In the heart of Europe, there is a small country that for over 1,000 years has been engaged in a cruel struggle with great powers and foreign rulers to keep its independence. It is the Republic of Hungary, the home of the Magyars, a people who are not related to any of their many neighbors: the Yugoslavs, the Austrians, the Rumanians, the Czechs and Slovaks, or the Russians.

THE LAND

As a result of World War I, Hungary was reduced to one-fourth of its former size. It is now a landlocked country.

The Danube River, Duna in Hungarian, which forms part of the Czechoslovak-Hungarian border, turns south and cuts through the country, flowing in a southerly direction. Most of eastern Hungary makes up an extensive lowland, the Great Plain (Alföld). To the south and west of the Danube lies Transdanubia (the country across the Danube). This is a region of undulating hills, wide valleys, and woods of beech and oak trees. To the northwest is the Small Plain, or Little Alföld (Kis Alföld).

In the north of Hungary, especially in the northeast, hills and ranges of low mountains stand out against the horizon. In the north central highland belt are mountains of volcanic origin—the Börzsöny, Cserhát, Mátra, Bükk, and Zempléni—separated by river valleys. These mountains have one of the largest cave systems in Europe, and many visitors come to explore the underground world of stalactites. Mount Kékes, at 3,330 feet (1,015 meters) the highest peak in the country, rises in the Mátra Mountains.

The Danube, which crosses the Little Alföld, breaks through some low hills and continues south through the Great Plain on its way to the Black Sea. It provides an important trade route between Hungary and its neighbors. The main tributary of the Danube is the Tisza River, which also crosses the entire country from north to south.

In western Hungary is Lake Balaton, at 230 square miles (600 square kilometers) the largest lake in central Europe. Often called the Hungarian sea, Lake Balaton attracts about 1,000,000 visitors a year who come to swim, sail, and fish in its lovely fresh, turquoise waters. Extinct volcanoes mark the skyline on the northern shore, and in the valleys nearby are old trees, rare plants, and exotic flowers. In the marshland at the southwest corner of the lake, migratory birds, including snow-white herons, pelicans, cormorants, bustards, and other rare birds, come to breed.

The climate in Hungary is continental, with seasons of almost equal length. More rain falls in western Transdanubia than in the eastern Great Plain, and in the west the winters and summers are more temperate than in the east. It is sunnier in Hungary than in other countries of the same latitudes, and the long, warm, sunny autumn helps produce fine fruits and sweet wine grapes.

Natural Resources.   Hungary has little mineral wealth. Some hard coal, considerably larger amounts of lignite, or brown coal, and natural gas are present. But additional amounts of coal, much of the country's oil, and coke and iron ore for steel production must be imported. Iron ore is imported mainly from the U.S.S.R. and Czechoslovakia and is shipped on Danube barges. Since the flat terrain provides Hungary with no source of waterpower, coal is used to generate electricity. The first Hungarian nuclear power plant began to operate in 1982. Extensive de-

Towns dating back to the Middle Ages are found throughout the scenic Hungarian countryside.

posits of bauxite, the raw material for aluminum, comprise the greatest mineral wealth of Hungary. Much of it is exported, since it takes large amounts of power to manufacture aluminum.

THE PEOPLE

In the late 9th century, a seemingly endless column of hundreds of thousands of people crossed the northeastern Carpathians into what is now Hungary. There were fierce horsemen wearing long felt coats; pointed, fur-trimmed caps; and leather boots. Their sabers, bows, and quivers hung from their silver-decorated belts. Women and small children sitting on carpets and furs were inside some of the large, covered wagons, pulled by long-horned oxen. Other wagons carried agricultural tools—iron plows, hoes, sickles—as well as the implements of armorers, saddlers, bow makers, potters, and silversmiths. Behind the wagons came herds of cattle, horses, water buffalo, and sheep. The cattle were driven along by dogs—big, white shaggy Komondors and lively little black pulis. The wave of people and cattle descended to the great plain.

Historians believe there were 500,000 Magyars in this invasion. They had come from the area north of the Black Sea. In about 10 years, these fierce horsemen absorbed or conquered the Slavic and Avar groups who had occupied most of the Carpathian Basin. The conquerors were the ancestors of today's Magyars, who are also known as Hungarians.

In contrast to the past, there are no large minorities in Hungary today. Germans account for about 0.5 percent of the population, and

Urban Hungarians often shop at outdoor markets for fresh fruits and vegetables.

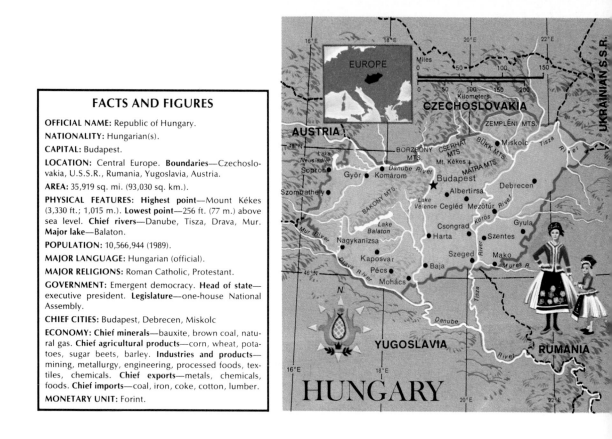

FACTS AND FIGURES

OFFICIAL NAME: Republic of Hungary.

NATIONALITY: Hungarian(s).

CAPITAL: Budapest.

LOCATION: Central Europe. **Boundaries**—Czechoslovakia, U.S.S.R., Rumania, Yugoslavia, Austria.

AREA: 35,919 sq. mi. (93,030 sq. km.).

PHYSICAL FEATURES: Highest point—Mount Kékes (3,330 ft.; 1,015 m.). **Lowest point**—256 ft. (77 m.) above sea level. **Chief rivers**—Danube, Tisza, Drava, Mur. **Major lake**—Balaton.

POPULATION: 10,566,944 (1989).

MAJOR LANGUAGE: Hungarian (official).

MAJOR RELIGIONS: Roman Catholic, Protestant.

GOVERNMENT: Emergent democracy. **Head of state**—executive president. **Legislature**—one-house National Assembly.

CHIEF CITIES: Budapest, Debrecen, Miskolc

ECONOMY: Chief minerals—bauxite, brown coal, natural gas. **Chief agricultural products**—corn, wheat, potatoes, sugar beets, barley. **Industries and products**—mining, metallurgy, engineering, processed foods, textiles, chemicals. **Chief exports**—metals, chemicals, foods. **Chief imports**—coal, iron, coke, cotton, lumber.

MONETARY UNIT: Forint.

there are also about 200,000 Gypsies, some of whom speak their mother language, Romany. A large Hungarian minority—almost 2 million people—lives in neighboring Rumania and has caused friction between the two countries because the Hungarian government complains about discrimination against the Rumanian Hungarians.

Way of Life. After World War II and the coming of Communism, the social upheaval in Hungary was enormous. Before the war, society was sharply divided between the ruling classes and the people. Political power was primarily in the hands of large landholders and industrial, military, and religious leaders. Their Hungary was known for its frivolous living style.

When the Communists took over in 1949, they nationalized most of the industry and collectivized the agriculture, and thus leveled differences in wealth. Living standards increased in the 1970s, with most people having second or third jobs, but the next decade witnessed a growing political, economic, and social crisis, reflected in the world's highest suicide rate and extremely high rates of divorce, alcoholism, and heart attacks. According to government figures, by the end of the 1980s, almost 40 percent of the population had incomes below the official poverty level.

Education is compulsory through 10 grades, and most children start school before the age of six. Secondary education can be pursued at more than 800 grammar, vocational, and technical schools. Admission to the universities in Hungary is difficult to obtain. Only the best students are accepted. For some years, children of workers and peasants were favored, but today student qualifications are the main criteria for admission.

No accurate statistics are available on religion in Hungary, but it is believed that about two-thirds of the Hungarians are Roman Catholics, and most of the rest are Protestants, mainly Calvinists. While the Communists held power, the church was strictly controlled by the state. In the late 1970s, the relations between the state and the Roman Catholic Church improved, and in 1978, Hungary established diplomatic relations with the Vatican.

One phase of life that all Hungarians enjoy is fine foods. It is both an art and a national pastime. Food is quite plentiful, and cooking, which makes use of spices mixed with meat, fish, and chicken, is superb. Hungary is often said to have more good restaurants than all of the rest of Eastern Europe combined. *Gulyás* (goulash) and chicken paprikás are famous dishes. Red paprika, made of peppers grown in Hungary, is the national spice. Hungary has wonderful native wines, fine apricot brandy, delicious salami, paté of goose liver, and a variety of delicate pastries.

Hungarians have always been avid sportsmen. A large percentage of the population are registered in sports clubs, where they participate in track and field events, swimming, water polo, soccer, fencing, weight lifting, gymnastics, shooting, boxing, and wrestling.

Language. Although a number of individual Hungarian words may sound familiar to Western ears, and though the Roman alphabet is used, the language itself is a unique one. It is not related to any of the Germanic, Romance, or Slavic languages. Instead it is one of the Uralic family of languages, which also includes Finnish and Estonian.

Stress in Hungarian is placed on the first syllable, and the letters of the alphabet always stand for the same sound, which makes pronunciation relatively easy. Because of the great flexibility of the language, translation from Hungarian encounters almost insurmountable obstacles. Many significant Hungarian literary figures are completely unknown except to Hungarians. The works of only a few have been translated. Sándor Petőfi, who died in 1849 at the age of 26, wrote fervent poems in praise of liberty and equality. The 19th-century novelist Mór Jókai wrote to give inspiration to a nation defeated by the Habsburgs of Austria. His thrilling stories are still very popular. Imre Madách, writing at the same time, expressed his ideas in poetic dramas of great power. His most famous philosophical drama, called *The Tragedy of Man,* tells the history of mankind as shown to Adam by Lucifer. The poet Endre Ady, who wrote in the early 20th century, revived ancient forms of Hungarian poetry to express in symbolic language of enormous force the need for change in Hungary. Hungarians consider Attila József to be the greatest modern poet. His works are scarcely known outside Hungary, however, because they are difficult to translate well. Hungary's best-known writer gained fame outside his homeland. He was Ferenc Molnár (1878–1952). His romantic plays such as *Liliom*—which became the musical *Carousel*—were great popular successes. One of the first leftist intellectuals who denounced Stalinism was the Hungarian-born Arthur Koestler, whose political novel *Darkness at Noon* (1940) is a brilliant analysis of totalitarianism. György Lukacs (1885–1971), a controversial Marxist thinker, was one of the outstanding personalities of European culture. Among the contemporary writers, the best-known is György Konrad, some of whose writings were suppressed in Hungary during the years of Communist rule. Some of his works were available in the West.

The development of Hungarian music came later than that of literature, but music and musicians from Hungary have enriched the Western world. Franz (Ferenc) Liszt, the 19th-century pianist, created the symphonic poem. He also composed concertos, sonatas, ballads, rhapsodies, and études that deeply influenced composers of the following generations. He became the first director of the Hungarian Academy of Music, which has since educated conductors and concert artists heard in many countries.

Two later towering figures in the music world, Béla Bartók (1881–1945) and Zoltán Kodály (1882–1967), studied Magyar folk music. Starting with folk music as his source material, Bartók went on to create 20th-century masterpieces for individual instruments and for the orchestra. Kodály's great choral works are also rooted in Hungarian folk music.

In Hungary, gypsy (*cigány*) orchestras delight people wherever they gather. Concerts and operas are always crowded. Many Hungarian operettas, such as those of Franz (Ferenc) Lehár, who wrote *The Merry Widow,* are very popular.

The Sciences. Hungary is proud of the large number of eminent scientists their small nation has produced. János Bolyai contributed to modern ideas of relativity and space physics. Ignaz Semmelweis, who discovered the cause of puerperal (childbirth) fever, is known in medical history as the savior of mothers. Two Hungarian physicists, Leo Szilard and Edward Teller, made significant contributions to the development of atomic energy while working in the United States. Three of the five Hungarian-born Nobel prize winners in science—Georg von Békésy, Albert Szent-Györgyi, and Eugene P. Wigner—lived and worked in the U.S.

CITIES

Budapest, the Capital. Budapest, the capital city, has about one fifth of the population of Hungary, and the whole metropolitan area accounts for over one fourth of the country's population. In north central Hungary, close to the border of Czechoslovakia, Budapest is one of the leading cities in Eastern Europe. At the hub of Hungary's vast network of roads, railways, and waterways, it is the gateway for travelers whether they come by plane, train, or Danube steamboat or hydrofoil.

The mighty Danube divides Hungary and also divides its capital. Buda, on the west bank, and Pest, on the east, were once independent cities. They were merged in 1873 and also joined with them was Óbuda, another old town on the hilly west bank of the Danube. Pest, built on flatland at the beginning of the Great Plain, is more modern than Buda. It is along the Danube on the outskirts of Pest that the city's factories, warehouses, and shipbuilding yards are located. More than 50 percent of Hungary's industry is concentrated in or near the capital.

A uniquely beautiful city, Budapest is graced by eight bridges that cross the Danube. Part of the city is situated on picturesque hills with wooded slopes and huge parks. There are 123 thermal springs within the city, making it the largest spa in the world. It is also a great cultural center, with many theaters, two opera houses, and three major symphony orchestras. And it boasts dozens of good restaurants and elegant, fashionable shops, the best of them on Váci Utca, an equivalent of New York's Fifth Avenue. In the middle of the Danube are islands, including the lovely Margaret Island, with its huge park and famous luxury hotel.

The imposing House of Parliament, completed in 1903, stands on the Pest side of the Danube.

Budapest offers a living picture book of Hungarian history. At its northern border are the excavated remains of Celtic settlements from the Copper Age. Close by, within the city limits, are the ruins of Aquincum, the capital of Roman Pannonia, where Valentinian II was proclaimed emperor in A.D. 375. Nearer the center of the city is a recently discovered Roman amphitheater built to hold about 16,000 spectators. Close to it are the ruins of the 4th-century Christian chapel that marked the first appearance of Christianity in the region.

There are also Romanesque, Gothic, and baroque buildings in Hungary. Castle Hill, the ancient seat of Hungarian kings, has been restored to its original style after being bombed in World War II. Next to it is the famous Gothic Coronation Church of Matthias, where the Hungarian kings were crowned. A part of the rebuilt Royal Palace became home to the National Library in the 1970's. A great museum is housed in one section of the palace. The Neo-Gothic Parliament Building, completed in 1903, stands by the river on the Pest side of the city.

Budapest has had public transportation since 1866, when horse-drawn trams were first introduced. Old-fashioned rattling streetcars still can be seen in the streets, but a modern subway built in the 1970's now takes care of a large part of public transport.

Other Cities. **Pécs**, in the south, is both a mining center and a university town. Around the city are Hungary's largest coal mines and uranium mines. Hungary's oldest university was founded there in 1367. Pécs also has a famous 11th-century cathedral. **Miskolc**, a growing industrial town, is the center of northern mining activity. **Debrecen**, in the east, is an old college city with historic buildings. **Szeged,** to the west on the Tisza River, has a neo-Romanesque Cathedral Square used for open-air drama and opera performances. Around the square is the Hall of Fame arcade with busts and reliefs depicting great Hungarians.

ECONOMY

Agriculture. Today, although Hungary has a higher percentage of land used for farming than any other European country, less than one-third of the people work on farms. Under Communist rule, almost all the farming was done on state farms or cooperatives where laborers received fixed wages. They raised wheat, rye, corn, potatoes, sugar beets, and tobacco, and were guaranteed an annual wage by the state in much the same way as were factory workers.

Members of collective farms were allocated small plots for their own use. They were permitted to market their produce from these lots. There were about 1.8 million such plots, at one time producing about one-third of all Hungarian food. With the end of Communist rule in 1989, Hungary established a policy of encouraging the development of a free-market economy. This policy will increase the number of private farmers cultivating private lands.

Vineyards thrive in Hungary's climate. Some grapes are grown for an unusual wine known as Bull's Blood.

Industry. Largely lacking in the raw materials for heavy industry, Hungary has sought sound industrial development in those industries requiring much skill but little material. Hungary's major industries include the manufacture of machinery, machine tools, and transportation equipment. Electrical appliances, agricultural machinery, trucks, and bicycles are among the products made. There is a growing chemical industry in Hungary, particularly of pharmaceutical products. Much of the agricultural wealth is processed into canned foods, wines, and beer.

Economic Reforms. In 1968, Hungary introduced a series of far-reaching economic reforms, called the New Economic Mechanism (also labeled as Goulash or Paprika Socialism). These reforms included the reduction of centralized planning, introduction of some private enterprise, and increased economic contacts with the West. Initially, the reforms produced a sort of economic miracle, and the country seemed the most vigorous and dynamic in Eastern Europe: Tens of thousands of Hungarians started to work as private home builders, repairmen, and craftsmen of various kinds; shops were full of Western goods; and joint ventures with Western companies were on the increase.

By the mid-1980s, however, the economic miracle began to show ominous cracks. The foreign debt of Hungary is one of the highest per person in the world. Inflation has brought great hardships to most of the people, particularly those who are either too old or do not have enough necessary skills to take on second jobs. According to Hungarian sources, three-fourths of all employed people in the late 1980s had to supplement their income by secondary employment, which raised their average work week to 72 hours.

In March 1990, the International Monetary Fund (IMF) approved more than $200 million in standby credit for Hungary. Inflation remained a serious problem, but American, Japanese, and other Western corporations began a number of large joint ventures in Hungary, generating needed capital and jobs.

GOVERNMENT

For 40 years, Hungary was a Communist state. Then, in 1989, a new constitution was endorsed that stripped the Communist Party of the monopoly on power that it had held for 40 years. The National Assembly is made up of 386 freely elected deputies from a wide array of parties. The Presidential Council was abolished, and the office of executive president was established as head of state. The president names the premier, who is the acting head of government. The Communist Party in Hungary renounced Marxism and changed its name to the Hungarian Socialist Party. The new party, which undertook sweeping reforms in an effort to gain broader popular appeal, fared better in the 1990 elections than many domestic and foreign observers had expected.

HISTORY

Hungarians date the beginning of their country from 896, the year of the Magyar conquest of the area. The area had seen many invaders before the Magyars. It was once a part of the Roman Empire and was later overrun by Huns, Slavs, and Germanic tribes. The Magyars established themselves in the region, and Stephen I (István in Hungarian) became the first Christian ruler. He asked the Pope for recognition as king of Hungary, and on Christmas Day, A.D. 1000, he was crowned with a crown sent by the Pope. Later he was canonized and became the patron saint of Hungary. For more than 900 years, the Crown of Saint Stephen was the crown of the kings of Hungary.

King Stephen organized his state into counties on the model of Charlemagne's empire. When German armies invaded Hungary, he drove them from the country. The Germans made many later attempts to conquer Hungary; each time they were defeated. In the 12th century, the Hungarians were threatened by the Byzantine (Greek) Empire, but this attempted take-over also failed.

In the 13th century, Mongols (Tatars) swept over Hungary, pillaging and burning the countryside and slaughtering half the population in two years. In 1301, the able Árpád dynasty, descendants of the founder of Hungary, died out, and after a period of struggle, the French Anjou dynasty began to reign. During the 14th century, under Charles Robert and Louis the Great, Hungary became the leading Central European power.

By the middle of the 15th century, the Ottoman Turks were threatening the Balkan Peninsula, and soon they began to raid Hungary. From 1443 to 1456 the great Hungarian military leader, János Hunyadi, fought them off. In 1456 he defeated Sultan Mohammed II at Belgrade (now the capital of Yugoslavia) and saved Hungary and Europe from the Turks for another 70 years. His son, King Matthias Corvinus, made Hungary one of the most powerful countries in Europe. His court attracted scholars and artists. He founded a university, the famous Corvina Library, and a fine museum. After his death in 1490, the nobles fought over who was to be his successor, and the country was filled with dissension. The peasants, oppressed by the powerful nobles, rose in revolt in 1514. The uprising was put down with great cruelty. This time the invading Turks found a weakened and divided country. In 1526, on the plains near Mohács, the Hungarian Army suffered a total defeat. Even today Hungarians, when pressed, will say jokingly, "Don't worry, more was lost at Mohács!"

The country was cut apart. Central and southern Hungary, including the capital, Buda, were occupied by the Turks for a century and a half. The west and north came under the Habsburg emperors of the Holy Roman Empire. All that remained of Hungary was Transylvania, now mostly in Rumania. The Transylvanian Diet enacted laws providing for extension of the freedom of religion to Calvinists, Lutherans, Unitarians, and Catholics, a revolutionary idea in the 16th century. The ruling Hungarian princes fought the Habsburg king and also secured religious liberty and constitutional rights from the Habsburgs for northern and western Hungary.

In 1686, Buda was recaptured from the Turks by Habsburg forces with the help of armies from other countries of Western Europe. The Turks were driven out of Hungary, but the entire country then fell under the domination of the Austrian Habsburgs. Hatred for Austria grew, especially when attempts were made to impose the German language and customs on the Hungarian people. In 1825, a movement was begun by Count István Széchenyi, a Hungarian statesman, to revive the oppressed nation morally, socially, and economically.

In 1848, revolutions erupted all over Europe. Hungary, under the leadership of Lajos Kossuth rose to demand independence from Austria.

Heroes' Square in Budapest is dominated by a monument to the Magyar conquest of the area now known as Hungary.

The Austrians, assisted by Russia, crushed the revolt and forced Kossuth into exile. The Hungarians made use of the tactics of passive resistance. They were so successful that the Habsburgs were forced to compromise. The Compromise of 1867 created the Dual Monarchy of Austria-Hungary, with Hungary accepting the Austrian Emperor Franz Joseph as king, but Austria agreed to recognize Hungary's internal autonomy.

THE 20TH CENTURY

After having tried to prevent the war, Hungary during World War I fought on the side of Germany and Austria. With the defeat came the loss of nearly 75 percent of Hungarian territory, one third of all the Magyar people, and half of the country's industry. A democratic revolution broke out but was unsuccessful. A Communist regime took over briefly. Soon, however, conservatives came back to power under Admiral Miklós Horthy, who reestablished the monarchy without a king. He ruled as regent. The Hungarians, determined to recover their lost territories, turned to Germany and Italy for help. From 1938 to 1941, Hungary, with the aid of Germany, was successful in regaining part of its lost territories. But in 1944 during World War II, the Germans, fearing the Hungarians would try to conclude a separate armistice with the Western Allies, invaded the country. The Soviet armed forces drove the German armies out of Hungary between 1944 and 1945. Hungary once again was forced to give up her old lands, and once again occupation brought wholesale destruction and violence.

In 1945, a democratic government was emerging in Hungary, and a republic was officially proclaimed. Land was distributed to the peasants.

Within a few years, however, the Communists took over. By 1949, a Stalinist dictatorship had been established under Mátyás Rákosi. Democratic institutions were abolished, and repression was widespread. Years of terror followed. After Stalin's death in 1953, Rákosi was deposed. Imrè Nagy, who succeeded Rákosi as premier, ended the reign of terror, released all political prisoners, and gave the people more and more freedom. The Russians, fearful of losing Hungary, helped Rákosi and later his right-hand man, Gerő, back to power. But the forces of freedom could not be contained. On October 23, 1956, a revolution broke out. The Freedom Fighters, as the rebel students and workers were known, were supported by the overwhelming majority of Hungarians. They briefly controlled Budapest, but they could not withstand a Soviet army. In 2 weeks of revolt, about 5,000–6,000 Hungarians were killed, 13,000 were wounded, and 20,000 apartments were destroyed. In the wake of the uprising, some 200,000 people left for the West, 40,000 were imprisoned, and about 280 were hanged, including Imrè Nagy. János Kádár became the head of the new Soviet-sponsored government.

After 1960, a delicate compromise between the nation and the Kádár government took shape. Kádár's economic and political liberalization and his policy of national reconciliation made him the most respected Communist leader, and Hungarians, for their part, took care not to overstep certain limits: not to challenge the relationship with the Soviet Union or the leading role of the Party. The compromise worked very well for over 2 decades. The average Hungarian, while still unwilling to accept Soviet domination and basically pro-Western because of ties of tradition, culture, and religion, became resigned to an inner neutrality. The improving living conditions, a relatively free travel policy to the West, and the absence of political repression made life in Hungary much more pleasant than in the rest of Eastern Europe.

But by the late 1980s, a sense of political dead-end had become pervasive. The aging Kádár seemed unwilling to step down, the Party was in disarray, and people were dissatisfied. At a dramatic national Communist Party conference in May 1988, however, Kádár was shifted to the newly created ceremonial post of president. He was succeeded by Karoly Grosz, who advocated economic reform. Kádár's death in July 1989 almost seemed to symbolize the enormous changes that were then sweeping across Hungary. As it introduced its own program for multiparty elections, Hungary helped to precipitate revolutionary changes in other East European countries, especially East Germany. Hungary's decision to open its borders created a route for tens of thousands of East Germans to escape westward through neighboring Hungary. Hungary also announced plans in 1990 to withdraw from the Warsaw Pact, speeding the end of the Cold War. Negotiations for the withdrawal of Soviet forces from the country are continuing, with many observers seeing good prospects for success.

In the past, Hungary outlasted the Ottoman Turks and the Hapsburg Empire, powerful opponents who defeated and subjugated Hungary. In the late 20th century, Hungary has outlasted domination by an even more powerful neighbor, the Soviet Union. The ability to survive under these foreign occupations is evidence that Hungarians live with a constant awareness of their past and faith in their future.

ISTVÁN CSICSERY-RÓNAY, University of Maryland

In Yugoslavia's Herzegovina region, the mixture of ethnic groups has led to a blending of architectural styles.

YUGOSLAVIA

Yugoslavia, the Land of the South Slavs, is the largest country on the Balkan Peninsula in southeastern Europe. In the course of its short history as a nation, Yugoslavia has been a kingdom, a dictatorship, an occupied territory, a Communist nation, and now an emerging multiparty democracy faced with ethnic and national forces that threaten to splinter its fragile unity. Yugoslavia's location astride one of the natural pathways between Europe and the Orient made it a land where cultures met and merged. A country of six contentious republics, five nationalities, four languages, three religions, and two alphabets, it was long held together by one party—the League of Communists of Yugoslavia.

THE PEOPLE

The six republics that make up Yugoslavia are Serbia, Croatia, Slovenia, Bosnia and Herzegovina, Montenegro, and Macedonia. (To complicate matters further, it should be remembered that Serbia is the home of Yugoslavia's largest minority group—most of the nearly 1 million Albanians who live in the autonomous province of Kosovo-Metohija.)

Languages. The five related South Slav peoples who live in the six republics are the Serbs, Croats, Slovenes, Montenegrins, and Macedonians. The four languages most widely spoken in Yugoslavia are Serbian,

Croatian, Slovenian, and Macedonian. Serbian and Croatian are usually referred to as one language—Serbo-Croatian—because they are so similar. Serbo-Croatian is the main language of Serbia, Croatia, Bosnia and Herzegovina, and Montenegro. But even a newcomer to Yugoslavia will be ready by now for an added complication—two ways of writing the language. Croatia, Slovenia, and parts of Bosnia and Herzegovina use the Latin alphabet. The others use the Cyrillic alphabet that is used by many other Slavic peoples, particularly the Russians.

Religion.   The different scripts reflect the conversion of the South Slavs to two branches of the Christian faith centuries ago. The Croats and Slovenes as well as some Bosnians were converted to Catholicism by missionaries from Rome. The remaining South Slavs were converted to the Eastern Orthodox Church and later formed the independent Serbian Orthodox Church. The Gospels were first translated into Slavic in the 11th century by the monks Cyril and Methodius, and it is from Cyril's name that the script derives its name. A third major religion—Islam—was introduced into large areas of present-day Yugoslavia by the conquering Turks between the 14th and 16th centuries.

Education.   The Yugoslavians have succeeded in making one nation out of so many different elements, and each of the republics and each of the peoples have a large degree of political and cultural autonomy. As a result, even the minorities—Albanian, Hungarian, Bulgarian, Czech, Slovak, Italian, Rumanian, Turkish, and Ruthenian—have schools in which instructors use the minority language. All Yugoslavians are required to attend school from the age of 7 to 15. Students who plan to continue their education at a university or technical school generally attend a gymnasium after 6 years of elementary school. There are over 100 schools and technical institutes for higher education.

The Arts.   Variety and age-old traditions are the hallmark of Yugoslavia's arts, as they are of every other aspect of the nation's life. Every educated non-Yugoslavian has heard of the great modern Croatian sculptor Ivan Meštrović and of the distinguished contemporary Bosnian writer, Ivo Andrić, who won the Nobel prize for literature. Yet few outsiders are aware of the great religious frescoes that decorate many of the monasteries and churches of Yugoslavia or of the nation's ancient literary traditions. The most fascinating of the old literary works are the *pesme*—epic poems about historical events—that are still sung or recited to the accompaniment of a gusla, a mournful sounding one-string instrument that is played with a bow. Between the bards of old and modern times hundreds of distinguished poets, playwrights, and novelists have contributed to the nation's literary heritage. In addition to Andrić, the best-known modern writers are Miroslav Krleža, a poet and playwright, and Milovan Djilas and Vladimir Dedijer, who are well-known for their observations on recent Yugoslavian history.

Way of Life.   The variety that is evident in every aspect of Yugoslavia's landscape and traditions is faithfully reflected in the daily life of the people. The bustling industrial cities of the nation offer their own dramatic contrast to the gentle pace of the almost timeless villages in the mountains, where life seems to go on as it has for centuries, almost untouched by plagues, invasions, wars, or changes in government. Changes are coming, however, even to the remotest corner of the land as roads, radios, telephones, and television link the people together.

Even now some generalizations can be made about the Yugoslavians. They are almost one in their passion for soccer—the national sport—and chess, the most popular indoor game. Yugoslavians are enthusiastic movie fans, and several Yugoslavian films and animated cartoons have won international prizes. But for many Yugoslavians the weekly trip to the market is still the highlight of a life devoted to hard work. For the visitor the market offers a colorful spectacle, with handsome people dressed in traditional costumes choosing among an attractive array of goods ranging from brilliant textiles to beautifully arranged mountains of red and green peppers.

Indeed, in Yugoslavia one can "taste" history, for each occupying force has left its mark on the local cuisine. In the north the most popular dishes reflect centuries of Austrian and Hungarian influence. The Turkish and Italian kitchens can be detected in other parts of the nation. If there is such a thing as a typical Yugoslavian meal it would be a blend of all these influences resulting in superbly seasoned soups called *čorbas,* followed perhaps by a stew or goulash dish. Grilled meats are often served, too. Delicious fruits from the slopes of Slovenia make a popular dessert, but Italian ice cream or *pita,* an Austrian-style strudel, may be served for dessert. Small, sweet cups of Turkish coffee may complete the meal or can be sipped at one of the *kafanas*—coffeehouses—that are everywhere. A universally popular drink is *šljivovica*—a potent plum brandy.

THE LAND

Yugoslavia shares its land borders with seven nations: Italy in the northwest, Austria and Hungary in the north and northeast, Rumania in the northeast, Bulgaria in the east, Greece and Albania in the south. The nation's long western coast faces the Adriatic Sea.

The Yugoslavians like to say that when God created the earth, He took all the leftover stones and put them on their land. In fact, all but about one fifth of Yugoslavia is covered by mountains, plateaus, and hills. The Alps that curve across Europe end as the Slovenian Alps of northern Yugoslavia. They are usually divided into the Karawanken and the Julian Alps. The 9,395-foot (2,863 meters) Triglav Peak in the Julian Alps is the highest point in the nation.

The Dinaric Alps, which extend from near Ljubljana in the north to the Albanian border in the south, cover about one third of the country. These limestone mountains and plateaus act as a formidable natural barrier separating the coastal lowlands from the interior. This barren limestone zone, which is known as the Karst, has a dry, forbidding appearance, although the region actually has an abundance of rain and snow. About 10 miles (16 kilometers) inland from the Gulf of Kotor is the "wettest place in Europe," because its annual rainfall averages 180 inches (457 centimeters). However, since limestone is porous, the water runs down through the rocks to form underground channels and rivers. The remarkable, 12-mile-long (19 km.) Postojna Cave outside Ljubljana was carved out of the limestone by one such river. The cave is known for the fantastic shapes of its stalactites and because it is the home of *Proteus anguineus,* a transparent, eyeless, fishlike creature.

Above ground in the Karst there is little vegetation. As a result there is little animal life, except for a few sheep and goats grazing on the

YUGOSLAVIA

FACTS AND FIGURES

NAME: Socialist Federal Republic of Yugoslavia.

NATIONALITY: Yugoslavian(s).

CAPITAL: Belgrade.

LOCATION: Southeastern Europe. **Boundaries**—Italy, Austria, Hungary, Rumania, Bulgaria, Greece, Albania, Adriatic Sea.

AREA: 98,766 sq. mi. (255,804 sq. km.).

PHYSICAL FEATURES: Highest point—Triglav (9,395 ft.; 2,863 m.). **Lowest point**—sea level. **Chief rivers**—Danube, Vardar, Sava, Drava, Morava, Tisza. **Major lakes**—Ochrida, Prespa, Scutari.

POPULATION: 23,724,919 (latest estimate).

MAJOR LANGUAGES: Serbo-Croatian, Slovene, Macedonian.

MAJOR RELIGIONS: Eastern Orthodoxy, Roman Catholicism, Islam.

GOVERNMENT: Socialist federal republic. **Head of government**—collective presidency. **Legislature**—Federal Assembly. **International cooperation**—United Nations, European Organization for Nuclear Research.

CHIEF CITIES: Belgrade, Osijek, Zagreb, Niš.

ECONOMY: Chief minerals—coal, iron, copper ore, bauxite, gold, zinc, natural gas. **Chief agricultural products**—livestock, maize, wheat, barley, rye, tobacco, hemp, sunflower products, potatoes, fruits. **Industries and products**—pig iron, steel, cement, chemicals, fertilizers, food processing, textiles, tourism. **Chief exports**—machinery and transport equipment, basic manufactures, chemicals, food and live animals. **Chief imports**—machinery and metal products, chemicals, iron and steel, electrical products.

MONETARY UNIT: Dinar.

scattered patches where enough soil remains for grass to grow. The larger patches are called *polje* ("fields"), but even these are difficult to farm because of heavy fall rains and spring floods caused by melting snow.

On the western side of the Dinaric Alps is the narrow coastal lowland called Dalmatia. Dry, sunny summers and winter rains have given the coastal region typically Mediterranean vegetation. On the terraced hillsides, olives, wine grapes, and figs are grown. Centuries of Italian occupation and influence are evident in the pastel-colored towns. The lovely coast attracts increasingly large numbers of vacationers each year. Many of the hundreds of islands off Yugoslavia's coast, which are actually the peaks of a submerged mountain chain, are also popular with tourists.

On the eastern, or inland, side of the Dinaric Alps the landscape changes more slowly and less dramatically. Since the mountains act as a shield to the warmer Mediterranean climate, the seasons are harsher there, with longer winters and hotter summers. The limestone is covered with soil, and rivers flow through the valleys rather than underground. The mountain slopes are forested, and crops are grown at the lower elevations and in the valleys.

Between Belgrade and the Greek border the country becomes increasingly rugged and mountainous. Historically these mountains have served as a refuge during the countless invasions that are part of the nation's history. Today the higher elevations are a source of timber and are used as a place to graze cattle. In the south, where the climate is milder, such crops as tobacco, rice, and cotton are grown in valleys.

The Vojvodina, as the large farm region of the northeast is called, is known as Yugoslavia's breadbasket because it is on this vast expanse of flat and well-watered land that grains are grown. According to an old saying, you can stand on a watermelon and see the entire Vojvodina. From such a perch it would be possible to see acres of wheat, corn, sunflowers, tobacco, and fruit being grown.

Rivers and Lakes.   The Vojvodina is actually a part of the fertile Danube lowland that extends into Hungary and Rumania. In ancient geological times the lowland was the floor of a vast inland sea that was gradually drained by the Danube River. The Danube, which cuts across Yugoslavia's northeastern corner, flows past Belgrade and cuts through the Carpathian Mountains at the Iron Gate, where the Yugoslavians and Rumanians are building a large hydroelectric dam and plant. Other rivers besides the Danube that contribute to the fertility of the Vojvodina are the Tisa and Sava. The most important river in southern Yugoslavia is the Vardar, which flows past Skopje on its way to its outlet in the Aegean Sea at the Gulf of Salonika. For thousands of years the Vardar has been an important route for invaders, traders, and travelers moving between Asia and Europe.

Yugoslavia's largest lakes—Prespa, Ochrida, and Scutari—lie across

Lake Bled, a popular tourist resort in northwestern Yugoslavia, lies in the shadow of the Julian Alps.

its southern frontiers. Scutari has the distinction of being the largest lake on the Balkan Peninsula, while Prespa is connected with the peninsula's deepest lake, Ochrida, by underground channels. The most unusual of Yugoslavia's lakes are the 16 Plitvice Lakes in Croatia. Since each lake is on a different level, the water falls breathtakingly from one to another.

ECONOMY

Yugoslavia's developing economy is based on its variety of natural resources. They include iron, copper, gold, lead, chrome, antimony, coal, zinc, bauxite (aluminum ore), natural gas, and oil. The rivers that tumble down the mountain slopes are being harnesssed to provide hydroelectricity, and the forests are a source of timber. And, of course, there is the rich farmland of the Vojvodina, which has made Yugoslavia self-sufficient in food production.

The willingness and freedom to experiment that distinguish Yugoslavia from most of the other Communist countries of Eastern Europe have had important results in both agriculture and industry. When the Communists came to power at the end of World War II, they followed the lead of the Soviet Union and collectivized the farmlands. Outside the Vojvodina, collectivization went against nature and tradition. Farms were too small and too scattered to be united efficiently. In addition, farmers regarded land ownership as a form of wealth and fought collectivization. In the 1950s, the effort to enforce collectivization was given up. A farmer may now own up to 25 acres (10 hectares) of land privately. The larger commercial farms are still run as collectives. The government has also made substantial efforts to help farmers combat the effects of the severe droughts that strike the nation on the average of every four years by providing drought-resistant grains, better fertilizers, and improved storage facilities. The result has been a production of grain surpluses that can be used in drought years. Other farm products like fruit and cattle are now produced in large enough quantities for export. Yugoslavian fruits, vegetables, and cattle are sold in Austria, Germany, and Italy.

In industry, Yugoslavia has also moved from a centrally directed economy to a decentralized, worker-run economy. In principle, the people of Yugoslavia are the owners of the nation's resources and industries. Every business that employs more than five employees is run by the workers, who elect a workers' council to set production quotas, direct the work, and decide on salaries and bonuses. A minimum salary is guaranteed to every worker. If the business earns a profit, it is divided among the workers according to their contribution to the job.

Workers' capitalism, as it is called, has been successful in Yugoslavia, although serious problems remain to be solved. There is a rather high level of unemployment, especially in the south, which has led large numbers of Yugoslavians to look for work outside their own country. And there is still a gap between the high standard of living enjoyed by the people of Croatia and Slovenia in the industrialized northwest and the inhabitants of the less-developed southern regions of Macedonia and Montenegro. Government efforts to build roads, railroads, and factories in the south may help to close the gap.

Despite such problems, Yugoslavia's industries already produce a variety of goods ranging from refrigerators to bottle caps. Ships and railroad equipment, shoes and textiles are exported to the other nations

The walled city of Dubrovnik was one of the Mediterranean's leading ports in the 16th and 17th centuries.

in the Communist world. Metals, wood products, tobacco, and processed foods are Yugoslavia's leading exports to the West. In addition to the money earned in foreign trade, Yugoslavia gains foreign currency from its workers abroad and from the constantly growing numbers of tourists visiting the country.

Cities, Regions, and Republics

The Coast. From the Istrian Peninsula in the north to Montenegro in the south, Yugoslavia's long coast is its chief tourist attraction. There are some 400 peninsulas, 60 islands, 550 sun-drenched islets, and historic towns, resorts, and festivals for visitors to choose from.

Pula on the Istrian Peninsula, for example, offers a nearly perfectly preserved Roman amphitheater built in the 3rd century to seat over 20,000 people. A little farther south along the coast is Rijeka, Yugoslavia's main seaport. The next stop might be Split, where the Yugoslav-born Roman emperor Diocletian built a palace in the 3rd century A.D. After his death the palace became a military settlement, a market, and then was divided into residences for countless families. The palace is still the heart of the city and is one of Yugoslavia's most famous landmarks.

Dubrovnik (formerly Ragusa) leads all the cities of Yugoslavia in popularity. Surrounded by its 1,000-year-old walls, the red-roofed buildings of the old city add warmth to the glistening whiteness of the buildings and streets. Here each summer a festival of plays, operas, concerts, and dances is held in a flawless setting where past and present meet. As a leading sea power Ragusa rivaled Venice and gave its name to posterity in the word "argosy," which means "ship of Ragusa." Trade with lands as distant as the Americas and the Indies brought wealth to the small city. This wealth was wisely used by the Ragusans, who vowed, *Non bene pro toto Libertas venditur auro*—"We would not sell our liberty for gold." Instead, an annual tribute to the Turkish sultan helped maintain Ragusa's freedom, and much of its wealth was used to make the city a more beautiful and better place to live. A hospital, orphanage, and old people's home were built in Ragusa by the 14th century, and, in 1416, Ragusa's government became the first in the world to abolish the slave trade. An island of independence and culture for centuries, Dubrovnik is now a charming resort, a busy seaport, and a glowing monument to the past.

As one moves south into Montenegro, one comes to Miločer, with its small, attractive palace—once the summer residence of the Serbian kings. Nearby is Sveti Stefan, a small resort made up of reconstructed houses. Some people say that Sveti Stefan was once a fishing village; others, perhaps more romantic, say that it was a pirate's hideway.

Slovenia. It is a tremendous leap in distance and spirit to Slovenia in northwestern Yugoslavia. The republic is so Central European in appearance and outlook that one could easily imagine one were in Austria, southern Germany, or Switzerland. The landscape is Alpine, with shimmering, snowcapped peaks, which are part of the Slovenian Alps; blue lakes; and rich orchards and pasturelands. The Slovenes are justifiably proud of their high standard of living, their industries, and their varied cultural achievements.

Slovenia's capital, **Ljubljana**, is an ancient city with its own gentle charm. It is well known for its concert and opera performances and as a starting place for visits to Yugoslavia's Alps, the Postojna Cave, the seaside, or beautiful Bled Lake, with its romantic fortress and even more romantic island, which is said to have been the home of the Slavic goddess of love.

Croatia. A road across nearly 100 mi. (160 km.) of lovely countryside links Ljubljana with **Zagreb**, the capital of Croatia. Croatia shares with Slovenia a certain Central European aspect and attitude that reflect both its history and its location. Today, although Belgrade is Yugoslavia's capital and largest city, Zagreb is the country's cultural capital and ranks as the second-largest city. A university, theaters, opera houses, art galleries, publishing houses, and film studios contribute to the city's traditionally active cultural life.

The landscape of Croatia is crowded with memories of the near and distant past. North of Zagreb in the Zagorje district are the Krapinske Toplice—hot springs that were popular when Romans ruled here. The countryside, which is dotted with castles and chateaus, is now best known as the area where Josip Broz spent his early years. As Marshal Tito, Broz led the Yugoslavians to freedom in World War II and became the nation's first president.

Serbia. The *autoput*—"highway"—that links Ljubljana to Zagreb contines to **Belgrade**, the capital of the republic and of the nation. Founded by the Celts in the 3rd century B.C., its location on the east-west route between Europe and the Orient has made Belgrade's history one of repeated destruction by warring armies and rebuilding by patient citizens. One's first impression of the city is that it is completely modern —broad avenues are flanked by tall glass-and-concrete office and apartment buildings. But a few reminders of the past have survived. By far the most impressive is the mightly Turkish fortress, the Kalemegdan. And in the National Museum, there is a priceless collection of objects from every period in Yugoslavian history, including such treasures as the 14th-century emperor Stephan Dušan's Law Code—the first of its kind in the

The historic Turkish fortress the Kalemegdan, in Belgrade.

Belgrade, Yugoslavia's capital and largest city, has many skyscrapers and modern apartment complexes.

Balkans. The long Turkish occupation of Belgrade can best be evoked at the Bajrakli Džamija—a mosque. Yugoslavia's largest city, Belgrade, is a center of industry and of government administration.

The soaring mountains, dark forests, and vast fertile plain of Serbia offer still other memories of the past. The Vojvodina takes its name from the military governors, *vojvodi,* who once ruled the region. Šumadija— a region of farms and forests south of Belgrade—contains Topola, the home of Karageorge, "Black George," the leader of the first important uprising against the Turks in 1804 and the ancestor of the kings who ruled Yugoslavia from 1903 to 1941. Not far away is Kragujevac, home of Miloš Obrenović, who led a successful uprising against the Turks in 1815 and whose descendants ruled Serbia almost continuously until 1903. A memorial park in Kragujevac recalls the most terrible event in the city's recent history—a day in 1941 when the Nazis shot 7,000 people.

Less-painful memories are associated with Niš, the birthplace of the 4th-century Roman emperor Constantine I, the Great; Novi Pazar, which contains the oldest (7th-century) church in Yugoslavia; and the nearby 13th-century monastery of Sopoćani, whose frescoes are considered among the finest in Europe.

Bosnia and Herzegovina. If there is one part of Yugoslavia that seems closest to one's expectations of what a Balkan country should look like, it is Bosnia and Herzegovina, with its magnificent mountains, rich legacy of historic sites, and startlingly Oriental towns. **Sarajevo**, the capital of the republic, exemplifies all these characteristics. Set in a narrow mountain valley, Sarajevo's clock tower and the spires of its minarets recall centuries of Turkish occupation. The most important moment in Sarajevo's long history took place on June 28, 1914, when a young Bosnian, Gavrilo Princip, shot and killed the visiting Austrian archduke Franz Ferdinand—an event that led to the outbreak of World War I.

Mostar, the provincial capital of of Herzegovina, is also set in a narrow valley and takes its name from the beautifully arched Stari Most—Old Bridge—that spans the Neretva River there. Nearby, one may see the elaborately carved tombstones of the Bogomils, a heretical sect that flourished briefly during the Middle Ages.

Montenegro. Because the center of this, the smallest Yugoslavian republic, is dominated by huge mountains, the Venetians called the entire region Monte Negro ("black mountains'). It is called Crna Gora in Serbo-Croatian. The Montenegrins are famous for their ferocity as fighters in the long struggle for complete independence. Once, in the 19th century, for example, a tiny Montenegrin force held off an army of 20,000 Austrians who had come to get men for the imperial army. Although independence has been won at last, tales like this one are still told in the majestic mountains between the coast and **Titograd**, the new and very modern capital city.

Macedonia. Ancient Macedon, the birthplace of Alexander the Great, is now known as Macedonia and is divided among Greece, Bulgaria, and Yugoslavia. A Turkish province from the late 14th to the early 20th century, Macedonia had previously been settled by the Greeks, Romans, and Slavs. Each of Macedonia's invaders has left his imprint on the mountainous land, but it is the unspoiled scenery as much as the relics of the past that attracts visitors.

The capital of Macedonia, **Skopje**, reflects little of the past, since the frightening day in July, 1963, when an earthquake struck and destroyed more than two thirds of the city and killed more than 1,000 people. A new Skopje has arisen around the shattered railroad terminal, which was left as a memorial.

HISTORY

When the Slavs moved out of their original home in the Carpathian Mountains in the 5th century A.D., the South Slavs moved into the region that is now named Yugoslavia for them. The longest and darkest chapters in their history are of subjugation to foreign rulers—Austrian, Hungarian, Italian, Turkish, and briefly in Napoleon's time, French. Yet, nothing in Yugoslavia's history compares in length or importance with the Turkish rule that began with the defeat of the Serbs at the battle of Kosovo Field in 1389 and soon was extended to include most of the region. The Turks ruled parts of Yugoslavia until early in this century.

In the early 19th century Serbia, which had suffered the most from Turkish rule, overthrew its oppressors. In 1830 Miloš Obrenović claimed the throne as prince of Serbia. A measure of freedom had been gained but the rivalry between the Obrenović and Karadjordjević families threatened the internal stability of the young nation. Nevertheless, Serbia became a leader in the Pan-Slavic movement, which aimed to unite all the Slavic peoples. In this role it threatened the Austro-Hungarian monarchy, which had replaced Turkey as the chief foreign power with territories and interests in Yugoslavia.

The Serbian rulers encouraged the formation of underground movements to bring about the overthrow of Austrian rule in such regions as Bosnia. It was one of these revolutionaries, Princip, who assassinated the Austrian Archduke in Sarajevo in 1914—a murder that led to World War I and the destruction of the 640-year-old Austrian monarchy and its vast empire. One of the new nations to appear on the map of Europe at the end of the war was the Kingdom of the Serbs, Croats, and Slovenes.

The kingdom faced tremendous problems. Age-old traditions of

Diocletian's Palace in Split, now used to house cafés, is one of many ruins dating back to Roman days.

separatism did not die easily, nor were the other parts of the young kingdom ready to turn over their power to the Serbian-dominated government. In 1929, King Alexander I tried to solve these problems by dissolving the parliament and transforming the government into a dictatorship called the Kingdom of Yugoslavia. Parliament was reopened in 1931, but the problems remained as various national groups, especially in Croatia and Macedonia, fought for more independence. Alexander's assassination in 1934 is usually attributed to Croatian extremists.

Alexander was succeeded on the throne by his young son Peter. Alexander's cousin Prince Paul acted as regent. The rise of Fascist power in Germany and Italy provided the regency with its greatest threat. In March 1941, after all its neighbors but Greece had fallen to Hitler and Mussolini, the Yugoslavian government signed a treaty with the Italians and Germans. The Yugoslavian people refused to accept the terms of the treaty. The government was forced to go into exile. And, perhaps more important, the German timetable for launching its invasion of the Soviet Union was seriously delayed because the German army now had to deploy troops in Yugoslavia to subdue the people. The Yugoslavians fighting from mountain hideouts in the armies led by Draža Mihajlović and Marshal Tito succeeded after four years in regaining Yugoslavia's freedom. The losses were staggering. One in every nine Yugoslavs was dead; cities and industries lay in ruins. But Yugoslavia was free.

In November 1945, the Communists under Tito's leadership formally took over the government. Yugoslavia began its postwar life as a faithful Soviet satellite. In 1948, serious economic and political differences caused a rift between the U.S.S.R. and Yugoslavia that jeopardized the very existence of the new South Slav nation. However, the Yugoslavian government overcame these difficulties and gradually assumed a position of independence. The nonaligned movement was formally inaugurated in Belgrade in 1961. Yugoslavia became a leader of the neutral "Third World" nations.

GOVERNMENT

In 1974, a new constitution was proclaimed in Yugoslavia. The people select the councils that administer all levels of government from the smallest district up to the federal centers. The Federal Assembly, as the legislature is called, is divided into two houses. The Federal Chamber consists of delegates of the working people of the six republics and the two provinces. The members of the Chamber of the Republics and Provinces are chosen from the assemblies of the republics and provinces.

An extraordinary Communist Party Congress in 1990 amended the constitution, relinquishing the Communist Party monopoly on power. Multiparty elections were proposed, and the premier, Ante Marković, formed a new party. The political liberalization has worsened tensions among the republics, with more-traditional Serbia favoring strong central controls, and liberal Slovenia seeking full Western-style democracy. The Slovenia Communist Party voted to secede from the national party, adding to the fragmentation. Large numbers of ethnic Albanians in Kosovo province have protested and rioted for greater freedom. Yugoslavia's challenge will be to maintain the nation's unity while recognizing that freedom and independence remain important to all Yugoslavians.

CAROL Z. ROTHKOPF, Author, *Yugoslavia, A First Book* and other books

A view of Albania's capital city, Tirana.

ALBANIA

The 18th-century English historian Edward Gibbon described Albania as "a country within sight of Italy which is less known than the interior of America." Now, some two centuries later, the interior of America has been thoroughly explored, settled, and voluminously described, but the world still knows little about the People's Socialist Republic of Albania, a Communist country in southeastern Europe.

THE LAND

Albania is a narrow strip of land on the west coast of the Balkan Peninsula. It is washed by the Adriatic Sea on the west, and wedged in between Yugoslavia on the north and east and Greece on the southeast and south. About 40 mi. (65 km.) away, across the Strait of Otranto, lies the heel of Italy's boot.

The country has three distinct landforms—coastal lowlands, hills, and high mountains. The long lowland coast has stretches of sandy beaches as well as many shallow lagoons and extensive marshes. The stagnant waters in the swampy areas held the constant threat of malaria. Some of these swamps have been cleared and reclaimed, but some work still remains to be done. Here and there along the coast can be seen the beginnings of the hills that cover the central part of Albania. The soil is often good, and the slopes of the lower hills are terraced and carefully cultivated. The valleys are broader here than in the mountains beyond. Some of the major cities and towns are located in this area.

The outstanding geographic fact about this country, however, is that nearly three quarters of its surface is mountainous and often quite inaccessible. The mountains rise to their greatest height in the 9,066-foot (2,763 meters) Mount Korab, in northeastern Albania. Throughout the centuries, the mountains have served as a natural fortress and refuge for the people. In fact, the Albanians called themselves Shqyptarë ("sons of the eagle"), and many still make their homes in the mountain valleys.

The mountainous nature of the country and the poor soil make it very difficult to grow enough food to feed the population. Wheat and corn are the main crops. Olives, figs, grapes, and citrus fruits are grown in the southern part of the country. Sugar beets, tobacco, and cotton are becoming more important. Livestock raising, particularly sheep, is most important, but the grazing land is often quite far from the village or farm.

Climate.   Although Albania is small, it has a surprising variety of climatic conditions. The coastal regions enjoy a Mediterranean climate, with mild, rainy winters and very warm, dazzling summers. But these mild temperatures are sharply altered in the hilly inland areas by the harsher climates of the central Balkan Peninsula. Some of the mountain areas are windswept and snow-covered in winter, with precipitation of up to 100 inches (254 centimeters) annually in the north. The summer months are cool and bright.

Lakes and Rivers.   Albania shares its largest lakes—Scutari, Ochrida, and Prespa—with Yugoslavia. Many relatively short rivers cross the country. Although they usually dry up in summer, many become raging torrents in winter. The most important rivers are the Drin, the Seman, and the Vijosa. Only one of Albania's rivers, the Bojana, is navigable. The Shkumbî River, which crosses the center of Albania, is thought of as the dividing line between the northern Albanians, who speak a dialect called Geg, and the southern Albanians, who speak Tosk.

THE PEOPLE

The Albanians are a homogeneous people. They speak Albanian, an Indo-European language that is written with the Roman alphabet. Even though two dialects are spoken, each group can understand the other. Since 1945, the official language has been based on the Tosk dialect and spelling.

Traditionally, the Gegs of the north have been thought of as reserved and taciturn, and they have a reputation as good fighters. Many are tall, handsome, and blonde, and all are credited with great courage in defending their mountain homes. Tosks, on the other hand, are a more affable, outgoing people. Since they lived in the path of Albania's many invaders, they met and mingled with other peoples. Whatever rivalries these two groups had in the past, they are united today by a common concern for their country.

A rich oral literature made up of folk songs, poetry, and proverbs plays an important part in the cultural life of the country. The poetry and songs are traditionally about love, honor, or the heroic deeds of the past The songs are often accompanied by the one-string lute called the *lahuta*.

Today folk music is often used as a means of propaganda, and specially written verses are distributed at meetings or sung on radio.

Religion. In 1967 the Albanian Government closed the country's mosques and churches and claimed that Albania was the first atheist state in the world. It was estimated, however, that about 70 percent of the people were Muslims, 20 percent Orthodox, or Eastern, Catholics, and 10 percent Roman Catholics. Christianity came to Albania in the 1st century A.D. When the Turks arrived in the 14th century, they brought the Muslim religion with them. Waves of conversion followed each Turkish victory until Albania had the largest number of Muslims in Europe. Today, many of the mosques and churches are used as youth-group centers, cultural houses, and even as restaurants.

Education. At the outbreak of World War I, after more than 500 years of Ottoman rule, Albania was one of the most backward in all of Europe. A little progress was made after independence with the building of more primary schools. It is in the field of education, in particular, that the Communist government has had considerable success. The former high rate of illiteracy has been reduced to the point where the government can now claim that everyone under 40 can read. School is compulsory for 8 years, and many children go on to secondary schools. Albania's first university was opened in 1957 in Tirana, the capital, with faculties in medicine, law, and other fields. There are teachers training colleges and an agricultural institution, as well as an institute of science.

THE ECONOMY

Albania has always been an agricultural country, with seven out of 10 Albanians making a precarious living from small farms. Primitive farm-

A busy market for farm products at Krujë in the mountains north of Tirana.

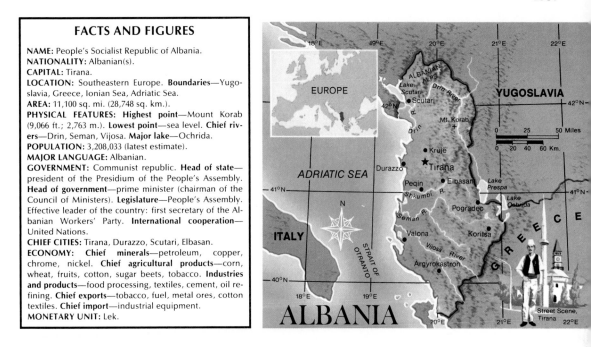

FACTS AND FIGURES

NAME: People's Socialist Republic of Albania.
NATIONALITY: Albanian(s).
CAPITAL: Tirana.
LOCATION: Southeastern Europe. **Boundaries**—Yugoslavia, Greece, Ionian Sea, Adriatic Sea.
AREA: 11,100 sq. mi. (28,748 sq. km.).
PHYSICAL FEATURES: Highest point—Mount Korab (9,066 ft.; 2,763 m.). **Lowest point**—sea level. **Chief rivers**—Drin, Seman, Vijosa. **Major lake**—Ochrida.
POPULATION: 3,208,033 (latest estimate).
MAJOR LANGUAGE: Albanian.
GOVERNMENT: Communist republic. **Head of state**—president of the Presidium of the People's Assembly. **Head of government**—prime minister (chairman of the Council of Ministers). **Legislature**—People's Assembly. Effective leader of the country: first secretary of the Albanian Workers' Party. **International cooperation**—United Nations.
CHIEF CITIES: Tirana, Durazzo, Scutari, Elbasan.
ECONOMY: Chief minerals—petroleum, copper, chrome, nickel. **Chief agricultural products**—corn, wheat, fruits, cotton, sugar beets, tobacco. **Industries and products**—food processing, textiles, cement, oil refining. **Chief exports**—tobacco, fuel, metal ores, cotton textiles. **Chief import**—industrial equipment.
MONETARY UNIT: Lek.

Street Scene, Tirana

ALBANIA

ing methods were used up to the time of World War II, and families would cooperate in some of the hard work of the farms. The women would often do the farming while the men were taking the livestock to graze on distant fields.

In the 1950s, the government had to start from scratch in a land devastated by war. A series of five-year plans, starting in 1951, set goals for the country. The first two plans were completed with Soviet money, aid, and technicians. A textile mill, sugar refinery, cotton-processing plant, tobacco factory, plywood plant, and several hydroelectric plants were built. In addition, the Soviet Union and the Soviet bloc began the exploitation of Albania's mineral deposits by drilling for oil and mining for copper, coal, and chrome.

However, there was little success in improving agriculture, mainly because of the shortage of machinery and the failure of the country's collectivization policy. Under this policy, Albania attempted to gather small farms into larger units under the supervision of the government, and thus increase production.

In the early 1960s, after the break with the Soviet Union over policy differences, Albania was still in need of outside help. China supplied financial aid and technicians to the Albanians, who by then had gained some industrial proficiency. Factories for the production of cement, plastics, glass, chemicals, and electric power tools were built. More land, particularly in mountain areas, was made available for agriculture. A more widespread use of tractors and farm cooperatives increased agricultural output—important in the nation that has the highest birthrate in Europe. Chinese aid terminated in 1978, and, in 1980, Albania signed trade agreements that made Yugoslavia its major trading partner.

CITIES

Tirana (Tiranë), the capital of Albania, centers on a plaza that bears the name of Albania's national hero—Skënderbeg Square. In January

Rugged mountains provide a scenic backdrop for Elbasan, an important city in central Albania.

1968, the residents of the city commemorated the 500th anniversary of Skënderbeg's death by placing a huge statue of him in the square. The wide, tree-shaded main street seems even wider because so few cars are seen on it. The wooded hills beyond lend a certain charm to the city, as do the delicate spires of old mosques. In the old section of the city, along the narrow streets, men can be seen wearing the baggy trousers and sashes of the Turks of bygone days.

A railroad line connects Tirana with its port city of **Durazzo** (Durrës), which is approximately 20 mi. (32 km.) away on the Adriatic Sea. Durazzo is the chief port of the country. Its beach was once the mecca of Eastern European vacationers seeking the sun, but is now becoming increasingly popular with Western Europeans.

Other important Albanian cities are **Scutari** (Shkodër) and **Valona** (Vlorë), which are about the same size as Durazzo.

HISTORY
The first people in recorded history to inhabit the area that is present-day Albania were the Illyrians, who set up a kingdom in the 3rd century B.C. The Illyrians were a sturdy people—peasants, warriors, and pirates. The Romans, irritated by the Illyrian pirate ships that harassed Roman trade, decided to remove the source of trouble, and conquered Illyria in 167 B.C. But the Romans were not able to penetrate the more-inaccessible mountain regions, whose inhabitants put up stiff resistance to foreign rule. After the Romans, a host of other conquering peoples and races invaded the country in the succeeding centuries.

The characteristic spires of mosques found in many Albanian villages reflect the country's large Muslim population. Most Albanian mosques and churches are now used for nonreligious purposes.

The Long Years of Turkish Rule

The people who had the greatest and most enduring influence in Albania, mainly because their rule was of such long duration, were the Ottoman Turks. The first Turkish invasion of Albanian territory took place in 1385 at the invitation of a petty ruler who had quarreled with one of his neighbors. The newcomers gradually extended their rule over most of the country, after overcoming a good deal of resistance. The most spectacular opposition to Turkish domination was led by the greatest Albanian hero, Gjergj Kastrioti, or Skënderbeg, as he is known.

Skënderbeg, the son of an Albanian nobleman, was sent as a hostage to the sultan's court. There he became a Muslim and joined the Turkish Army, in which he had a distinguished career. However, he knew that his people had not fully submitted to Turkish occupation, and he decided to return to Krujë, his family home. He reconverted to Christianity. The Albanians were quick to recognize him as their natural leader. For a quarter of a century, Skënderbeg fought a number of highly successful defensive battles against large Turkish armies. His death in 1468 marked the end of resistance on any large scale, although it took the Turks many years more to conquer the whole country. Skënderbeg has been a symbol of freedom to the Albanians and the mainspring of the modern national independence movement.

The Albanians paid dearly for the struggle they put up against the Ottomans. Thousands were killed in battle; many of their ancient cities and towns were destroyed; the country's economy, trade, and crafts came to a standstill. The many anti-Turkish revolts that took place later and the suppression that followed contributed to the general decline of the country.

Independence

Albania declared itself an independent state in 1912. It was one of the last countries of southeastern Europe to break away from the dying Turkish empire. In 1914, a German prince, Prince Wilhelm zu Wied, was made ruler of Albania. When World War I broke out 6 months later, Wilhelm left the country. During this war Albania was occupied at one time or another by the armies of several countries.

In the years that followed, the country had a rather chaotic existence. A leading figure in the immediate postwar years was Bishop Fan Noli, who headed a reform government. He was overthrown by Ahmet Zogu, who, after a struggle, emerged as president in 1925 and then as the self-styled King Zog in 1928. He ruled the country as a dictator, and his years in office were marked by some abuses and a number of real achievements. The strong centralized government encouraged education and in some ways strengthened the national economy.

Zog formed a close alliance with Italy in an attempt to counter Yugoslavia's ambitions regarding Albania. He accepted financial aid from Italy and encouraged Italian investments. But when the Italian Fascist leader, Benito Mussolini, embarked on a policy of expansion, more and more concessions were demanded from Zog. In 1939, 5 months before the outbreak of World War II, the Italians occupied Albania and forced Zog into exile. The Germans took over Albania after Italy's defeat in 1943 and ruled for just over a year.

A resistance movement, divided into Communist and nationalist branches, grew up during the war years. Under the German occupation and during the last stages of the war, these two groups struggled for power. The civil war that followed was won by the Communist forces. Known as the National Liberation Movement, and helped by Yugoslav partisans, they set up their own government in Tirana. Their leader was Enver Hoxha.

In the next few years, the Communists were busy building their administration and removing all centers of opposition to their rule. The close ties they had with Yugoslavia ended abruptly when Yugoslavian President Tito quarreled with Stalin and broke away from Soviet domination. Albania decided to seek the Soviet Union's protection by becoming its satellite. Economic, technical, and military assistance was the reward for this step.

When the Soviet Union, in the mid-1950s, decided to renew its friendship with Yugoslavia, there was a distinct cooling off of Soviet-Albanian relations. Finally there was a complete break between the two countries.

Left without a single ally in Europe or elsewhere, Albania found a welcome friend in the People's Republic of China. The Chinese and Albanian leaders were in agreement on Communist doctrine. And since China seemed too far away to pose any threat to Albanian independence, its aid was even more welcome.

Albania broke its last tie with the Soviet Union after the invasion of Czechoslovakia by Warsaw Pact forces. Albania had been an inactive member of the pact since 1961, and, in 1968, the Albanian legislature renounced its obligations under the pact. In 1977, Albania ended its relationship with China, soon resuming trade with Yugoslavia.

GOVERNMENT

Albania is entirely controlled by one party—the Albanian Workers' Party (the Communist Party). The legislative body, the People's Assembly, meets for only a short time each year. In its absence, its affairs are handled by the Presidium, whose chairman serves as Albania's head of state. The chairman of the Council of Ministers, or prime minister, serves as the head of government. Real political power, however, rests with the first secretary of the Albanian Workers' Party.

ALBANIA AND THE OUTSIDE WORLD

Albania has known only a few years of independence, but advances in those years have been major ones. However, Albania has been more reluctant than any other European Communist government to reduce the powers of the state and allow the people greater freedoms. Protests have been met by force, but it is clear that not even the hard-line Albanians are completely immune from pressure for change.

The breakup of the Eastern bloc has further isolated Albania, leaving it without the resources for development. A small-scale exodus of Albanians began in mid-1990, similar to the beginnings of the successful uprisings in neighboring countries. The architect of Albania's isolation and strict Stalinist policies, Enver Hoxha, died in 1985. Whether his successors can maintain his unyielding grip on the country remains to be seen.

Reviewed by ANTON LOGORECI, British Broadcasting Corporation, European Services

One of the many impressive government buildings in Sofia, the capital of Bulgaria.

BULGARIA

Highway E-5, the modern road from Belgrade, Yugoslavia, to Istanbul, Turkey, is built over the old Roman road to the Near East. Running southeast across the country, this road, originally paved with stone slabs and four or five steps wide, once separated two Roman provinces. Today these provinces are united as the People's Republic of Bulgaria, a country facing great change that is in the eastern section of the Balkan Peninsula on the Black Sea.

The Roman road linked the Western and Eastern Roman empires. Later, it was an avenue for the peoples invading the eastern parts of the empire, and still later, a part of the Crusaders' route to the Holy Land. After the Crusaders, the warriors of Bulgaria and the soldiers of the Byzantine Empire (successor to the Eastern Roman Empire) used the road to reach the fields where they met in a succession of bloody battles. During the nearly 500-year-long occupation of Bulgaria by the Ottoman (Turkish) Empire, the Turks used the road to maintain their iron grip on Bulgaria.

Along Highway E-5, as elsewhere in Bulgaria, there is evidence of settlers and travelers from earlier times. Ancient tombs, Roman stone columns, ruins of Roman spas, Byzantine monasteries, and Turkish mosques dot the countryside. But the travelers and invaders left more than archeological remnants and historic monuments. They left a people accustomed to violence, disorder, and hardship. They also left a wealth of legend and superstition.

Today one may still see a collar of blue beads with a rosebud pattern hanging from the hood of a taxi. These collars, used in the hope of warding off the evil eye, once adorned the necks of horses. In the villages Bulgarians still celebrate Saint George's Day, the holiday of herdsmen and shepherds. A lamb is killed and wine is spilled to bring good health. When the lamb has been eaten, the bones are collected. Half are buried in an anthill, so that the sheep will multiply like ants; the rest are thrown into the river so that milk will flow like water.

HISTORY

Bulgaria's violent and tragic history began in the 7th century A.D. when the Bulgars, a fierce warring group of horsemen, rode out of Central Asia. They seized lands near the Danube, and some spread south to conquer the Slavs. Instead they adopted the Slavic customs and language and were gradually assimilated.

The First Bulgarian Empire, founded in 679, lasted until 1018. During this period Christianity was introduced into Bulgaria. In the 9th century disciples of two Christian missionaries, the brothers Cyril and Methodius, who are known as the Apostles of the Slavs, came to Bulgaria. They brought with them an alphabet and a written language and literature. This alphabet, called Cyrillic, is shared by the Russian, Serbian, Macedonian, and Bulgarian languages, and to this day it provides a strong cultural tie between the people of Bulgaria and those of the Soviet Union.

Bulgarian culture flourished during the First Empire, but war with Byzantium went on constantly, and in 1018 Bulgaria was defeated and became part of the Byzantine Empire. In 1186 the brothers John and Peter Asen led an attack on Byzantium and started Bulgaria back on

Women work a collective farm. Bulgarian agriculture is the most collectivized in eastern Europe.

the road to independence and power with the establishment of the Second Bulgarian Empire. During most of the Middle Ages the Bulgarian czar ruled the major part of the Balkan Peninsula. But in 1395 Bulgaria was overrun by the Turks, who were to rule the country for nearly 500 years. During those 5 centuries of terrible tyranny many Bulgarian towns and villages were destroyed. People were taxed so heavily that they did not have enough to eat. Bulgarians still have an intense hatred for the Turks and great affection for the Russians, who drove the Turks out in a war that started in 1877. Nevertheless, the years of Turkish domination have left traces in the food, names, customs, dress, art, and architecture of Bulgaria.

Modern Bulgaria began in 1878 with the Treaty of San Stefano and the Congress of Berlin, which ended the Russo-Turkish War. Russia reestablished the medieval frontiers of Bulgaria, but other European powers objected, and only the northern part of the country remained independent. In 1885 the southern part broke away from Turkey, and the country was reunited at last.

But wars continued. In the two bloody Balkan Wars of 1912–1913 Bulgaria first gained, but ultimately lost, considerable territory. In World War I Bulgaria joined with Germany and Austria-Hungary against the Allies. Again land was lost. Three wars in 6 years left the Bulgarians defeated, bitter, and impoverished.

In 1941 Bulgaria joined Italy and Germany and declared war on Great Britain and the United States. They did not declare war on the Soviet Union. The king succeeded in keeping his country from active participation in the war, and Bulgaria was the only one of the Axis powers that managed to save its Jewish population.

On September 5, 1944, a few days after Bulgaria had begun peace talks with Great Britain and the United States, the Soviet Union declared war on Bulgaria and occupied the country. An armistice was signed in Moscow. A government friendly to the Soviet Union was set up. All opposition was ruthlessly stamped out. Hundreds of high government officials, intellectuals, and other opponents of Communism were put to death or jailed. The young king, Simeon II, was exiled. Georgi Dimitrov, a Moscow-trained admirer of Russian leader Joseph Stalin, became the first Communist premier of Bulgaria.

Since 1946, when Bulgaria was declared a People's Republic, it has been one of the Soviet Union's most consistent allies in the Eastern bloc. A new constitution was established in 1971 under which Todor Zhivkov became the first secretary of the Communist Party and chairman of the Council of State. He remained in power until 1989, adhering to strict Communist ideology and isolating Bulgaria from the West. The economy stagnated under his rule as the country passed through a series of five-year plans. The security forces remained a powerful presence in Bulgaria, and cooperation with Moscow was very close. Dissidents were assassinated, even overseas, and Bulgarian newspapers and other media were tightly controlled.

In 1989, Zhivkov, then the longest-serving leader in the Eastern bloc, resigned with little warning. He had continued to resist political liberalizations and was facing growing pressure as a result of the changes sweeping neighboring countries. In early 1990, Zhivkov was arrested on charges of misusing government property, inciting ethnic hostility, and

FACTS AND FIGURES

OFFICIAL NAME: People's Republic of Bulgaria.

NATIONALITY: Bulgarian(s).

CAPITAL: Sofia.

LOCATION: Southeastern Europe. **Boundaries**—Rumania, Black Sea, Turkey, Greece, Yugoslavia.

AREA: 42,823 sq. mi. (110,912 sq. km.).

PHYSICAL FEATURES: Highest point—Musala Peak (9,596 ft.; 2,925 m.). **Lowest point**—sea level. **Chief rivers**—Danube, Maritsa, Iskar, Struma, Mesta.

POPULATION: 8,972,724 (1989).

MAJOR LANGUAGE: Bulgarian.

MAJOR RELIGION: Bulgarian Orthodox.

GOVERNMENT: Emergent democracy. **Head of government**—executive president. **Legislature**—National Assembly. **International cooperation**—United Nations, Warsaw Treaty Organization, COMECON.

CHIEF CITIES: Sofia, Plovdiv, Varna, Burgas.

ECONOMY: Chief minerals—coal, copper, manganese. **Chief agricultural products**—wheat, corn, barley. **Industries and products**—processed foods, light machine tools, oil. **Chief exports**—machinery and equipment, tobacco, fruits, vegetables, metals. **Chief imports**—raw materials, heavy machinery, vehicles.

MONETARY UNIT: Lev.

misconduct in office. Under Zhivkov, the large ethnic Turkish population had been forced to adopt Slavic names and make other cultural concessions, causing tensions and contributing to labor unrest and political dissent. With Zhivkov gone from the scene, the pace of reform in Bulgaria increased.

GOVERNMENT

A constitution modeled on the Soviet one was adopted, and the People's Republic of Bulgaria was officially proclaimed by the National Assembly on September 15, 1946. The Communist Party monopoly on power was revoked in January 1990, and by March the party had undergone restructuring and even changed its name in an effort to gain popular support. The constitution was amended in March 1990, with parliament electing former Communist Party general secretary Petar Mladenov to the newly powerful post of executive president. Mladenov resigned in July under pressure from students and opposition groups, although the renamed Communist Party had won a majority in June parliamentary elections. Protests against alleged Communist corruption continued.

On August 1, 1990, the National Assembly chose opposition leader Zhelyu Zhelev to succeed Mladenov as president. Zhelev had been expelled from the Communist Party in 1965 after he questioned some of Lenin's theories. He heads the Union of Democratic Forces (UDF), a 16-party coalition of opposition groups. His election ended a 6-week impasse with the Socialist Party (the former Communists).

EDUCATION

When the Turks were driven out by the Russians, more than 90 percent of the people over school age could not read and write. Today there is almost complete literacy. School is compulsory for all children between the ages of 7 and 16. Under the Communist regime, Bulgarian students were prepared for their role as workers in the Communist society. All students were required to work part of the time in farming or industry.

There was strict control of the whole school day as well as of all extracurricular activities. Students remained in the *zanimalna*, a type of prolonged study hall, until parents finished work. There was also the *internat*, a boarding school for children whose parents could not care for them. Greater freedom and more practical education will be the goal of new student organizations and political opposition groups that formed in Bulgaria in 1989.

RELIGION

Under the Communists, the churches could have nothing to do with education, youth movements, or social services. They could not own property, and the appointment of all priests and church officials was approved by the government. Although religious practices were discouraged by the government, most Bulgarians cling to their Eastern Orthodox faith. The Turks in Bulgaria, who make up about 9 percent of the population, are Muslims. There are also small Jewish, Roman Catholic, and Protestant minorities.

The Church of St. Nedelja on Lenin Square in Sofia dates to the Middle Ages.

An icon portraying Ivan Rilsky, the 10th-century founder of the Rila Monastery in western Bulgaria. The monastery now houses a museum.

THE ARTS

Because of the difficulty of the language, few of the great Bulgarian writers are known to the rest of the world. A novel by Ivan Vazov, *Under the Yoke* (1894), gives such a remarkable picture of life in Bulgaria under the Turks that it has been widely translated and read all over the world.

Bulgarians are intensely proud of their opera. They have a great many fine singers, particularly bassos. Opera stars travel freely and often appear in Western nations. In a country with about the same population as the city of New York, there are 5 opera houses, 2 official music theaters for light opera, and 12 symphony orchestras.

Contemporary art in Bulgaria has not approached the greatness of the country's ancient icon art. Icons, small religious images painted on wood, were introduced into Bulgaria with the adoption of Christianity. The icon artists reflected in their work the great imagination and the love for brilliant colors that were seen also in the beautiful embroidery, weaving, and wood carving done by the peasants.

THE LAND

Throughout Bulgaria's bloody history, the Bulgarian peasant continued to work his small farm and to drive his oxen across his fields. (Oxen, according to Bulgarian legend, could be as swift as the fastest horse, but they choose not to move quickly for fear of damaging the earth they love.) The peasant was helped in his work by his wife and children. His wife left his side in the fields only when she was about to give birth. She usually returned to the fields the next day.

Since the reforms of 1989–1990, Bulgarian farmers have been freed from most of the restrictions imposed by the Communist government. By government decree, farmers are free to choose their methods of farming and to export their produce. A special bank was established to provide funds to support small farms, and there is no longer a limit on the amount of private land a farmer can cultivate.

Bulgaria is divided into two main agricultural regions by the Balkan Mountains. In the north is the Danubian Plateau, where wheat and other grains, sugar beets, and sunflowers are grown. In the fertile Maritsa River valley, south of the Balkan Mountains, the winters are mild and rainy and

Plovdiv in south central Bulgaria is the center of the country's wine-growing region.

Modern hotels are being built in many Bulgarian cities to attract Western tourists and hard currency.

the summers dry and very hot. Tobacco, grapes, cotton, and rice are harvested there. Fruits and vegetables are cultivated in both regions.

Roses are one of Bulgaria's most valuable crops. Thousands of varieties are grown in the famous Valley of Roses, in the southern foothills of the Balkan Mountains. More than 200 lb. (90 kg.) of petals may be used to produce 1 oz. (30 g.) of attar of roses. This oil, which comes to the surface when rose petals are boiled in water, is extremely expensive and is used in making fine perfumes.

INDUSTRY

All industry and trade, as well as agriculture, were brought under government control by the Communists. As part of the economic and political reforms of 1989–1990, leaders are proposing a gradual shift to a market economy.

Timber from the mountains and hydroelectricity from the rivers are only two of Bulgaria's resources. Coal, lignite, iron ore, lead, zinc, copper, uranium, pyrites, chromite, manganese, petroleum, and natural gas are also found. In recent years, Bulgaria has had one of the highest rates of economic expansion of all European countries. Steel and electric power production have been greatly increased. At Varna and Burgas, on the Black Sea, there is a growing oil and petrochemical industry. Electric trucks, hoists, and electric motors, light machine tools, small ships, railroad cars, cement, and a large variety of processed foods are also produced and exported. More than three-fourths of all exports go to the Soviet Union and Eastern European countries.

The sandy beaches of Bulgaria's Black Sea coast have been transformed into popular resort areas.

EAST MEETS WEST

After centuries of facing the East, the Bulgarians are more and more attracted to the West. They have trade missions traveling throughout the world in an effort to attract markets for their products. They are attempting to bring foreign investments and capital into Bulgaria. The Bulgarians are too practical to let their worry about the importation of Western democratic ideas interfere with their desire for Western currency, sophisticated machinery, and modern business techniques.

One of the most successful efforts to bring Western currency into the country has been the use the Bulgarians have made of their great natural advantages—the magnificent beaches, beautiful mountain ranges, and more than 500 mineral springs. Bulgaria has built a tourist industry that brings more than 5,000,000 visitors to the country each year. On the shores of the Black Sea, the Bulgarians have constructed their version of Miami Beach in Florida or the Riviera in France. Visitors flock to resorts called Zlatni Pyassatzi ("golden sands"), Slunchev Bryag ("sunny beach"), and many smaller communities. In addition to seacoast resorts, Bulgarians and visitors enjoy the hiking and winter sports in the picturesque mountains and delight in drinking the water and taking the baths at the many spas.

SOFIA, THE CAPITAL

The co-existence of East and West and of medieval and modern that makes Bulgaria so fascinating is seen in all the major cities. Sofia, the capital, beautifully situated 1,820 feet (555 meters) above sea level, looks

The Banya Bashi Mosque, a Sofia landmark, dates to the 16th century.

out onto the towering peaks of the Vitasha Mountains. The city is filled with gardens, parks, and tree-lined boulevards. It is also filled with monuments and museums devoted to past and present: the remains of a Roman tower than can be seen in the basement of a Sofia department store; the Church of Saint Sophia, built during the 3rd and 4th centuries; the Monument to the Red Army; the Archeological Museum; the Museum of the Revolutionary Movement; the Museum of Ecclesiastical History; and many others.

In the present cafés of Sofia one may sip Turkish coffee or sample yogurt, a Bulgarian food that is famous all over the world. One may also order Coca-Cola, for Bulgaria was the first Soviet-bloc country with its own Coca-Cola bottling plants. If one is hungry, there are a host of aromatic and flavorful native dishes that combine delicious vegetables and meats with oriental spices and herbs. One may dine on bean or cucumber soup, carp stuffed with nuts, a lamb kebab or *giuvetch* (stew), and a dessert of melon or berries.

Though cafés resound with Western popular music, the famous native dance, the *horo,* is still danced to the music of bagpipes. Supermarkets, cafeterias, and motels have come to Bulgaria, and dollars are more sought after than Soviet rubles. Yet as Bulgaria changes, becoming modern and industrialized, its bonds to the Soviet Union remain strong. These bonds have been forged by affection and by a shared history and culture, as well as by political, military, and economic ties.

Reviewed by RADO L. LENCEK
Associate Professor, Department of Slavic Languages, Columbia University

A rugged mountain pass in northwestern Rumania.

RUMANIA

The Socialist Republic of Rumania, on the Balkan Peninsula, is one of the younger nations in Europe. Though the land was settled more than 2,000 years ago, the nation known as Rumania has existed for only a little more than a century. From the late 14th until the mid-19th century the country consisted of two principalities, Moldavia and Walachia. In 1859 these provinces were united and named Rumania. Today Rumania includes, in addition to the two original territories, the regions of Banat, Transylvania, Bukovina, and Dobruja.

Until December 1989, Rumania was one of the satellite countries of the Soviet Union, with which it shares a long border. Rumania frequently sought to forge its own brand of socialism, often diverging from Soviet policy. Since the 1989 revolution, Rumania has been working to broaden its cultural, linguistic, and economic ties to the West while trying to resolve its own internal problems.

THE PEOPLE

The heart of modern Rumania was imperial Rome's Dacia. The Dacians were conquered by the Romans in the early years of the 2nd century. Rome established colonies in Dacia, and they were garrisoned by Roman legions. Most Rumanians, about 85 percent, are believed to be descendants of the Dacians and the Roman colonists. Their name comes from the word ''Rome.''

Language. Unlike their neighbors in Yugoslavia, Hungary, and the Soviet Union, the Rumanians trace their ancestry to the Latin-speaking peoples and are related to the French, Italians, Spanish, and Portuguese. The Rumanian language is basically a Latin language to which, over the years, the Rumanians added bits of the Slavic languages spoken by their neighbors.

Religion. The Communist government of Rumania discouraged religious observance but allowed people to worship if they chose. It regulated the church as much as possible, paying church salaries and maintenance. The Rumanian Orthodox Church includes 90 percent of the people. The remainder are Roman Catholics, Calvinists, Jews, and Lutherans. The Jewish community, once sizable, has been sharply cut by emigration to Israel. About 10 percent of the people once worshiped in the Eastern Catholic Church, but in 1948 the government abolished this church and transferred its property to the Rumanian Orthodox Church.

Education. The Rumanians traditionally regarded their country as an island of French culture in the Balkans. Prior to the establishment of the Communist government in March, 1945, Rumania looked to France for cultural, social, and educational inspiration. Schools were patterned on those of France, and French was a required second language.

When the Communists took over the country, the educational system was changed. General education was made free and compulsory for 10 years, for children from 6 to 16. Workers and peasants were brought

The exterior walls of the 15th-century Sucevita monastery are richly decorated with frescoes.

into the schools, so that almost everyone learned to read and write. The secondary school system was expanded to include, in addition to the traditional academic schools, technological and teachers' training schools. At the university level, institutions were established to stress training useful to the state—teaching and technology. The study of Russian was compulsory for many years.

In the early days of Communism, teachers and scholars thought to have "unhealthy" social views were replaced by party members. As the need for trained personnel grew in the 1950s, some of the purged teachers were brought back. Since the 1989 revolution, academic excellence has regained its importance, and Marxism-Leninism is no longer the primary focus of academic education. Technical expertise and economic development are now major educational goals. There are some 140 institutes of higher learning, including 7 universities and a number of institutes that specialize in technical training.

Culture. Rumania has a rich folklore, going back centuries. It found expression in lyric poetry, ballads, folktales, mystery plays, traditional New Year and Nativity plays, and in many other forms. Folk music and amateur theatricals have long flourished even in the most remote parts of the country.

Since drama has long been a major form for Rumanian literature, it is not surprising that the outstanding Rumanian writer of today is a playwright. Eugène Ionesco makes his home in Paris, and his plays are performed throughout the world.

Many Rumanian writers and composers left Rumania to create some of their best works in France, to which they were drawn by its congenial intellectual atmosphere. However, most of them retained, through their work, a close identification with their native land. This is true of composer Georges Enesco. Enesco, who died in 1955, was a composer, violinist, and teacher. Perhaps his best-known orchestral work is the *Rumanian Rhapsodies.*

The most prominent Rumanian artist was Constantin Brancuşi, the sculptor, who traveled on foot from Rumania to Paris, where he worked until his death in 1957. His art, found in the great galleries of the world, sought to capture "the essence of spirit" of the subject. His lovely sculptures of birds eternally poised in flight are elegant, deceptively simple, thin shafts of marble or brass. The museums of Bucharest and Craiova exhibit works done by Brancuşi when he was young.

Centuries before Brancuşi, Rumanian folk art took the form of embroideries, pottery, and architecture. There are numerous folklore displays in places such as the Village Museum in Bucharest and the ethnological museums in Bucharest, Cluj, Sibiu, Jassy, and other cities.

The outstanding achievements of early Rumanian art were the monasteries in the Moldavian towns of Voroneţ, Humor, Arbore, Moldoviţa, and Suceviţa. Simple and severe in architectural outline, these monasteries have frescoes covering their entire outer walls. These mural paintings, extraordinary displays of creativity and acute observation, depict religious stories, historical events, and local spiritual legends. Although they are more than 4 centuries old, they have retained their brilliance and freshness. No one knows the secret of this remarkable preservation.

Country Life. Nearly 30 percent of Rumania's people still work in agriculture. Most of them live in or near small villages. Village life has

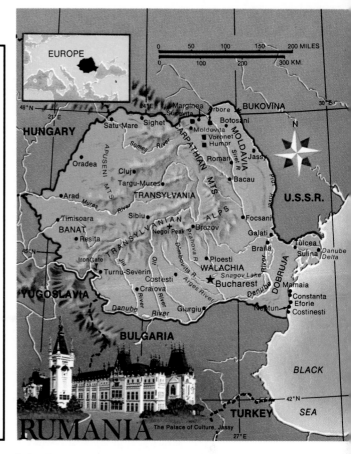

RUMANIA

The Palace of Culture, Jassy

FACTS AND FIGURES

OFFICIAL NAME: Rumania.

NATIONALITY: Rumanian(s).

CAPITAL: Bucharest.

LOCATION: Southeastern Europe. **Boundaries**—USSR, Black Sea, Bulgaria, Yugoslavia, Hungary.

AREA: 91,700 sq. mi. (237,500 sq. km.).

PHYSICAL FEATURES: Highest point—Mt. Moldoveanu (8,346 ft.; 2,544 m.). **Lowest point**—sea level. **Chief rivers**—Danube, Mures, Olt, Jiu, Siret, Prut.

POPULATION: 23,153,475 (1989).

MAJOR LANGUAGE: Rumanian.

MAJOR RELIGION: Rumanian Orthodox.

GOVERNMENT: Emergent democracy. **Head of state and government**—executive president. **Legislature**—Grand National Assembly. **International cooperation**—United Nations, Council for Mutual Economic Assistance (COMECON), Warsaw Treaty Organization.

CHIEF CITIES: Bucharest, Braşov, Constanţa, Timişoara.

ECONOMY: Chief minerals—oil, natural gas, salt, coal, lignite, iron, copper, bauxite, chromium, manganese, uranium. **Chief agricultural products**—corn, wheat, sugar beets, barley, vegetables, grapes, fruits. **Industries and products**—oil, methane gas, pig iron, steel, coke, chemical fertilizers, paper, food, textiles, machinery, household appliances. **Chief exports**—oil and oil products, cement, agricultural products, timber, tractors, ships, equipment for cement mills, chemical factories, oil fields and refineries. **Chief imports**—iron ore, industrial coke, metals, electrical equipment, electric motors, television sets, industrial and agricultural equipment.

MONETARY UNIT: Leu.

changed greatly since World War II. While there were improvements in sanitation and other modernizations that brought electricity, radio, and television to the countryside, the government of Nicolae Ceauşescu launched a campaign designed to tear down ancient villages, replacing them with high-rise developments. This program incited great popular discontent.

Under the rule of the Communists, the schools, libraries, and churches were emphasized as social and political centers. Yet the weekly *şezătoare* (the communal get-together), with dancing, music, and gossip, persists. It is part of a waning tradition, as is the wearing of the beautifully decorated, homemade peasant costumes. But there are still remote areas where blouses and dresses embroidered in lively patterns and rich colors are handed down for generations, and where wealth is measured in such treasured possessions as embroidered clothes, home-woven blankets, and carpets.

Since Rumania hopes to become an important exporter of grain, an attempt is being made to keep too many people from leaving the villages. Even so, the villages are slowly disappearing as the young depart for the rapidly expanding cities. The sleepy town, with its small homes, large gardens, horse-drawn carriages, numerous churches, coffeehouses, neighborhood stores, and open-air markets is becoming a part of Rumania's past.

Food on the farms is good but simple. There are fresh eggs, cheeses, vegetables, and always *mămăligă*, a cornmeal dish that is eaten twice or

The modern resorts lining the Rumanian Black Sea coast are popular tourist destinations.

even three times a day, often in combination with cheese, salted fish, or bacon. Still a part of Rumanian tradition is the distillation of plum brandy (ţuica) each fall. At harvesttime the pungent odor of distilling plum hangs over each village.

City Life. Originally, more than three fourths of all Rumanians lived on farms, but the drive to industrialize brought many workers from the farms to the cities. City population doubled in little more than 20 years, and the number of cities with populations over 100,000 has grown more than threefold.

Most of the city-dwellers now live in new high-rise apartments with adjacent shopping centers. But many are housed in homes that once belonged to the wealthy or middle-class families. A house designed for one family may become the home of three or four families, who often come to the city accompanied by their farm animals. The government is working to provide badly needed housing for the workers, technicians, and government officials who crowd into the cities.

Rumanians travel to work by bus or other public transportation, or by bicycle or motorbike. Because public transportation is crowded and expensive and there are few automobiles, the people do not travel far from their homes. Movie theaters, public gardens, and restaurants—all within walking distance—are invariably crowded in the evenings.

Although salaries are low, people flock to movies and sports events for diversion. Rumanians, urban or rural, love to watch soccer and other spectator sports. Every town has at least one soccer team and one stadium, and this is true also of the larger villages. Most Rumanians tend to be sports spectators rather than participants. Excellence in sports is an aim of the government, and the Communist Party sponsors organized recreational activities under the auspices of the youth organizations. The young people, however, tend to enjoy such frowned-upon diversions as rock music, dancing, or Western movies much more than organized exercise classes and "voluntary work" on farms or building sites.

Vacations for many workers and students are provided by the government. Resort towns in the mountains and on the Black Sea are crowded during the summer when most of the industrial workers enjoy organized vacations.

Housewives in the cities spend considerable time marketing for food and preparing meals. Even though Rumania grows such fine fruits and vegetables, there are food shortages in the cities, since much of the best food is exported. However, city people still enjoy good food and drink. Many of their favorite dishes are of Turkish, French, or Russian origin. *Imam baiyldi* is a dish of eggplant stuffed with spiced meat or vegetables and covered with tomatoes. The delicious dish takes its name from the legend of the Turkish priest (*imam*) who fainted (*baiyldi*) with pleasure after taking a taste.

THE LAND

On the map Rumania looks like a round pouch with a wide opening in the lower right. The opening is on the Black Sea. Rumania borders on four countries: Bulgaria in the south, Yugoslavia in the west-southwest, Hungary in the west-northwest, and the Soviet Union in the east and north.

Rumania's terrain is about one-third mountains, one-third hills and plateaus, and one-third plains. But these rather neat divisions give no indication of the great beauty and diversity of the country, the extraordinary drama of the high mountains, and the bountiful riches found in all its areas.

Mountains. The Carpathian Mountains form a majestic semicircle that shelters an elevated plateau. This is the Transylvania tableland, a high area with a cool climate, rich in forest and mineral resources.

The Carpathians become the Moldavian Carpathians in the east, the Apuseni Mountains in the west, and the Transylvanian Alps in the south. Numerous fairly low passes break through the high mountains. Rumania's highest peak, Negoi, rises 8,361 feet (2,548 meters) in the Transylvanian Alps. There are many other peaks almost as lofty.

A girdle of lower hills gradually descends from the ring of mountains. In the spring these hills are carpeted with flowers—narcissus, anemones, crocuses, daffodils, and forests of lilacs. Sweeping down from the hills are the great, well-watered plains of Rumania. In the east are the Moldavian plains. In the south the Walachian plains are the site of vast oil deposits. To the southwest is the small Banat plain.

Rivers. It is in the arc of the Carpathian Mountains that most of Rumania's many clear, swift-flowing rivers rise. The Olt, Jiu, Siret, Prut, Arges, Dîmbovița, and others are tributaries that join the Danube on its way to its delta on the Black Sea.

The mighty Danube is Rumania's chief river. Only it and one tributary, the Prut, are navigable. The Danube not only waters some of Europe's richest soil, but it is also a main artery of national and international commerce. Galați and Brăila, two inland ports on the Danube, are used for loading wheat, while the port of Giurgiu is the outlet for the Rumanian oil fields. The Danube forms part of the border with Yugoslavia and almost the entire border with Bulgaria. Near the beginning of the boundary with Yugoslavia, the river foams through a deep gorge, the Iron Gate. It is here that Rumania and Yugoslavia are jointly constructing one of Europe's largest hydroelectric plants.

The many other rivers of Rumania are great potential sources of power. They are now used for floating logs down from the great forests that supply the masses of conifers, oaks, and beeches for Rumania's timber industry.

Wildlife.   Rumania has a fascinating variety of wildlife. Surefooted chamois clamber over the highest peaks. Deer, foxes, bear, wolves, lynx, boars, and smaller animals fill the woods. Eagles and falcons can be seen hovering above the crags. The lovely lakes of the Dobruja region, just west of the Black Sea, teem with fish.

The Danube's broad, marshy delta, where the river empties into the Black Sea, is entirely within Rumania. This area, more than 1,000 square miles (2,600 square kilometers), is an immense natural park. It is a paradise for waterfowl. Swans, pelicans, egrets, cormorants, flamingos, wild duck and geese, night herons, and many others abound. More than 60 varieties of fish live in the many channels of the delta.

Sportsmen come to Rumania to hunt stags, bear, and wild boars. They come to observe the many varieties of game and birds in their natural setting, and to go fishing. Strict game laws regulate hunting and fishing, and rare animals and birds in the Danube Delta are protected in many reservations and sanctuaries.

Climate.   Rumania has a continental climate. In general there are plenty of rainfall, severe winters, hot summers, and long autumns. In the southwest there is a mild Mediterranean-type climate, and in the uplands of Transylvania the climate is usually moderate. But in many of Rumania's inland cities it may be intensely hot in summer; and in the winter when the north wind, called the *crivăț*, blows, it can be cruelly cold.

Resources.   Rumania is potentially one of Europe's wealthiest countries. The fertile land makes Rumania a natural granary. The Danube and other rivers provide a plentiful supply of fish. The vast forests supply abundant timber for building, paper production, and export. Among the many varieties of trees are the firs that grow in high altitudes. Their wood is prized for its resonance and is used in the manufacture of musical instruments.

Mineral wealth is scattered throughout the mountains of Rumania. There are copper, manganese, uranium, lead, zinc, bauxite, kaolin, sulfur, gold, and salt. The most important mineral product is petroleum. Drilled principally in the Prahova Valley around Ploeşti, crude oil from Rumania ranks second only to the Soviet Union's in Europe's total production. Pipelines from the oil fields run from Ploeşti to Bucharest, Constanţa, and Giurgiu. Other petroleum resources are near Bacău.

In the Transylvania area of Rumania there are the largest natural gas reserves in Europe. Coal is mined in the Jiu River valley, and iron ore is found in several areas.

AGRICULTURE

When the Communists came to power in 1945, they launched a program to nationalize agriculture. They believed the large landowners were to blame for the lack of progress on the farms. A major part of the land was taken over directly by the state. Some was divided into small holdings to be worked in farm cooperatives under state direction, but most of the better land was held for the huge state farms.

Farmers, long proud of owning their bit of land, however poor, sometimes had to be forced into collectives. Full collectivization did not take place until 1962. The introduction of tractors and other mechanical equipment, the use of chemical fertilizers, and the general upgrading of methods increased yields. Rumanian agriculture suffered from mismanagement and inefficiency, however, and severe shortages were experienced in the months after the revolution of 1989. Rumania is nevertheless one of the world's leading corn producers, and large amounts of wheat, rice, potatoes, cereals, and fruits are potentially available to ease the situation.

INDUSTRY

Before World War II Rumania was primarily an agricultural nation. Since the end of the war, Rumania has concentrated on mining and heavy industry. Industrial development was begun to produce goods needed by the Soviet Union and has been pursued relentlessly since 1948. The drive transformed Rumania from an underdeveloped farming country into one of the most industrially advanced in Europe.

The strides have been spectacular. Industrial output has increased at a rate 2 or 3 times faster than the growth rate in the major industrial countries of the world. The output of steel has increased 10 times since the late 1940s. Similar records have been made in the production of manufactured goods. The output of crude oil, long the country's main source of energy and wealth, has doubled since 1939, but the limited reserves are not expected to last through the 1990s, and imports in the early 1980s about equaled production.

Building materials, chemicals, natural gas, heavy machinery, electrical products, tractors, locomotives, and automobiles are produced in quantity. The production of electrical power has increased also.

The cost of the rapid industrialization has been great. Other branches of the economy, such as agriculture and particularly the production of consumer goods, have been disregarded. More clothing, shoes, and household goods are becoming available, but they are still expensive and relatively scarce. Transportation and communication have improved since 1948, but they are still insufficient for the modern industrial country Rumania aims to be.

During the decade beginning in the late 1940s no person of middle-class origin could hold a position of responsibility. The measures taken were so drastic that experienced managers and professionals were often displaced by poorly trained or untrained workers. Another severe handicap was Rumania's total economic dependence on the Soviet Union.

Since 1955, the Rumanian government has embarked on a different path. The professional classes have been brought back into the system. Wages and benefits for workers have increased. Trade and cultural contacts with the West have been actively sought. As a result the people support the purposes and economic policies of the government, and production has increased steadily. Today Rumania faces the problem of improving the quality of its industrial goods to compete successfully in the Western markets, with which it now conducts half its external trade.

BUCHAREST, THE CAPITAL

The capital and largest city of Rumania stands on a plain in southern Rumania. All the main roads converge there, and Bucharest is the governmental, artistic, cultural, and economic hub of the country. Bucharest is a modern city of about 2,000,000 people. It has numerous skyscrapers and blocks and blocks of modern houses; vast sections of the city that consisted of ancient hovels were torn down in the early 1960's to make way for modern apartments. A city center was built around and includes the former royal palace. The circus hall, a circular building of concrete and glass, seats 2,500 spectators. It is always filled with crowds watching native or visiting circuses.

Documents trace the importance of Bucharest back to the 14th century when it was the seat of the Walachian princes. Today's city, however, shows the strong French influence of the 19th century. The city has Parisian-style boulevards shaded by lime trees and bordered by miles of red, yellow, and white roses. On the outskirts are the lovely Baneasa forest and park, the Snagov lake and forest, and a number of other inviting lakes.

The city has much historic architecture. The Curtea Veche Church is of the 16th century; the Church of the Patriarchy and the Mihai Voda Church were built in the 17th century; and the Stavropoleos and Cretulescu churches are examples of 18th-century styles. There is also the 18th-century Mogoșoaia Palace, which is now a museum of feudal art.

Before World War II Bucharest was known throughout Europe as

A scene in downtown Bucharest, the capital and leading city of Rumania. Modern office and apartment buildings are found all over the city.

the Paris of the Balkans. It was a glittering, sophisticated city, filled with cafés, theaters, palaces, and luxury hotels. Today little remains of this prewar elegance, although in recent years some of the old gaiety has been recaptured. Today there are some good restaurants. People gather in cafés. Young Rumanians dance to Western music in nightclubs, and theaters are crowded.

OTHER CITIES

Cluj is Rumania's second largest city and an important industrial and educational center. It has a rich historic past and is the chief city of Transylvania, which before World War I was a part of Hungary. Many of its residents are of Hungarian descent. Located in the foothills of the Apuseni Mountains, Cluj is a popular winter resort. It has a number of institutions of higher learning and an important medical center. Some of its churches date back to the 14th and 15th centuries.

Constanța, Rumania's chief seaport on the Black Sea, is one of the country's oldest cities. It has important archaeological exhibitions that relate to its founding more than 2,500 years ago by the Greeks. Later, under the Romans, it served as an important trading post. The ancient Roman poet Ovid (43 B.C.–A.D. 17) spent the last years of his life in exile here. There is a Roman ruin noted for its mosaics, and other Roman remains are found nearby. In more recent times Constanța suffered from a serious lack of fresh water. Water was hawked by peddlers who sold it by the jar from carts. Today Constanța is a modern city with a modern water system.

On the outskirts of the city are many resorts that have sprung up to accommodate the tourists who are attracted by the sunshine, the miles of fine, sandy beaches, and the warm, blue waters. The new resorts are at Mamaia, Eforie, Costinești, Neptun, Jupiter, and Venus, all on the southern Black Sea coast.

Jassy, the ancient seat of the Moldavian princes, is a major administrative and economic city. The Rumanian cultural renaissance of the 19th century flowered there, and the city is still a cultural center. The well-known Cuza University is located there. In Jassy, too, is the 17th-century Trei Ierarhi Church, a jewel of stone architecture. The Golia Church of the same century is a fine example of Moldavian art. The 20th-century Gothic Palace of Culture houses a museum of ethnography, history, and art.

Timișoara was the site of a massacre by soldiers that provoked the 1989 revolution. It is an ancient town of historical interest, with sites such as the 14th-century Huniady Castle nearby. A breathtaking road runs through the Transylvanian Alps and the Carpathians from Timișoara, in western Rumania, to **Brașov,** in central Rumania. Ruined medieval castles dot the heights, and there are Gothic churches with massive walls. In Brașov there is a superb 14th-century cathedral and an ancient town hall. There are also important truck and tractor factories in Brașov.

Ploești is the main center of Rumania's oil industry. There Europe's petroleum industry began in 1857. So important were the oil wells and refineries of this area that during World War II costly low-level Allied bombing raids were conducted to cut off this vital source of fuel for Germany's war machine. Just north of Ploești is the lovely Prahova Valley with its picturesque mountain resorts and lovely lakes.

The 14th-century Corvins Castle dominates the skyline of Hunedoara, an important steel-producing city.

HISTORY

For some 23 centuries Rumania has suffered because of its strategic location on the Balkan Peninsula. Over and over again it has been conquered and occupied. In the 2nd century A.D. the Romans made Dacia, the region northeast of the Danube, one of their most prosperous colonies. Toward the end of the 3rd century, Goths, Huns, and Slavs invaded the area. Bulgaria was the conqueror during the 7th and 8th centuries, and it was at this time that Eastern Christianity was introduced. Later warriors from Asia invaded the land.

Moldavia and Walachia, the principalities that until the 19th century made up the country that is now Rumania, were briefly united with Transylvania by Michael the Bold at the end of the 16th century. But he could not withstand the might of the Turks, and they occupied Walachia and Moldavia. Transylvania was returned to Hungary.

Moldavia and Walachia began to gain a measure of independence after 1856. In the same year, the European powers guaranteed Moldavia and Walachia autonomy. In 1859 the two provinces were united as Rumania, under the rule of Alexandru Ioan Cuza. He was forced to abdicate in 1866, and the throne went to Carol I, of the German House of Hohenzollern-Sigmaringen. Violence and unrest continued to plague the country. The peasants were desperately poor and political corruption was widespread. Foreign countries continued trying to interfere in Rumanian affairs. Complete freedom from Turkish control had been won at the end of the Russo-Turkish War (1877–78), but some land had been ceded to Russia. Carol I tried desperately to transform his small nation into an independent Rumania. Some industries and railroads were built, but most of the power stayed in the hands of the great landowners.

As a result of the Second Balkan War (1913), Rumania won a large part of Dobruja from Bulgaria. After World War I, when Rumania sided with the Allies, Rumania doubled in size. It received Transylvania from Hungary and Bessarabia from Russia.

Between the two world wars there was constant friction among the various ethnic groups, and economic conditions were bad. Crown Prince

The palace that houses the State Council of Rumania includes one wing devoted to a national art museum.

Carol gave up the throne in favor of his son Michael in 1925, only to take it back in 1930. In 1938 Carol set himself up as a dictator, but he soon came into conflict with the Iron Guard, a terrorist organization with strong sympathies for Nazi Germany.

During World War II, Rumania was caught between Nazi Germany and the Soviet Union. After Carol was forced to abdicate by the pro-Nazi government, Michael returned to the throne in 1940, but a dictator, Ion Antonescu, was in control of the government. German troops occupied the country, and in June 1941, Antonescu wiped out the Iron Guard and declared war on the Soviet Union. In 1944, as the Soviet armies advanced, King Michael overthrew Antonescu and entered the war on the side of the Allies. The Soviet Union occupied and seized control of Rumania.

The Communist takeover caused a social, economic, and political revolution. The first leaders concentrated on destroying the power of the old ruling classes, chiefly the landowners, and reversing the country's anti-Russian viewpoint. In 1947 King Michael was forced to give up the throne again and go into exile. Prominent anti-Communists were sentenced to prison and the only opposition, the National Peasant Party, was outlawed.

Rumania had never known democratic rule but was all too familiar with dictators. Thus the establishment of a small, all-powerful group in control of the government was nothing new. In 1952 Gheorghe Gheorghiu-Dej became premier, and in 1955 he became head of the Rumanian Communist Party. He ruled as chief of state and head of the Party until his death in 1965. His successor, Nicolae Ceaușescu, who came to power in 1965 as president of the State Council and secretary general of the Communist Party, began a program to set Rumania free from its total commitment to the wishes of the Soviet Union, without severing the close ties that bound his country to its powerful neighbor. His rule was ruthless, and he placed family members in key positions of power in the government. He ruled through an extensive network of fiercely loyal secret police and informers.

RUMANIA AFTER THE REVOLUTION

The uprising of 1989 in Rumania was the only revolt in Eastern Europe that was met by massive force. Thousands of people died in the fighting, provoked in part by a massacre by government soldiers of protesters in Timişoara. Nicolae Ceauşescu had created a regime that was as much a cult of personality as it was a doctrinaire Communist dictatorship. His wife and son were hated by many Rumanians, and the brutal Securitate security police were fanatically loyal to Ceauşescu until the very end.

Unlike other East European revolutions, Rumania largely replaced a Communist dictator with other Communists. Many continue to fear that the revolution was "stolen" from those who sought true freedom and democratic rule. Still, it is not uncharacteristic that Rumania would choose a distinct path from its neighbors. Rumanian armed forces did not take part in the 1968 invasion of Czechoslovakia by Warsaw Pact forces, and Ceauşescu often advocated a separate path to socialism.

Rumania under the Ceauşescu government maintained good relations with China during the Sino-Soviet split and tried to cultivate economic relations with the West. It opposed the Soviet invasion of Afghanistan in 1979. It also pursued its own course of economic development and refused to gear its production of finished goods to coincide with the needs of the Soviet economy.

Rumania remains a country of striking contrasts. When pro-democracy protests grew in Bucharest in 1990, the new government called upon thousands of pro-government coal miners, who descended on the city, beating students and foreigners while the police just watched. The desire for modern democratic government had come into conflict with the forces of what remains a traditional society.

Rumania's internal conflicts are taking place at a time that there is also conflict with neighboring countries. Tensions with Hungary have risen over Rumanian treatment of ethnic Hungarians in Rumania's Transylvania region. Moldavia, now a republic of the Soviet Union, contains many ethnic Rumanians who feel stronger bonds to Bucharest than to Moscow. As is the case throughout Eastern Europe, nationalist tensions and political uncertainty in Rumania are complicating the transition to a free multiparty government.

Perhaps more than any other formerly Communist country, Rumania suffers the legacy of its former ruler. Ceauşescu's police had infiltrated every segment of society, creating fear and suspicions that have been slow to disappear. The degree of corruption under the Ceauşescus is just beginning to come to light, and Rumanians will no doubt keep a watchful eye on their new leaders. Rumanians, who have lived under conquerors from Romans to Russians, are proud to have taken their future into their own hands.

GOVERNMENT

Rumania was controlled by the Rumanian Communist Party until 1989, when a popular uprising overthrew the Ceauşescu regime. An interim government, the National Salvation Front, was established and made promises to hold free multiparty elections. Student groups and new political parties were formed, and in January 1990, the Communist Party was temporarily banned in Rumania.

STEPHEN FISCHER-GALATI, Editor, *Romania*

A parade in Moscow's Red Square.

UNION OF SOVIET SOCIALIST REPUBLICS

The Union of Soviet Socialist Republics is the colossus of the Eurasian continent. With one seventh of the earth's land area, it ranks as the world's largest nation. This immense country, which now spans over 170 degrees of longitude—nearly half the globe—gradually grew outward from a small area around Moscow. In 1917, when the Bolshevik Revolution ended the rule of the Russian czars, the U.S.S.R. became the first Communist-governed state. Uniting nearly 100 different nationalities, the Soviet Union is as rich in population as it is in natural resources. The predominantly agricultural Russia of the czars has become a mighty industrial power.

THE PEOPLE

In the Soviet Union each person is a Soviet citizen and at the same time has his own separate nationality. He belongs to one or another of about 100 different national groups living in the Soviet Union. The people within each group share the same language, culture, and historical experience. Nationality is important to a Soviet citizen—he is very conscious of being Georgian, Lithuanian, Russian, or whatever he is. This situation differs from the United States' "melting pot," in which people from many nationalities, while proud of their origins, have gradually come to regard themselves as more American than anything else. This happened in America because people had left their home countries and settled in a new nation. In the Soviet Union, however, most of the national groups still live in the specific area where they have always lived. As the Russian Empire expanded its territory over the centuries, many non-Russian peoples came under the rule of the czars. When the Communists took power in 1917, they reasserted control over these peoples.

For governing purposes, the Soviet Union is divided into 15 republics, each corresponding to one of the major nationalities. The Russians —a Slavic people—are the largest national group, and their republic stretches from west of Moscow clear across Siberia to the Pacific. Until recently the Russians made up more than half the country's total population. Now the Russian population is decreasing in proportion to other national groups, especially those in the Caucasus and Central Asia. The Russians, however, remain the most influential group. They control the Communist party. Lenin, the first leader of the Soviet Union, was a Russian. Although his successor, Joseph Stalin, was a Georgian, he was careful in public to refer to the Russians as the "most outstanding" of the Soviet nationalities.

In addition to the Russians there are two other major Slavic groups in the U.S.S.R.—the Ukrainians and the Belorussians. Their languages and cultures are similar. The three groups together make up nearly three quarters of the overall Soviet population. The Ukrainians are the country's second largest group. They were not strong enough to establish an independent state and have been dominated by Poles and Russians, against whom they often rebelled. This experience has made them particularly aware of their national identity. The Belorussians, a much smaller group who live in the northwestern part of the country, have a less developed national feeling.

The Moldavian Republic borders on Rumania, and its people speak Rumanian. Along the Baltic Sea are three small republics—Estonia, Latvia, and Lithuania—which differ from one another as well as from the Slavs in language and religion. The Estonians speak a language related to that of the nearby Finns. Traditionally, the Estonians and Latvians have been Protestants, while the Lithuanians have been Catholic. The Baltic republics were independent from the end of World War I until World War II, when Soviet troops brought them under Russian rule once again. In appearance and culture, these republics are the most European part of the U.S.S.R. Their capital cities contain many Gothic-style buildings and picturesque narrow, winding streets. Their people have long been fine woodworkers, weavers, and leather craftsmen, and this tradition carries over into the manufacture of attractive, modern fabrics and furniture that are used all over the country.

FACTS AND FIGURES

OFFICIAL NAME: Union of Soviet Socialist Republics.

NATIONALITY: Soviet(s).

CAPITAL: Moscow.

LOCATION: Eastern Europe and north and central Asia. **Boundaries**—Barents Sea, Kara Sea, Laptev Sea, East Siberian Sea, Chukchi Sea, Bering Sea, Okhotsk Sea, Japan Sea, North Korea, China, Mongolia, Afghanistan, Iran, Caspian Sea, Turkey, Black Sea, Rumania, Hungary, Czechoslovakia, Poland, Baltic Sea, Finland, Norway.

AREA: 8,649,498 sq. mi. (22,402,200 sq. km.).

PHYSICAL FEATURES: Highest point—Mount Communism (24,590 ft.; 7,495 m.). **Lowest point**—Batyr Depression near the Caspian Sea, 433 ft. (132 m.) below sea level. **Chief rivers**—Volga, Ob-Irtysh, Yenisei, Lena, Amur, Ural, Syr Darya, Amu Darya, Dnieper, Don, North Dvina. **Major lakes**—Caspian Sea, Aral Sea, Lake Ladoga, Lake Baykal.

POPULATION: 288,742,345 (1989).

MAJOR LANGUAGES: Russian (official); Slavic languages; Indo-European languages; Altaic, Uralian, and Caucasian languages.

MAJOR RELIGIONS: Russian Orthodoxism, Islam, Judaism, Protestantism, Georgian Orthodoxism, Roman Catholicism.

GOVERNMENT: Communist state. **Head of state**—Executive president. **Legislature**—two-house USSR Supreme Soviet.

CHIEF CITIES: Moscow, Leningrad, Kiev, Tashkent, Kharkov, Gorky, Novosibirsk, Kuibyshev, Sverdlovsk, Minsk, Tbilisi, Dnepropetrovsk.

ECONOMY: Chief minerals—coal, petroleum, natural gas, manganese, lead, zinc, nickel, mercury, potash, phosphates. **Chief agricultural products**—wheat, potatoes, sugar beets, cotton, sunflowers, flax, other grains. **Industries and products**—heavy machinery, iron and steel, vehicles, textiles, food processing, mineral fertilizers, communications equipment, lumbering, fishing. **Chief exports**—petroleum and petroleum products, natural gas, metals, wood, agricultural products, manufactured goods. **Chief imports**—grain, agricultural products, machinery and equipment, steel products, consumer goods.

MONETARY UNIT: Ruble.

CONSTITUENT REPUBLICS OF THE SOVIET UNION

REPUBLIC	CAPITAL	AREA (sq. mi.)	(sq. km.)	POPULATION (estimate)
Armenia	Erivan	11,306	29,283	3,317,000
Azerbaijan	Baku	33,436	86,599	6,614,000
Belorussia	Minsk	80,200	207,718	9,942,000
Estonia	Tallinn	17,413	45,100	1,530,000
Georgia	Tiflis	26,911	69,699	5,201,000
Kazakhstan	Alma-Ata	1,049,200	2,717,428	15,842,000
Kirghizia	Frunze	76,642	198,503	3,967,000
Latvia	Riga	24,695	63,960	2,604,000
Lithuania *	Vilna	26,173	67,788	3,590,000
Moldavia	Kishinev	13,012	33,701	4,111,000
Russian Soviet Federated Socialist Republic	Moscow	6,592,800	17,075,352	143,090,000
Tadzhikistan	Dushanbe	54,019	139,909	4,499,000
Turkmenia	Ashkhabad	188,417	488,000	3,189,000
Ukraine	Kiev	233,100	603,729	50,840,000
Uzbekistan	Tashkent	172,700	447,293	17,973,000

* Lithuania declared independence March 1990, a claim not recognized by Moscow.

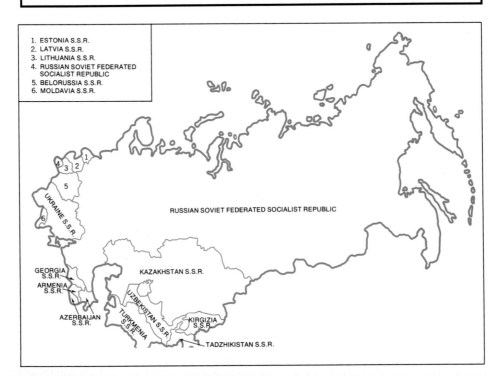

1. ESTONIA S.S.R.
2. LATVIA S.S.R.
3. LITHUANIA S.S.R.
4. RUSSIAN SOVIET FEDERATED SOCIALIST REPUBLIC
5. BELORUSSIA S.S.R.
6. MOLDAVIA S.S.R.

Many nationalities with long histories live in the Caucasus mountain region between the Black and Caspian Seas. The main ones are the Georgians, the Armenians, and the Azerbaijani. The Georgians, a quick-witted, temperamental people, can be very charming and very fierce. They have an old and distinguished culture of which they are justifiably proud. In its warm climate, Georgia produces tea, tobacco, fruits, and good wines. Many resourceful Georgian farmers travel 1,000 miles (1,609 kilometers) to Moscow with their fresh produce at a time of year when their goods bring high prices on the market. The Armenians, farther south, trace their history to the beginnings of Christianity. Over the centuries they have suffered under the Turks, Persians, Mongols, and others who invaded their area. The same was true for the Muslim Azerbaijani.

Most of the Soviet Union's Muslim Turks live in Central Asia in a huge area that used to be called Turkestan. In the 1920's it was divided into five republics—Kazakhstan, Uzbekistan, Turkmenia, Kirghizia, and Tadzhikistan. The people in the first four republics are descendants of Turkic nomads who roamed the deserts and steppes. The Tadzhiks are related to the Persians. Progress in literacy and economic development has been very noticeable in Soviet Central Asia. Many new industries have been established. The Soviet Government sees to it that the living standard of its Central Asian peoples is better than that of the related peoples just across the border.

Soviet Jews, who number between 1,000,000 and 2,000,000, do not have their own republic, but have been assigned Birobidjan, an autonomous region in eastern Siberia. Most Jews, however, live in the western part of the country. In Czarist Russia, the Jews lived under harsh restrictions and were often persecuted. Under the Soviet regime, anti-Semitism has persisted. Between 1970 and 1982, about 260,000 Soviet Jews were permitted to emigrate. Then the emigration stopped and did not resume until the late 1980's.

There are many small nationalities scattered over the vast territory of Siberia. The Chukchi, for example, inhabit the Chukchi Peninsula in the far northeast. They were, and to some extent still are, reindeer herders leading a nomadic life and sleeping in deerskin tents called *yarangi.* The government encourages them to settle in one place by offering to pay part of the cost of building houses for them. Until relatively recently many of the small northern nationalities suffered from serious diseases, and their numbers were declining. Now, they receive better medical treatment, and their economic and cultural conditions have improved. The government even commissioned written languages to be created for them and books to be written in these languages.

In the late 1980's several nationalities have used the political liberalization under Mikhail Gorbachev to press their specific claims. The Crimean Tatars, forcibly removed to Central Asia after World War II, wanted to return to their homeland; Baltic republics asked for more autonomy; and Armenia and Azerbaijan were locked in a territorial dispute.

Religion

One of the first acts of the revolutionary government that came to power in 1918 was the disestablishment of the Orthodox Church. The 1936 Constitution of the Soviet Union guarantees "freedom of religious worship and anti-religious propaganda" to all citizens. The emphasis has

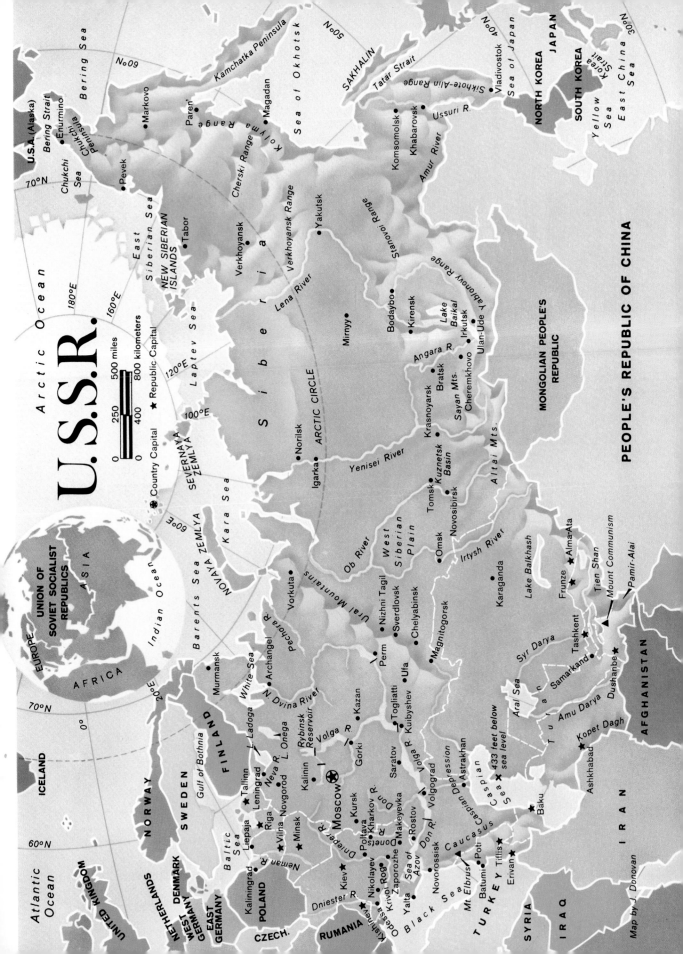

The GUM department store, a Moscow showplace.

A civil wedding ceremony in the U.S.S.R., where formal religions are not recognized.

been on the second half of this curious statement. The Communist Party considers religious belief to be unnecessary, and students are taught that God does not exist. People attending church services have at times been subjected to severe official pressure to abandon their religion.

Historically the Orthodox Church was the faith of the Eastern Slavs —Russians, Belorussians, and Ukrainians. The Roman Catholic Church flourished in Lithuania and Western Ukraine, while the Latvians and Estonians were mainly Protestants. The Jews, who live mainly in European Russia, have been persecuted by the czars and by the Communists. Early Christian churches existed in Georgia and Armenia, while some Buddhists made their home in the easternmost part of the country. For political reasons, the Soviet government has always allowed the Muslims of Central Asia to follow their own faith with comparatively little state interference.

The new policy of "glasnost" (openness) of the late 1980s, however, has made it quite clear that, despite years of suppression, religion in the Soviet Union is far from dead. The government began to show an increasing tolerance to religious beliefs and actions and even returned some church property, and high Communist officials participated in the 1988 celebrations of 1,000 years of Christianity.

Education

Before the Bolshevik Revolution of 1917, over three quarters of the people in Russia could neither read nor write. Most of the illiterates were peasants, some were workers, and there were virtually no schools for these groups in the prerevolutionary society. The situation has changed dramatically, and schooling has become available to everyone.

Soviet youth today show a tremendous desire to learn. As one of them said, "We understand that nothing can be done without knowledge." For knowledge opens the way to the kinds of jobs in the arts, sciences, and professions to which the young people aspire.

After the revolution, Lenin told the young people, "It is not enough to understand what electricity is; it is necessary to know how to apply it to industry and agriculture." Since then, the Soviet leaders have continued to emphasize that learning must be of practical value to the society, and this has been their guideline in setting up a new educational system in which all schools in the country are run by the government.

Most toddlers, and even babies, are placed in day nurseries because their mothers work. For slightly older children there are kindergartens. Compulsory schooling begins at the age of 7 with first grade and is supposed to continue to at least age 17, although many youngsters, especially in the villages, drop out before then.

The school program stresses mathematics and science, the Russian language, literature, and history. In the fifth grade pupils begin to study a foreign language, usually English or French. Children in the non-Russian republics also study their own native language and culture. Boys and girls alike get polytechnical, or "shop," training. Two Communist Party-sponsored organizations are active in the schools—the Pioneers, for children aged 9 to 14, and the Komsomol (Young Communist League), for those in their late teens and early 20's.

A student who has completed the eighth grade may go on to complete the last two years of general secondary education; go to a specialized

A kindergarten playground in a small town in Siberia.

A Muslim school on the Registan Place in Samarkand, Central Asia.

Moscow University in Moscow has a skyscraper campus.

As early as kindergarten, Soviet schools stress Marxist theory and respect for Lenin and the motherland.

vocational school where he can also get a high school diploma; or get a job and take courses in the evening.

Many young people would like to go to a university or a higher institute, but there is room for only about one out of every five who graduate from high school. In practice, students from the cities have a better chance of being accepted than young people from the villages, where the quality of schooling is much lower. The Soviet people take pride in the fact that higher education in their country is tuition-free and that students receive allowances to help cover the cost of books and daily living.

Perhaps the most important thing about Soviet education is that it has tried to raise rapidly the educational level of a whole population, and in this it has made real achievements.

Soviet Science

On October 4, 1957, the Soviet Union launched the world's first earth satellite, Sputnik I, and in 1961 it launched the first manned satellite, carrying astronaut Yuri Gagarin. These events drew world public attention to the achievements of Soviet science and technology over the years. Yet, rather than competing with the United States in manned flights to the moon, the Soviet leaders in recent years have concentrated on space exploration with unmanned rockets and instruments.

From a late start in developing the atomic and hydrogen bombs, the U.S.S.R. has become one of the world's two nuclear superpowers. It uses nuclear power for submarines and for icebreaker ships in the Arctic Ocean. Soviet scientists have made distinguished contributions in the fields of plasma physics, thermoelectricity, and the physics of the earth.

A monument to Sputnik I, 1957, the first vehicle to orbit the earth.

They have done extensive research in the Arctic region. Soviet geologists have gained much knowledge of the country's mineral resources, especially in the remote areas of Asian Russia. In medicine there has been experimentation with the possibilities of transplanting organs and tissues.

The Soviet Union has built on a distinguished prerevolutionary Russian tradition in science, which included work by Dmitri Mendeleev in chemistry, Ivan Pavlov in physiology, and Konstantin Tsiolkovsky in the theory of rocket motion. The Communist leaders early recognized the importance of science for building up the country's industry and for its military development. They provided facilities for Soviet scientists and emphasized mathematics and science in the secondary school curriculum to prepare young people for careers in these fields.

The Soviet political and economic system is highly centralized, and this gives it some advantages in undertaking crash programs to attain certain goals. Its leaders can concentrate resources and manpower on an important project to a degree that the United States can do only in wartime. This is why Stalin's scientists were able to develop an atomic bomb by 1949 and a thermonuclear bomb by 1953 (just after his death)—long before Western leaders expected this to happen.

The Arts

The Soviet Union inherited a great Russian literature. Such classics as *War and Peace* by Leo Tolstoi and Fëdor Dostoevski's *Crime and Punishment* are read all over the world. These are two of the brightest stars in a whole constellation of fine writings of the 19th century, an extraordinarily rich period in Russian literature.

It began with the "golden age" of poetry from 1815 to 1830. In this short span Russia produced not only its finest poet, but one of the giants of world literature—Aleksander Pushkin. Russian poetry before him had an artificial and antiquated quality. Pushkin developed his own poetic style that was at once flowing, musical, and measured. He was a national poet in that he created a new literary language for Russia and used Russian life, folklore, and history in his compositions. His poetry was sensitive to people's problems and to the inequalities between the upper and lower classes in Russia. His most popular work is the novel-in-verse *Eugene (Evgeni) Onegin,* whose central character is a St. Petersburg dandy who lived a gay life similar to Pushkin's own life in his early years.

Pushkin encouraged and influenced Nikolai Gogol (1809–52), who became the country's first truly imaginative prose writer. Gogol was a realist who saw his society just as it was—an unjust order governed by corrupt and bungling *chinovniki* ("bureaucratic officials"). In his two masterpieces, the novel *Dead Souls* and the play *The Inspector General,* he satirized the world of officialdom and nobility and showed sympathy for the weak and underprivileged. Through satire, Gogol expressed his feeling that Russia was in need of a moral awakening. In the 19th century there were many sensitive people from the educated classes who felt a responsibility toward the whole of Russian society. They saw the damaging effect of autocratic rule by the czar and felt they should help bring about reform. Many of them turned to literature as a means of expressing their social criticism. Criticism had to be phrased carefully to get by the censors and still be understandable to the reading public. The critical writer always risked the danger of imprisonment or exile to a remote area.

"The Feast of the Intercession of the Virgin (Pokrov)," a wooden icon of the late 15th century from Novgorod. (A La Vieille Russie, New York-Paris.)

Three prose writers of the second half of the century stand out—Ivan Turgenev, Fëdor Dostoevski, and Leo Tolstoi. In 1852 Turgenev published *Sportsman's Sketches,* in which he portrayed the serfs as having more of a sense of humanity than their masters. Between 1855 and 1860, when the czar was preparing to abolish serfdom, Turgenev wrote several novels expressing the reforming enthusiasm that had taken hold of Russian society at that time. The young radicals liked his novels until he published one called *Fathers and Sons,* whose hero, Bazarov, they took to be an unflattering portrait of themselves. The young radicals were indignant—they said Bazarov was not a hero but a caricature. Turgenev replied that he had not intended this and was surprised by their reaction. Unflattering or not, his portrayal really did catch the spirit of the intellectual youth of that period. Many called themselves Nihilists, meaning that they did not accept any authority or any principle on faith.

Fëdor Dostoevski and Leo Tolstoi—two giants in literature—could not have been more different in their writings and personalities. Yet both underwent profound spiritual changes in their lives. When he was in his 20's, Dostoevski (1821–81) belonged to a radical discussion group that criticized existing conditions in Russia. He was arrested and sent to Siberia for 4 years of hard labor. While in Siberia he became a convert to the Orthodox religion, feeling that this would bring him closer to the Russian people. His most famous novels, *Crime and Punishment, The Idiot,* and *The Brothers Karamazov,* are novels of ideas—profound psychological studies with religious overtones. It has been said that Dostoevski " 'felt ideas' as others feel cold and heat and pain." During much of his life Dostoevski was poor, physically ill, and in mental anguish. His own suffering is reflected in his writings.

Count Leo Tolstoi (1828–1910), on the other hand, was a member of the nobility. Although he, too, criticized the rule of autocracy, his writings early won him wide fame, and this helped to protect him from arrest. *War and Peace* is a vast and vivid picture of how upper-class people's lives were affected by events at the time of Napoleon's invasion of Russia in 1812. Another famous Tolstoi novel, *Anna Karenina,* shows the tragic consequences for people of a love that transgressed the moral and social laws of the late 19th century. In his later years Tolstoi condemned both the Church and the State as organized forms of compulsion for man. He turned to the fundamental teachings of Christ and the principle of non-violence as the way to resist evil.

By the middle of the 19th century Russian music had also come into its own. European musical forms were joined to Russian musical themes, and there emerged compositions with a distinctive national flavor—such as Mikhail Glinka's opera *Russlan and Ludmilla,* and the works of Nikolay Rimsky-Korsakov and Modest Mussorgsky. Later in the century, composer Peter Tchaikovsky expressed the romantic movement in music, and his compositions won great popularity throughout the world.

When the Bolshevik Revolution came in 1917, many writers, composers, and artists did not want to live under a Communist regime and left the country. Those who stayed took part in the creative experiments of the 1920's, when all sorts of ideas and artistic styles were tried out. Poets, actors, painters, and architects took their talents out in the streets and created public "happenings"—parades, theatricals, and poetry readings for the masses. Writers wrote about the turmoil of those post-civil war days with relatively little censorship.

This freedom came to an end at the beginning of the 1930's. Stalin imposed severe controls in all areas of Soviet life. The Party dictated a new outlook for literature and art called Socialist Realism. Writers were expected to glorify Communism and write glowingly about what the Communist Party was doing to build up the country. The writer's message had to be easily understandable to large numbers of people, many of whom were just learning to read. The writer was to create positive heroes who would set a good example for Soviet citizens in their daily lives. Complex stories about a person's inner conflicts were frowned upon.

The result was that most of the literature in the Stalin period was monotonous. An outstanding exception was Mikhail Sholokhov's four-part novel, *The Quiet Don,* about the effect of world war, revolution, and civil war on the Cossacks who lived along the Don River.

The Soviet Government controlled the press, and it simply did not publish those writers who went against the Party's directives. Some writers wrote "for the drawer" (meaning, for a later time when chances of publication might be better). One of these was Russia's great 20th-century poet, Boris Pasternak. Pasternak was miraculously spared during the Great Purges, but other writers with whom the Party found fault were arrested and sent to the forced labor camps.

Painting was also expected to portray the Soviet people in a happy light. Abstract art was not permitted. Music was restricted as well, and some works by Sergei Prokofiev and Dmitri Shostakovich were not performed in those years.

By 1953 it seemed as if the creative arts had been crushed by censorship and repression. The death of Stalin, however, brought a change of climate for the artists in the Soviet Union. The period came to be known as the "Thaw," from a novel of that name by Ilya Ehrenburg, published in 1954. Ehrenburg dared to refer to the terror and the purges and was critical of Socialist Realist art. He and others began to call for more freedom of expression. This frightened the Party, and within a few years the "thaw" ended, but many writers continued to publish their works in "samizdat" (underground "publishing," usually done on antiquated manual typewriters) and abroad. In 1957, Boris Pasternak's now-famous novel, *Doctor Zhivago*, appeared in the West. The next year, Pasternak was awarded the Nobel prize for literature but was forced by the government to decline it. *Doctor Zhivago*, about a sensitive man's reaction to the Bolshevik Revolution, is considered by some a work of genius.

A performance of the Bolshoi Ballet, considered one of the finest in the world.

Much attention also has been focused on Alexander Solzhenitsyn, whose great talent came to public light in 1962 when his short novel *One Day in the Life of Ivan Denisovich* appeared with the personal approval of Khrushchev. It made a tremendous impact, being the first book published in the Soviet Union to describe a prisoner's life in the forced labor camps. It reflected Solzhenitsyn's own experience as a prisoner. In 1964, however, Solzhenitsyn came under attack by the Party. Two further novels, *The First Circle* and *The Cancer Ward,* were not passed by the censors and were published abroad. In 1970, he, too, was awarded the Nobel prize. The Soviet press denounced the award as politically inspired. *The Gulag Archipelago, 1918–1956,* which describes in detail the Stalinist prison system, appeared in Paris in 1973. It caused a tremendous uproar, and Soviet authorities forced Solzhenitsyn to emigrate. Since the mid-1970s, Solzhenitsyn has lived in Vermont, although in 1990, President Gorbachev restored his Soviet citizenship.

In the post-Stalin period, poets have had a great influence on the Soviet people, especially the younger generation. In the early 1960s, Yevgeny Yevtushenko, Andrei Voznesensky, Bella Akhmadulina, and others who were then in their 20s recited their verse before thousands of appreciative listeners. These poets sensed intuitively that people were fed up with political slogans, dishonesty, and bureaucracy and wanted to restore the value of human relationships. When Yevtushenko said, "my need is for us to gaze into each other," he spoke for millions of his countrymen.

Next to poetry the Soviet people especially love the ballet, which has long been the pride of Russia. Many dream of going to the Bolshoi Theater in Moscow and seeing *Swan Lake* or *Giselle.* The Bolshoi has a ballet school where talented youngsters get rigorous dance training. The very best of them usually enter the Bolshoi, and the other graduates join ballet companies in major cities around the country.

Mikhail Gorbachev's call for greater openness provoked an impressive flourishing of all arts, but especially of literature, film, and theater. Books and movies dealing with subjects that were off limits for decades began appearing. Anatoli Rybakov's *Children of the Arbat,* written in the 1960s, was published in 1988 and hailed as a masterpiece. The novel illuminates a short period of Stalin's rule and contains a fascinating intimate portrayal of the dictator himself. The movie *Repentance,* a mesmerizing allegory of Stalinism and the halfhearted de-Stalinization process, has been seen by millions of Soviet citizens. Many works, long forbidden by Soviet authorities (including *Doctor Zhivago*), are being published, and new talent is being cultivated in the rather unfamiliar atmosphere of increased tolerance.

Food

Since they live in a severe climate, it is not surprising that Russians are hearty eaters and drinkers. Their soups are usually thick, with lots of cabbage and other vegetables, potatoes, meat, or fish in them. Two favorites are borsch and *shchi.* A clear bouillon is always accompanied by something more substantial such as piroshki (little filled pastries).

Black bread, kasha (a cereal made from buckwheat or other grain), potatoes, and cabbage have long been basic to the Russian diet, and in years of war people subsisted on these things alone.

The busy marketplace in Tiflis, the capital of the Georgian Republic.

These fruit vendors are Uzbeks from Tashkent, capital of Uzbekistan.

Even now, fresh fruit and vegetables are hard to get in wintertime, and Russians look forward to the abundance of summer.

Country cooking can be tasted at its best at a peasant wedding banquet on a collective farm. There one finds homemade cheeses, meat jelly, and boiled meats, porridge, omelets, pies filled with pot cheese, gelatin desserts, and several kinds of pancakes.

In Moscow an elegant meal at one of the good restaurants would start with *ikra zernistaia*—fresh caviar—and vodka. The main dish might be *osetrina* (sturgeon, the fish from which the best caviar comes), or it might be *kotleta po kievski,* an unusual chicken dish named for the Ukrainian city of Kiev. This is made by rolling a flattened chicken breast around a finger of seasoned butter. The rolled chicken breast is then dipped in bread crumbs and quickly deep-fat fried until it is golden brown. Outside the U.S.S.R. this dish is known as "Chicken Kiev." Other popular main courses are the Georgian *shashlyk,* chunks of lamb pierced by a skewer, and the Central Asian *plov,* a mutton and rice dish. Dessert may be the Ukrainian *vareniki,* bite-sized cherry dumplings.

In the late 1980's a number of privately and cooperatively-owned restaurants and cafés opened in major Soviet cities, especially in the Baltic republics, as a response to the call for restructuring of the Soviet economy. These new establishments generally provide much better food and service than the state-owned restaurants.

Recreation and Sports

For two decades after World War II, the Soviet people worked six and seven days a week rebuilding their damaged industries and cities. Only recently have they had time for leisure and recreation. The Russians are a hardy people who love the out-of-doors, even during their long, cold winters. On snowy weekends the hillsides near Moscow are bright with skiers. Cross-country skiing is also popular. In Moscow's spacious Gorky Park, the walkways are flooded for skating.

In the summertime people head for the dacha, which may be a rented room in someone else's country house or a whole cottage of one's own. There they tend vegetable gardens and stroll through the forest in search of edible mushrooms. It is a real dacha treat to eat freshly gathered mushrooms that have been lightly cooked, seasoned, and served in a sour cream sauce.

The young people enjoy exploring their vast and varied land. From Moscow they go north to visit Leningrad and the old cities along the Baltic or south to swim in the warm waters of the Black Sea and to climb in the Caucasus mountains; southeast to see the deserts and ancient monuments of Soviet Central Asia and eastward into the wilderness of Siberia, which is rugged enough for the most venturesome of explorers. Everywhere there are different nationalities and cultures, so that going to these places is somewhat like visiting another country. Still, it does not take the place of a real trip abroad, and many Soviet people resent the fact that their government permits only a very small number of them to visit other countries.

Among the indoor pastimes, watching television takes up a fair amount of time. There are many serious educational programs, some intended for children. On the lighter side, TV presents sports events, feature movies, and quite a few live performances of theater, music, and ballet.

These trained dogs and their handlers are part of the famed Moscow Circus.

Swimmers in Moscow seem to enjoy the 81-degree F. (27 degrees C.) water temperature.

The game of chess is a passion for many people. Not only do they play it themselves, but when national or international tournaments are held in Moscow, the chess fans avidly follow every move the players make.

City teen-agers enjoy meeting their friends at a favorite café, where the custom is to eat ice cream and sip mild mixtures of fruit juice and wine, and sometimes dance to the latest tunes. They are fond of Western popular music. Of New Year's Eve, a Moscow girl said, "We like to gaze into a bowl of water or a mirror and tell each other's fortune. We love the evening of May Day when there are fireworks and floodlights, and cars are banned from the main streets so people can walk and dance under the lights."

On some collective farms there are regular movies, and a troupe of actors or musicians occasionally comes to visit. But mostly the peasants have to be resourceful and create their own entertainment. Even in the remote villages, the accordion and the balalaika—a traditional guitarlike instrument—now get competition from the transistor radio.

Organized sports activities have an important place in Soviet life. The Communist Party's view is that sports are not just for fun, but have a social value as well. They help to develop people who are healthy in outlook as well as in body, who will work well at their jobs, and be responsible citizens. There are some 200,000 sports clubs throughout the country, co-ordinated by the central government, with a total member-ship of over 50,000,000. A person usually joins one of these clubs at his place of work or study. Promising athletes are given intensive training so they can compete in international sports events. Moscow hosted the 1980 Summer Olympic Games, which were boycotted by some Western na-tions, including the United States, because of Soviet actions in Afghani-stan. (The Soviet Union and its allies boycotted the 1984 Summer Games, which were conducted in Los Angeles.) Soccer is the favorite team sport throughout the Soviet Union. Basketball, volleyball, gymnastics, track and field, and speed skating are also popular; and there are various national sports, from local versions of wrestling in Central Asia and the Caucasus to reindeer and dog sled races in the far north.

THE LAND

To comprehend a land the size of the Soviet Union requires a huge effort of the imagination. One cannot easily picture a landscape that covers as much area as the Soviet Union does. It becomes a little more comprehensible when one realizes that the 50 United States would fit into the U.S.S.R. two and a half times. And the Soviet Union's vast east-west extent becomes a little easier to imagine when one learns that the U.S.S.R. covers so many time zones that when it is midnight on the European frontier, it is 11:00 in the morning on the Bering Strait. The Soviet Union offers other dramatic contrasts in its range from north to south, for the nation extends from the Arctic to the subtropics.

The overwhelming fact about Soviet geography is its size, and the nation's size is matched by its strategic location as a natural bridge across Eurasia. Geographers traditionally have divided the vast Eurasian land-mass into two "continents"—Europe and Asia. The line dividing the two follows a line marked by the Ural Mountains and the Volga River. (A separate article about the VOLGA RIVER will be found in this volume.)

The western fourth of the Soviet Union, which is often called European Russia, covers about 2,000,000 square miles (5,180,000 sq. km.), comprising the eastern half of Europe. The remaining three quarters of the Soviet Union covers most of northern and part of central Asia. This area is often called Soviet Asia.

Together the two parts of the Soviet Union have about 37,000 miles (59,530 km.) of frontiers, of which approximately 27,000 miles (43,440 km.) are coastline. A glance at these coasts is a reminder of one of the most important facts about the Soviet Union—its northerly location and its relatively isolated position.

The long eastern and western coasts of North America open on to two of the world's major oceans—the Atlantic and the Pacific—making contact with the other continents comparatively simple. The Soviet Union's longest coastline, however, is on Arctic seas, where ice makes navigation impossible during most of the year. In this region only the port of Murmansk, whose waters are warmed by the North Atlantic Drift of the Gulf Stream, is open the year round. Other northern ports may be open as little as 2 months a year. Along the Soviet Pacific coast, the most important port is Vladivostok, but it, too, is threatened by fog and ice.

The Baltic Sea in the northwest and the Black Sea in the southwest—neither of which is totally controlled by the Soviet Union—provide the nation with its most important trade routes to Europe. Leningrad, the port closest to the centers of population and trade, is open only from May to October. The more westerly Baltic ports of Kaliningrad and Liepaja, however, are ice-free during most of the year. From its warm water ports at Odessa, Nikolayev, Novorossisk, Poti, and Batumi on the Black Sea, the U.S.S.R. is linked with some of its satellites in Eastern Europe via the Danube and with the Mediterranean via the Bosporus and the Dardanelles. On its southern frontier the Soviet Union shares the Caspian Sea with Iran.

The land borders of the Soviet Union touch 12 nations, but this does not diminish the sense of isolation that is caused by forbidding geographical features such as rugged mountains and empty deserts. It is only along the Soviet Union's borders with the nations of Eastern Europe that geography has permitted easy contact, and it is these contacts that have provided the traditional route by which European culture entered and stimulated the life of the Eurasian giant.

Landforms

The Soviet Union is made up mainly of an enormous lowland interrupted and fringed by mountains. The vast lowland is usually thought of as being divided into several parts. The Great Russian lowland in the west is separated from the West Siberian Plain by the Urals. The Turan lowland lies southeast of the Caspian Sea. Moving west to east the West Siberian Plain rises to become the Central Siberian Plateau, and then the land rises even higher in the East Siberian Highlands.

The Urals, which form the major north–south range, have never acted as a barrier, since they can be crossed easily at several points. The Caucasus mountains between the Black and Caspian seas are a more formidable barrier. The snowcapped mountains contain Mount Elbrus, the highest peak in Europe. Mountains frame the borders of the Soviet Union from the Carpathians in the west through the Crimean Mountains, the Caucasus, and the Kopet Dagh. Along the southeastern borders of So-

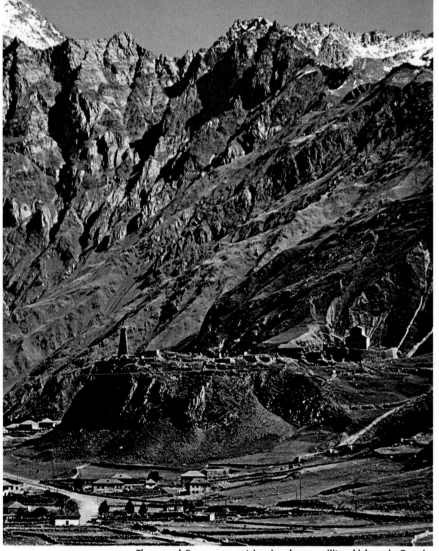

The rugged Caucasus mountains rise above a military highway in Georgia.

viet Central Asia one comes to the highest mountain systems in the country—the Pamir-Alai and the Tien Shan. Moving east, the Altai and Sayan mountains border southern Siberia. The eastern part of the nation is dissected by several mountain ranges.

Climate and Vegetation

The climate of the Soviet Union may be categorized as "continental," with its extremes of cold winters and rather hot summers. But as with every other aspect of Soviet geography, one simple category is not sufficient to describe the subtle varieties that exist in the enormous country. From north to south the climate and vegetation of the Soviet Union can be divided into four broad zones—Arctic-tundra; taiga, or humid forest, zone; dry-fertile region; and strips of subtropical land and desert.

The Arctic north is, of course, subject to the most extreme cold. Winters are long and bitter. Summers are short and cool. Only hardy scrub plants and lichen grow easily, providing food for reindeer grazed by the nomads. In the northeastern part of this zone mineral resources such as coal and nickel help to make up for the lack of good soil and a long growing season.

The Estonian port of Tallinn, ice-free most of the year, handles Soviet trade with Western Europe.

The taiga zone, as the coniferous forest region is called, stretches across the Soviet Union in a broad belt covering about one half of the nation's land area. Here, in a zone with a fairly typical continental climate, is one third of the world's forest land and a major Soviet resource —timber.

Moving south across forests of mixed pines and deciduous trees, the climate grows somewhat milder, and one reaches the Soviet steppe zone with its fertile soil. The black earth of the steppe stretches in a band from the western border to the Altai Mountains. Here fields of wheat, corn, and cotton seem to stretch to the very edge of the earth.

On the southern coast of the Crimea, in Moldavia, and in the coastal lands south of the Caucasus there is a region of subtropical climate where it is possible to grow such crops as tea and citrus fruits. A significant part of the Soviet Union—about 18 percent of the land—is desert. This extremely dry and hot region, which may have as little as 4 inches (10 centimeters) of rain a year, reaches from the Caspian Sea through the Turan lowland to the mountains of Central Asia. Parts of the desert are irrigated so that crops can be raised.

Rivers and Lakes

The Soviet Union has a wide and useful network of rivers, which have since earliest times provided water links across a land that still suffers from a shortage of highways and railroads. Many of the rivers have now also been harnessed as a source of hydroelectric power. The most important rivers of European Russia are the Pechora, the Dvina, Neva,

Neman, Dniester, Dnieper, Don, and the Volga—Europe's longest river. The value of these rivers for transportation has been increased by canals linking them to each other and eliminating strenuous overland trips. The mightiest rivers of Soviet Asia are the Amur, the Yenisei, the Lena, and the Ob-Irtysh system. The Syr Darya and Amu Darya bring moisture to the parched lands of Soviet Central Asia.

In addition to having the longest river and the highest mountain in Europe, the Soviet Union contains the world's largest lake—the salty Caspian Sea. Lakes Ladoga and Onega in the northwest are the largest freshwater lakes in Europe. Lakes Baikal and Balkhash in Soviet Asia are also unique since they are the largest on the Asian continent. Aside from distinctions of size, the lakes of the Soviet Union are important as a source of fish and as a part of the nation's transportation system.

Natural Resources

The Soviet Union's spectacular growth into one of the world's leading industrial nations is based on its wealth of natural resources. Virtually every major mineral is found in the Soviet Union, which is the world's leading coal and iron producer and a major oil producer.

Coal, the traditional fuel of industry, is found in many different parts of the Soviet Union. The leading fields are the Donets Basin (Donbas) in the eastern Ukraine, the Kuznetsk Basin (Kuzbas) in southern Siberia, at Karaganda in northern Kazakhstan, and near Cheremkhovo, west of Lake Baikal. Iron, which with coal is required for the manufacture of steel, is also found in several different parts of the nation. The most important deposits are at Krivoi Rog, near Kursk, and in the Kuzbas.

The Soviet Union is a major producer of oil and natural gas. The

A horse-drawn sleigh is useful in the snows of the northern U.S.S.R.

oldest fields are at Baku on the Caspian Sea. Other fields have been found between Volgograd and the southern Urals, in the western Ukraine, on Sakhalin island off the northeast coast, and in Siberia.

In addition to these minerals, the Soviet Union has the world's largest deposits of manganese; large copper reserves; bauxite, nickel, lead, zinc, magnesium, and the rare metals gold, silver, and platinum. Two important nonmetallic minerals—apatite and potassium salts—are also mined in the U.S.S.R. Apatite is used in the manufacture of phosphate fertilizers, and potassium salts are used in chemical production.

It appears that the only industrially important resources that the Soviet Union lacks are tin, tungsten, and rubber—lacks that can readily be made up through imports.

ECONOMY

A much more serious handicap for the nation as a whole is created by what seems at first to be an advantage—size and location. The U.S.S.R.'s generally extreme climate and shortage of fertile farmlands relative to the size of the population have created problems for the government throughout Russian and Soviet history.

Agriculture

Providing the people with enough food has been a colossal problem for the country's leaders, both under the czars and under the Communists. There are two major reasons for agriculture's lagging far behind industry. One has to do with land and weather conditions. Although the Soviet Union is a very large country, it has relatively little fertile soil. Where the soil is at its best, as in the black earth region of the Ukraine, there is often not enough rainfall for a good crop. Farther north, the rain is plentiful, but the growing season is short.

The other reason for the persistent agricultural lag is that the country's rulers have traditionally distrusted the peasantry and have been unwilling to grant it real independence. Even after the abolition of serfdom in 1861, most peasants continued to live in serflike conditions. They were heavily taxed, did not have enough land, and suffered restrictions on their freedom of movement. Shortly before the Bolshevik Revolution, steps were taken to strengthen the individual farmer, but the reform was too late and too little to remedy the situation. Stalin's solution to the agricultural problem was to force the peasants into a nationwide system of collective and state farms. Resistance by the peasantry to this move was widespread. Without the incentives of private ownership and profits, agricultural output fell so low that there was famine.

By the middle of 1990 severe shortages of even the most basic foodstuffs were apparent in Moscow. Lines for bread and other commodities and empty store shelves were evident in spite of increased food imports. Distribution problems and broader economic troubles were considered to be largely responsible.

There are two types of farms in the Soviet Union—collective and state. The collective farm *(kolkhoz)* is made up of several villages and the land around them, which averages about 7,000 sown acres (2,830 hectares) altogether. A village often has just one road, wide and unpaved, with the houses lined up along it and the fields stretching beyond. In European Russia the houses tend to be weathered log cabins that some-

Workers on a collective farm in the Crimea set out tobacco plants.

times have decorative wood carving around their windows. In Georgia the houses are of stone, and in Central Asia adobe is often used.

On a collective farm the government owns the land but leases it to the farm. The peasants work the fields communally with pooled equipment and sell most of their produce to the state, which sets the price. Earnings are calculated according to the amount of work each person has done for the farm. In theory, the *kolkhoz* is a co-operative whose members elect their chairman. In practice, the farm chairman is usually selected by local party officials, and his election by the farmers is a formality. He has authority not only over production, but also over the farmers themselves.

The state farm (*sovkhoz*) is organized like an agricultural factory. It is both owned and operated by the government, and its workers receive a set monthly wage, paid vacations and sick leave, and a pension, just as city workers do. There are now more state farms, and they cultivate a much larger part of the sown land (about half of it) than in Stalin's time.

On both the *kolkhoz* and the *sovkhoz*, each family is permitted to have its own vegetable garden as well as a cow, a few pigs, and some chickens. These private plots—usually half an acre to an acre (⅕–⅖ hectare)—can really be considered a third type of farm, existing alongside the *kolkhoz* and *sovkhoz*. Although they comprise only about 3 percent of the total cropland, they provide a large part of the country's vegetables, meat, and dairy products. The farmers give a lot of time and effort to cultivating their plots—not only to feed their own families better, but also to add to their cash earnings. They take their produce to a farmers' market where prices are not government-controlled and prices are higher than those paid by the state.

Farm machinery has helped Soviet farmers to increase their productivity.

It is a wonderful experience to visit one of the large, colorful, and bustling farmers' markets in Moscow in the summertime. Among other things there are fresh berries, jars of honey of all flavors, and crocks of white pot cheese and of *smetana* (similar to sour cream). Several peasants beckon to the customer at the same time, each offering a taste of his tempting produce. There is often lively bargaining over prices before the final purchase is made.

In the early 1980s private plots, which cover only about 3 percent of the total sown area, supplied one-third of the country's meat, milk, eggs, and vegetables; one-half of all fruit; and up to two-thirds of potatoes, an important staple of the Russian diet. The leadership of Mikhail Gorbachev has encouraged private initiative, but the vast agricultural system seems impervious to change, and the Russian people still complain about scarcities, long lines for basic foodstuffs, and the poor quality of many goods.

Industry

The Soviet Union is one of the most industrialized nations in the world. Nonetheless, the industrial output of the U.S.S.R. has been declining, despite the efforts of Gorbachev to restructure the economy. As the Soviet society becomes more open, western analysts are discovering that the economy is much more fragile than previously thought. Excessive military spending and ineffective central planning have crippled many sectors of the economy.

In 1914, several years before the Communists took power, Russia had become the world's fifth largest industrial producer. Railroad building in the late 19th century had stimulated the construction of some large metalworking and machine-building factories, especially in St. Petersburg (now

Russian caviar, packed for export in large canneries, comes from sturgeon caught in the Caspian Sea.

In the Belorussian city of Minsk, production-line workers assemble farm machinery in a state-owned factory.

Rugs and textiles are important products of Samarkand in Central Asia.

Leningrad). Moscow was then the center of the textile industry. Progress had been made in developing the iron and coal of southern Russia, the mineral resources of the Urals, and the oil of Baku on the Caspian Sea.

After World War I, the Revolution of 1917, and the civil war, industrialization was resumed in 1928 with the launching of the 5-year plans. Stalin achieved a high rate of industrial growth by concentrating on a few goals. He wanted more iron, steel, coal, and oil—machinery for heavy industry and weapons for defense. He neglected other aspects of the economy, with the result that industrial progress was very uneven. The emphasis for decades was on quantity rather than quality. If goods were shoddy, they were accepted anyway because of shortages.

On the other hand, the Soviet Union under Stalin and his successors developed the less settled frontier regions of Central Asia and Siberia. The electric power system is rivaled only by that of the United States. Several of the world's largest dams are in the Soviet Union, as are the world's longest transmission lines. The world's first atomic power station was opened in the U.S.S.R. in 1954, and by the 1980s the country had about 40 nuclear reactors. A major nuclear disaster took place at the Chernobyl reactor in 1986, resulting in more than 30 immediate deaths and the evacuation of some 130,000 people.

In the 1980s the Soviet Union continued to be a military superpower, but it became more and more obvious that the rigid central economic planning was wasteful and inefficient, and that the country had no chance to catch up with the technologically developed Western countries without profoundly changing the economy. The last years of the Brezhnev era were a period of general stagnation, but when Mikhail Gorbachev became head of the Party in 1985 he almost immediately began to call for reforms. He surrounded himself with a number of bright economists and within a few years was able to formulate the main points of his "perestroika" (restructuring).

The major goal was to make individual Soviet enterprises more autonomous, to give them more freedom and at the same time more responsibility for their performance. In a planned economy, a company is totally dependent on central authorities, which determine where to buy materials, what to produce, and where to sell it. This system encourages inefficiency, because the company does not have to compete with anyone, and since workers cannot be fired, they know they will get their wages regardless of how well or badly they work. Under "perestroika," unprofitable companies would suffer financially, and failure to produce would result in wage cuts.

A number of new laws were promulgated in order to make it possible for individuals or small groups to start their own enterprises. Restaurants, taxis, recycling centers, and repair shops were set up in many places, but party bureaucrats often hampered these new initiatives. Another goal of "perestroika" was to fight against shoddy products. Better quality control was introduced in many companies, but it was often resented by workers and led to drops in production.

The Soviet Union also wanted to attract foreign companies, and for that reason a new law was promulgated that made it possible to start joint ventures, with the Soviet government owning 51 percent of the shares. One of the first companies to make such a deal was McDonalds, which introduced their "Big Macs" to the Muscovites in 1988.

What did not change in "perestroika" were various social benefits, such as the minimum of three weeks of vacation (with trips to tourist resorts often partially paid for by the trade unions), free medical service, free education and specialized training, sick pay, and pensions after retirement.

CITIES

More than 20 cities in the Soviet Union have populations exceeding 1,000,000. Some of these, such as Novosibirsk and Dnepropetrovsk, are heavily industrial and have little to interest the tourist. The chief goals of foreign visitors are the capital, Moscow, the old capitals Kiev and Leningrad, and Central Asian cities such as Tashkent and Bukhara.

Moscow

Moscow, the capital of the Soviet Union, is above all a place of contrasts and bustling activity in which one can see the many changes that have taken place in Soviet life. Once called "The City of 40 Times 40 Churches," its skyline was dominated by cupolas. Now, the eye is drawn high up to the gray spires of the several skyscrapers that Stalin built. One is the Ministry of Foreign Affairs, and another is Moscow University, towering above the Lenin Hills. Alongside old log houses on the back streets, there now exist block after block of modern apartment buildings, creating whole new suburbs on the outskirts of the city.

Moscow's sidewalks are always crowded. Bundled up for the cold winter, people tend to look alike. In summer the differences in dress and nationality are striking. There are peasant women wearing head scarves and carrying sacks and open baskets who have come in for the day to sell their fresh produce. They rub shoulders with city-dwellers, many of

A pedestrian arcade in the world-famous Moscow subway.

This poster in Moscow stresses the call of the Soviet motherland.

One of the Soviet Union's popular resorts on the Black Sea at Yalta.

The 19th-century Cathedral of St. Isaac in Leningrad is now a museum.

whom wear attractive Western-style clothing. People hurry to and fro, for this city is the political and administrative center of virtually everything that goes on in the Soviet Union.

The heart of Moscow is the Kremlin ("fortified palace") from which the city originally grew. It is enclosed by a massive brick wall built in the 15th century. Inside are splendid cathedrals where the czars of Russia once were crowned and palaces where at times they lived and entertained. The cathedrals are now museums, and the palaces have been turned into congress halls, government offices, a museum, and a theater. There is one modern building completed in 1961, the Palace of Congresses, where large and important meetings are held. The Kremlin, closed to the public in Stalin's time, is now a favorite place for tourists from all over the country and abroad. They stand in line, sometimes for hours, to see the body of Lenin in the mausoleum just outside the Kremlin in Red Square.

Moscow has many theaters, of which the Bolshoi opera and ballet and the Moscow Art Theater are the most famous. At the conservatory of music, the world-renowned musicians give concerts and lessons. In the Tretyakov Art Gallery, founded by two brothers of that name, there are many beautiful old Russian icons—religious paintings on wood.

The Belfry of Ivan the Great in the Kremlin dates from the 15th century.

Leningrad

Leningrad is a city of unusual grandeur and spaciousness. Its majestic river, the Neva, is bounded by elegant palaces and huge squares. Its main avenue, the Nevski Prospekt, is one of the most handsome in Europe. From an island in the river, a golden stiletto spire thrusts up into the vast northern sky, which is often overcast and mournful in mood. Leningrad is a relatively young city—about 100 years younger than New York City. Begun in 1703, the town was originally named St. Petersburg after the apostle Saint Peter, but everyone understood that it was really the city of another Peter—the czar, its founder—who was a far from saintly person. There still exists the simple wooden house in which Peter the Great lived during the first years of building the town.

The city owes its elegant style to an architect of Italian origin, Rastrelli. His grandest creation, the huge Winter Palace, stretches at great length along the Neva. Within it is the famous Hermitage Museum, originally the royal family's private art collection.

The Communists celebrate St. Petersburg as the birthplace of the Revolution of 1917, after which the city was renamed in honor of Lenin. Leningrad was an industrial center even before the Revolution; it manufactured the country's first tractors, turbines, and ships. A place of sad memory is the Piskarevsky Cemetery, the mass grave of some of the 600,000 Leningraders who died during the 900-day siege in World War II.

Kiev

Kiev, the capital of the Ukraine, was the capital of old Russia—the place, as the chronicles say, "from whence the Russian lands took their beginnings." High on the hillside overlooking the river is a statue of Prince Vladimir holding a large cross. He introduced Christianity into Russia in the 10th century. The name of Kiev's main street, the Kreshchatik, is thought to come from the verb *krestit,* meaning "to christen," because Prince Vladimir christened his 12 sons in a brook that flowed through the valley where the street now is. During World War II the Kreshchatik was almost completely destroyed, as was much of Kiev during a 2-year occupation by the Nazis. Kiev is the center of Ukrainian culture, which reached its highest expression in the work of the 19th-century poet Taras Shevchenko.

Tashkent

Old Tashkent in Central Asia was a one-story city of flat roofs and adobe walls, with a labyrinth of narrow, winding streets. The windows of houses faced on an inner courtyard, and the outside wall was windowless to keep the women from looking at and being seen by men who passed. In those days Uzbek women never appeared in public without a *chachvan,* a heavy veil, over their faces. After the czar's army conquered Central Asia in the 19th century, a Russian section of Tashkent gradually took shape. In the last few decades many new buildings were constructed, so that by 1966 the modern section comprised one fourth of Tashkent. That year the city suffered a serious earthquake. More than 28,000 buildings in Tashkent were damaged. Fortunately there was little loss of life. The Soviet Government is devoting considerable resources and attention to rebuilding Tashkent, which is the leading cultural and economic center of Soviet Central Asia.

Kiev, on the Dnieper River, once the capital of old Russia.

Produce from small household plots, sold at open-air markets, equals the output of the huge collective farms.

Ancient ruins at Echmiadzin, a cultural center of old Armenia.

HISTORY

The history of what is now the Soviet Union began more than 1,000 years ago with the founding of two small principalities called Novgorod and Kiev. Before that there had been many groups of people living on the vast plain stretching from the Baltic Sea all the way to the Pacific Ocean. They had come in waves from Europe and Asia, and they were able to move around with ease on the Russian plain because of its large network of rivers and the absence of effective mountain barriers. Among these peoples at various times were Scythians, Sarmatians, Goths, Huns, and Khazars. Some remained essentially nomadic, while others settled down and engaged in trade and cultivation. But after a few centuries most of them were expelled by a new wave of invaders, and this pattern was repeated several times over a thousand years.

One group was able to make a permanent place for itself. These were the Slavs. By the 8th century A.D. they had spread out along the predominantly north–south river roads of Russia and founded a number of trading towns, of which the two most important were Novgorod and Kiev. They encountered another group that at first fought them and then came to share power with them in these towns or helped to protect them. These were the Varangians, or Norsemen, who had come from across the Baltic. The ancient chronicles say that in the 9th century, when there was a revolt in Novgorod, a Norseman named Rurik was invited to come in and restore order and became the prince of Novgorod. Shortly afterward his successor, Oleg, went south and took over Kiev, thereby establishing the ruling dynasty of Kievan Russia.

Kievan Russia. Kiev carried on a lively trade with Byzantium, the Eastern Roman Empire, which had its capital in Constantinople. Furs, honey, wax, and tar as well as war captives to be sold into slavery were transported down the Dnieper River and across the Black Sea to Constantinople and there exchanged for silks, spices, wine, and gold.

Through these contacts with Constantinople, which was also the center of the Greek Orthodox Church, Prince Vladimir of Kiev was converted to Christianity in 988. This was to have important consequences for Russia. Its art and architecture were much influenced by Byzantium. It adopted the Greek alphabet for its written language. Perhaps most important, with the Orthodox Church came the Byzantine idea that a prince rules by authority of God and cannot be challenged by anyone on earth. Russia's czars continued to rule according to this principle until 1917.

The princes of Kiev did not succeed in unifying the lands and tribes around them, and the real unification of Russia began later and to the north, but not before Russia had been invaded by another outside group, the Tatars, commonly known as the Mongols.

The Tatar Rule. "No one knows for certain," says the Russian chronicle, "who they are or from where they come, or what their language is, or race, or faith, but they are called Tatars." They came from Asia, where Genghis Khan had already built a vast empire, and his grandson Batu was looking for new lands to conquer. In 1237 his army of horsemen stormed over the principalities of Russia, burning cities and killing inhabitants. They sacked Kiev itself and pushed westward almost to Vienna, then turned back and set up a headquarters in Russia on the lower Volga River. From this encampment the Tatars ruled Russia for almost 250 years.

They forced the Russian princes to pay them heavy taxes. They demanded total obedience, and any protests were harshly put down. To keep the Russians divided, the Tatars played one prince off against another. One result of this was that the Russian princes absorbed into their own government some of the Tatar despotic ways of governing.

The Tatar rule was altogether disastrous for Russia. Not only did it lay waste the land and the civilization that had begun in Kiev, it also deepened Russia's isolation from Europe. Just when Europeans were starting their renaissance of scientific and cultural growth, the Russians were effectively cut off from these developments. Moreover, they lost for good what little democracy they had in the Kievan period—including the city assemblies in which the men had gathered in the main square to shout out their opinions on various matters.

Russia Under The Czars

The Growth of Moscow. It was Moscow that finally gathered up enough strength to overcome the Tatars. The city was begun in the middle of the 12th century as a trading post on a riverbank. For a long time its princes were the most humble and obedient vassals of the Tatar khan. They often journeyed to the Volga to pay him rich tribute. All the while, however, they were gradually enlarging their territory, seizing land from other princes, using diplomacy where possible, and moving into unclaimed forests. Then they began to fight the Tatars. But it was not until almost 1500 that the Tatar Empire had weakened to the point where it could no longer extort taxes from the Russians.

The Grand Duke Ivan III (known as the Great) ascended the throne in 1462 and completed the process of bringing all the principalities under Moscow's rule. In 43 years he tripled Moscow's domain. By that time Byzantium and its capital, Constantinople, had been overrun by the Turks. This had two major results in Russia. When Ivan married the niece of the last Byzantine emperor, he concluded that Moscow was the true heir to the Byzantine Empire. He began to call himself "czar," which is the Russian for Caesar. Secondly, the Russian Orthodox Church declared that it was no longer part of the Greek Orthodox Church. It said that because Constantinople was in Muslim hands, Moscow had become the "third Rome," where Christianity would survive.

Why did Moscow, rather than some other principality, succeed in unifying Russia? One reason is that Moscow was well placed geographically for both river and overland trade. More important was the ruthlessness and determination of its princes in their policy of expansion.

The 16th-century czar Boris Godunov is buried in this cathedral at Zagorsk.

Autocratic Power.   During the 16th century Russia continued to expand, especially down the Volga and eastward to Siberia, and settlers moved into these areas. The Moscow Kremlin was enlarged and made more splendid. The power of the czar increased, and the freedom of the Russian people declined still further. Governing in the autocratic manner of the Tatars, the czar weakened the position of the boyars (the hereditary nobility), the only group that might have opposed him. He took land from them and gave it to his own followers, often the men who won battles for him. In this way he created a new class of landowners who were totally dependent on him and obliged to give him service. In theory the peasants were at liberty to move around as long as they paid their taxes. But they usually had gotten in debt to their landlords for loans received, so that in fact they really were not free to leave the landlords' estates. In this way serfdom became widespread in Russia.

Ivan IV, who ruled in the second half of the century, was called Ivan "The Dread," or "Terrible." He truly was dreaded, for his was a reign of terror. By the time of Ivan's death in 1584, the country was in turmoil, its people discontented. The next 29 years were a "Time of Troubles." Ivan's sons died, and several men tried to claim the throne. The Swedes and Poles took advantage of the chaos to invade the country. In the end, a national assembly was convened, and in 1613 it elected 16-year-old Michael Romanov to be the czar. The Romanov family was to govern Russia for the next 300 years.

Peter the Great.   Under the first three Romanov czars, order was gradually restored in the government. The outlying areas were brought back under Moscow's control. The next Romanov, Peter the Great, opened Russia once again to European influences and made his country a major European power. Peter was a giant among the czars, both physically (standing over 6½ feet—2 m.—tall) and in what he accomplished for Russia. He fought the Swedes for many years and wrested from them land on the Baltic and the Gulf of Finland. There, on a swamp, he began in 1703 to build a new capital, St. Petersburg. It became Russia's window on Europe.

Peter wanted to use the knowledge and skills that Europe possessed to overcome Russian backwardness. To this end, he journeyed to Holland and England and elsewhere. He studied these countries' shipyards and even learned the shipbuilding trade himself, as well as other skills. Upon his return home he decreed many changes. Russia's noblemen and merchants were ordered to shave off their beards and exchange their caftans for European dress. Those who refused to shave had to purchase a beard license. Peter set up schools for the study of mathematics, engineering, and foreign languages. He had foreign books translated and founded the first Russian newspaper. Foreign technicians and craftsmen were brought in. The Army and Navy were modernized, and the government administration was reorganized along Swedish lines.

The main burden of Peter's conquests and reforms fell on the peasant-serfs. By this time they were bound to the land by law. This meant that the nobleman was sure to get peasant labor to till the land on his estate, and the czar was sure of getting the peasant taxes he needed. But Peter also made demands of his noblemen, requiring them to attend his new schools and serve either in the armed forces or the civil administration.

Petrodvorets, summer home of Peter the Great, is known for its fountains.

Nobility and Peasants—a Widening Gap. After Peter the Great came 37 years of weak leadership. The Russian nobility took advantage of the situation and persuaded the czar to release them from obligatory service to the state. With plenty of wealth and free time, the nobility entered its "golden age," under Empress Catherine the Great in the second half of the 18th century. European culture was fashionable in high society. Catherine herself corresponded with the French philosophers Voltaire and Diderot and admired their ideas. In Europe these ideas helped to bring about more political freedom for the people. But this did not happen in Russia.

At the other extreme from the glittering life in court were Russia's 34,000,000 peasants (of a total population of 36,000,000). The majority of them were serfs on noblemen's estates, and the rest lived in similarly poor conditions on lands belonging to the royal family. Upon hearing that freedom from service had been granted to the nobility, many peasants anticipated that they too would be set free. When this did not come about, their discontent increased.

By the turn of the century, some people had begun to realize how unhealthy the situation in Russia was. Czar Alexander I at first talked of making fundamental changes. He even asked his advisers to draft a constitution and a plan for emancipating the serfs. But soon the Czar's attention was absorbed by war against the armies of Napoleon, and little came of these promising beginnings.

Revolt and Reaction.   Napoleon's invasion of Russia in 1812 brought the Russian people together in the common goal of expelling him. They burned everything in his path so that his army would have no food or shelter. Even Moscow was deserted and in flames when Napoleon reached it. He was forced to retreat, and countless numbers of his soldiers died in the bitter cold of the great expanses of Russia. Russian troops followed the retreating French Army and in 1813 triumphantly entered Paris. Russia had become one of the strongest nations in Europe. In alliance with the leaders of Austria and Prussia, the Czar set himself up as the guardian of European order.

A handful of young officers of the Guards returned to Moscow from Paris inspired by French political ideas. Some among them concluded that the only way to end serfdom and gain political freedom in Russia was to overthrow the czar. They formed secret societies and plotted. When Alexander died in 1825, they tried to prevent his brother Nicholas, a supporter of autocracy, from ascending the throne. Their revolt was quickly suppressed. Since it took place in December, they became known as the Decembrists and inspired later Russian revolutionaries.

Nicholas I proved to be as severe as his opponents had feared. A suspicious man, he created a large secret police and a network of informers. The universities were still further restricted in what they could teach. There was censorship of printed material, and dissent was punished. In spite of this repressive atmosphere, Russian literature began to flourish, and young radical intellectuals developed political and social ideas that were eventually to have an enormous impact on Russia.

The condition of the peasants worsened. Their numbers increased, while the amount of land and their primitive farming techniques remained the same. Nicholas was afraid to come to grips with the problem lest the whole state fall apart.

After the Emancipation.   The end of serfdom came after the country's defeat in the Crimean War in 1856. The war resulted from competition with Britain and France to take over territories formerly occupied by the Ottoman (Turkish) Empire. Russia's large armies were no match for the smaller but better equipped French and British forces. This revealed how weak Russia really was. Alexander II became czar in 1855 and decided that major changes would have to be made right away or Russia's power and prestige would decline still further. His Emancipation Proclamation set the serfs free in 1861. In the opinion of many Russians this and other reforms that followed did not go far enough in changing the situation. The revolutionaries became even more convinced that the Czar would have to be overthrown. One group among them engaged in terrorist acts and finally succeeded in assassinating Alexander II in 1881.

Alexander III was czar for 13 years and was followed by Nicholas II, who ruled until the Bolshevik Revolution of 1917. They were the last two czars of Russia. Fearful of the growing revolutionary movement, they both relied largely on censorship, the secret police, and the use of force, as their predecessors had. In some ways, however, Russia was going through a period of growth. Russian industry made great strides after 1870. Peasants migrated to the factories to become workers. Cities developed in new areas of manufacture, mining, and oil drilling.

Under Catherine the Great, Russia had acquired large slices of Polish land and reached the shores of the Black Sea. Its settlers had begun to spread out into the vast spaces of Siberia. In the next period, Russia took over Transcaucasia (now divided into the Georgian, Armenian, and Azerbaijan republics), and under the last three czars it expanded into Central Asia and acquired more land on the Pacific. The non-Russian peoples who had come under the czar's control were subjected to Russification—pressure to have them learn Russian and adopt the Orthodox religion.

In 1904–5 Russia suffered another humiliating defeat, this time in a war with Japan. It came at a time when popular discontent was already at the boiling point. Workers in St. Petersburg, Moscow, and elsewhere went on strike. There were peasant uprisings, too. The strike spread to the railwaymen, and in October, 1905, the country was virtually at a standstill. The Czar finally sent troops to disperse the demonstrators and restore order in the countryside. Hundreds of people were killed.

Nicholas realized that some concessions would have to be made. He granted such basic rights as freedom of speech and the right to assemble and to form unions and political parties. He established a lawmaking national assembly, called the Duma. But he kept the final power of decision for himself; and when the Duma went against his wishes, he could overrule it or dissolve it. In the next 2 years it was twice dissolved. This situation was totally unacceptable to the people who favored extreme changes. Finally in 1917, in the midst of World War I, when Russia was experiencing heavy losses and disorder, the revolutionaries seized the opportunity to impose their own solution on the country.

THE REVOLUTION

Lenin and the Revolutionary Movement. Lenin, whose real name was Vladimir Ilich Ulyanov, was brought up in a family that was deeply religious and loyal in its feeling for the czar. But in 1887, at the age of 17, his older brother, who had joined a group of underground revolutionaries, was hanged for taking part in an attempt on the life of Czar Alexander III. To understand his brother's act, Lenin began to study the ideas of the revolutionary movement.

When he was in his early 20's, Lenin discovered the ideas of Karl Marx. A German who lived most of his life in England, Marx was a major social thinker of the 19th century. He saw the history of mankind as divided into several periods. In each period a small group of powerful people took advantage of the rest of the people by exploiting their labor. Eventually, when life got unbearable for the oppressed, they rose up and overthrew their oppressors, and a new period of history began. In Marx's own time, it was the factory workers who were being exploited. They worked long hours for low wages, while the capitalist factory owners received large profits. Marx predicted that the living standard of the workers would decline under capitalism because profits would rise and wages decline, and eventually machines would put more and more people out of work. Inevitably, said Marx, the workers would unite to destroy the capitalist system. In its place would come communism. It was to be an ideal society, without classes, without exploitation, in which all the people shared ownership of the factories and farms and received the benefits of their labor.

Marx's ideas had tremendous appeal to people everywhere who were discontented with existing conditions. Lenin became a Marxist and spent his time writing books and articles about how a revolution could be achieved in Russia. Twice in the 1890's he was exiled to Siberia for his writings. Then he went to Western Europe, where the czarist police could not seize him. In 1898, Lenin joined with other Marxists to form the Russian Social Democratic Labor Party. Its members could not agree on how to apply Marxism to Russian conditions, which differed greatly from the society that Marx had known in Western Europe. In 1903, the disagreement led to a split into two groups—Lenin's Bolsheviks (meaning "majority") and the Mensheviks (meaning "minority"). The Mensheviks wanted a party that was open to everybody, one in which members would be free to express their opinions. The Bolsheviks insisted on a small and tightly-knit party, taking in only dedicated people who would accept without question the decisions of the party leaders. Lenin thought that the workers would not unite and make a revolution on their own initiative. The revolution would have to be started and led by a small group of disciplined revolutionaries who knew what was best for everyone. This group was the nucleus of the future Communist Party.

1917. Toward the end of World War I, the czarist government simply collapsed from exhaustion, corruption, and lack of support. Its army had gone into battle in 1914 ill-equipped and poorly led and suffered a series of shattering defeats by the Germans and the Austrians. As the war progressed, food grew increasingly scarce in the cities.

In 1917 two revolutions took place in Russia. The first one began on March 8 (February 23 on the Russian calendar then in use) in Petrograd, as St. Petersburg was renamed at the start of the war). Breadlines turned into riots, and strikes broke out all over the city. Police and soldiers were ordered to fire at the rioters; instead many came over to the opposition side. Finally, Czar Nicholas II had to abdicate, and a Provisional Government was formed, consisting of members of the Duma. It placed the Czar under arrest and declared Russia to be a republic. What the people yearned for most was peace, yet the Provisional Government went on trying to fight the war.

Lenin was in Switzerland when the February revolution began. Understandably he was eager to reach the scene of action, but to do so he had to cross Germany, which was then Russia's enemy. The Germans reasoned that Lenin's presence back home would help to weaken the Russian war effort, so they offered to transport him in a sealed railway car up to Germany's northern border. From there he went through Sweden and Finland, and arrived in Russia in April.

By this time, soviets ("councils") of workers' and soldiers' deputies had been formed in Petrograd and all the larger cities and towns in Russia, and many of them were behaving as if they were the real governing bodies. Lenin told his followers in the soviets not to recognize the Provisional Government and to demand the transfer of "all power to the soviets." The goal in sight, he said, was peace, bread, and land.

By autumn the Bolsheviks had achieved a majority in both the Petrograd and Moscow soviets. Lenin decided it was the right moment to seize power. On the morning of November 7 (October 25 on the old calendar) the Bolsheviks took over the main government buildings in Petrograd. A new government was formed, with a cabinet called the Soviet of Peoples Commissars. Lenin was its chairman, and a fiery and brilliant young man named Leon Trotsky became Commissar of Foreign Affairs. The Bolshevik Revolution was an accomplished fact.

The Soviet Union: 1917 to 1953

Consolidating Communist Power.   One of the first things that Lenin did was to take Russia out of the war. He paid an enormous price for peace. In the March, 1918, treaty of Brest-Litovsk with Germany, Russia gave up eastern Poland, the Baltic states (Estonia, Latvia, and Lithuania), and Finland, and agreed to recognize the Ukraine as independent. These areas contained nearly one third of the country's population and arable land and one half of its industry. Public opinion in Russia was horrified. With Germany's defeat at the end of World War I, the Soviet Government gradually recaptured the Ukraine, but it did not regain the Baltic states and the parts of Poland that had been lost until just before World War II.

Inside Russia, opposition to the Communist Government began to grow among several groups of people—the businessmen, the landowning nobility, the Orthodox Church, and officers of the disbanded imperial army. They joined to support the White armies that fought the Communist Red army in a civil war that went on for nearly 3 years. The fighting was savage, leaving hundreds of thousands dead. Britain, France, the United States, and Japan all sent troops and arms onto Russian territory to help the Whites. Even so, the Whites lost the civil war. One reason was that the Red Army under Trotsky's leadership had become an effective fighting force. Another reason was that the White armies were widely separated from one another geographically, and their leaders could not agree on a common political program. They failed to win the support of the peasants, who were caught between the opposing sides and suffered at the hands of both. There could be no challenge to the new Soviet Government from Czar Nicholas II, since he and his wife and children had been executed in July, 1918.

The civil war was won, but the country all around was devastated. Famine was widespread. Factories lay in ruin, transportation had broken down, and agricultural output was way down. The peasants were especially discontented because their grain and other crops had been taken from them by force to feed the soldiers and city people.

When the Communists first seized power, they took ownership of large factories, farms, banks, public utilities, and railroads, and they banned private trade. But with the economy so battered by war, Lenin realized that the country needed a "breathing spell" in which to recover. This was why he introduced the New Economic Policy (NEP) in 1921. Private shopkeepers once again opened their doors. Peasants and small manufacturers were allowed to sell their products for whatever price they could get on the market. By 1929 industry and agriculture were producing as much as they had on the eve of World War I. Lenin intended the NEP to be a temporary retreat from his goal of building Communism. But he died in 1924 before he could work out a program explaining just how Russia could industrialize rapidly and create a new society.

The Early Stalin Period.   Within the Party it was generally expected that Trotsky would take Lenin's place. He was easily the most respected man after Lenin himself, and he had done a brilliant job of leading the Red Army to victory in the civil war. Trotsky's main rival was Joseph Stalin. In 1922 Stalin had been named General Secretary of the Communist Party. This enabled him to place his supporters in key posts within the Party and government, and with their help he became strong enough to compete with Trotsky for the leadership.

In addition to their great personal rivalry, Trotsky and Stalin disagreed profoundly about what the Party's basic policy should be. Trotsky believed that the Bolshevik Revolution would be followed by similar Communist revolutions in the advanced industrial countries of Western Europe. When those countries became Communist, they would then share their technology with the Soviet Union, enabling it to industrialize. Stalin believed that his nation could industrialize without help from outside. Moreover, he thought it would have to do so, since he did not see any sign of successful Communist revolutions elsewhere.

By 1927 Stalin succeeded in having Trotsky expelled from the Party. Two years later Trotsky was deported from the country, and in Mexico in 1940 he was assassinated by an ice-pick blow on the head.

In 1928, Stalin launched an economic and social revolution. The government took control of the entire economy and drew up a series of five-year plans for its development. The emphasis was on developing industry—factories, machines, mining, electricity, and transportation. To build these facilities, people worked long hours, often in the cold and without enough food. Much work was also done by prisoners, whose numbers soon reached hundreds of thousands. To enforce his policies, Stalin used methods as authoritarian as those of Peter the Great. Furthermore, his victory over his rivals signaled the end of the cultural and artistic freedom of the 1920's and the beginning of a long period of intellectual stagnation, brainwashing of generations of children, and stifling of all creative initiative.

Stalin forced the peasants to join large collective farms. Their own lands and farm animals and tools became common property. They all had to work the fields together and sell their produce to the government for much less than they could have received in open market competition. The peasants rebelled against this policy. They went so far as to slaughter half the country's farm animals rather than give them up to the collective farms. Many peasants were arrested and sent into forced labor on industrial projects and in the mines of Siberia. Many died of starvation. Yet this was only the beginning of the terror.

In the middle 1930's, for reasons that are hard to understand, Stalin grew suspicious of almost everyone, even his close colleagues. From 1936 to 1939 there took place a Great Purge as dreadful as any in the history of Russia. Millions of people simply vanished from sight. Party officials, old Bolshevik heroes, engineers, scientists, economists, writers, high military men, and many others were arrested on false charges of trying to overthrow the Soviet Government and restore capitalism. They were executed or sent to the forced labor camps, where conditions were so bad that many soon died.

Throughout this terror, Stalin's industrialization went forward. By 1940 the Soviet Union was producing far more iron, steel, coal, and oil than at the start of the first five-year plan. Only the United States and Germany outranked the U.S.S.R. in steel output. But these economic achievements were soon to suffer a terrible blow from the invasion of Hitler's army.

World War II. Stalin had grown increasingly fearful that Nazi Germany would invade his country. In 1934 the Soviet Union joined the League of Nations and for a period began to negotiate with England and France about possible collective security arrangements against the

Nazis. When the Nazis marched into Austria in 1938 and Czechoslovakia in 1939, neither France nor England intervened. Stalin decided in 1939 to sign a treaty with Germany itself in which both sides agreed not to attack each other. Stalin reasoned that this would give him more time to arm his country for the war that he felt would eventually come. The same treaty included a secret agreement to divide Poland. When Germany invaded Poland in September 1939, the Red Army quietly moved in from the other side and took eastern Poland. Soviet troops captured the southeastern part of Finland, but only after a heroic resistance by the Finns; and they also occupied the Baltic states, which had been free republics since the end of World War I.

On June 22, 1941, in spite of the treaty and without warning, Hitler invaded the U.S.S.R. The Red Army at first was no match for the Nazis, who easily advanced to the gates of Moscow and Leningrad by October of that year. They were prevented from entering those cities, but went on moving eastward across the Ukraine to the Volga, where one of the fiercest battles of the war took place in Stalingrad (now Volgograd), in the winter of 1942–43. From then on, Soviet troops began to push the Germans back. The Red Army entered Berlin in May 1945.

World War II is known as "The Great Patriotic War" in the Soviet Union. In the course of it, close to 20,000,000 Soviet people were killed. In Leningrad alone, which endured a 900-day siege, it is estimated that more than 1,000,000 people died, largely from starvation. Although the Soviet Union received approximately $11,000,000,000 worth of lend-lease assistance from the United States during the war, the war damage to the Soviet economy was enormous. Stalin was determined that his country would immediately begin to climb the steep road of economic recovery and reach an even higher level than before. He did not let the war-weary Soviet people rest at all, but prodded them on to more hard work. Again the emphasis was on heavy industry, and consumer goods received little attention.

The Cold War. At the end of World War II, Stalin took back all the areas that Russia had lost during World War I, and incorporated them into the Soviet Union. These included eastern Poland, Bessarabia (part of Rumania), and the three Baltic states, which the Red Army had briefly occupied before the Nazi invasion of the Soviet Union.

The Soviet Union was in a strong position to exert its influence in Eastern Europe. As its troops helped liberate one country after another from the Germans, Stalin gave his support to local Communist parties and saw to it that these parties soon came to power. By 1948 there were Communist governments dominated by the Soviet Union in Albania, Bulgaria, Czechoslovakia, Hungary, Poland, Rumania, and East Germany. (Yugoslavia, which emerged from the war as a Communist nation, became too independent to satisfy Stalin, and in 1948 relations between the two nations were strained almost to the breaking point.) The relationship between the U.S.S.R. and the East European nations was a source of deep disagreement between the Soviet Union and its wartime allies, the United States and Britain. The American leaders were particularly insistent that the people of Eastern Europe be able freely to choose their own governments. Stalin, on the other hand, wanted to ensure that these governments would not pose a threat to the Soviet western borderlands, which had been invaded so often throughout Russia's history.

"The Motherland" monument commemorates the Soviet defense of Stalingrad during World War II.

This and other issues of disagreement led the Western countries and the Soviet Union to become increasingly distrustful of each other. The United States responded to Soviet actions in Eastern Europe by agreeing to support Greece and Turkey against any possible Soviet threat. In 1949, the United States also took the initiative in forming the North Atlantic Treaty Organization (NATO) for the nations of Western Europe, Canada, the United States, Greece, and Turkey. They were to come to each other's assistance in case of attack by an outside power. (The equivalent East European group, the Warsaw Treaty Organization, was formed in 1955 by the U.S.S.R, Albania, Bulgaria, Czechoslovakia, East Germany, Hungary, and Rumania, presumably because of the threat of remilitarization in West Germany.) This period of mutual distrust and tension between the U.S.S.R. and the Western world became known as the Cold War.

Inside the U.S.S.R. during the Cold War years, the Soviet people lived under controls more strict than usual. They were told that the Soviet Union had won its "Great Patriotic War" all by itself, without any assistance from the Western nations. Western culture was pronounced decadent, and Soviet culture proclaimed superior to all others. In the words of the British leader Winston Churchill, an "iron curtain" had descended, cutting the Soviet people off completely from contact with the West.

The Post-Stalin Years

The long Stalin era came to an end with his death on March 6, 1953. The immediate problem was who would succeed him, for Stalin had not designated a successor, and the Soviet system had no formal provision for choosing one. Several men competed with one another, and Nikita Khrushchev emerged the victor. In 1964, Khrushchev himself was toppled and succeeded by Leonid Brezhnev as First Secretary (later changed to General Secretary) of the Party and Alexei Kosygin as Premier.

One outstanding event in Khrushchev's career was his spectacular attack on Stalin in a long speech to the 20th Party Congress in 1956. Called the "secret speech" because it was never published in the Soviet Union, its contents nevertheless became widely known both inside the country and around the world. It was a great shock to the Soviet people who, in spite of their suffering under Stalin, regarded him with awe and respect. Suddenly they were told by Khrushchev that Stalin had ordered the arrest and torture and killing of countless innocent countrymen. There followed a campaign to de-Stalinize Soviet life. Pictures and statues of Stalin were removed. Almost everything named after him was renamed. His body was even taken out of the mausoleum in Red Square, where it had lain in honor next to Lenin's.

Soviet citizens no longer felt the mass terror that they did under Stalin. Most of the forced labor camps were closed and their political prisoners allowed to return home. There was some easing of the strict controls over people's lives. The "Stalin Constitution" of 1936 was replaced by a new Constitution in 1977. People were able to speak out somewhat more freely than in Stalin's time, and it became possible to criticize bureaucratic officials and practices.

The choice of Mikhail Sergeyevich Gorbachev to be General Secretary of the Communist Party in 1985 marked a dramatic shift in power from the older to the younger generation of Soviet leaders. At the age of 54, Gorbachev was one of the youngest men ever to rise to the top leadership of the Soviet Union.

Soon after he took over, Gorbachev began to push energetically for economic, political, and social reforms. One of his first campaigns was a war on alcoholism, which had become a plague of the Soviet society, causing innumerable economic losses and contributing to a decline in life expectancy. This crackdown led to dismissals of hundreds of corrupt local officials, but also to an increase in home distilling and bootlegging of alcohol.

War on alcoholism was only the first step, however. The two words that summed up Gorbachev's policy were "glasnost"—which means openness, intellectual liberalization, and loosening of ideological controls—and "perestroika," or economic restructuring. Implementing these, Gorbachev initiated a new period in Soviet foreign policy. After a decade of very cold relations with the United States, the two superpowers concluded a treaty in 1987 eliminating intermediate nuclear missiles, and in May 1988, Soviet troops began to withdraw from Afghanistan, where they had been fighting Moslem guerrillas since 1979. Gorbachev impressed Western politicians as a new type of Soviet leader—very intelligent, capable, and less interested in ideology than in promoting international cooperation. Unlike his predecessors, he always traveled to the West with his elegant wife, Raisa, did not avoid journalists, and had a sense of humor.

Gorbachev's ambitious, revolutionary plans for the Soviet society have many supporters but also many opponents, including both conservatives and radicals. The power and prestige of the Communist Party is at an all-time low, and Gorbachev is relying more on his newly expanded presidential powers than on his position as general secretary of the Communist Party for his authority. The party itself is fragmenting and one of Gorbachev's main rivals for power, Boris Yeltsin, has resigned from the Party. Gorbachev's personal prestige received a boost in 1990, when he was awarded the Nobel Peace Prize.

Radicals, such as Yeltsin, who was recently elected president of the Russian Republic of the U.S.S.R., charge that changes are being implemented too slowly. Conservative, old-line Communists argue that changes are coming too quickly. Still, in September 1990, Gorbachev's closest economic advisers submitted a plan to him that called for the virtually complete dismantling of the Communist economic structures within 500 days. The plan would put banks, stock markets, farmland, and business enterprises into private hands.

As economic problems mount, internal divisions and ethnic tensions that were formerly suppressed by the central government are rising to the surface. Soviet troops have been sent to several regions to quell open warfare between rival groups who are fighting over disputed land and treatment of ethnic minorities. Lithuania declared its independence in March 1990, and the other Baltic republics have declared their intention to become independent.

In the former Eastern bloc, Hungary and Czechoslovakia have demanded that the Soviet Union withdraw its troops from their territory, and it has been agreed that a unified Germany will remain in NATO, depriving the Soviet Union of its ally East Germany. With all of these pressures, the Soviet Union has been forced to reevaluate its position in world affairs. Rather than confronting the West as it did for 45 years during the Cold War, Gorbachev has led the Soviet Union to a much more moderate stance. The two superpowers have demonstrated astonishing cooperation in the U.N. Security Council, giving that body new influence and effectiveness. The Soviet Union is also seeking to join the mainstream world economy and to increase trade with the West.

GOVERNMENT

The Supreme Soviet is the national legislature. After decades of merely rubber-stamping decisions of the Communist Party leadership, it has begun to undertake meaningful debate on important issues. In 1989, for the first time, its members were chosen by the people from candidates that included challengers endorsed by non-Communist parties.

Each of the 15 republics in the Soviet Union also has its council of ministers and supreme soviet, and there are soviets on the lower levels of the province, district, and town.

COLETTE SHULMAN
Editor, *We The Russians*

VOLGA RIVER

VOLGA RIVER

Most major European rivers flow through several countries, taking on different characteristics as they cross new borders. The Volga is Europe's longest river, but for its entire 2,293-mile (3,685 kilometers) course, it never leaves Russian soil. The Volga is the most important river in the Soviet Union. It is part of a far-flung network of waterways that connects the Caspian Sea with the Baltic, the Black Sea with the White. Huge hydroelectric stations along the river have harnessed its waters to provide electricity and irrigation for vast areas of the Volga Basin. The Volga carries about one half of the Soviet Union's river freight, taking food and raw materials to the industrial north and bringing heavy machinery, manufactured goods, and lumber back to the agricultural south.

THE UPPER VOLGA

Leaving its source in the Valdai Hills, the Volga grows in volume as it flows through several lakes. It is navigable almost from its source, though in winter long stretches of the river are frozen and in summer short spans become so shallow that movement of anything but timber is impossible. Small boats can begin the downriver voyage at the town of Rzhev, where the river turns northeast. Larger craft start the trip at Kalinin, some 100 miles (160 km.) farther downstream. Almost from its source, too, there are dams on the Volga. The Volga Reservoir, between Kalinin and Kimry, is the first link in a chain of man-made lakes including some of the biggest in the world. At one end of the reservoir, a canal connects the Volga with the Moskva River at Moscow. The canal gave the capital of the Soviet Union access to the great northern and southern seas, making the city an important port though it lies hundreds of miles inland from any sea.

Still flowing northeast, the Volga passes another power dam at Uglich and then reaches the Rybinsk Reservoir, or Rybinsk "Sea." Many villages had to be moved or evacuated before the land could be flooded, and some Russians who were farmers before 1941 became fishermen instead, earning their livings on this 1,800-square-mile (4,700 square kilometers) lake.

THE MIDDLE RIVER

Near the industrial city of Yaroslavl, with its textile mills, chemical plants, and shipyards, the Volga begins to flow east. Passing another large dam and power station at Gorodets, the river reaches Gorki (formerly Nizhni Novgorod). Renamed in 1932 for the great Russian writer Maxim Gorki, the city was famous for centuries for its annual trade fair. East and West met on the banks of the Volga to exchange not only grain, spices, bright silks, and other products, but also their different cultural traditions.

Until about 1900, many of the goods traded at Nizhni Novgorod were placed on barges and hauled downriver by teams of men working on shore. These men were called *burlaki,* and "The Song of the Volga Boatmen" still evokes the heavy straining rhythm of their work.

Below Gorki, the river widens considerably, and there, instead of the pine forests characteristic of the upper Volga, high bluffs on the "European" bank face vast expanses of Asian steppeland on the other. At Cheboksary, the river enters the three-branched Kuibyshev Reservoir, which covers 2,300 square miles (6,000 sq. km.) of land. On the arms of the reservoir are two cities that are landmarks in Russian history. Kazan, on the northern arm, faces east, and still reflects the heritage of the 13th-century Tatar invaders of Russia. From the minaret of Kazan's 200-year-old mosque, the Muslim call to prayer is still heard daily.

In 1552 Kazan was captured from the Tatars by the army of Ivan the

Caviar from the Caspian Sea is processed in factory boats that sail up the Volga River to markets.

Terrible. Starting from Moscow, the army used the Volga as the highway of Russian expansion, taking city after city along the river until they reached Astrakhan on the Caspian Sea.

Ulyanovsk (formerly Simbirsk), on the reservoir's southern arm, was the birthplace of Alexander Kerensky, who headed the Russian Government after the March, 1917, revolution, and also of Lenin (Vladimir Ilyich Ulyanov). Lenin led the October revolution that overthrew Kerensky's government the same year and established Communist rule in Russia. Today, in the city named for him when he died, a statue of Lenin stands on a hill high above the Volga, fully dominating the landscape.

Before the river leaves the reservoir, its power is tapped again by another hydroelectric station at Zhigulevsk. Just past this dam, the Volga flows around the Zhiguli Mountains in a great, sweeping curve called the Samara Bend.

THE LOWER VOLGA AND THE DELTA

Flowing southwest, the Volga reaches Saratov, a city whose traditions have been heavily influenced by the many Germans who have lived there. In 1763 Empress Catherine the Great, a German by birth, offered free land and local self-government to any German who would settle along the Volga and aid the development of Russia. The German community flourished, and by 1917 there were some 750,000 Volga Germans living in and around Saratov.

About 200 miles (320 km.) downstream is Volgograd. In 1942–43, when the city was still called Stalingrad, its location made it a major Nazi objective. If Stalingrad could be taken, the Russian supply lines on the Volga would be cut. After a heroic resistance in which the city was almost totally destroyed, the Nazis were defeated. Today, in the Volgograd Hills, there is a colossal memorial to the soldiers who died defending Stalingrad.

The Volzhskaya Power Station near Volgograd is the second most powerful in the world. The river was deepened when it was built, allowing even more cargo and tourist ships to ply the Volga. There are also many fishing boats on this part of the river, which abounds in carp, pike, herring, and sturgeon that come up from the delta.

Astrakhan, the last major city on the Volga, is a port and the center of the caviar industry—75 percent of Russian caviar is processed there, after it is taken from the delta sturgeon. From Astrakhan, a 120-mile-long (190 km.) dredged channel gives oil tankers, coal- and grain-bearing barges, and passenger steamers access to the Caspian Sea.

Below the city, the many-fingered delta of the Volga reaches out toward the Caspian. Among its hundreds of winding channels and crosschannels, there is a wildlife sanctuary where animals are safe and birds can nest among the reeds. The delta's varied plant life includes a rare, bright scarlet lotus.

Europe's longest river has been called "the big river" and "Mother Volga," but it is more than an artery of traffic and more than a source of power. It is a great stream in which many civilizations have mingled, and it carries not only large quantities of freight, but the burden and glory of Russian history as well.

Reviewed by MARVIN KALB, Diplomatic Correspondent, CBS News
Author, *The Volga—A Political Journey Through Russia*

ILLUSTRATION CREDITS

The following list credits, according to page, the sources of illustrations used in volume 4 of LANDS AND PEOPLES. The credits are listed illustration by illustration—top to bottom, left to right. Where necessary, the name of the photographer or artist has been listed with the source, the two separated by a dash. If two or more illustrations appear on the same page, their credits are separated by semicolons.

1 © Chip & Rosa Maria de la Cueva Peterson
3 © Ian Yeomans/Woodfin Camp & Assoc.
4 George Buctel
6 © Harry Griffiths/Photo Researchers
7 © E. Preau/Sygma
8 © Yoshiaki Matsuda/FPG Int.
9 Herbert Fristedt
10 © Chip & Rosa Maria de la Cueva Peterson
11 Walter Hortens
13 Multi-Media Photography, Inc.
14 Multi-Media Photography, Inc.
15 Carlsberg Breweries
17 Multi-Media Photography, Inc.
18 © Weinberg-Clark/The Image Bank; Susan Heimann
19 Ernst Z. Roghkopf
21 S. E. Hedin
23 Norwegian Embassy Information Service
24 Norwegian Embassy Information Service
27 Mulvey-Crump Associates, Inc.
29 E. C. Johnson—De Wys, Inc.
30 © J. Messerschmidt/Leo deWys Inc.
31 © Steve Vidler/Leo deWys Inc.
32 © J. Messerschmidt/Leo deWys Inc.
33 Multi-Media Photography, Inc.
35 Mulvey-Crump Associates, Inc.
36 Editorial Photocolor Archives, N.Y.; Floyd Norgaard—Lenstour Photo Service
38 Henry I. Kurtz
41 Frank Schwarz—Lee Ames Studio
42 © M. Desjardins/Photo Researchers
43 © Swedish Tourist Board, New York
44 Jerry Frank
45 Marvin Newman—Multi-Media Photography, Inc.
46 © J. Braennhage/Leo deWys Inc.
47 Herbest Fristedt
49 S. E. Hedin
51 Pete Turner
52 Multi-Media Photography, Inc.
53 I. Holmasen—Ostman Agency
54 © Jim Pickerell/Black Star
55 Floyd Norgaard—Lenstour Photo Service
56 © Mike Yamashita/Woodfin Camp & Assoc.
57 Walter Hortens
59 © F. Gohier/Photo Researchers
60 © Jim Pickerell/Black Star; Sven Samelius/Ostman Agency
61 Multi-Media Photography, Inc.; Kay Honkanen—Ostman Agency
62 Pete Turner
63 Floyd Norgaard—Lenstour Photo Service
65 © Robert Frerck/Click, Chicago
66 © Robert Frerck/Odyssey Productions
67 V. Lefteroff—De Wys, Inc.
69 Douglas Lyttle
70 © Michael Howard/Leo deWys Inc.
73 © Robert Frerck/Odyssey Productions
74 Jerry Frank
76 J. Blatter—F. & N. Schwitter Library
79 Victor Englebert
81 George Buctel; Diversified Map Company
82 Dick Huffman—Monkmeyer Press Photo Service
83 Victor Englebert
84 © Steve Vidler/Leo deWys Inc.
85 © Joachim Messerschmidt/Leo deWys Inc.
87 © Robert Frerck/Odyssey Productions
88 © Robert Frerck/Odyssey Productions
90 © Mike Busselle/Leo deWys Inc.
91 © Robert Frerck/Odyssey Productions
93 Charles Shapp; © Nik Wheeler/Black Star
95 © Robert Frerck/The Stock Market
96 © Robert Frerck/The Stock Market
96 Alan Band Associates
97 Jerry Frank
99 The Metropolitan Museum of Art, Bequest of Mrs. H. O. Havemeyer, 1929. H. O. Havemeyer Collection

100 Hans Hanau—Rapho Guillumette Pictures; The Metropolitan Museum of Art, Bequest of Mrs. H. O. Havemeyer, 1929. H. O. Havemeyer Collection
101 Editorial Photocolor Archives, N.Y.
102 Alan Band Associates
103 Katherine Young
104 Virginia Carleton—Editorial Photocolor Archives, N.Y.
105 © Robert Frerck/Odyssey Productions
106 © J. Pavlovsky/Sygma
107 © Robert Frerck/Odyssey Productions
108 © Robert Frerck/The Stock Market
109 © Robert Frerck/The Stock Market
111 © Robert Frerck/Odyssey Productions
112 © Robert Frerck/Odyssey Productions
114 Fritz Henle—Photo Researchers
117 © Steve Vidler/Leo deWys Inc.
119 Archivo Mateu
120 Archivo Mateu; Duchscherer—Monkmeyer Press Photo Service
121 George Buctel
123 Mulvey-Crump Associates, Inc.
124 © Steve Vidler/Leo deWys Inc.
126 © Leo deWys Inc.
127 Diversified Map Company
128 © Lael Morgan/Click-Chicago
129 © Arthur Hustwitt/Leo deWys Inc.
130 Bettina Cirone
131 Renzo Cantagalli
132 Renzo Cantagalli
133 Grolier Photo Library
135 Renzo Cantagalli
137 © Cotton Coulson/Woodfin Camp & Assoc.
139 Renzo Cantagalli
141 © Alfred Tessi/The Image Bank
142 Editorial Photocolor Archives, N.Y.
143 Alan Shayne/Photo Researchers
144 © Randy Wells/The Stock Market
145 © Giorgio Ricatto/Shostal Assoc.
146 Douglas Lyttle
147 Susan Heimann
148 © Monkmeyer Press Photo Service
149 F. & N. Schwitter Library
150 Herbert Fristedt; Ernst Z. Rothkopf
152 © Piergiorgio Sclarandis/Black Star
154 © Roberto Koch, Contrasto from Picture Group
155 Grolier Photo Library
156 © John G. Ross/Photo Researchers
157 Charles Shapp
158 Editorial Photocolor Archives, N.Y.
159 Editorial Photocolor Archives, N.Y.
159 Herbert Fristedt
161 Charles Shapp
163 Gianni Tortoli—Photo Researchers
164 Mulvey-Crump Associates, Inc.
166 © D. Brogioni/Picture Group
168 © Shostal
169 © M. Courtney-Clarke/Photo Researchers
171 © Cotton Coulson/Woodfin Camp & Assoc.
172 © Robert Frerck/Woodfin Camp & Assoc.
173 © J. Messerschmidt/Bruce Coleman Inc.
174 A. Earle Harrington
175 Walter Hortens
176 F. & N. Schwitter Library
177 Frank Schwarz—Lee Ames Studio
178 © J. Messerschmidt/Leo deWys Inc.
179 © Giansanti/Sygma
180 Tony La Tona—Lenstour Photo Service
181 Editorial Photocolor Archives, N.Y.
182 © D. Rawson/Photo Researchers
183 George Buctel
185 © Art Resource
186 Linda Bartlett
187 © Grolier, Inc.
189 © Chuck O'Rear/Woodfin Camp & Assoc.
190 © Comstock

191 © Harry S. Zolindakis
192 Michael A. Vaccaro
193 © Susan McCartney/Photo Researchers
194 © Klaus D. Francke/The Stock Market
196 G. Tomisch/Photo Researchers
197 Stern/Monkmeyer Press Photo Service
198 Editorial Photocolor Archives, N.Y.
199 © Michael Howard/Leo deWys Inc.
200 © Harry S. Zolindakis
201 © Steve Vidler/Leo deWys Inc.
202 Editorial Photocolor Archives, N.Y.
203 © Harry S. Zolindakis
204 © Harry S. Zolindakis
207 Harrison Forman
208 © Ray Manley/Shostal
210 © Harry S. Zolindakis
211 © Harry S. Zolindakis
212 © Chris Niedenthal/Black Star
213 © Momatiuk/Eastcott/Woodfin Camp & Assoc.
214 © Chris Niedenthal/Black Star
215 © Wendy Chan/The Image Bank
216 © Susan McCartney/Photo Researchers
217 George Buctel
218 © Chris Niedenthal/Black Star
219 © Chris Niedenthal/Black Star
220 S. E. Hedin
221 S. E. Hedin
222 E. Henriksson—Ostman Agency
223 Eliott Erwitt—Magnum Photos
224 S. E. Hedin
225 © Philppot/Sygma
226 © Walter S. Clark/Photo Researchers
229 Dankwart von Knobloch—Lenstour Photo Service
231 © Fridmar Damm/Leo deWys Inc.
232 © Chris Niedenthal/Black Star
233 © Eastcott-Momatiuk/Woodfin Camp & Assoc.
234 © Eastcott-Momatiuk/Woodfin Camp & Assoc.
236 © Marvin E. Newman/The Image Bank
239 © Fridmar Damm/Leo deWys Inc.
240 S. E. Hedin—Ostman Agency
242 © Bill Weems/Woodfin Camp & Assoc.
243 Frank Schwarz—Lee Ames Studio
246 S. E. Hedin
247 Editorial Photocolor Archives, N.Y.
250 © Richard D. Stradtmann/The Image Bank
252 © Dr. Hans Kramarz
255 Diversified Map Company; Frank Schwarz —Lee Ames Studio
256 © World Films Enterprise
258 © Robert Frerck/Odyssey Productions
260 Jerry Frank; © Porterfield-Chickering/Photo Researchers
262 © Berlitz, from Kay Reese
264 Bjorn Klingwall—Ostman Agency
266 K-A Schwartzkopf—Ostman Agency
267 George Buctel
268 © J. Legroux/Leo deWys Inc.
269 © Leo deWys Inc.
272 Editorial Photocolor Archives, N.Y.
273 © Steve Benbow/Woodfin Camp & Assoc.
274 Harrison Forman
275 George Buctel
276 Bulgarian Tourist Office
277 Bulgarian Tourist Office
278 Bulgarian Tourist Office
279 © Margot Granitsas/Photo Researchers
280 © David Burnett/Leo deWys Inc.
281 Harrison Forman
282 Pete Turner
283 © Editura Ştiinţifică şl Enciclopedică
285 Walter Hortens
286 © Editura Ştiinţifică şl Enciclopedică
290 Harrison Forman
292 © Editura Ştiinţifică şl Enciclopedică
293 © Editura Ştiinţifică şl Enciclopedică

295 Fusco—Multi-Media Photography, Inc.
297 Diversified Map Company
299 Jere Donovan
300 S. E. Hedin—Ostman Agency; A. J. Antuck
302 S. E. Hedin—Ostman Agency
303 S. E. Hedin—Ostman Agency; © Arthur Treadgill/Leo deWys Inc.
304 Editorial Photocolor Archives, N.Y.
306 A La Vieille Russie, New York–Paris
308 Burt Glinn—Magnum Photos

Cover photo: © ZEFA/Leo de Wys

310 S. E. Hedin—Ostman Agency; Bjorn Bolstad—Peter Arnold
312 Luis Villota; S. E. Hedin
315 Burt Glinn—Magnum Photos
316 © M. Bertinetti/Photo Researchers
317 Inge Morath—Magnum Photos
319 S. E. Hedin
320 Marilyn Silverstone—Magnum Photos
321 © Claus Meyer/Black Star; © Tass from Sovfoto
322 Erich Lessing—Magnum Photos

324 Mary Ann Joulwan; Luba Paz
325 S. E. Hedin—Ostman Agency; S. E. Hedin
326 Herbert Fristedt
328 Editorial Photocolor Archives, N.Y.; © Sovfoto
329 Bjorn Bolstad—Peter Arnold
331 Warren Slater—Monkmeyer Press Photo Service
333 Editorial Photocolor Archives, N.Y.
340 © Vance Henry/Taurus
343 Wesley McKeown
344 © Jonathan T. Wright/Bruce Coleman Inc.